READINGS IN
THE HISTORY OF
MUSIC IN PERFORMANCE

READINGS IN
THE HISTORY OF
MUSIC IN
PERFORMANCE

Selected, translated, and edited
by Carol MacClintock

INDIANA UNIVERSITY PRESS
BLOOMINGTON & LONDON

Manufactured in the United States of America

Library of Congress Cataloging in Publication Data
Main entry under title:

Readings in the history of music in performance.

    1. Music—Performance.   2. Music—History and criticism—Sources.
I. MacClintock, Carol Cook, 1910–
ML457.R4   780'.9   78–9511
ISBN 0–253–14495–7   1   2   3   4   5   83   82   81   80   79

To My Husband

Contents

vii

Part III *The Seventeenth Century*

Part IV The Eighteenth and Early Nineteenth Centuries

PREFACE

The value of historical documents in any area is incontrovertible; for music history and the performance of music they are of particular importance. The current, ever-increasing interest in the performance of music in earlier periods points up the need for documents and contemporary accounts describing *how* music was to be performed and what the accepted conventions and actual practices were in former times. This collection of texts and translations from historical sources was therefore compiled with a view to providing materials that would be informative and helpful to interested amateurs as well as to performers and students, not only in the study of music history but also in the study of the history of music in performance, or "performance practice," as it is usually called.

The student working on the interpretation of early music needs not only dictionary-type reference books—those that consist of brief explanations of terms—but also sources of larger scope that explain methods and techniques, describe performances or give eyewitness accounts of music-making, and convey some idea of attitudes toward and usages of music in periods other than our own; in short, that establish perspectives on the performance of early music.

The selection of readings in this volume is admittedly far from encyclopedic, for untranslated source materials abound;[1] rather it is designed to present a general overview of musical thought and practice in various earlier periods and to cover some of the essential and often vexing problems that arise in the performance and interpretation of early music. In working with music of the past one finds that very few, or no directions are given, and that the notation on the page is merely the barest bones of the music: the flesh and blood remains to be supplied. Only by turning to documents of the past can one begin to know what constituted a concert in other times, how musicians performed their music, how their audiences heard it, and what liberties may have been taken with it. For example, a composition for five or six parts from the late sixteenth or early seventeenth century, ostensibly for voices alone, may be performed equally well, according to Praetorius, by only one or two concertato voices with the other parts played by instruments, or with all the parts taken by instruments, often of the most diverse kinds. Questions of tempo and changes of tempo in choral music of the same periods are also troublesome for the modern choral conductor; however, theorists such as Vicentino and Mersenne make it clear that variations in tempo in concerted groups are essential to express the words—though Vicentino says this way of proceeding cannot be written down! Passages such as Muffat's description of Lully's bowing are necessary for the performance of Lully's music and other works of that period, and Leopold Mozart's chapter on optional ornaments enables today's performer to play a composition correctly in the style of Mozart's day. In matters such as these an extract of some length may clarify the whole problem, for the rights of the interpreter before 1850 were considerably greater than they are today.[2]

These readings on the performance of Western music cover the period from the late middle ages to the early part of the nineteenth century. The style and the sound of music in the Classical and Romantic eras is now somewhat remote from our minds and ears, and even here, in periods that are relatively familiar, it is wise to seek information from then contemporary sources.

It is my hope that readers will find these selections both helpful and interesting, and above all that they will be encouraged to read further in the extensive literature that exists on this subject.

Here I wish to express my appreciation of the interest, enthusiasm, and encouragement shown by the students in my classes in Performance Practice, which spurred me on to undertake this task. I also acknowledge with thanks the assistance of Michael Braunlin with the Latin translations, James Carrier's fine music examples, and the unfailing help and encouragement of my husband, Lander MacClintock, not only in the matter of translations from the sources in modern languages but in every way.

NOTES

1. See Mary Vinquist and Neal Zaslaw, eds., *Performance Practice: A Bibliography* (New York: W. W. Norton & Co., 1970).

2. M. Pincherle, "On the Rights of the Interpreter in the Performance of 17th- and 18th-Century Music," *The Musical Quarterly* (XLIV) 1958, pp. 145–66.

Part I *Before 1500*

1. The Late Middle Ages

Jerome of Moravia (Hieronymous de Moravia) was a musical theorist who lived in the latter half of the thirteenth century. He worked in Paris and became a member of the Dominican order, whose monastery was then in the rue St. Jacques.

His Tractatus de musica, *a very comprehensive work, is based mainly on earlier writers and, in a way, sums up the practice of the periods preceding his own, from Plato and Aristotle to Johannes de Garlandia. Jerome was apparently attempting to give an overview of the entire field of musical knowledge. Besides his theoretical discussions based on previously existing sources, he includes two chapters that are original and deal with music of his own time: Chapter 25,* De modo faciendi novos ecclesiasticos et omnes alios firmose sive planos cantus, *on singing; and Chapter 28,* De tetrachordis et pentachordis musicis instrumentis, *on instruments then in use. The latter is particularly important for information on tuning the* vielle.

Chapter 25, part of which is translated here, provides valuable information on thirteenth-century performance practice of ecclesiastical music. Jerome discusses ornamentation to be used and describes three kinds of "harmonic flowers," or trill-like ornaments. Although his descriptions and rules are sometimes obscure, he conveys unequivocally that ornaments were widely used.

SOURCE: *Charles Edmond Henri de Coussemaker,* Scriptores de musica medii aevi nova *series, 4 vols. (Paris, 1864–76), vol. I, pp. 91–94.*

JEROME OF MORAVIA
from *Tractatus de musica*

De modo faciendi novos ecclesiasticos et omnes alios firmos sive planos cantus.

. . . All notes in ecclesiastical song are governed by certain rules. First: whenever there are extra syllables and words, the meter thus being interrupted, and there are four notes descending or ascending, separately or in ligature, then the first is a *longa*, the second is a *breve*, but the third, or penultimate of the phrase, and the fourth, the final note, are longer; thus: [♩ ▪ ♩·♩·]

If these same notes are repeated, then the first will be a *breve*, the second a *longa*, and the third and fourth as before, because variation of the manner removes boredom and induces adornment. [▪ ♩ ♩·♩·]

If there are five notes, then in like manner they are varied, because the first is always a *longa*, the second a *breve*, the third a *semibreve*, the fourth and fifth longer, as before. [♦♦♦♦♩·♩·]

If there are six notes, then the first, second, third, and fourth are *semibreves* like the preceding, the fifth and sixth as before. [♩♩♪♪♪♩·♩·]

Should there be more than three notes in descending, then the first, second, penultimate, and final as above; the others are the very shortest (*brevissime*) notes.

Second: in regard to the fact that notes in conjunct figures may be joined in the melody but separated in the singing: this disjunction is not an ending, but is called a "breathing" and is nothing more than the appearance of an end, or the existence of an *instantia*.[1]

Third: no short note may be taken up by a *reverberation* unless it be one of the aforesaid five notes that are measured in a special way, which then are performed in different manners.[2]

Some of them are made by the beating of a semitone, others of a tone, and still others with reverberation of different kinds.

The shortest reverberation is an extremely rapid anticipation taken before a following note, which, by this means, is halved.

Fourth: although no short note may be embellished except those measured in a special way, sometimes a *breve* may be resolved into three shorter notes.

The "harmonic flower" *[flos harmonicus],* or ornament, however, a fitting grace of the voice or sound, is a very swift and stormlike vibration.

Some ornaments may be long, others open; indeed, some are sudden.

Long ornaments are those whose vibration is steady and does not exceed a semitone.

Open ornaments are those whose vibration is steady and does not exceed a whole tone.

1. "*Instans* is taken to be the smallest indivisible sound that can be perceived clearly and distinctly." *Tractatus*, Ch. xxv, *Scriptores* I, p.89.
2. Jerome refers here to para. 3 under the first rule above.

The sudden ones are those whose vibration is at first steady, but in the middle and at the end most swift, and does not exceed a semitone.

The quality and diversity of these ornaments may be shown on the organ in this way: When we play a chant on the organ, and if we want to ornament a certain note of that chant, let us say low G, then that note is held open and immobile; but at the same time we strike—not the note immediately below it, or low F, but the A above; from this rises beautiful and graceful harmony, which we call *florem harmonicum*.

Therefore, when immobile keys set up the vibration of a semitone, and that vibration is steady, then it is the ornament that is called "long"; but when they include a tone, and the vibration is neither slow nor sudden, but is in between, then it is the open embellishment. But when the ornament consists of a semitone and the vibration at the beginning is steady, but in the rising and falling becomes very swift, then it is the "sudden" ornament.

Fifth: it must be noted that the aforesaid ornaments ought not occur on notes other than the five notes measured singularly, but differently, for the long ornaments ought to occur on the first, penultimate, and final note on the rising semitone. But if certain other manners are established in descending, the second note of the syllable should have an open embellishment; but sudden embellishment is not other than a *plica longa*. Among these, and immediately following, short notes are placed for the beauty of the harmony.

Sixth: because reverberation should precede those ornaments by tones or semitones on all the five notes except the final, which is taken as the beating of a semitone, it may be finished with the stormy note [*nota procellaris*], which is indeed nothing more than a slow vibration over a semitone; whence it stems from the family of "long" embellishments.

It is called "stormy" because it rises without interruption, just as a storm raised by the breeze over a river does not disturb the water. Likewise the *nota procellaris* ought to occur in singing with the appearance of motion but without interruption of the sound or voice. Certain of the French observe this manner of singing in certain songs, though not in all, in which they delight the nations. . . .

It does not appear that one can speak well or sufficiently about the other procedures unless one were to speak specifically of all the manners from which song arises. Therefore unison singing, as the first and principal thing, must be mentioned. If the unison passage has more than two notes, all are *semibreves* except the penultimate and final, which are taken up in reverberation; even when only two notes are in unison they may serve one or more syllables or words.

Also, when two notes are distant from each other by a semitone or tone, ligated or free, they may be joined by a third note, which is called the middle note, and it is most often a *semibreve*. However, the first note, when it is a *breve*, may properly be resolved into three very short notes, which appear to the sense to fall more rapidly among the aforementioned notes. Sometimes also they make an upward *plica longa* from the first free descending note in the middle, as before. But in the ascent they make a reverberation on the second note.

Also, when two notes stand apart a semitone or ditone, joined or free, the second, either *semibreve* or *breve*, may be resolved into three very short notes, which are joined in singing. Sometimes, however, in descending from the first note a *plica longa* is made downward to the middle note, from which a reverberation is made to the third note, as before; and conversely in ascending. Or, what is more common, reverberation is made on the third note.

Likewise, where the notes are separated through a *diatessaron* in descending, a *plica longa* descends from the first to the second note; but from the third note a reverberation is made to the fourth note. But in ascending, reverberation occurs on the fourth note. From the *diapente* the same occurs among certain notes as it does with the *diatessaron*, ascending and descending; but the reverberation then is made on the tone above the fifth note.

In order that ecclesiastical song may be performed by two or even more singers, after the proper manner, five things are necessary for the singer.

First, the chant should be studied carefully by all the singers, and they should agree with one accord in the quality or quantity of harmonic time, either according to the ancients or the moderns.

Second, as far as possible let them all be good singers and choose for themselves a conductor to whom they shall pay diligent attention; and let them follow his every rule for notes and pauses; for this is best.

Third, lest the natural disparity of voices lead to disharmony, let the voices have different qualities, i.e., the chest, the throat, or the head.

The voice that forms notes in the chest we call "of the chest." Those in the throat are "of the throat"; and those voices formed in the head are "of the head."

Chest voices are best for deep notes; those of the throat for higher notes; and those of the head for the highest. Generally, heavy, low voices are chest voices; subtle and very high ones are head voices; those in between are throat. They all must maintain their individuality during singing.

However, since all voices gain their vigor from the chest, it is therefore necessary that a chant never be begun too high, especially by those having head voices; rather they should place in the chest a note deeper than the others as a basis for their own part—yet not too deep, which is to shout, or not too high, which is to shriek, but in between, which is to sing. Thus, let them always begin so that the melody might not be subject to the voice, but the voice to the melody; otherwise beautiful notes cannot be formed.

But if anyone desires to understand more beautiful notes, let him hold this rule: that he despise the song of none, however unskilled, but attend diligently to the singing of all. For just as the mill wheel makes a strident sound, unaware of what it itself is doing, it is impossible for a rational being to desire all his acts to be directed to their proper end; but sometimes, at least by fortune or by chance, he might perform a beautiful note.

And when he will have heard a pleasing note, let him diligently retain it, that he might make use of it. However, the chief obstacle to producing beautiful notes is sadness of the heart, for then no note is or can be strong; it comes indeed from the joyousness of heart, because melancholy persons can have beautiful voices but cannot indeed sing with beauty.

The Traité de deschant by an unknown musician, called Anonymous XIII by Edmond de Coussemaker, was most likely written some time during the fourteenth century, according to Manfred F. Bukofzer, although other scholars have placed it in the thirteenth. No date of origin appears in the manuscript from which it was taken by Coussemaker (B. N. Paris, fonds latin 1474).

Anonymous's little treatise is of practical importance in the history of contrapunctus supra librum *or* déchant sur le livre, *which was becoming widely used at that time. The singer was expected to be able to add a discant at sight to a tenor or bass; therefore our writer gave explicit rules for intervals and kinds of movement.*

The little work is written in Old French, which would seem to indicate it was intended for the instruction of singers who had little or no Latin. Whatever its intention, it provides an interesting insight into systematic musical instruction for performers of its time.

Source: *Charles Edmond Henri de Coussemaker,* Scriptores de musica medii aevi nova series, *4 vols. (Paris, 1864–76), vol. II, pp. 496–98.*

ANONYMOUS XIII

Treatise on Discant

Whoever wishes to understand the art of Discant must know that there are xiii kinds of song, that is: unison, half-tone, tone, tone and a half; two tones, two tones and a half; three tones, three tones and a half, which are a fifth; [half-tone with fifth, tone with fifth, tone and a half with fifth], two tones [with fifth], two tones and a half with fifth, which make an octave.

It is a unison when the tenor and discant are both on a line or a space like this [Ex. 1].

A half-step is ordinarily to be sung between *mi* and *fa,* or when one limits a tone in a manner divided thus: *la sol la* or *sol fa sol,* the middle note being raised a half-tone by means of a square ♮, which is placed before it, and it is pronounced *fa mi fa.* Whenever a round b is set in some place one must say *fa,* both in plain chant as well as in discant; and where there is a square ♮, one should say *mi* or the equivalent sound, for round b and square ♮ are provided to make a half-tone from a tone and a tone from a half-tone.

A tone is found between all the notes except *mi fa,* as in *ut, re, mi, fa, sol, la* and the converse.

Two tones are found between *re fa* and *fa la,* and the converse.

Two tones and a half are between *ut fa, re sol, mi la,* and the converse.

Three tones are between the *fa* of F fa ut and the *mi* of B fa ♮ mi, also in other places where they may be found.

Three tones and a half are between *ut sol, re la,* which make a fifth, or between the *mi* of E la mi and the *mi* of B fa ♮ mi, and conversely.

A half-tone with a fifth is between the *re* of D sol re and the *fa* of b *fa* ♮ *mi.*

A whole tone plus a fifth is between the *ut* of C fa ut and the *la* of A la mi re: or between the *re* of D sol re and the *mi* of B fa ♮ mi.

A tone and a half with a fifth falls between the *ut* of C fa ut and the *mi* of b fa ♮ mi.

Two tones with a fifth are between the *ut* of C fa ut and the *mi* of b fa ♮ *mi.*

Two tones and a half [with fifth], which make an octave, are between the *ut* of C fa ut and the *fa* of C sol fa ut.

Further, one should know that of these aforementioned xiii kinds are made xiii harmonies, three perfect and four imperfect, and six dissonances. The three perfect ones are: unison, fifth, and octave. The imperfect are two thirds and two sixths. The six dissonances are two seconds, two fourths, and two sevenths.

A half-tone and one tone are two seconds.

A tone and a half, and two tones are two thirds.

Two tones and a half, and three tones are two fourths.

[A tone and a half or two tones with a fifth make two sevenths.]

The third made up of a tone and a half-tone requires a unison after it, and that of two tones, a fifth after it.

The sixth, and the half-tone with a fifth require a fifth after them, and that of a tone with a fifth requires an octave after it.

Who wishes to sing an octave against his tenor should say, contra *ut, fa;* contra *re, sol;* contra *mi, la,* eight notes above the tenor or whatever it may be; and in the same way contra *fa sol la* as contra *ut re mi,* for *fa sol la* is considered as *ut re mi.* Who wishes to sing a fifth against his tenor should say contra *ut, sol;* contra *re, la;* or similarly, as being five notes above the tenor.

Who wishes to take a third should say contra *ut, mi;* contra *re, fa;* contra *mi, sol;* contra *fa, la;* and the contrary, three notes from the top down.

Who wishes to take a sixth should say contra *ut, re* or *la;* contra *re, mi;* contra *mi, fa;* contra *fa, sol;* contra *sol, la* six notes above the tenor.

Wishing to make a good discant, one should begin and end with a perfect accord, that is: by unison, fifth, or octave. He should see how the tenor moves: if it rises at the beginning, as *ut, re, mi,* etc., the first [note] ought to be an octave; and if the tenor descends, as *re, ut,* or *mi, ut,* or *la, sol,* the first note should be a fifth, but let this be on obliquely descending notes.[1] And one should never say or take two fifths, nor should he take two octaves, one after the other, nor rise or fall with the tenor, for they are perfect.

But with imperfect accords, thirds and sixths, one may descend two or three notes, or more if need be, providing they are on obliquely moving notes: for there are three kinds of notes, that is, obliquely moving, not oblique, and tending to be oblique.

The obliquely moving notes are like this: [example lacking] on which one should sing third, fifth or sixth, octave, both at the beginnings of the discant as well as in the middle; also [staff without notes] on which one should sing fifth, octave or third, fifth.

Also, on the [non-oblique notes] [——] one should say fourth, third, etc.

---

1. *notes appendans* ≡ *en pente,* or sloping = oblique motion.

Likewise, on the [——] one should say octave, third, etc.

Notes tending to be oblique occur when the tenor rises one note or two, or three, by degrees, and at the end should there be one note descending, all the previous ones are tending to be oblique, as here: [staff without notes].

If it is the beginning of the song, the first and last [accords] should be an octave, and the middle ones sixths; or in the middle of the song the first and last a fifth, and the middle ones thirds. The first ones are sixths and the final ones octaves, or the first are thirds and the final a fifth. And one should make only two or three thirds or sixths, one after the other, without a middle [accord].

Further, if the tenor rises three notes by degrees or by leap, as here: [Ex. 2] the first ought to be an octave, the second a fifth; if it is the end of the song, the final note should be a unison; if it is in the middle of the song, the last note should be a third.

If the tenor rises by one degree, as here [Ex. 3], if it is the end of the song, [use] octave, fifth, third, unison; if it is in the middle, octave, third or fifth; and the others thirds.

Moreover, if the last note is more than a step, as here [Ex. 4], octave, fifth, or third, and the last one a third, below the tenor; or the first one an octave, and the other middle ones sixths and the final one a third; and if it is the end of the song, the last is a unison.

In all rising ligatures, if the tenor rises five or six notes altogether, one should use the rule of the three- or four-note ligatures given above.

Also, if the tenor should descend three notes by degrees, as here [Ex. 5], if it is the beginning of the song, the discant is octave, sixth, octave or fifth, third, fifth; if in the middle, sixth, sixth, octave, or third, third, fifth, or third, sixth, octave, etc.

If [the tenor] skips a step, as here [Ex. 6], third, fifth, octave; or thus [Ex. 7], third, sixth, octave.

If the tenor descends four notes stepwise, as here [Ex. 8], if it is at the beginning of the song, there are three discants, that is: octave, sixth, [sixth], octave; or fifth, third, third, fifth; or fifth, third, sixth, octave.

If it is in the middle of the song, there are six discants: three sixths and the final [interval] an octave; or three thirds and the last a fifth; or sixth, octave, sixth, octave; or third, fifth, [third, fifth]; or third, third, sixth, octave; [or third, sixth, sixth, octave]. If the tenor descends five or six notes, one can use the rule of three or four as given earlier.

Also, in song there are three exceptions, of which the first is, if the tenor has *re fa*, etc., or *sol mi*, as here [Ex. 9], and the discant were

octave, fifth, octave—which would be *sol fa sol,* or *la sol la*—the middle
note is not altered [chromatically].

The second is, if the tenor descends two tones and a half, as here
[Ex. 10], if the first discant note is a third, it should and would be much
better for it to descend one tone in order to have a fifth than to rise two
tones to have an octave, for the third is then [in its place and is pleas-
ing].[2]

Also, the third exception is, if the tenor should rise two tones and a
half, as here [Ex. 11], if the first discant note is a tenth, it is allowed and
is better to rise one note to make an octave [with the tenor] than to
descend two tones to have a fifth.

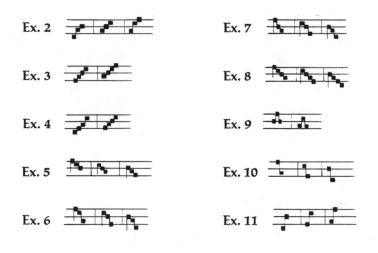

Ex. 2

Ex. 3

Ex. 4

Ex. 5

Ex. 6

Ex. 7

Ex. 8

Ex. 9

Ex. 10

Ex. 11

2. The French is "en parchon et en fleurs," which presents some problems of exact translation, but it seems to mean the above.

2. The Early Renaissance

Conrad von Zabern (b. Zabern, Alsace ?), was a musician, musical scholar, priest, and theologian. He held the post of Professor at Heidelberg around 1470, where he lectured on music. Little is known of his life except that he wrote an essay on the monochord and its use, which was published by Peter Schöffer in Mainz about 1473. His other known work is De modo bene cantandi choralem cantum . . . , *also published by Schöffer in 1474. A second edition appeared in 1509.*

In De modo bene cantandi *Conrad points out the faults and deficiencies of choirs of the day and exhorts the singers to improve their ways. The six rules for good choir singing constitute the main portion of the work. They indicate very clearly some of the problems of performance in the late fifteenth century.*

SOURCE: *Jul. Richer, ed., "Zwei Schriften von Conrad von Zabern,"* Monatshefte für Musikgeschichte XX, Jhrg.8, No. 7 (1888):95–108.

CONRAD VON ZABERN
from *De modo bene cantandi*

Six requirements for good singing:

1. Concorditer (to sing with one spirit and accord)
2. Mensuraliter (to sing in proper measure)
3. Mediocriter (to sing in middle range)
4. Differentialiter (to sing with discrimination)
5. Devotionaliter (to sing with devotion)
6. Satis urbaniter (to sing with beauty and refinement)

1. To sing with one accord: each singer must put forth his voice at the same moment and in the same degree, without anyone anticipating or holding back. As examples, the angels sang together the night of Christ's birth; also, the three children in the fiery furnace who with

their three voices praised God as with one. To acquire this habit, the singers should observe one another carefully, especially when the choir is large and the place of performance spacious.

2. To sing in proper tempo it is necessary that one give each note its value and not hold one longer than another. This is often wrong because the singers often hold the higher tones excessively long.

3. To choose a medium range for each song is reasonable, because in a large choir it usually happens that it is difficult for all to sing the very high or very low notes, and therefore one must do without some of the voices. It is therefore important that the leader should give the starting note in the proper range, so that a melody may lie in a range about eight or nine steps above or below it.

4. To sing with discrimination means to observe fittingly the necessary requirements for the church services and the church year. This is accomplished (a) through the selection of different tempos; (b) the practice of using different pitches.

In regard to (a), in general a high feast is to be sung in a very slow tempo; on Sunday and single feasts in a moderate tempo; and daily services in fairly rapid tempo. Such a gradation has a good basis in the authority of the Council of Basel. Also it falls to the choir leader to make clear at the beginning the tempo to be held to. On one and the same day one sings the high service with greater ceremony than that of the private Mass, and due to the coincidence of different liturgical relations on the same day the *officio de festo* must be performed more pompously and solemnly in contrast to the *officia de feria*, which will be sung in a faster movement. (b) On joyous feasts one chooses a somewhat higher tone, which however does not too much exceed the middle range. For funeral services both in the Mass as well as in the Vigils and Vespers, one sings in a low and serious tone.

5. To sing with devotion it is necessary (a) for each singer to maintain the notes firmly, as they are written and handed down from the blessed Father. Also, one should not divide single notes into several parts, nor leap to the upper fifth or lower fourth or some other consonance, nor deviate from the written notes in a kind of discant. All such digressions destroy the devotion of the hearer and easily cause confusion in the choir.

(b) During the singing it seems suitable that the singers, if it is necessary, and usual, uncover their heads or bow humbly, just as the usual genuflection at the proper time.

(c) In the service one should use no melodies except those that come from the Holy Father, otherwise the servants of the Devil would be introduced. So, many school Rectors certainly have the Devil in their service when they borrow worldly songs and sing to them the text of the Gloria, Credo, Sanctus, and Agnus, and I do not know whom it pleases. This causes not only great vexation to the believer in Christ, but it also leads the young fleshly minded people to think less of the kingdom of God than of the dance hall, where they have heard the same kind of singing.

6. The beautiul and well-bred manner of singing has the title of *urbanus* (urbane) and *urbanitas* in contrast to *rusticus* (rustic) and *rusticitas*, because city people ordinarily have more delicate manners than do country people. Now there certainly are people so affected by Nature with rustic ways that it is impossible to enumerate them; but those most perceptible and frequent must here be cited in order to enable one to avoid them; for one cannot avoid evil if one does not know it. Therefore it is necessary for such avoidance careful self-examination of all that has been written in our notes, and to be conscientious and faithful. . . . Thus, who wishes to sing beautifully and edifyingly will never be thoughtless and inattentive, but rather will examine himself and his voice; in this way he will avoid more readily the unbeautiful things that will now be enumerated.

(a) The first bad habit is the addition of an *h* to vowels in words that do not have an *h*: for example, in Ky-ri-e e-lei-son, where one often hears "he he he" sung on the *e*, like the butcher when he drives his sheep to market. Likewise, one hears thousands of times a "ha, ha," "ho, ho" in words that have no *h*. This certainly cannot be called elegant and beautiful singing: rather I call it rustic.

(b) A second bad habit (again *rusticitas*) is to sing through the nose, which makes a voice very *un*beautiful. The nasal passages are never associated with the development of the human voice; so it is not a small sign of lack of education if one is not contented with the mouth and the ordinary natural tools, but emits the voice through the nose.

(c) Another crude manner is unclear pronunciation of the vowels, which makes the singing unintelligible to the hearers. In this most of the clerics are to blame, for they sing as if they had mush in their mouths and make scarcely any difference between *e* and *i*, and *u* and *o*. I have often heard sung instead of *Dominus vobiscum*, "vabiscum"; instead of *Oremus* (Let us pray), "Aremus" (Let us plough), so that I say to my neighbor "No, we will not plough now." And in fact from Frankfort to Coblenz and from there to Trier I have made the frequent observation that *e* and *i* are not clearly pronounced and clearly differentiated, especially by students. Therefore the Rectors should justly refrain from this daily, so that they do not carry this error into old age.

(d) Another bad habit is that when the pitch of a vowel sustained below a series of notes and held for a long time does not remain true but wanders and varies during the singing. This sounds very bad, yet it is a very common error, as one can perceive every day.

(e) A very common sign of poor training is the horrid wavering up or down of the pitch. The one as well as the other is detestable, the more so because it attracts attention and is disturbing in the highest degree. It spoils the correct singing of the others, just like an out-of-tune string disturbs the tuning of the clavichord. Whoever has this shocking habit should desist entirely from singing until he has procured relief; and it should not be neglected as long as there is hope of correction.

(f) Another common habit is the violent squeezing out or pushing of the voice, which injures the beauty and sweetness of the singing in the highest degree. I know some persons who, though better trained than others in singing, nevertheless destroy their singing because of this error, for they are convinced that they sing well; however they have never been shown how blameworthy that manner is.

(g) A particularly striking crudity is that of singing the high notes with a loud tone, indeed with full lung power. And truly, if there is a person who, by nature, has a heavy, trumpetlike voice, it makes a great disturbance in the whole choral song and appears as though the voices of several oxen were mixed in with the choir. And I have also heard in a Collegium that singers with full, heavy voices scream on the high notes from pleasure in strength, so that one thinks that they want to burst the windows or knock them out of their frames. I must say that I have long been astonished by this crudity, and have therefore been led to make the following little rhyme.

Ut boves in pratis
Sic vos in choro boatis

(As the cattle in the field,
So bellow those in the choir)

In order to comprehend this error, one must know that whoever sings well must use his voice in three degrees. The low notes are to be sung entirely from the chest, the middle ones with moderate strength, the high ones with a soft voice. And the change from one to the other must not be sudden, but gradual, according to the movement of the melody. Who does otherwise manages without understanding, doing as he pleases. Let us take an example. Everyone knows that an organ, no matter what size, has a variety of pipes. large, medium, and small, and that the larger ones are not only deeper but also fuller, the smaller not only higher but also thinner and more delicate. . . . The monochord has only one string of one strength, yet it produces very different characters—notes of full, moderate, and soft sounds, according to each pitch of the scale. Why should a man not imitate this string and be able to modulate his voice in many ways? Each bad habit disfigures the song, first of all, then tires the singer, and third, makes him hoarse and incapable of singing. For the windpipe is a delicate organ and easily injured by violent use, often through singing high notes loudly. On the contrary, by singing softly, avoiding abuses, one benefits by being able to sing considerably higher than by unnatural straining of the voice.

(h) Another bad practice is that of intoning liturgical chants which belong together on entirely different pitches, often when a single overall pitch can be maintained without difficulty for the choir. This can be done in the case of the *Kyrie* and *Gloria in excelsis* with the *Et in terra*. . . .

(i) Another fault is sluggish singing, without life and emotion, such as an old woman groans who is near death, so that one thinks he hears sighing rather than singing. One must avoid both extremes; bawling too loud and singing too faint-heartedly; according to the old saying, "For too little and too much spoils the performance."

(k) Finally there is still to censure the unseemly movements of the body, such as: not standing still, but swaying from side to side; raising one's head too high; bending one's head considerably to the side; drawing one's mouth crookedly to one side; not opening one's mouth wide enough; etc. All such are to be avoided in order that those who see it will not be irritated or moved to laughter instead of devotion.

The Banquet of the Oath of the Pheasant, given by Philippe the Good, Duke of Burgundy and Brabant, on February 17, 1453 in the city of Lille, was a spectacular event. Both Olivier de la Marche, in his Mémoires, and Mathieu d'Escouchy, in his Chroniques, agree in describing a most unusual musical entertainment performed between the courses of the meal, or entremets. The chroniclers describe quite faithfully the instruments and the kinds of music performed, even the attire of some of the performers, but they mention only a few titles of the works that were sung or played. The composer of one chanson, Sauvegarde de ma vie, has yet to be identified, but Je ne vis oncques la pareille is ascribed to Dufay in one source, to Binchois in another, and is anonymous in nine other sources; because this chanson exists in so many manuscript sources, we must assume that it was well known and very popular. The chasse, which de la Marche describes as being so realistic, may have been Gherardello's Tosto che l'alba, a charming caccia.

Accounts such as this unusually complete description shed light on the role of music in festivals and banquets in the fifteenth century and increase our meager knowledge of the instruments used and the kinds of compositions that were deemed suitable.

SOURCES: *Olivier de la Marche,* Mémoires, *and Mathieu d'Escouchy,* Chroniques, *in Publications de la Société de l'Histoire de France, vols. 120, 219.*

OLIVIER DE LA MARCHE AND MATHIEU D'ESCOUCHY
from *Mémoires* and *Chroniques*

Banquet of the Oath of the Pheasant

This fête began with a joust. . . . Each one did his best in the tournament, and when it was over, each one withdrew. Then at the proper hour, they gathered in a hall, where my lord had prepared a rich banquet; and there my lord, accompanied by princes and chevaliers, lords and ladies, finding the banquet ready to be served, went to see the entremets which had been prepared. . . . In this room were three covered tables, one of medium size, one large, and the other small. On the medium one a church with a cross was erected, where there was a bell ringing and four singers, who sang and played the organ when their turn came. . . .

The second table, which was much larger, had first of all, a large pastry, in which were twenty-eight persons playing different instruments, each when their turn came. . . .

When everyone was seated, the bell of the church, which was the first entremets of the principal table, rang loudly. After it ceased three small boys and a tenor sang a very pretty song; and when they had finished it, from the pastry, which was the first entremets of the long table, a shepherd played a musette in a new manner. . . .

After this a horse entered walking backwards, richly covered with vermilion silk. On it two trumpeters were seated back to back, without a saddle; they were clothed in coats of grey and black silk, with hats on their heads, and they wore masks. They led the horse backwards up and down the hall while they played flourishes on their trumpets. And to accompany this entremets were sixteen chevaliers clothed in livery.

This entremets finished, the organ in the church was played, and in the pastry a German cornett was played very curiously; and then a goblin or monster of strange appearance entered. . . .

[This being concluded] those in the church sang, and in the pastry a *douçaine* played with another instrument, and after it four *clairons* sounded very loud and made a joyous fanfare. . . . After their flourish Jason appeared in full armor. . . .

At the conclusion of this mystery the organ in the church played for about the length of a motet, and after that, from the pastry, three sweet voices sang a chanson, which was called *Sauvegarde de ma vie.* Then after the church and the pastry had each played four times, through the great door where the other entremets had entered, came a stag, marvelously large and handsome; it was white with large golden antlers and was decked with a rich cover of vermilion silk. Mounted on the stag was a youth about twelve years old, I think, dressed in a short crimson robe, with a little scalloped black hat, and wearing nice slippers. The child held onto the horns of the stag with both hands. And as soon as they entered the hall, the youth began to sing the *dessus* of a chanson in a high clear voice, and the stag sang the tenor, without there being anyone else besides the child and the stag. And the chanson they sang was *Je ne vis oncques la pareille.* While singing they made a tour of the tables, and then departed. This entremets pleased me and I watched it gladly. . . .

After this fine entremets of the white stag and the boy, the singers in the church sang a motet, and in the pastry a lute was played, accompanied by some good voices. And the church and the pastry always performed between the entremets.

As soon as the organ in the church had played, four minstrels in the pastry played flutes. Then, in the highest part of the room, a flying dragon appeared, all fiery, and flew the length of the hall, passing above the assembly, and disappeared; and no one knew what became of it.

After the dragon two blind men played viols, and with them a lute in good accord; and then a young demoiselle from the retinue of the duchess sang . . . and it was a fine and sweet melody to hear.

[The next entremets was of Jason sowing the dragon's teeth.] This mystery finished, they played the organ in the church, and in the pastry they performed a *chasse,* such that one seemed to hear little dogs yelping and hunting dogs baying, and sounds of horns, as if they were in a forest; and this *chasse* ended the entremets of the pastry.

Such were the worldly entremets of this feast.

Part II The Renaissance

3. Music in Daily Life

Giovanni Boccaccio (1313–1375) was one of the first Humanists and a most prolific writer, both in prose and in verse, in Italian and in Latin. His best-known work is The Decameron, *a collection of one hundred stories, original tales, traditional stories, folk tales, and romantic histories original with Boccaccio and repeated from many sources.*

The setting is as follows: The city of Florence has been attacked by an epidemic of the plague, to escape which a group of well-born ladies and gentlemen, ten in all, have gone into the country at Certaldo. There to pass the time, each person tells a story on each of the ten nights; hence, the title, The Decameron. *The stories are connected with short descriptions of the life of the group at Certaldo, and in a number of them descriptions of music-making occur—reflections of such activities in normal social life.*

SOURCE: *Giovanni Boccaccio, "The First Day, Novella X," "The Seventh Day, Novella X," in* The Decameron *(1348–53).*

GIOVANNI BOCCACCIO
from *The Decameron*

The First Day, Novella X

[After supper] the queen ordered the musical instruments to be brought, and that a dance should begin, led by Lauretta, with Emilia singing, accompanied by Dioneus upon the lute; Lauretta immediately complied, and Emilia sang a *canzona* in a very fascinating manner.

The song being ended, to which they had all responded, though the words occasioned some speculation, and after a few other little dance songs, a good part of the night being now spent, the queen thought proper to put an end to the first day. . . .

The Seventh Day, Novella X

. . . Here Lauretta, having been made queen . . . gave them liberty till supper. The company then arose, and while some went to wash their feet in the cool stream, others took a walk upon the green turf, under the cover of the spreading trees, and Dioneus and Fiammetta sat singing together the song of Palamon and Arcite. Thus all were agreeably employed till supper; when the tables were set forth by the side of the fountain, they sat down to the music of a thousand birds, and their faces fanned all the while with cool, refreshing breezes coming from the little hills around them, they supped with the utmost mirth and satisfaction. Taking a walk afterward round the valley before the sun was quite set, they began their march back to the palace, talking all the way of a thousand different things, which had either occurred in this day's discourse, or the preceding, and arrived there as it grew dark. Refreshing themselves after their walk with wine and sweetmeats, they indulged in a dance by the side of the fountain; sometimes, for variety, they danced to the sound of Tindarus's bagpipe, and sometimes to other more usual instruments. . . .

Baldassare Castiglione (b. 1478) was a scholar as well as a courtier and gentleman. He received a classical education at a humanist school at Milan and at the court of il Moro, Ludovico Sforza. After Sforza's fall in 1499, Castiglione served under Francesco Gonzaga, Duke of Mantua. In 1504 Castiglione became a member of the court of Guidobaldo di Montefeltro, Duke of Urbino, where he served as diplomatic envoy and also in military expeditions. In that court, under the influence of the duchess Elisabetta Gonzaga and Emilia Pio, the arts and courtly manner flourished; according to Bembo, Castiglione was outstanding among "the most noble talents" in that circle, where poetry, music, and theatrical pieces were composed and performed.

Castiglione's major work, Il cortegiano (1528), is a monument of highest historical and literary importance. Based on the courtly life at Urbino, Castiglione purports to describe the ideal courtier, incidentally describing the life and thought of this period of the Renaissance. The work is in four books, each relating an evening's discussion supposed to have taken place in March 1507. The participants are all personages connected with the Urbino court, including the duchess, Bembo, Giuliano de' Medici, the poet Bibbiena, and many other artists, musicians, and men of letters. Each of them is called on to help describe the qualities of "a perfect courtier." The first book contains the discussion of knowledge of music as a desirable attribute, along with such other virtues and accomplishments as refined and gentle speech, skill in riding, courage in feats of arms, understanding of the art of painting, and the ability to write well. The role of music is shown here to have been of considerable importance.

SOURCE: *Baldassare Castiglione,* Il cortegiano, *Books I and II, 1528; trans. Leonard Eckstein Opdyke as* The Book of the Courtier *(New York, 1905, 1929).*

BALDASSARE CASTIGLIONE
from *The Book of the Courtier*

Here everyone laughed, and the Count began anew and said, "My lords, you must know that I am not content with the Courtier unless he be also a musician and unless, besides understanding and being able to read notes, he can play upon divers instruments. For if we consider rightly, there is to be found no rest from toil or medicine for the troubled spirit more becoming and praiseworthy in time of leisure, than this; and especially in courts, where besides the relief from tedium that music affords us all, many things are done to please the ladies, whose tender and gentle spirit is easily penetrated by harmony and filled with sweetness. Thus it is no marvel that in both ancient and modern times they have always been inclined to favour musicians, and have found refreshing spiritual food in music."

Then my lord Gaspar said:

"I admit that music as well as many other vanities may be proper to women and perhaps to some that have the semblance of men, but not to those who really are men; for these ought not to enervate their mind with delights and thus induce therein a fear of death."

"Say not so," replied the Count; "for I shall enter upon a vast sea in praise of music. And I shall call to mind how it was always celebrated and held sacred among the ancients, and how very sage philosophers were of opinion that the world is composed of music, that the heavens make harmony in their moving, and that the soul, being ordered in like fashion, awakes and as it were revives its powers through music.

"Thus it is written that Alexander was sometimes excited by it so passionately, that he was forced almost against his will to leave the banquet table and rush to arms; and when the musician changed the temper of the tune, he grew calm again, lay aside his arms, and returned to the banquet table. Moreover I will tell you that grave Socrates learned to play the cithern at a very advanced age. And I remember having once heard that Plato and Aristotle would have the man of culture a musician also; and they show by a host of arguments that the power of music over us is very great, and (for many reasons which would be too long to tell now) that it must needs be taught from childhood, not so much for the mere melody that we hear, but for the power it has to induce in us a fresh and good habit of mind and an habitual tendency to virtue, which renders the soul more capable of happiness, just as bodily exercise renders the body more robust; and that music is not only no hindrance in the pursuits of peace and war, but is very helpful therein.

"Again, Lycurgus approved of music in his harsh laws. And we read that in their battles the very warlike Lacedemonians and Cretans used the cithern and other dulcet instruments; that many very excellent commanders of antiquity, like Epaminondas, practiced music; and that those who were ignorant of it, like Themistocles, were far less esteemed. Have you not read that music was among the first accomplishments which the worthy old Chiron taught Achilles in tender youth, whom he reared from the age of nurse and cradle? and that the sage preceptor insisted that the hands, which were to shed so much Trojan blood, should be often busied with the cithern? Where is the soldier who would be ashamed to imitate Achilles, to say nothing of many other famous commanders whom I could cite?

"Therefore seek not to deprive our Courtier of music, which not only soothes men's minds, but often tames wild beasts; and he who enjoys it not, may be sure that his spirit is ill attuned. See what power it has to make (as once it did) a fish submit to be ridden by a man upon the boisterous sea. We find it used in holy temples to render praise and thanks to God; and we must believe that it is pleasing to Him and that He has given it to us as most sweet alleviation for our fatigues and troubles. Wherefore rough toilers of the field under a burning sun often cheat their weariness with crude and rustic song. With music the rude peasant lass, who is up before the day to spin or weave, wards off her drowsiness and makes her toil a pleasure; music is very cheering pastime for poor sailors after rain, wind and tempest; a solace to tired pilgrims on their long and weary journeys, and often to sorrowing captives in their chains and fetters. Thus, as stronger proof that melody even if rude is very great relief from every human toil and care, nature seems to have taught it to the nurse as chief remedy for the continual wailing of frail children, who by the sound of her voice are brought restful and placid sleep, forgetful of the tears so proper to them and given us in that age by nature as a presage of our after life."

As the Count now remained silent for a little, the Magnifico Giuliano said:

"I do not at all agree with my lord Gaspar. Nay I think, for the reasons you give and for many others, that music is not only an ornament but a necessity to the Courtier. Yet I would have you declare in what way this and the other accomplishments that you prescribe for him, are to be practiced, and at what time and in what manner. For many things that are praiseworthy in themselves often become very inappropriate when practiced out of season, and on the other hand, some that seem of little moment are highly esteemed when made use of opportunely."

Then the Count said:

"Before we enter upon that subject, I wish to discuss another matter, which I deem of great importance, and therefore think our Courtier ought by no means to omit; and that is to know how to draw and to have acquaintance with the very art of painting.

"And do not marvel that I desire this art, which today may seem to savour of the artisan and little to befit a gentleman; for I remember having read that the ancients, especially throughout Greece, had their boys of gentle birth study painting in school as an honourable and necessary thing, and it was admitted to the first rank of liberal arts; while by public edict they forbade that it be taught to slaves. Among the Romans too, it was held in highest honour, and the very noble family of the Fabii took their name from it; for the first Fabius was given the name *Pictor*, because—being indeed a most excellent painter, and so devoted to painting that when he painted the walls of the temple of Health—he inscribed his own name thereon; for although he was born of a family thus renowned and honoured with so many consular titles, triumphs and other dignities, and although he was a man of letters and learned in the law, and numbered among the orators—yet he thought to add splendor and ornament to his fame by leaving a memorial that he had been a painter. Nor is there lack of many other men of illustrious family celebrated in this art; which besides being very noble and worthy in itself, is of great utility, and especially in war for drawing places, sites, rivers, bridges, rocks, fortresses, and the like; since however well we may keep them in memory (which is very difficult), we cannot show them to others.

"And truly he who does not esteem this art, seems to me very unreasonable; for this universal fabric that we see—with the vast heaven so richly adorned with shining stars, and in its midst the earth girdled by the seas, varied with mountains, valleys, and rivers, and bedecked with so many divers trees, beautiful flowers, and grasses—may be said to be a great and noble picture, composed by the hand of nature and of God; and whoever is able to imitate it, seems to me deserving of great praise. . . ."

Then my lord Gaspar Pallavicino said:

"There are many kinds of music, vocal as well as instrumental: therefore I should like to hear which is the best of all, and at what time the Courtier ought to perform it."

Messer Federico replied:

"I regard as beautiful music, to sing well by note, with ease and in beautiful style; but as even far more beautiful, to sing to the accompaniment of the viol, because nearly all the sweetness lies in the solo part, and we note and observe the fine manner and the melody with much greater attention when our ears are not occupied with more than a single voice, and moreover every little fault is more clearly discerned,—which is not the case when several sing together, because each singer helps his neighbour. But above all, singing to the viol by way of recitative seems to me most delightful, which adds to the words a charm and grace that are very admirable.

"All fretted instruments also are pleasing to the ear, because they produce very perfect consonances, and upon them one can play many things that fill the mind with musical delight. And not less charming is the music of four bowed viols, which is most sweet and exquisite. The human voice lends much ornament and grace to all these instruments, with which I would have our Courtier at least to some degree acquainted, albeit the more he excels with them, the better,—without troubling himself much with those that Minerva forbade Alcibiades, because it seems that they are ungraceful.

"Then, as to the time for enjoying these various kinds of music, I think it is whenever a man finds himself in familiar and beloved companionship and there are not other occupations, but above all it is fitting where ladies are present, because their aspect fills the listener's heart with sweetness, renders it more sensitive to the tenderness of the music, and quickens the musician's soul.

"As I have already said, it pleases me well that we should avoid the crowd, and especially the ignoble crowd. But discretion must needs be the spice of everything, for it would be quite impossible to foresee all the cases that occur; and if the Courtier rightly understands himself, he will adapt himself to the occasion and will perceive when the minds of his hearers are disposed to listen and when not. He will take his own age into account: for it is indeed unseemly and unlovely in the extreme to see a man of any quality,—old, hoary, and toothless, full of wrinkles,—

playing on a viol and singing in the midst of a company of ladies, even though he be a passable performer. And the reason of this is that in singing the words are usually amourous, and love is a ridiculous thing in old men,—albeit it is sometimes among its other miracles to kindle frozen hearts in spite of years."

Then the Magnifico replied:

"Do not deprive old men of this pleasure, messer Federico, for in my time I have known old men who had right perfect voices and hands very dexterous upon their instruments, far more than some young men."

"I do not wish," said messer Federico, "to deprive old men of this pleasure, but I do wish to deprive you and these ladies of the pleasure of laughing at such folly. And if old men wish to sing to the viol, let them do so in secret and only to drive from their minds those painful thoughts and grievous troubles with which our life is filled, and to taste that rapture which I believe Pythagoras and Socrates found in music. For just as the arms of a smith, who is weak in his other members, become stronger by exercise than those of another man who is more robust but unaccustomed to use his arms,—in like manner ears practiced in harmony will perceive it better and more speedily and will appreciate it with far greater pleasure, than others, however good and sharp they be, that are not versed in the varieties of musical consonance, because these modulations do not penetrate ears unused to hearing them, but pass aside without leaving any savour of themselves; albeit even the beasts have some enjoyment in melody.

"This then is the pleasure it is fitting old men should take in music. I say the like of dancing, for in truth we ought to give up these exercises before our age forces us to give them up against our will."

Discorso sopra la musica *is one of eight short essays contained in a codex in the Library of the Archivio di Stato in Lucca. The manuscript was written and compiled about 1628 by Vincenzo Giustiniani, a Roman nobleman who, although he was not a professional musician, was a cultured dilettante interested in all the arts and very knowledgeable about music. His accounts of music and musicians are reliable, and his little* Discorso *provides considerable information about musical activities during the period 1570–1628 and much that is of interest regarding the changing styles of musical performance. His account of the musical activities at the courts of Mantua and Ferrara around 1575 shows clearly that music played a very large part in court entertainments. It also shows that not only had the practice of singing* diminutions *become the ac-*

cepted style but also the newer expressive manner was being practiced. The singers at the two courts were famous for their sensitive renditions and undoubtedly contributed to the new style of solo singing. Giustiniani's description gives the reader an excellent idea of the requisites for performing choral and solo music of the period.

SOURCE: *Vincenzo Giustiniani,* Discorso sopra la musica, *trans. Carol MacClintock, in* Musicological Studies and Documents 9 *(Rome: American Institute of Musicology, 1972), pp.69–70.*

VINCENZO GIUSTINIANI
from *Discorso sopra la musica*

In the Holy Year of 1575, or shortly thereafter, a style of singing appeared which was very different from that preceding. It continued for some years, chiefly in the manner of one voice singing with accompaniment, and was exemplified by Giovanni Andrea napoletano, Signor Giulio Cesare Brancaccio, and Alessandro Merlo romano. These all sang bass with a range of 22 notes and with a variety of passagework new and pleasing to the ear of all. They inspired the composers to write similar works to be sung by several voices in the manner of a single one accompanied by some instruments, in imitation of the above-mentioned and of a certain woman called Femia. But they achieved greater invention and artifice, which resulted in some Villanellas which were a mixture of Madrigals in florid style and Villanellas. Many books of these by the aforementioned authors and by Orazio Vecchi and others are seen today. But as the Villanellas acquired greater perfection through more artful composition, so also every composer, in order that his compositions should satisfy the general taste, took care to advance in the style of composition for several voices, particularly Giaches Wert in Mantua and Luzzasco in Ferrara. They were the superintendents of all music for those Dukes, who took the greatest delight in the art, especially in having many noble ladies and gentlemen learn to sing and play superbly, so that they spent entire days in some rooms designed especially for this purpose and beautifully decorated with paintings. The ladies of Mantua and Ferrara were highly competent, and vied with each other not only in regard to the timbre and training of their voices but also in the design of exquisite passages delivered at opportune points, but not in excess

(Giovanni Luca of Rome, who served also in Ferrara, usually erred in this respect). Furthermore, they moderated or increased their voices, loud or soft, heavy or light, according to the demands of the piece they were singing; now slow, breaking off with sometimes a gentle sigh, now singing long passages legato or detached, now groups, now leaps, now with long trills, now with short, and again with sweet running passages sung softly, to which sometimes one heard an echo answer unexpectedly. They accompanied the music and the sentiment with appropriate facial expressions, glances, and gestures, with no awkward movements of the mouth or hands or body which might not express the feeling of the song. They made the words clear in such a way that one could hear even the last syllable of every word, which was never interrupted or suppressed by passages and other embellishments. They used many other particular devices which will be known to persons more experienced than I. And under these favorable circumstances the above-mentioned musicians made every effort to win fame and the favor of the Princes their patrons, who were their principal support.

4. On Singing and Ornamentation

Adrian Petit Coclico (1500–1563) was a Flemish composer and teacher of music at Wittenberg, Germany. In 1547 he joined the capella of Duke Albrecht of Prussia as both singer and composer, but left that post in 1550 because of a scandal. He then settled in Frankfort-am-Main, where he met the publisher Montanus, who brought out Coclico's Compendium musices *in 1552. Thereafter he opened a school in Nuremberg; then in 1554 he was at Wismar. He moved about until 1556, when he became a member of the chapel of Christian III of Denmark, a position he held until his death.*

In his Compendium *Coclico calls himself a pupil of Josquin des Près, and he may indeed have a right to that claim. His description of Josquin's teaching seems to have the ring of truth, but Coclico also claims to have been a member of the Papal chapel, to have lived in a number of cities in France, to have been imprisoned for heresy, etc., all of which cannot be substantiated.*

The examples Coclico gives as being Josquin's may not be by that master; nevertheless they are representative of the style of the time and thus of value to the student of vocal ornamentations of that period.

Source: Compendium musices descriptum ab Adrian Petit Coclico discipulo Josquini de Pres, *1552, facs. ed., ed. M. Bukofzer (Kassel: Bärenreiter [Documenta musicologica], 1954), unpaged.*

ADRIAN PETIT COCLICO
from *Compendium musices*

Concerning Refinement and Ornamentation, or Pronunciation in Singing

To the young boy wishing to learn the art [of singing] well and elegantly, I advise him first to select a teacher who, by natural instinct, sings beautifully and smoothly and makes music beautiful by ornamenting his phrases; shunning the hawkers, who, by their shouting and other unsuitable things, bring most noble music to be hated by man. Who therefore has found in his youth such a teacher, will become a singer, like those seen in Belgium, Hainaut, and France, who have a singular gift in singing above those of other nations.

Several princes of musicians have lived among those people: Josquin des Près, Pierre de la Rue, Jacob Scampion, and others, who employed the most admirable and smooth passages that are to be admired. The memory of those men still remains in the schools of those regions and is continued by scholars of music, for their disciples faithfully imitate their preceptors. And so the German boy ought to take care to imitate his learned teacher while his voice is youthful, for the changed boy's voice achieves the art of singing well only with difficulty, or rarely; what is learned in youth never becomes lost in forgetfulness.

Since there are truly very few in these regions who understand the suavity of these outstanding old masters, I have decided to write out several examples that may be applied to all passages, but the words or syllables below the notes are omitted.

However, at first it is difficult to sing these with the throat unless the boy sweats and labors considerably, and works very hard; and he should repeat them daily until he understands the precepts and use of this art, so that he does not move the tongue, but pronounces them from the throat correctly and ornately. This is the first passage, as Josquin taught it to his pupils.

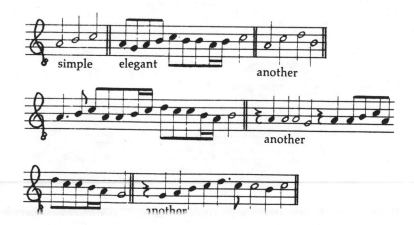

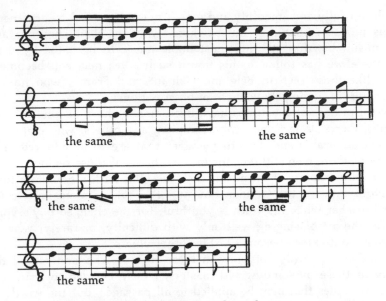

And we can sing this way in all other cadential passages.

Elegantia on the chanson *Languir me fault.*

Another example in Duo.

C'est a grant tort

Another example. Canon of 4 voices from 1.

This cannot be done correctly in the bass except in a time and place where the tenor happens to descend below the bass, etc. Because the bass is the foundation of all the other parts, when it does not remain fixed, species occur in the song that offend the ears. Similarly, it occurs in counterpoint when the bass is not singing or pronouncing well, or intoning badly.

Very little is known of the life of Giovanni Camillo Maffei, and that little is contained in his own Lettere, *published in Naples in 1562. He was born in the village of Solofra near Naples and spent his whole life in the Campagna and in Naples itself. For many years he was in the service of Giovanni da Capua, conte d'Altavilla, whose court at the end of the sixteenth century was one of the centers of Neapolitan culture.*

Maffei was a doctor of medicine, a learned philosopher, after the manner of the late Renaissance, and, in addition, a very accomplished amateur musician and singer in great demand, as we can tell from his letters.

It was at the request of his patron and in his capacity as doctor, philosopher, and singer that Maffei wrote his treatise on singing in the form of a long letter. In the first part he describes the anatomy, the physiology, and the physics of the voice and pays homage to Aristotle and Galen; this section has little value for the modern student. But the second part, in which he expounds his method of self-training and of ornamenting the music, which he calls "cantar di gorga o di garganta," roughly translated as "singing diminutions or passages," is of much interest and even value to the present-day student. Maffei's precepts regarding vocal practice are for the most part good, but his third rule, to seek out Echo when practicing, seems somewhat impractical! His discussion of the requirements for good passaggi *and the rules for placement of diminutions are enlightening and helpful to today's singers who may wish to revive the art of diminution. Also, in his discussion of types of voices, he remarks in passing that the virtuoso singers of his time possessed extraordinary ranges, for a good singer could "sing bass, tenor, and other voices with great ease" and perform passagework "now in the bass, now in the mezzo, now in the alto"—which explains why certain arias and madrigals by Caccini, Rasi, and other composers have such extended ranges.*

I have been unable to find modern equivalents for several of Maffei's technical terms and have been forced therefore to leave them in the original Italian; for example, fistola cimbalare, which most likely means glottis.

SOURCE: Delle lettere del Sor Gio. Camillo Maffei da Solofra, Libri Due ... Napoli, 1562, *Letter I, as printed in N. Bridgeman, "Giovanni Camillo Maffei et sa lettre sur le chant,"* Revue de Musicologie, *July 1956:10–34.*

GIOVANNI CAMILLO MAFFEI

Letter on Singing

To the most illustrious S. Conte d'Alta Villa:

The sweet harmony of the fine singing that is heard in your lordship's house at the hour devoted to such pursuits has perhaps appeared to be the reason for asking me about the voice and the method and right use in order to make vocal diminutions without a master. But seeing in these two requests the possibility of not only expressing myself badly but of talking too long, I came to the opinion that I should demonstrate them to your lordship on paper rather than by word of mouth. And I am sure just as much as it will annoy a person who does not understand, just so much will your lordship derive pleasure from it.

[A long philosophical discussion based on classical writers on the function of breathing and its mechanics is omitted.]

If your lordship were to say to me, "You have told me about the heart, the lungs, the throat, and about breathing; now speak a little about how the voice is produced," I would answer that to produce voice, repercussion of the air is necessary, as in the definition that has been given; and for this to occur it was necessary to create at the top of the throat many cartilages, many sinews, and many muscles, so that the cartilages, alternately closed and opened by the sinews and muscles, should give the effects already described. That is, should draw air from the lungs and should make voice. And in order that your lordship should be completely satisfied, be contented to hear how it is done.

The top of the trachea (or windpipe) is composed of three cartilages, of which the largest appears to us as a shield; and it is the "knot" that is seen in the neck of every man, which is hard in order to protect that place, like a shield. So it is called "shield cartilage"; and inside this there is another, for better protection if the first is not sufficient, and it has no name. Inside of this one in the middle, there is still another, called the *cimbalare* [glottis], shaped like the tongue [reed] of a bagpipe; and here is produced the repercussion of the air and the voice; not as Homer said in the text, in that line of verse *Clamorem emisit quantum caput huic sapiebat.* And because movement is necessary, so as to be able to close or open these cartilages as need be, Nature has made, from the sinews descending from the head to the stomach, a branch there, together with its muscles, which I have talked about. And these sinews are called "reversing," since they return from the stomach to the cartilages. And their movement is so responsive that they serve the brain in the same way that the bridle of a horse serves the rider. Because this matter is difficult and obscure, I would like to give an example very effective in clearing it up.

As in the bagpipe three elements are seen, the bag of wind, the arm that presses the bag, and the pipe of the instrument, adding a fourth element, the reed of the pipe, which is held in the mouth; the fingers of the hand are placed so as to be able to close and open the holes, according to the tone desired.

So in the voice similar things may be recognized. The hollow of the chest and the lungs where the air is stored is like the bag, and the muscles of the chest are like the arm, and the windpipe can, without any doubt, be likened to the pipe; the cartilage called the *cimbalare* is the reed of the bagpipe, and the sinews and muscles, which alternately close and open, do the work of the fingers.

Applying this illustration in more detail. I say just as the sound reverberates in the large cavity of the bagpipe because of the air that is propelled from the fingers that control the holes, the sound re-echoes and changes according as it pleases the player. In the same way the voice sounds in the instrument because of the air that is forced from the chest into the throat, where it strikes and impinges upon the *fistola cimbalare*, being dilated or shrunken by the sinews and the muscles according as the person who is producing the voice wishes. So, your lordship will say to me, "The tongue, the teeth, and the lips are not necessary for voice?" I answer that voice is very different from articulated speech, because the voice expresses only the vowels *o, i, u, e, a,* and to utter these sounds nothing other is necessary than what we have said. But speech, whose task is, by joining the consonants to the vowels, to make syllables (let us say, for examples, *to, ba, se, non*) and from the syllables to make words, speech requires other circumstances. From this, since this result cannot be achieved without the help of the tongue, teeth, and palate, as is clearly seen, it follows that such members are not necessary except for articulated, connected speech. When people say to me, "Since the material of the voice is air, what does it mean when sometimes the air emerges as in breathing, that it does not make voice?" I would say to him that, generally speaking (to talk as Galen talks), the material of the voice is exhaling, but speaking more exactly, it is very copious exhalation which is given violently. Since that is what is needed to make voice, it must issue forth with violence, which does not happen when we are breathing normally.

But it is now time to return to Aristotle's definition, after having touched upon what was necessary to make it clear. It went like this: (1) The voice is a sound caused by the mind, by repercussions in the air, made in the throat with the intention of conveying a meaning. We cannot use sound in general because though all voice is sound, not all sound is voice, as the sound of a bell demonstrates. And all the rest that follows points out the difference, because when he says "caused by the mind" he differentiates it from the sounds that are not caused by the mind. (He means by mind, as I have said, principally the imaginative faculty.) And when he says "it is caused by the repercussion of air in the throat," he is differentiating voice from those sounds which, while they result from the repercussions of the air, are not made in the throat. And last of all, when he says "with the intention of conveying a meaning" he makes them different from the repercussions made in the throat without signifying any meaning, like coughing.

I remember (says your lordship) to ask to what animals it is granted to have voices? I answer briefly that voice is granted only to those animals that possess a throat and lungs. So flies, crickets, grasshoppers, butterflies, and all other insects, because they have no throats, are without voices, and that noise or whispering they make when they fly is not voice, but the sound made by their wings as they strike the air. And for the same reason fish have no voice because they have no lungs; they not only have no voice but do not breathe, and may Pliny pardon me for this. I am not speaking of dolphins, whales, dogfish, and many other fish that have lungs and breathe out of the water. And so that your lordship may be completely satisfied, you should know that voice, sound, and speech are three very different things, as Aristotle says in his books on "the kinds of animals," and this is the difference. Voice is differentiated from sound because to make voice a throat is necessary, which is not needed to make sound; it is also different from speech because in making voice the throat is sufficient, but in speaking not only the throat is needed but also the lips, the tongue, the teeth, and the palate, without any defects at all, because otherwise words could not be uttered. So if certain animals have a voice and cannot speak it is for no other reason than that they do not have these members, or if they have them they are not suitable for the task. So it is granted only to Man to speak, for all three members properly adjusted are granted to Man alone. And if your lordship were to ask me if there are any animals (I do not speak of Man, to whom speech is appropriate) who share in this, I would answer what Aristotle says about it; that is, that all four-legged creatures have been denied speech, and only to some birds has it been granted, those who have a rather large and flexible tongue, as is seen in the so-called *Pappagalli* [parrots] and as the magpies clearly demonstrate.

"But," the musicians will say to me, "since such a great diversity of voices is perceptible, inasmuch as nature produces them, large and small, harsh and sweet, high and low, and artistry changes them, please tell me, what is the reason for this diversity?" So, wanting to explain the reason to these people, as well as to your lordship, more briefly than Aristotle and Galen have written, I will reply.

The differences among the voices are three (as Galen says in his books on the medical art): these are, great and small, harsh and smooth, high and low. And Aristotle writes (in his book on the generation of animals) in like manner, though he adds another difference, that is, rigid and flexible, meaning by this the "unsoft" (I am forced by lack of the proper term to call it this). Though this fourth difference can be classified with the second, nevertheless I will speak of it apart.

These then are the natural species of voices, and if others should be found, like the hoarse, the graceful, the thick, and others, they can easily be reduced to one of these four. I don't want to speak of the voice called "black" by metaphor.

Beginning with the small and the large, it is right that I return to what was said in the beginning of this discourse; that three things join in producing voice, as in every other human activity—the material, the master, and the instrument; meaning by the master the potentiality of the mind, the imaginative faculty; the motive is the chest, and the material is the air; for the instrument, the throat and lungs. So when the instrument is large, and there is much air, the powers of the mind are sturdy; as a result the voice becomes great. Great expirations cause great repercussion in the throat, from which comes the largeness of the voice, as is seen in the great horns, where much breath and power is necessary. And if the rule is true that a thing is known by its opposite, this can be the cause of the small voice, since when the throat is narrow and small, the air only a little, the voice is made necessarily small. And this should be said about people to whom Nature has granted one or the other. For if a man with a big voice tried to make it small or make a small one big, he could accomplish it in his own way by adding or taking away the things we have talked about. But because I have much to say about the deep voice and the high one, I pass on to that subject.

I say that even though the deep and the high voices are different from the large and the small, that is no reason why they should not exist together, for it often happens that the same voice is large and deep, large and high, deep and small, high and small. I will not go into the various opinions of the ancients on this subject but only express the pure truth in company with my Aristotle, the true secretary of Nature. I say that the big voice is caused by the slow movement of the air in the throat, as the high voice is carried by the swift movement; it is clear that because of its speed the latter is heard better and is more penetrating than the former. Speaking of this swift and slow movement, I say that two things together cause them. The first is the air, as something set in motion by the mind. The second is the mind, as the cause of the movement of the air. And these two things have the following correspondence and proportion between them: when the air in motion advances and resists the potential movement, the movement of the air is slowed and in consequence the voice necessarily becomes deep. And when, on the contrary, the power of the mind anticipates and is stronger than the air so that it spins it out and moves it, then the voice necessarily becomes high. This is the reason why boys and girls have small and high voices, since their throats are small and the air contained in them only a little, and when it is moved swiftly by the mind it makes the voice high. And when your lordship says to me, "If this reason was the real one, it would follow that all newborn animals would have high voices; but it is clearly seen (in addition Aristotle says so) that calves and cows have deep voices and not high ones," I would answer in the same way, by informing you that the same philosopher wrote that calves and cows have larger throats than any other animals, so the air contained in them must necessarily be great, and that the strength of their chests is weak and slack. This happens to calves because of their tender age, which does not give them much strength; and in cows because of their sex, naturally weak and hoarse. And so, following the same reasoning, one must conclude that since for the aforesaid reason the air moves slowly, in this and every sort of animal the voice becomes deep. And if on further consideration your lordship should seek the reason why these animals change their voices from deep to high when (contrary to the others) they reach maturity, I would say that when the animals grow older they gain great strength. For which reason the air, however much it is, is moved with velocity. From this results the high voice, and the same must be said about the deep and the high voices, insofar as Nature provides. If a person in his own way wants to fake it with the voice called *falsetto*, he can do so by making the movement of the air faster. And this way of faking a voice is granted only to a man, especially when he is talking and desires to persuade, to move someone, and to impose his will.

And if your lordship wants to know which of these voices is the most perfect and suitable for a gentleman, I would say, the deep voice, because Aristotle tells one that perfection of the voice, or any other thing, consists in being the best and exceeding all others. So since the deep voice is the best and exceeds others, it should be esteemed the most perfect, most noble and generous.

Now I will talk about the rough and smooth voices briefly so as not to bore your lordship. I say that both of these voices are caused by the internal surface of the throat. When the surface is smooth and when it is perfect and properly proportioned, it makes the voice smooth and equal. And, if because of some infection of the surface or for lack of proper proportion of the throat, it makes the voice become hoarse, harsh, and unequal.

There remains for me to speak of the voices called rigid and flexible by Aristotle. These words and terms are Latin and we do not have a proper term in Tuscan. However, to make things clearer, by the "flexible" voice you must understand (as it were) a pliable voice, that is, one that is varied sweetly, so that the ear is satisfied. By the "rigid" voice should be understood a hard one that varies in no way, so the ear is disturbed when it hears it. Some persons would reduce this kind of voice to the rough and the smooth, because one is caused by the natural surface of the throat and the other by the construction of the throat. Leaving Galen aside, who does not talk about it, I turn to Aristotle, who mentions this voice. So I say that these voices result from the actual material of the throat; and by the "throat" I mean all the parts we have mentioned which unite in producing voice. So if the throat is soft, it will produce a flexible, pleasing, and variable voice, but if it chances to be hard, it will produce a rigid and harsh voice.

When the instrument is hard it cannot yield (as would be necessary); and when it is soft, yielding easily, it can form and imitate every sort of voice. Thus it occurs that there are many people who can sing nothing but the bass, and many others who are inclined to sing and can sing only one voice of the concert, to the great annoyance of the hearer. On the contrary, others are found who sing bass, tenor, and other voices with great ease, and decorating, diminishing, perform passagework now in the bass, now in the mezzo, now in the alto—all beautiful to hear.

You will perhaps say to me, "Now that you have mentioned the *passaggi*, setting aside your Aristotle, talk a little while about decorating with the throat." So I will tell you that neither the ancients nor the modern writers have ever had a method of making the throat suitable or adaptable for singing, nor are they deserving of reproaches for this. The former, as the first inventors of beginning music, the latter, because the thing is extremely difficult, neither has been willing (or better, able) to express it. For anyone who tries reasonably to talk about it must be not only a musician but also a learned physician and philosopher. But leaving the fine words to him who likes to chirp, and considering carefully the production of the voice, I say that the voice is only a sound caused by the minute and controlled repercussion of the air in the throat with the intention of pleasing the ear. It is clearly seen that sound is a genus apart, since every cultivated singing voice is a sound but not every sound is a cultivated voice.

It is also clearly seen that other details make a difference, because when you say that the virtuoso voice [*voce passeggiata*] is "small" and trained with the intention of pleasing the ear, it is made different from the small voice heard in laughter and in like manner in coughing, which though it is small [*minuta*], is not educated [*passeggiata*], nor does it please the ear. It is different also from that voice which imitates with control and ornament, bearing each syllable in the mouth, as a person would do when he says, for example, *Amore, fortuna,* etc., on the five notes ut, re, mi, fa, sol, giving each syllable a note, because this voice, though it is small and controlled and pleasing to the ear, is produced with the intention of meaning something, that is, of conveying the feeling of the words. This voice cannot and should not be called "virtuoso voice" [*voce passeggiata*], which is produced only to please the ear. Nor, because I have given so much brevity to this definition, should one say that such a voice is different from the others inasmuch as it is reduced to the flexible, consisting as it does in going from bass to *alt*, and descending from *alt* to bass with the diminutions and orderly repercussion of the air. So it can only be produced by a pleasing and soft instrument. It becomes clear to everyone that to those to whom Nature has not given the soft and pliant throat, one not adapted to make diminutions, these rules of mine may be useful to them only a little or not at all.

Now that it has been said what voice is, and to which of the aforesaid voices it is reduced, I want to talk about the place where the diminutions are made. It is the same place where voice is formed, that is, the cartilage called *cimbalara*, as we have seen, which, when it is constricted or dilated by the sinews we have mentioned, in the manner which your lordship will understand, breaks and strikes the air so minutely that the desired singing is produced by every one. Now I come to expounding to your lordship the rules about singing that should be applied.

The first rule, then, is that the person who desires to sing should avoid, as a capital enemy, any affectation, because it is of major ugliness in music and in the other branches of knowledge, and we should play music with less pretention. I need adduce no other reason than experience, which we encounter every day. Many people, because they can sing four notes gracefully, put so much self-love into it when they sing that the hearers joke about it, and after they have sung throughout all the city they develop with their feet what they have developed with their throats and go about so proud and conceited that they are rather avoided than esteemed. So avoid complacency without giving people to understand that you are making or wanting to make a profession of it.

The second rule is that the hour when you should do the exercises should be in the morning, or four or five hours after having eaten; because at the time when the stomach is full the pipe of the throat cannot be as polished and clean as is necessary to produce that clear and calm voice, which is more than any other thing necessary in singing embellishments.

The third rule is that the place where you practice should be solitary or where Echo answers, as in some shady valley or rocky hollow where she answers anyone who talks; and her singing along with the singer can easily demonstrate if the diminutions are good or not, and can be critic *viva voce*.

The fourth is to make no movement in any part of the body except in that *cimbalare* cartilage, because if those people appear ugly to us who, when they sing, shake their heads, tremble in their legs, or move their hands and feet, we must be sure that we appear ugly to others when we do the same thing. And we see many such persons who, caring little about the rule, or because they have never become aware of it, cannot by any means stand still when they are singing; and so be warned about this.

The fifth rule is to hold a mirror before your eyes so you may become aware of any ugly expression you might make in singing.

The sixth rule is to extend the tongue so that the tip touches the base of the lower teeth.

The seventh, that you should keep your mouth moderately open, no wider than when you are conversing with friends.

The eighth is that you should let out the breath a little at a time with the voice, and take care that it does not go out through the nose or through the palate, for each would be a great mistake.

The ninth is that you should talk with those people who sing very easily, because listening to them leaves certain images in the memory that are no small help.

The tenth is, that you should do these exercises many times without doing as some people do, who, when they do not fulfill their intentions in two or three attempts, immediately stop and complain about Nature, which has not given them the aptitude and the disposition that are necessary. So when they attribute to Nature what should be attributed to their own laziness they make a great error. Thus I am certain that a pupil warned about his voice by Echo, and of his pronunciation by the mirror, helped by a continual exercise and also by listening to the people who sing easily, such a pupil will acquire the *passaggi* in every sort of madrigal and motet.

But because we need some written examples of these rules by working on which one can acquire little by little that disposition of the throat, I have printed these notes, and reduced in orderly fashion what I have already said. The pupil—after the hour when he has digested his meal and has gone to some resounding valley, or cave, or some other place where, holding a mirror before his eyes, he has extended his tongue in the correct way, and has held his head still and every part of his body— he then should propel the breath little by little in these notes, keeping the letter O in his mouth, for the reason I will explain later.

These are the notes, and they are arranged in such a way as to constitute an easy beginning to our enterprise, at which point I must say that in no way should one pass from one passage to another without having understood the first one thoroughly and practiced it. And I must say also that if I have provided no clef in these examples, I did so in order that one can begin on any note, that is, ut, re, mi, fa, sol, la; thus ascending or descending, either in the space or on the lines. And to these I add this other, for sometimes these fifths and octaves, which are contained in all the diminutions, may be varied greatly; one can interchange them, taking now the beginning or the middle of a passage with the end of another, and sometimes the contrary. First the simple notes are to be sung, then doubled in speed, without saying at this time in what place and on what syllable of the madrigal the passage will be sung, since for the moment I write only the manner of acquiring the disposition and formation of the ornaments. But because the pupil will feel little satisfied, or not at all, if after having gained the proper disposition of the throat, with industry, using the method I have described, he cannot apply the *passaggi* in madrigals or anything else he might sing, I have written out this madrigal [*Lasciar il velo*] and will talk about the many rules which are necessary for this project.

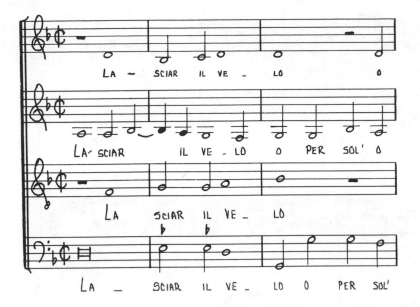

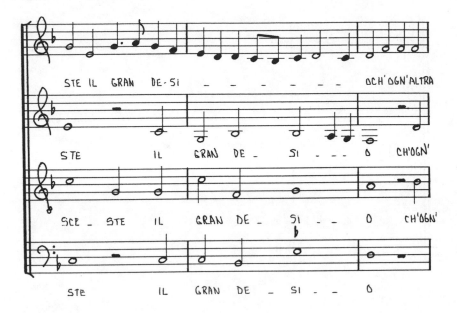

I know that this madrigal is old, but I have given it only as an example so that the good singer, in everything that is set before him to sing, may observe the rules that are observed in it; and so that they may be more clearly understood, here they are written out by me.

The first rule, then, is that diminutions are made in no other place except in the cadences; since the harmony is coming to an end in the cadences one can ornament very pleasingly without disturbing the other singers. But one is not prohibited for this reason, before reaching the cadence, from passing from one note to another with some variation or decoration, as we see in the printed madrigal, where it can be tolerated and where it seems to be fitting.

The second rule is that in one madrigal you should not make more than four or five diminutions, so that the ear, enjoying the sweetness rarely, becomes ever more desirous of hearing it. This would not happen if you sing decorations continually, because the diminutions, instead of pleasing, would become tiresome when the ear is saturated with them. We see this every day because we see many people who, without observing semitones and accidentals and without expressing the words as they are written, attend to nothing except making *passaggi*, persuading themselves that the ear will be pleased in this way; hence they become annoying and are blamed by everyone.

The third rule is that the diminution should be made on the penultimate syllable so that the end of the word will be the end of the ornamentation.

The fourth is that the diminution should be made on the word and syllable where the vowel *O* occurs rather than any of the other words. And so that this rule may be better understood, I say that there are five vowels (as everyone knows), among which some, like the *U*, strike the ear with a frightful tone, so that when you ornament on it you seem indeed to be imitating a howling wolf. So I can only wonder at those who make *passaggi* on the first syllable of the madrigal that begins "Ultimi miei sospiri." I can only wonder, I say, both because one should not begin by diminishing and because the vowel increases the dismay and darkness of the tone. And some, like the *I*, when you use it in diminutions, sound like a little animal bleating because it has lost its mother. However, we may grant that for the sopranos many diminutions on this vowel would be less ugly than for other voices. The other vowels that remain can be used without scruples, but when you make comparisons among them, I say that *O* is the best, because with it the voice is made rounder; and with the others, in addition to the fact that they do not unite so well with the breath, they make the diminutions sound like laughter. However I do not insist upon this rule and trust to the good judgment of the singer.

The fifth rule is that when four or five people sing together, while they sing, one should yield to another; because if two or three should make diminutions at the same time the harmony would be disturbed. And how much is included in this rule is clearly exemplified in the madrigal I have given.

I think that at this point I have accomplished what your lordship ordered me to do, because now all musicians, after obeying all my orders, will be able on their own initiative to perform diminutions. Now I want, for their satisfaction and my own, to set down some passages which they can sing with some grace. I shall follow this plan: first I will present the cadences and afterwards the diminutions (I am talking about the first one) because if I were to try to set down all those with which a cadence can be varied, I would fill the page with *passaggi* to be played rather than sung. I am adding "Vago augelletto" decorated in its melody.

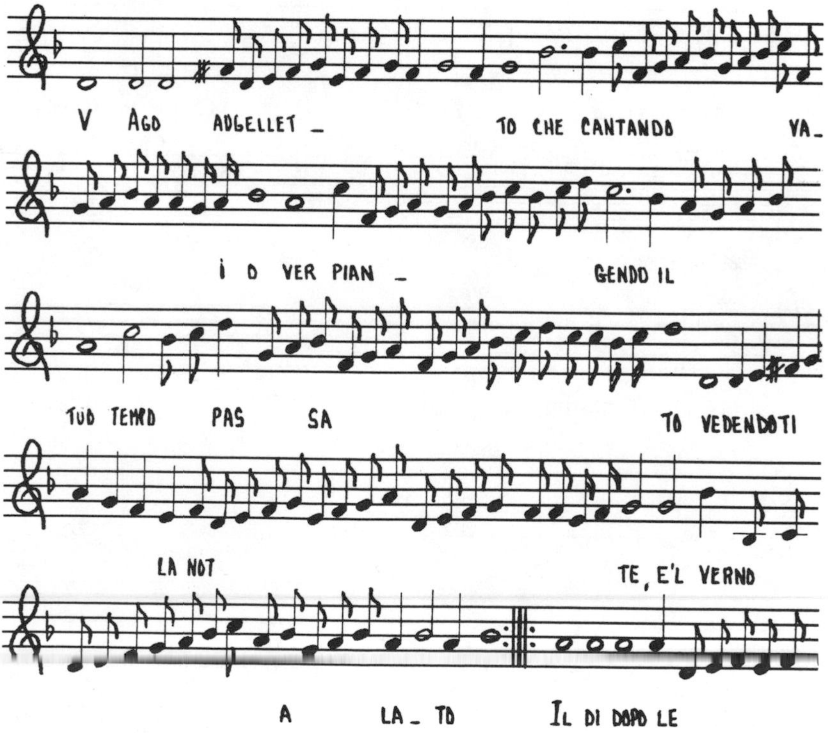

V AGO ADGELLET _ TO CHE CANTANDO VA_

I O VER PIAN _ GENDO IL

TUO TEMPO PAS SA TO VEDENDOTI

LA NOT TE, E'L VERNO

A LA _ TO IL DI DOPO LE

SPAL LE EI MESI GRA _

_ i i SE UOM' i TUOI GRA

VOS'AFFANI GRAVOS' AF FAN _ _ _ NI SAI

COSI SA. PES _

SI IL MIO SIMI _ LE STA _ TO VERREST' IN GREMB'A

QUESTO SCON _ SO _ LA

TO A' PA-TIR SECO DOLORO _ SI GUA _

_ i, GUA _ i i

IO NON SO SE LE PAR _ TI SARIAN PA

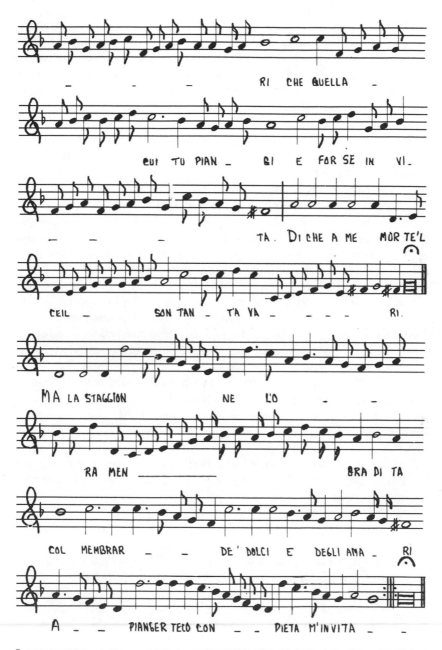

I am certain many envious people will judge this new work of mine to be not only vain but also constructed on a false assumption. "Vain," they will say, because ornamentation comes from Nature; "false," because while diminutions are being made, many false notes are committed. So I answer briefly that it is certainly true that the disposition of the throat comes from Nature, but that being able to learn the method of ornamenting with diminutions without these rules of mine is something impossible, because if Nature grants the aptitude, Art dictates the method, without which nothing good can be done.

I say in addition that Nature being a most liberal Mother, has given every man the capacity of being able to accomplish this task (I am not now speaking of some tongue-tied wretch, Nature's bastard, who is not deserving of the gift), but because they are unwilling to observe the rules and to do the work, doing injury to themselves, they are said to be unworthy of this power. And that this is true, I would like these envious people to prove, for I am sure that if they would, they could accomplish what they blame their own laziness for, unless they are so unfortunate that they were brought into the world only to speak evil. And briefly I reply that it is very true that mistakes are made in diminishing, but the diminution with its speed and its pleasing quality hides the defects in such a way that neither harshness nor falseness can be known. For this reason I know of no advice to give these envious people, except to be silent and to learn, because in the end the true method of singing in a courtly style is to please the ear and to sing in the ornamented style. And of this opinion are Gio. Domenico da Nola, Gio. Ant. Filodo, Sig. Stefano Lando, Sig. Rocco, and finally Gio. Tomasso Cimelli, who, in addition to the fact that they could restore music if it were to be lost, exhibit modesty, kindness, and virtue, and every other quality that characterizes an angelic and godly spirit. Come now, let him who does not know it, learn it.

And now to show how good I am, that I want to serve and help even the tongue-tied in this fine enterprise, I am adding the finest and safest remedies to get a good voice that I have used in my profession.

A useful means of getting a good voice is to use the methods that Nero, whom music pleased so much, did not disdain to use in order to sing more sweetly (as Suetonius mentions, quietly).

A good remedy is to place a leaden plate on your stomach as this same Nero did. Also good are the following pills, especially when the voice is spoiled by too great humidity: take four dried figs, remove the skin, take a half dram of calamint and also a scruple of gum arabic, and grinding everything up in a mortar, make balls, one of which you should keep in your mouth night and day, continually. Here is another. Take a dram of licorice and two of incense and also a dram of saffron, and grinding everything together, mix with it a little wine or grape juice. It should be used a little at a time. Cabbage soup is useful for the same effect.

And not inferior to these, for roughness of the voice, take senna, eating it in the cane with a knife; and an equally approved remedy is "lochsano di Mesoe," as is also gargling with a little sandrac and squill vinegar and some honey. I have spoken briefly about the things taken by mouth when the defects of the voice are due to humidity in the throat. When you want some external remedy you can use the following inhalant without going into salves, unguents, and other greases, because they are annoying and ugly things. Take a mixture of incense, sandrac stirace, and mint, and burn it on charcoal, inhaling the fumes through the nose and the mouth.

And when by chance the voice is bad because of a dry throat, which happens rarely, take oil of violet and mix it with sugar so both together become like honey, then swallow this a little at a time, and especially when you go to bed you should take a spoonful. And chicken broth is good for this purpose also; and dried figs with lots of liquid. I have tried briefly to remind people who need remedies to show how liberal I am in my profession and in everything of mine. I kiss your lordship's hand.

Hermann Finck (1527–1558), great-nephew of Heinrich Finck, was a German composer and organist. He probably received his early training as a member of the Chapel of King Ferdinand of Bohemia. He entered Wittenberg University as a student in 1545; from 1554 he was allowed to teach music to students there, and in 1557 he was appointed organist at the university. He died there on December 28, 1558.

Finck was a composer of some reputation, as the few remaining works from his pen show. He is said to have been in advance of his time in form and expression. His important work, however, was the theoretical treatise Practica musica, *published in 1556. It is in one volume, divided into five books in which he deals with theory and practical music. Finck's work reflects the taste of his time and gives some information about his contemporaries. In the fifth book—*De arte eleganter et suaviter cantandi *(On the Art of Singing Elegantly and Sweetly)—Finck gives advice to would-be singers and dos and don'ts for performance; he also devotes some space to ornamentation, or* coloraturae, *and gives musical passages in use at the time for practice.*

SOURCE: Practica musica Hermanni Finckii, exempla variorum signorum, proportionum et canonum, judicium de tonis, ac quaedam de arte suaviter et artificiose continens (Wittenberg, 1556), Book V.

HERMANN FINCK
from *Practica musica*

On the Art of Singing Elegantly and Sweetly

At the beginning, let those who practice music see whether the music is in four or more voices, and that each voice be assigned to a select and suitable singer. For example, a discant singer sings with a tender and soothing voice, but a bass with a sharper and heavier one; the middle voices sing their melody with a uniform sound and pleasantly and skillfully strive to adapt themselves to the outer voices.

Let there be another care among singers: the manner and way of beginning. The beginning should not sound different than the conclusion, and the voices should not waver, but, as in organs rightly put together, the harmony should remain tranquil and steady. For it is a great unpleasantness for a voice to be now tense, now relaxed, especially if one or more err in *Arsi* and *Thesi* and base confusion results, and in no wise is the symphony pleasing.

Then, lest one voice blunt or disturb another by its own sound, it should be seen to that the discantus and the alto not rise higher than they should, or that no singer strains his voice; for many singers change their tone colors, becoming black in the face and come to the end of their breath. I myself have seen with indignation excellent singers become debased and deformed, with distorted and gaping mouths, with head tossed back, and with bleating and barbaric cries, which (with preconceived opinion) they hold bellowing and singing to be one and the same thing, they ruin and deform the most beautiful music. What a deplorable sight!

Basses, indeed, make raucous noises, like a hornet enclosed in a leather pouch, or they exhale like a pierced balloon. What pleasantness is there, what charm? How can this kind of singing please? For singing does not arise out of bellowing, rather you receive all sounds from your mind and intelligence. Let them correct these mistakes; a beautiful song can be sung and brought to performance by such delightful, thoroughly refined, and well-blended voices that one could not ask for it to be better.

For no song is embellished by roaring and screaming; rather with spirit and understanding must the voices be united: the higher a voice rises the quieter and lovelier should the note be sung; the more it descends, the richer the sound, as in an organ, wonderfully assembled of different kinds of pipes structured of greater and lesser ones; the greater do not drown out the lesser, nor do the lesser, by their sharp sound, overcome the greater; as a result harmony and consonance flow equally into the ears, so that one voice like another, the high as well as the low, become soft, gentle, and clearly understood, whereby the hearts of the hearers are filled with wonder and the mind is pleasantly affected. If these principles please in the case of organs, how much more ought men, who are capable of reason and intelligence, strive and contend so that they learn to shun cacophony and to form and vary their voices elegantly.

It will be useful to remember also, that if in the beginning of a song there occurs an elegant fugue, this ought to be proffered by a clearer and more distinct voice than is usual; also that the subsequent voices ought to be delivered in the same way, if they arise from the same theme that the first singer has sung. This ought to be observed in all the voices when new fugues arise, so that coherence and the system of all the imitations can be heard.

Further, let the text be suitably underlaid, not so that it is directly under the note-head, as in Chant, but so that a singer has the text under-laid in his part, and the others likewise have it suitably placed in their parts. This also should be observed: if the notes exceed the text [i.e., syllable or word] by their number, you should not carry on *a*, *o*, or *u* in the mouth, but always those [syllables] that adapt to and fit with *i* or *e* if possible. Also you should not cram a foreign clausula into a song, *filled with coloratura*, unless you are in firm control of the matter, lest cacophony result, such as fifths, octaves, and open fourths. Nor should you seize upon a clausula that you have heard sung by a distinguished master, and try to use it wherever you please. This error cannot be as well ex-pressed in words as by examples placed before your eyes, so that every-one can see how base and monstrous methods of singing daily assault our ears.

There are many also who are self-learners, who, having had no in-structor, sing as they please, and without scruple incorporate organ embellishments, even if they are incorrect, in their songs; by this they tear apart some of the most beautiful songs, just as a young puppy tears apart rags.

The manner of adding embellishments depends on skill, natural suit-ability, and the singularity of the individual ornament. Each has his own manner. There are many who are of the opinion that the bass should be embellished, others say the discantus; but in my opinion embellishments both can and should be applied to all the voices; but not throughout, only at indicated places; also not in all voices alike, only on the proper degrees. And let them be done in their turn, in such a way that each embellishment can be clearly distinguished from the others, yet so that the entire work is uniform.

I have divided the *coloraturae* into two categories: those of the throat and those of the tongue. The tongue-*coloraturae* are used in solmization without text, in such a way that the degrees ut, re, mi, fa, sol, la are not sung with a full mouth, but rather flow easily and naturally from the mouth, very delicately and at the same time separated.

The *coloraturae* of the throat are employed when the text is sung. Presently, however, several who make the *coloratura* of the throat not dissimilar to the bleating of a she-goat, make a serious mistake; for no pleasure, nor distinction, nor suitability of the embellishment is heard, but only rumbling and a confused and ugly racket is heard. The law and nature of *coloraturae* requires that all those notes formed within the cheeks and delivered distinctly and clearly can be heard. Therefore I shall give examples of all the uses of *clausulae*, and how they can be embellished.

And this also should be noted, that when an end is made to the song, let no one change anything of it (it is for artists to correct songs) lest the melody of the song be disturbed by cacophony.

Also let this be observed, that when the song is ended, let all the other voices grow silent at the same time; the bass, however, can be protracted as far as the measure of a *longa*, a thing which lends itself well to symphonies.

What those who preside over choruses and groups of singers must do, and in what sort of voice the singing should be, however, will be found in the next book, where I shall consider the method of inventing and composing fugues; after I have made more clear the acceptability and nature of modes. In this place let it be enough to say that in a chorus *coloraturae* cannot be added without poor results, for when one part is assigned to several to sing, the *coloraturae* will become very difficult, whence both the pleasantness and the nature of the sound are obscured.

It remains now that the *clausulae* be given that are presently used most often in the best works and of whose use by necessity must be employed sparingly. The true nature and quality of these I have added (although foreign to the inexperienced ear and even to the matured one). You will be able to use these *clausulae* at your discretion, not only on those tones on which they are written, for their use extends far and wide, through the second, third, fourth, higher and lower. But you must take care that you keep your eyes and mind fixed on the tones *mi* and *fa* as if on a target, lest one be confused with the other; for all music depends on these two notes. I would treat this more learnedly and more quickly were it not unnecessary in my estimation; for whoever has progressed this far, so that he can employ these properly (if he not be devoid of reason), there is no doubt but that he can attain adroitness and even speed by daily practice.

I shall give therefore some *coloraturae* of the fixed *clausulae*.

uel

uel sic.

uel sic.

uel sic.

uel.

Ludovico Zacconi (1555–1627), musician, theorist and Augustinian priest, worked mainly in Venice, although he spent the years 1593–1618 in Vienna in the service of the Archduke Charles. In 1619 he returned to Venice, where he passed the remainder of his life. His great work, Prattica di musica, covered many years, the first part being published in 1592 (reprinted 1596) and the second part in 1619. This very comprehensive work, divided into four books, totaling 251 chapters, treats of everything from the rudiments of music, counterpoint, proportions, rules for singers, ornamentation, instruments and their tuning, to a long and important list of instruments then in use. It is one of the three most valuable and informative treatises on musical practice of the first half of the seventeenth century, the others being Cerone's El Melopeo (1613) and Mersenne's Harmonie universelle (1636).

Zacconi's chapter on florid singing and ornamentation, then at its height and employed in both sacred and secular music, is extremely valuable for today's performers of music of this period.

SOURCE: *Ludovico Zacconi,* Prattica di musica utile et necessaria si al compositore . . . si anco al cantore *(Venice, 1596), Book I, Ch. 66, "Che stile si tenghi nel far di gorgia . . . ," pp.58ʳ–61.*

LUDOVICO ZACCONI

from *Prattica di musica*

The Manner to Be Observed in Making Diminutions and the Use of Modern Passages

However much the things that were embellished by artifice have become old-fashioned, those of today are just as much embellished by the detailed studies of many, because clever talents always find new ornamentations. So whoever looks at this or that piece, even though it was embellished by careful study and long, serious effort, will find new beauties have been added to the ornaments. Therefore, not to enlarge upon the unsuitable thing that some do, I will not speak of particular embellishments that have been added to the works of Art and Nature, but will say only that Music has always been beautiful and becomes more so each hour because of the diligence and study by which singers enhance it; it is not renewed or changed because of the figures [i.e., notes], which are always of one kind, but by graces and ornaments it is made to appear always more beautiful.

The graces and accents are made by the breaking up of the notes each time that one adds, in a *tactus* or a half, a quantity of figures that are suitable to be uttered with velocity. These render such pleasure and delight that we seem to hear just so many trained birds, who with their singing steal our hearts and leave us well contented with their song.

These persons, who have such quickness and ability to deliver a quantity of figures in tempo with such velocity, have so enhanced and made beautiful the songs that now whosoever does not sing like those singers gives little pleasure to his hearers, and few of such singers are held in esteem. This manner of singing and these ornaments are called by the common people *gorgia*; this is nothing other than an aggregation or collection of many eighths and sixteenths gathered in any one measure. And it is of such nature that, because of the velocity into which so many notes are compressed, it is much better to learn by hearing it than by written examples, because one cannot write down the measure and tempo in which it has to be delivered without error.

It consists rather in tempo and measure than in moving with speed, since if *presto* or *tardo* must be a prescribed value, all of it will be of no value. Two things are required for him who wishes to enter this profession: chest and throat; chest, in order to be able to carry such a large number of notes to a correct end; throat, to produce them easily. Because many persons have little capacity of either chest or flanks, they have to stop their design in four or six figures, or interrupt them in the middle. Or they do not finish at all, because they take so much time preparing the breath that they cannot be on time when necessary. And others, because of defects of the throat, cannot separate the notes vigorously; that is, they cannot enunciate the notes well enough for it to be recognized as *gorgia*.

Some achieve this easily; these are the ones Nature teaches and brings out. Others achieve it by work, and these are the ones who have mastered it by diligent study. The first will always be more elegant and will delight more than the second; but those on whom Nature bestows it and Art refines it, are above all others most felicitous in this profession. . . .

Whoever wishes to sing *gorgia* should be warned that he must do them well, or leave them alone if they cannot be done perfectly, for there is nothing that has more need of good results and perfect measure than this; every least defect that is caught and recognized spoils and ruins that which is beautiful in itself, and in place of pleasure or delight it causes not only boredom and fatigue but also scoffing and bantering.

Each time a singer wishes to find out if he is succeeding in his diminutions, he first will try them in company with other singers, and those who have no companions on their parts can try it when all the voices form a full harmony; and this is the way one practices, so that one can sometimes be heard. To succeed, as I say, one must be judge of himself, and man in judging himself often, not to say always, fails to obtain a sincere and honest opinion; it is therefore good to seek from faithful friends their opinion as to whether or not he gives them pleasure and succeeds well. And this is said because many believe they can do it, yet do so little that one can say they do almost nothing. I have seen some who, with shaking of the voice and movement of the head, believe they are succeeding, and are not; others say they must do better, and they do worse; auditors would listen to such a singer more willingly if he sang the music as written so that they would not hear it sung so wretchedly. Therefore I say that to let others judge you and willingly listen to their opinion protects one from many stumbling blocks and dissuades one from abuses and errors.

The most beautiful and perfect thing sought in diminution is tempo and measure, which embellishes and seasons the collection and aggregate of figures; whoever departs from measure and tempo loses at the end because of a fine scattering of notes without results.

This, then, is the most difficult thing about *gorgia*; and it needs study and diligence rather than mere desire to put so many figures together. That singer will always be praised who, with a few ornaments, makes them at the right moment, somewhat spaced out, rather than the one who waits very late or barely arrives in time. . . .

One should therefore take care first to do the ornament well, then to measure it in tempo, so that it will please and satisfy everyone. And the first rule should be that in beginning any song the other parts should not make diminutions until after the first singer has been heard, because it is usually said that the high voice pleases most in contrast to the low, and one voice alone gives little delight; many voices together make a sweet and graceful harmony, as everyone knows. . . . Therefore the sweetness of the *gorgia* is born in that beautiful and succinct movement the parts make when only one of them moves with velocity.

The beginning, then, if not common and consecutive to all the parts, should always be delivered with simple and straightforward ornaments, so that the entrances of the other parts can be clearly heard; this is most delightful because unexpected, and even more so when they appear suddenly.

To explain better how unseemly it is to begin a part with *gorgia* when the other parts are silent, I say that everyone can make diminutions singing alone; however the hearers do not receive from those ornaments all the pleasure they would if they were accompanied by the other parts. . . . The beauty and difficulty consist in pleasing others without difficulty or dissonance; the player of any game is not praised for playing alone, but for playing well and getting along with others.

Further, that singer who at the beginning overshadows singers he does not know by his *gorgia* not only is worthy of reprimand, because of trying to make people believe that he knows something, but also brings shame and dishonor on himself. For if he encounters someone who performs better than he, he may enter in the midst of his labors with a new style, and thus remove all that he has gained. Therefore those who must sing in these circles do much better and wisely not to show immediately what they know. Because one can learn in every place and time, one should wait a little to listen, and then, having heard, begin little by little to bring forth his beauties; thus, awakening the hearers to new delights, he acquires immortal fame.

The singer also should be careful at the end of any song not to do what many mediocre and inexperienced singers do in this profession; they make such copious ornamentations that they wish to display everything at the end, and have left the whole middle section empty and dull. Therefore one who sings *gorgia* should show his valor not only at the end of a piece but also in the middle, where he must show his bold heart with audacity.

We must not omit the vice of those who, having made *gorgia* their friend, wish to do some little thing in each measure; and by singing them, even though the ornaments may be good, they spoil the syllables and words.

Therefore to avoid many errors, besides other rules I want to give you this warning; that you take care to do passagework on the semibreves, particularly when they accompany syllables, because the nature of their speed does not admit long diminutions, and they do not support breaking up except in these and other like circumstances [Ex. 1]. Therefore, any time you find them as below accompanying a single syllable,

Ex. 1

you can ornament securely, for the effect of the passage will always be more beautiful. Diminutions in minims, being of longer values and somewhat slower, will make it easy to do whatever you want, provided the syllables or the words are not spoiled.

Likewise, if you find several minims together, the group can be ornamented, whenever it is convenient for the singer and the words are not obscured. With semibreves and breves and other long notes, because they naturally require more time, many beauties can be put together to ornament them as one pleases; or one can use them in places where needed under a syllable or a word.

Ex. 2

In order to facilitate progress, and to see if one has acquired facility, let him try singing the figures of an easy duo and force himself to utter the figures in such a tempo as to leave no defect or lack in them, particularly in *chromas* [16ths]; in this way, let him learn how to pronounce in *gorgia*. If he wants to gain a good style in it, let him take one of the aforesaid duos where there are many small swift notes. Then if in this he finds himself secure, let him sing a single syllable, so that he may see where the difficulty lies. He should then practice it one, two, three, or more times until he sees that he is making progress.

However, if he has great difficulty and finds it hard to pronounce the aforesaid syllable, he must make himself sing it many times, so that he acquires a habit of singing it well. He should also take care to sing the syllables as bright and round as he would if he were sol-fa-ing them, or singing only a syllable of some word. By this he makes them so familiar and common that he knows how to sing syllables promptly, and not only those he has studied.

From that exercise a principle of moving the voice with velocity is born; for then one can, without a teacher, introduce *gorgia* and passages according to his ability.

Likewise, to facilitate his progress and to set his feet on the path of becoming a professor and real master, one should want to do well. It is necessary then that in every example or piece he sing all the five vowels, which are *A E I O U*; because some of them must be pronounced closed, as *I* and *U*, others half open, as *E* and *O*, and one wide, as *A*. He will find that I and U are easily said, and that with a bit of work one can master *E* and *O*; but that the *A* demands more breath than all the others and one works harder to pronounce it.

By practicing these, no problems will ever arise; because all the Italian words, and a great part of the Latin, end in vowels. And in order not to omit anything in this matter, because of the great zeal and desire I have to help the singer, I say also that the *tremolo*, that is, the trembling voice, is the true gate to enter the passages and to become proficient in the *gorgia*; because the boat moves with greater ease when it is first pushed, and the dancer leaps better if first he prepares for the leap.

The *tremolo* should be short and beautiful, for if it is long and forceful it tires and bores. And it is of such a nature that those who employ it must always use it, so that it becomes a habit. The continual movement of the voice aids and voluntarily pushes the movement of the *gorgia*, and admirably facilitates the beginnings of the passages. This movement I am speaking of should only be made with proper speed, and lively and vehemently.

The end of any ornamentation should be just and complete; the middle notes all equal and continual, so that one does not hear the beginning more than the middle and the end, nor the end more than the beginning and middle, because each obscuration that one makes, besides demonstrating timidity, takes away pleasure. And if there were anyone who, taking pleasure in assiduous and detailed study and enjoyment of my first examples, made himself master of them, I have written these others that you see [Ex. 3], to give him opportunity to ornament these simple ones and a few others that are longer.

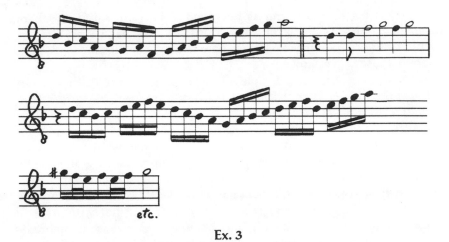

Ex. 3

The places that invite singers to make ornaments and passages are the cadences, which are of such a nature that if one does not do them well, one spoils them and takes away every beauty, and fills our ears with deformities. Therefore to show you some cadences, I have made the following examples.

Ex. 4

Further, one must be able to ornament a cadence, and happy is the singer who can do it well. . . . One can use not only the first manner [in Ex. 5] but the second as well in its proper mode and place.

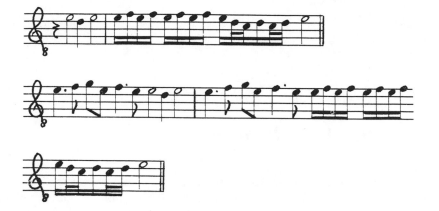

Ex. 5

5. Rules for Performers and Composers

Nicola Vicentino (1511–1572), a pupil of the famous Adrian Willaert, was a learned musician as well as a priest. He lived and worked for many years in Ferrara, where he was connected with the house of Este, and particularly with Cardinal Ippolito d'Este. A true Renaissance man, he was interested in the musical systems of antiquity and attempted to revive the Greek genera and modes. L'antica musica . . . (1555) contains not only his investigations into ancient music but also his attempts to apply the Greek genera in music of his own time; much of his music is therefore highly chromatic and enharmonic.

Vicentino invented an arcicembalo *with six keyboards to provide perfect tuning in every key. Several pieces of music were composed for it. He also made an* arciorgano *on similar principles.*

His treatise still holds much of value today, especially his chapters on counterpoint, imitation, fugue, all of which antedate Zarlino's great work, Istitutioni armoniche. *Vicentino gives practical advice for performance also, as in this extract, where he makes clear that dynamic changes, as well as variations in tempo, are important to enhance the music.*

SOURCE: *Nicola Vicentino, L'antica musica ridotta alla moderna prattica (Rome, 1955), Book IV, Ch. 42.*

NICOLA VICENTINO
from *L'antica musica*

Rules for Singing in Concert Any Kind of Composition

Compositions differ according to the subject on which they are made, and very often certain singers are not aware of this, singing any composition whatever without any consideration and always in their own way, according to their nature and practice. Works that are written on various subjects and various fantasias carry within them different manners of composition, and so the singer must consider what the musical poet has in mind, and whether the poet writes in Latin or the vulgar tongue, and with his voice express the composition and use diverse ways of singing, like the diverse manners of composition. If he will use such ways, he will be judged by auditors who are men of judgment to have many styles of singing and demonstrate that he has an abundant and rich store of manners of singing by the disposition of *gorgia*, or diminutions, together with the compositions, according to the *passaggi* appropriate to them. But there are some singers who, when they sing, demonstrate to their hearers their lack of judgment and consideration when they encounter a passage that is serious and sing it in a lively manner, and then, on the contrary, they sing an animated passage in a sad manner.

Such [performers] as these will point out that the diminutions, which are of the kind used in more than four voices, will appear good [only] if they are done in appropriate places and in tempo; because the diminution always loses many consonances and strikes many dissonances, even though it appears delightful to the auditor who is not a musician. Nevertheless, there is a loss of harmony; and in order that the harmony not be lost and that the good arrangement of the diminution may be demonstrated by the singer, it will be more satisfactory if, during the diminution, the instruments that are playing the piece play it as it is notated, without embellishments, so that the harmony cannot be lost with the diminution, for the instruments will keep the consonances in their proper form. And as to those who wish to embellish a composition singing and playing together, if both do not make the same diminutions at the same time they will sound well together. Then in the compositions which are sung without instruments, the diminutions will be good in compositions for more than four voices, because wherever a consonance is lacking, the other part will have it in the octave or unison and there will not be a poverty of harmony, for the singer will move among the parts, now with unisons, now with seconds, thirds, fourths, fifths, sixths, and octaves, touching now in one part, now in another, various consonances and dissonances which, because of the velocity of the singing, will appear good when they are not.

And every singer will take care, when he sings lamentations or other compositions of a sad nature, not to make any diminutions, because then the sorrowful composition would appear joyful; and the opposite is true also, for he should not sing in a sad manner the joyful things, either in the vulgar tongue or in Latin. And he should take care in concerting the secular pieces to attempt to give pleasure to the hearers, and he should sing the works in conformance with the ideas of the composer, and with his voice express in those intonations accompanied by the words the appropriate passions—now gay, now sad, sometimes sweet and sometimes harsh, and adhere to the pronunciation of the words and notes in using the embellishments [*accenti*]. And sometimes one uses a certain way of proceeding in the composition that cannot be written down—such as to sing *piano* and *forte*, and to sing *presto* and *tardo*, moving the measure according to the words to demonstrate the effects of the passions of the words and of the harmony. And it should not appear strange to anyone, this manner of changing tempo [*mutar misura*] suddenly in singing, since it is so understood in performance that where it is necessary to change tempo it is not an error. And the composition sung with changes of tempo is more pleasing in its variety than that which is sung without being varied all the way to the end. And a trial of this manner of singing will prove it to everyone, for in secular pieces it will be found that such procedure will please the hearers more than when the measure continues always unvaried.

The tempo [*moto della misura*] should move according to the words; slower and faster, and one will consider that in the middle and end of compositions the measure may be changed by the proportion of equality, even though it may be that some have the opinion that when beating the measure *alla breve* one should not change the tempo; yet in singing, it *is* changed. And this is not a great error, for just as when the proportion of equality ceases one returns to another tempo, so for the manner just described changes of tempo are not inconvenient in any composition. The practice of the orator teaches this, for one sees how he proceeds in an oration—now he speaks loudly, now softly, and slower and faster; and this way of changing the tempo has an effect on the mind. So one sings music *alla mente* to imitate the accents and effects of the parts of the oration—for what effect would the orator make if he recited a fine speech without arranging his accents and pronunciation, with fast and slow movements, and speaking softly and loudly? That would not move his hearers. The same should occur in music; for if the orator moves his auditors with the aforesaid manners, how much more would music, recited in the same manner, accompanied by harmony and well united, make a greater effect.

The experience of hearing the organ intone notes accompanied by their harmonies without words teaches us that music is wonderful to hear; how much more excellent would music be if the singers could, with the pronunciation of the words and the tones, intone and sing a composition as accurately as does the organ! Now, if the singers cannot reach such just intonation, at least let them be diligent in according together, more than they are able to do in their concerts.

And music sung *alla mente* will be more welcome than that sung *sopra le carte*. Let them take the example of the preachers and the orators. If they recited a sermon or oration from the written page it would not have any grace, nor be well received by the audience, for the [expressive] glances together with the embellishments greatly move an audience when they are used together; and beautiful and learned compositions move even more those who are expert in the profession than those who are not practicing musicians and only natural, and deprived of artistic judgment, which can be gained only with effort. And let the bass singer take care to accord well with the octave of all the parts so the concentus of all will be perfect, for in this is contained perfect harmony.

Gioseffo Zarlino (1517–1590), the most learned theorist of the late sixteen century, was trained in his youth to be a priest. He was admitted to minor orders in 1539 and became a deacon in 1549. In that year he moved from Chioggia, his birthplace, to Venice, where he soon became known for his learning and attainments. His great interest, however, was music and he became a pupil of Adrian Willaert, with whom he studied for several years. In 1565 Zarlino was elected maestro di cappella of San Marco, a post he retained until his death. During these years he taught many pupils who became famous, among them Nicola Vicentino and Cipriano de Rore.

Zarlino was a composer as well as a theorist, but very few of his compositions have been preserved. His major works, on which his fame rests, are the Istitutioni harmoniche *(1558, reprinted 1562, 1573),* Dimostrationi harmoniche *(1571, reprinted 1581), and* Sopplimenti musicali *(1588), three books that cover all of musical theory. A complete edition of all three was published in 1589.*

In his chapter on cadences, a part of which is presented here, he sets forth the usual practice of the time, and makes clear that the raised seventh degree, or leading tone, is understood to be invariably raised in final cadences, even though no accidental appears—a point that has often been misunderstood in modern performance of sixteenth-century music.

SOURCE: *Gioseffo Zarlino*, Istitutioni harmoniche *(Venice, 1573), Pt. III, Ch. 51, pp. 241–52.*

GIOSEFFO ZARLINO
from *Istitutioni harmoniche*

On the Cadence

Inasmuch as mention was made in the previous chapter of the cadence, which is the most beautiful part of the cantilena, when one finds some cantilenas that may be deprived of cadences one hears in them a certain imperfection; for that reason those cantilenas that contain such cadences give more pleasure than do those which are deprived of them. Therefore having spoken of cadence and discussed the syncope, inasmuch as most cadences are formed by the syncope, it appears to me that this is the time and place to speak of cadences before going further. Now I shall say what they are, and demonstrate the kinds of cadence and explain how they are to be used.

The cadence, then, is a certain action that the parts of the cantilena perform together, which denotes either a general repose of the harmony or the completion of the sense of the words on which the cantilena is composed. Or we can say that it is a middle, or final termination, or distinction of the argument of the words. And the cadence is very necessary in the harmonies, because when there is none they lack (as I have said), a necessary and great ornament, both to distinguish the parts as well as to separate the portions of texts. It is not, however, to be used except when it arrives at a clausula or period contained in the text, prose or verse; that is to say, in that place where its member or one of its parts terminates.

Hence the cadence has as much value in music as does the period in an oration, and one can truly call it the period of the cantilena. It is used in many different places, not just one, so that by variety the harmony is more grateful and pleasing. The musical cadences should coincide with the ends of periods in the text, and not be placed on any note whatsoever, but on the proper and regular notes of the mode of the composition; these will be demonstrated in the Fourth Part, where I will speak of them separately.

One should observe that cadences in plainsong are made in one part only; but in *canto figurato* other parts are added. In the first they denote the end of the sentence in the words; in the second, they are used not only to mark the end of the sentence but sometimes to carry out a certain order begun by the composer. Those of the *canto figurato* are of two kinds: that is, those that terminate with two parts on the unison, and those that finish on the octave. And although there are some others that finish on the fifth, on the third, and on divers other consonances, they are not however to be called absolute cadences except in a certain manner, and with an addition; that is, "imperfect cadences." All the kinds of cadences are found in two manners: they are either simple or diminished. The simple ones are those in which the parts proceed by similar figures, or notes, and do not contain any dissonance; and the diminished ones are those which contain various kinds of notes and some dissonances between the parts of the cantilena; and there are at least two parts that move by contrary motion.

The first kind of cadence, then, ended by a unison, is that which contains a progression that two voices of a cantilena make, one against the other; of these one ascends and then descends, or descends only, with the notes moving stepwise; and the other descends, then ascends by step in a similar way. The second kind has the lower part distant from the upper part a minor third; and in the third kind each of these parts come together in a single note, that is, in the same sound. This cadence can be made also in other ways, but it makes little difference how one makes it, provided the final notes with their antecedents be joined in the aforesaid manner, as one may see from the example below.

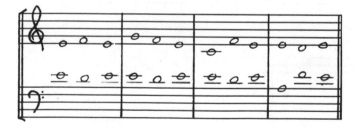

Ex. 1

The diminished cadences terminated by the unison are those that follow a similar procedure; but they are made with different kinds of notes, among which is found the syncope, the second part of which, coming on the downbeat, is dissonant, that is, a second, after which the minor third is sounded immediately, and it finishes on the unison [Ex. 2].

Ex. 2

And because practical musicians ordinarily diminish that part of the cadence that contains the syncope, if it is convenient, in order to express the words, before I go further I wish to show such diminutions; and they will be given below.

Ex. 3

Here each composer should be warned, in order that he not fall into error, that any of the cadences shown here are written properly in the notes of one mode only; nevertheless they can be made also in any other mode, where they will be most convenient, provided that the rule given above in chap. 38 be observed: to go from the imperfect consonance to the nearest perfect one. Therefore of necessity in the penultimate notes of this consonance the third should be minor; which will always be heard when they make the movement to the unison with one voice descending by step of a tone, and the other by a similar movement of the major semitone. And it can always be done in any place without putting in the sign of the chromatic tone (♯) to change the interval of a tone to a semitone; because in the part which makes the movement that ascends from the penultimate note to the final, the semitone is always intended to be placed, provided that the other part does not descend by a similar interval, for then the semitone could not be placed in two parts, that is, in the lower part and in the upper, because the minor interval of a semiditone would be heard, which would be dissonant, But Nature has provided for this, because not only the learned musicians but also the peasants, who sing without any art, proceed by the interval of the semitone. And these are the proper cadences. However, if their first interval is a fifth, and the second a semiditone, the last should finish on the unison, as seen below [Ex. 4]. It would not be possible *not* to call them cadences, unless it could be said that they were so called improperly.

Ex. 4

The cadence terminated by the octave is made in this fashion: the first, second, and third notes of the upper part and the first, second, and third of the lower part move in contrary motion by degrees; and the second notes are a major sixth apart and the octave is the final. However there may be some difference of movement between the first and second notes—the upper notes moving by degrees while the lower part moves by leap, or sometimes by degrees. The second interval will always be a major sixth and the final one an octave. And it is always good if one part, either upper or lower, will move by a semitone and the other by a tone, as in the other kinds of cadences, simple or diminished. Diminished cadences, to be sure, have a syncope in which the seventh is heard in the second interval, that is, on the downbeat; but the simple cadence is always consonant, because the notes move equally, as one may see in these examples.

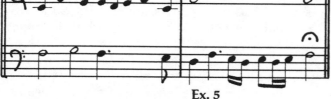

Ex. 5

One can see how the parts may be exchanged in the cadence; the lower part may be placed in the upper, and the upper part placed in the lower, for they correspond by an octave.

Besides these two kinds of cadences, there is another, terminated by the octave or by the unison. This one is made when the notes of the lower part and those of the upper part are placed a ditone apart, causing the lower part to descend by the leap of a fifth, or ascend by step, as is seen [in Ex. 6].

Ex. 6

These cadences [in Ex. 7] are likewise of two kinds: simple and diminished, as can be seen. Those which are simple have equal notes; the diminished ones have different note values, among which is found the syncope, which has in its second part the fourth, after which the major third follows immediately, as I have shown. These cadences are not much used in compositions for two voices, because ascending leaps, and descending also, are more suited to the lowest part of any composition for several voices, where we see them often so used. And when we use them, we always place them in the middle and not at the end of the cantilena; but sometimes necessity will require us to [place them at the end], that is, when we wish to have the parts in sequence or imitation, or when there is no other way to have a passage that is easy to sing, with a pleasing modulation. It must be said that I wish this to be advice rather than precept, because if one should write this also in the beginning and in the end, it would not be an error.

Ex. 7

Girolamo Diruta (b. ca. 1550) was an organist, theorist, and member of the Frati Minori. He is said to have received his early musical training from one Battista Capuani, a Franciscan monk, in the monastery at Correggio. In 1582 Diruta went to Venice, where he remained until 1593, studying with Zarlino, Costanza Porta, and Claudio Merulo. Diruta is said to have been known as Merulo's "principal pupil." In 1597 he was serving as organist at the cathedral of Chioggia and in 1609 as organist at the Gubbio cathedral. A famous organist in his time, today he is known for his treatise on organ playing—Il Transilvano—which is the first of its kind to attempt a systematic approach to fingering and style of playing the organ. It was published in two parts, the first appearing in 1592, the second in 1609. It was reprinted in 1513, 1597, and 1612, with other editions published by the house of Vincenti in Venice in 1615 and 1625.

The work is in the form of a dialogue between the Prince of Transylvania (Il Transilvano) and Diruta. The Prince asks questions (all the proper ones), and the teacher explains. Diruta covers scales, note values, hand position, and the fingering of scales and passages; at the end of the first part Diruta gives a number of musical examples, including some by Merulo, Giovanni Gabrieli, Luzzaschi, Guami, and others. The second part deals with composition, ornaments, transposition, the use of organ stops, and other things organists ought to know. He also includes some musical compositions.

SOURCE: Girolamo Diruta, Il Transilvano. Dialogo sopra il vero modo di sonar organi & instrumento da penna . . . (Venice: Vincenti, 1597), pp.4–7.

GIROLAMO DIRUTA
from *Il Transilvano*

Rules for Playing the Organ Properly with Dignity and Grace

DIRUTA. The rule that I want to give you for playing organs properly may seem somewhat obscure at first sight, and difficult; but illustrated with my clear examples it will become most clear and easy. To begin, the rule is founded on several precepts. The first is, that the organist must be seated at the middle of the keyboard. The second is, that he should not make any actions or movements of his person but should hold his body and head erect and gracefully. The third is, that he should allow the arm to guide the hand, and that the hand should always be straight in relation to the arm, neither higher nor lower than it is. This will occur when the wrist is held somewhat high, because thus the hand will be level with the arm. And what I say about one hand is valid for the other. Fourth, the fingers should be held evenly above the keys, but somewhat curved. In addition, the hand should be held lightly and easily over the keys, for otherwise the fingers will not be able to move with agility and promptness. And finally, the fingers should press the key and not strike it, and the fingers should rise as much as the key rises.

Even if these rules appear of little or no importance, one should hold them to be of great account because of their usefulness, since they cause the harmony to be sweet and smooth, and the organist is not inconvenienced in playing.

TRANSILVANO. The rules given appear good at first sight, and I believe they will be not only useful, but most useful and necessary. But I should like to know what takes away from the harmony—the upright position, or the head twisted, the fingers level or curved?

DIR. I will say that none of these take away from the harmony, rather that from them one sees the seriousness and agility of the organist; and from the observance of these rules that I have given you are born the lightness and grace of Signor Claudio Merulo da Coreggio. On the contrary, one who twists about or hunches over the keyboard resembles a ridiculous *poseur* in a comedy. And from this arises another difficulty, for the labors of such a person do not succeed as they should, nor with that grace with which they should be made, because anyone who plays capriciously and misuses the art (so to speak) gives cause for difficulties in it. And more than a few times I have encountered such people who said the work was difficult, and I said it was very easy; and having taught them these rules and principles, they saw that, not from the difficulties of the works but from ignorance, they had been unable to find the way, and so was born their inability to play.

TRANS. And the works of these other worthy men, did they succeed as well as those of Signor Claudio?

DIR. There is no doubt about it; nor would my rule be called a "general rule" if one could not play all kinds of works and, I will further add, those that are composed for other instruments, such as the works and rules composed by Messer Girolamo of Udine, *maestro* of the concerts of the most illustrious Signoria of Venice. And also those of the most virtuous and obliging Giovanni Bassano, in whose works you will find every kind of difficult diminution, both for cornetto and violin, and even passages to be sung; these would not be suitable for the organ if one did not observe this rule.

TRANS. Most excellent! But let us return to the instructions you gave me earlier, both because it is very bad to play without dignity, as you say, and to make a thousand movements with the body, things that move the auditor to laughter instead of pleasing his ears by the sound. Let us leave this matter for the moment and turn to the other instructions. What does it mean, "the arm must guide the hand" and the hand remain level, and all the other things you said.

How the Arm Guides the Hand

DIR. This perhaps, and without any "perhaps," is the most important of all. If you have ever considered those who have bad hand positions, they appear to be crippled, because one sees only those fingers that strike the keys, with the others hidden; also, holding the arm so low that it is below the keyboard makes the hand appear to hang from the keys. All this comes from the hand not being guided by the arm, as it should be. Therefore it comes as no surprise that such persons, besides the exertion they undergo in playing, do not do anything well. But if I should describe to you a hand that has the effect of lightness you would understand how it must be guided by the arm, and also how the hand is cupped and the fingers arched.

Manner of Cupping the Hand and Arching the Fingers

But this is more easily demonstrated than the other. Know then that to cup the hand is a manner of drawing back the fingers somewhat, by which, at the same time, you will see the hand cup and the fingers arch. This is the way one should present the hand over the keyboard.

Manner of Holding the Hand Soft and Flexible

To tell you how you should keep the hand soft and flexible over the keyboard, I will give you an example. When one slaps a person's cheek in anger, great force is used. But when one wishes to caress or fondle a person, one does not use force but keeps the hand soft in the same way we caress a child.

TRANS. With this example I understand fully how to hold the hand. But tell me the effect that is made by pressing the keys, and that of striking them.

Effect of Pressing, and That of Striking the Key

DIR. The effect of pressing the key is this: it makes the harmony conjunct. On the contrary, to strike the key makes it disjunct, as you can see in [Ex. 1]; it is like a person who takes a breath after every note in singing, particularly in quarter and eighth notes. Looking at this example you will see in the eighth notes that singing them, as I have described, causes an eighth rest between one note and the next, as in [Ex. 2].

Ex. 1, good.

Ex. 2, poor.

This is exactly what happens to the awkward organist who, by raising the hand and striking the keys, loses half the harmony. Many fall into this error, among them clever players, for when they wish to make a beginning on the organ they place, then raise their hands from the keyboard in such a way that they will make the organ remain silent for the space of a half measure, so that it appears they are playing a quilled instrument and are about to begin a *saltarello*.

TRANS. You speak truly, for I have heard this ugly effect not a few times; but I thought it was due to the one who pumped the bellows that the wind was interrupted. This information should be of great value. Now I begin to understand the difference between playing an organ and a clavicembalo or other quilled instrument, and that between playing dances and music.

Why Players of Dances Do Not Succeed in Playing the Organ

DIR. That is true. And because of this the holy Council of Trent has prohibited the playing of *pass' e mezzos* and other dance pieces, to say nothing of lascivious *canzone*, on organs in the church, since it is not proper to mix sacred and profane things; and it appears that the organ cannot tolerate being played by such performers. And if it should happen that these players of dances attempted to play musical pieces, they would not be able to keep from striking the keys on the organ (and one could not hear anything worse); and because of this the dance musicians never, or rarely, will play musical works on the organ well. On the other hand, the church organist will never play dances well on quilled instruments, because the manner is different, as I have said.

TRANS. This is certainly excellent information, and I believe that it would not be unwelcome to the players of dances, for they also could derive some benefit from it.

DIR. Indeed, it should be most welcome to them, for it would be of the greatest use to them, and they would learn to play more easily and lightly, if, however, besides this they would observe the other rules I have given about the hand, except the striking and leaping with the hand to give grace and style to their dances.

TRANS. Very good. But could it not be possible that one who plays dances well should play music on the organ and likewise the organist should play dances well?

Manner of Playing on Organs, and Dances on Quilled Instruments

DIR. I have already told you, but I will make it more clear. Listen. I say, the player of dances wishing to play music on the organ should observe all the rules already cited about holding and shaping the hand. But the organist, wishing to play dances, needs to observe the rules, yes, except, however, in regard to leaping and striking with his fingers. This is conceded him for two reasons; first, because the quilled instruments must be struck in order for the jacks and the quills to play better; second, to play the dances with grace in that style, the organist wishing to play dances is permitted to strike with the fingers, just as any other player. But the dance musician, wishing to play music on the organ, is not permitted to strike with the fingers.

How to Play Quilled Instruments Musically

TRANS. This fine distinction in playing music and dances pleases me; but I would like to understand something else: Why is it that many organists do not succeed in playing musically on quilled instruments?

DIR. I could give you many reasons, but I will give you only the most important ones. To begin with the first, I say the instrument should be quilled equally, and [the jacks] should jump easily, and should be played in a lively manner so that the harmony is not lost. It should also be adorned with hemiolas and graceful accents. And the same effect, that the wind produces in supporting the harmony, should be made with the quilled instruments. For example, when the organist plays a whole note or a half note on the organ, its entire harmony is heard without striking the key more than once; but when you play the harpsichord such a note will lack more than half of its harmony. It is then necessary to fill in this lack by lightly restriking the key, rapidly and with dexterity of the hand, several times. In short, whoever wishes to play with polish and grace should study the works of Signor Claudio, in which you will find what you need for this.

It remains for me to tell you what are the good and bad fingers, because of the good and bad notes, as being necessary for organists as well as for the player of dances. But we will speak of them on another occasion.

TRANS. I beg you, because you say it is so necessary to know about the good and bad fingers, and the good and bad notes, to tell me without going further.

What Are the Good and Bad Fingers, and Notes

DIR. Very well, since you ask me. I do not want to deny you anything that will satisfy you. Know then, that the knowledge of the fingers is the most important thing that I have yet spoken of, and whatever anyone says, such knowledge is of the greatest importance. They are in error who say little to point out which finger is to be used for good notes and bad notes.

Now look: we have five fingers on the hand. The first is called thumb, the second, index; the third, middle; the fourth, ring finger; the fifth, auricular. The first finger plays the bad note; the second, the good; the third, the bad; the fourth, the good; and the fifth, the bad. The second, third, and fourth fingers are those that do all the work in playing the black keys. What I say of one hand is valid for the other. The black keys progress in the same order, that is, good and bad, as you will understand from the example below.

B C B C B C B C B C B C B C B C B

Ex. 3

TRANS. I believe this rule would enable one to play infallibly. But tell me, which finger should one use to play the first note in the above example?

Dir. If you want to play it with the right hand, take the first note with the second finger, which is a good finger, and the second note with the third, for it is a bad finger, as is the note, as we have seen. The third note should be played with the fourth finger, for it is good, as is the note; then continue with the third and fourth fingers on to the end of the scale. The final note will be played with the fourth finger, and this must always be observed in ascending. In descending, begin with the fourth finger and follow with the third and second to the end, where you will see your example terminate naturally with the second finger, without any error.

Trans. Then you are saying that one begins with the second finger on the good note, and continues with the third and fourth, so that the middle finger must accompany the fourth in ascending, and the second in descending with the right hand.

Why the Middle Finger Is Used More Than the Others

Dir. You have understood perfectly. However, I must tell you that the third, or middle finger, has to play all the bad notes both ascending and descending, for one cannot do anything without it—ascending, descending, and leaping, nor can one play *groppi* or *tremoli* without it. Sometimes there are bad notes that leap by wide intervals, and also narrow ones, such as skips of thirds, fourths, and fifths. In this case one can play them with the first and fifth fingers, as you please, and as it may be comfortable for either hand.

But it remains for me to tell you about the movement of the left hand, in which you should observe the same order of the fingers, good and bad. When the notes ascend, the first note will be taken by the fourth finger, and followed by the third and second, always ending with the second, because it is its actual ending.

But in descending, the first note will be taken with the second finger, and it will be followed by the third and the second, ending with the fourth. And so, ascending and descending, one uses the second and third fingers of the left hand.

Trans. But please tell me why one should not ascend with the first and second fingers, nor descend with the third and fourth, inasmuch as many good players do it that way.

Why One Should Not Ascend with the First and Second Fingers nor Descend with the Third and Fourth Fingers of the Left Hand

Dir. The doubt that you express is of great importance, and, with respect to those good players that you speak of, I say that this way is better than theirs. Now, learn that in ascending with the thumb, or large finger, it is all right on the white keys, when one plays in a key with B-natural; but if there are B-flats, it means you must play the black keys, which are shorter than the white, with the thumb. This is very inconvenient, as you will find from experience, and therefore to play with the third finger allows more agility and facility.

Neither should one descend in any way with the fourth finger, because there is not as much strength in the fourth finger of the left hand as there is in the fourth finger of the right hand, as you know. However, some capricious players ascend with the second and first fingers and descend with the third and fourth. They can do it, although it is greatly to their disadvantage. One should, however, observe the rule of the good fingers on the good notes, the bad fingers on the bad notes, otherwise it will not be satisfactory, as you will find in trying this [Exx. 4 and 5], and other examples that I will give you.

Ex. 4, with B flat.

Ex. 5, with B natural.

TRANS. Certainly one cannot deny that your way is more correct, and easier than the others, both in regard to the first finger as well as the fourth; for in truth the large finger is farther from the black key, so that it is difficult to touch the black key and inconveniences the whole hand. This does not happen if the third finger is used. And the experiment on the B-natural of the second example [Ex. 5] works very well with the thumb, but truly causes infinite trouble with the B-flat.

DIR. Now, since you have made this experiment, it will not be inappropriate for you to do this other, that is, with all kinds of short notes, for you will find it necessary to observe the good and bad notes. For greater clarity I willl give you different examples [see Ex. 6]. Those notes that must be played with the good finger are indicated by the letter B (*buono* = good) and the bad ones with the letter C (*cattivo* = bad). You will always find that the beginning of all the kinds of short notes must be taken with the good finger, except those that have a rest of the same value as the note, as you will see in the third example.

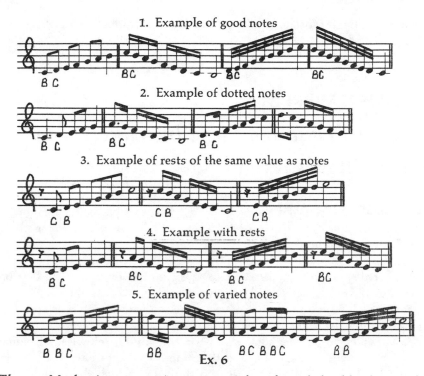

1. Example of good notes

2. Example of dotted notes

3. Example of rests of the same value as notes

4. Example with rests

5. Example of varied notes

Ex. 6

Thomas Morley (1557–1603) was one of the acknowledged leaders of the English madrigal school at the end of the sixteenth century and highly esteemed by his contemporaries. After Morley's death Ravenscroft eulogized him as "he who did shine as the Sun in the Firmament of our Art, and did first give light to our understanding with his Praecepts." For a long time Morley was organist at St. Paul's and later at the Chapel Royal under Queen Elizabeth. There is speculation that he was acquainted with Shakespeare, for whose plays he wrote one, perhaps two, songs. His fame rests both on his musical works—the charming madrigals and canzonets, a respectable body of sacred music, a book of instrumental Consort Lessons—and on A Plaine and Easie Introduction to Practicall Musick *of 1597.*

A Plaine and Easie Introduction *stands out as the most important English instruction book on sixteenth-century music, known throughout the musical world and used for the best part of the next century. Written in dialogue, it not only instructs but also conveys a good deal of information on contemporary musical life. Morley's discourse on forms and styles of musical composition, in the excerpt given here, presents a catalogue of the kinds of music then in favor and some description of the character of each.*

SOURCE: *Thomas Morley*, A Plaine and Easie Introduction to Practicall Musick *(London, 1597)*, Pt. III.

THOMAS MORLEY

from *A Plaine and Easie Introduction to Practicall Musick*

[Polymathes has asked the Master "to discourse unto us at large all the kinds of music, with the observations which are to be kept in composing of every one of them."]

MASTER: . . . I say that all music for voices (for only of that kind have we hitherto spoken) is made either for a ditty or without a ditty. If it be with a ditty it is either grave or light; The grave ditties they have still kept in one kind, so that whatsoever music be made upon it is comprehended under the name of a Motet.

A Motet is properly a song made for the church, either upon some hymn or anthem or such like, and that name I take to have been given to that kind of music in opposition to the other which they call Canto Firmo and we do commonly call Plainsong; for as nothing is more opposite to standing and firmness than motion, so did they give the Motet that name of moving because it is in a manner quite contrary to the other, which after some sort and in respect of the other standeth still.[1] This kind of all others which are made on a ditty requireth most art and moveth and causeth most strange effects in the hearer, being aptly framed for the ditty and well expressed by the singer, for it will draw the auditor (and specially the skilful auditor) into a devout and reverent kind of consideration of Him for whose praise it was made. But I see not what passions or motions it can stir up being sung as most men do commonly sing it, that is, leaving out the ditty and singing only the bare note, as it were a music made only for instruments, which will indeed show the nature of the music but never carry the spirit and, as it were, that lively soul which the ditty giveth. But of this enough; and to return to the expressing of the ditty, the matter is now come to that state that though a song be never so well made and never so aptly applied to the words yet shall you hardly find singers to express it as it ought to be, for most of our churchmen, so they can cry louder in their choir than

1. Morley's explanation is incorrect.

their fellows, care for no more, whereas by the contrary they ought to study how to vowel and sing clean, expressing their words with devotion and passion whereby to draw the hearer, as it were, in chains of gold by the ears to the consideration of holy things. But this for the most part you shall find amongst them; that let them continue never so long in the church, yea though it were twenty years, they will never study to sing better than they did the first day of their preferment to that place, so that it should seem that having obtained the living which they sought for they have little or no care at all, either of their own credit or well discharging of that duty whereby they have their maintenance. But to return to our Motets, if you compose in this kind you must cause your harmony to carry a majesty, taking discords and bindings so often as you can, but let it be in long notes, for the nature of it will not bear short notes and quick motions which denote a kind of wantonness.

This music (a lamentable case) being the chiefest both for art and utility is, notwithstanding, little esteemed and in small request with the greatest number of those who most highly seem to favour art, which is the cause that the composers of music, who otherwise would follow the depth of their skill in this kind, are compelled for lack of *Maecenates* to put on another humour and follow that kind whereunto they have neither been brought up nor yet (except so much as they can learn by seeing other men's works in an unknown tongue) do perfectly understand the nature of it; such be the new-fangled opinions of our countrymen who will highly esteem whatsoever cometh from beyond the seas (and specially from Italy) be it never so simple, condemning that which is done at home though it be never so excellent. Nor yet is that fault of esteeming so highly the light music particular to us in England, but general through the world, which is the cause that the musicians in all countries (and chiefly in Italy) have employed most of their studies in it; whereupon a learned man of our time, writing upon Cicero his dream of Scipio, saith that the musicians of this age, instead of drawing the minds of men to the consideration of heaven and heavenly things, do by the contrary set wide open the gates of hell, causing such as delight in the exercise of their art to tumble headlong into perdition.

This much for Motets, under which I comprehend all grave and sober music. The light music hath been of late more deeply dived into so that there is no vanity which in it hath not been followed to the full; but the best kind of it is termed Madrigal, a word for the etymology of which I can give no reason; yet use showeth that it is a kind of music made upon songs and sonnets such as Petrarch and many poets of our time have excelled in. This kind of music were not so much disallowable if the poets who compose the ditties would abstain from some obscenities which all honest ears abhor, and sometime from blasphemies to such as this, "ch'altro di te iddio non voglio," which no man (at least who hath any hope of salvation) can sing without trembling. As for the music it is, next unto the Motet, the most artificial and, to men of understanding, most delightful. If therefore you will compose in this kind you must possess yourself with an amorous humour (for in no composition shall you prove admirable except you put on and possess yourself wholly with that vein wherein you compose), so that you must in your music be wavering like the wind, sometime wanton, sometime drooping, sometime grave and staid, otherwhile effeminate; you may maintain points and revert them, use Triplas, and show the very uttermost of your variety, and the more variety you show the better shall you please. In this kind our age excelleth, so that if you would imitate any I would appoint you these for guides: Alfonso Ferrabosco for deep skill, Luca Marenzio for good air and fine invention, Horatio Vecchi, Stephano Venturi, Ruggiero Giovanelli, and John Croce, with divers others who are very good but not so generally good as these.

The second degree of gravity in this light music is given to Canzonets, that is little short songs (wherein little art can be showed, being made in strains, the beginning of which is some point lightly touched and every strain repeated except the middle) which is, in composition of the music, a counterfeit of the Madrigal. Of the nature of these are the Neapolitans or *Canzone a la Napolitana*, different from them in nothing saving in name, so that whosoever knoweth the nature of the one must needs know the other also; and if you think them worthy of your pains to compose them you have a pattern of them in Luca Marenzio and John Ferretti, who, as it should seem, hath employed most of all his study that way.

The last degree of gravity (if they have any at all) is given to the Villanelle or country songs, which are made only for the ditty's sake for, so they be aptly set to express the nature of the ditty, the composer (though he were never so excellent) will not stick to take many perfect chords of one kind together, for in this kind they think it no fault (as being a kind of keeping decorum) to make a clownish music to a clown-ish matter, and though many times the ditty be fine enough, yet because it carrieth that name Villanella they take those disallowances, as being good enough for plough and cart.

There is also another kind more light than this which they term Balletti or dances, and are songs which being sung to a ditty may like-wise be danced. These, and all other kinds of light music (saving the Madrigal) are by a general name called "airs."

There be also another kind of Balletts commonly called "Fa las." The first set of that kind which I have seen was made by Gastoldi; if others have laboured in the same field I know not, but a slight kind of music it is and, as I take it, devised to be danced to voices.

The slightest kind of music (if they deserve the name of music) are the Vinate or drinking songs, for, as I said before, there is no kind of vanity whereunto they have not applied some music or other, as they have framed this to be sung in their drinking; but that vice being so rare among the Italians and Spaniards, I rather think that music to have been devised by or for the Germans (who in swarms do flock to the University of Italy) rather than for the Italians themselves.

There is likewise a kind of songs (which I had almost forgotten) called Giustinianas and are all written in the Bergamasca language; a wanton and rude kind of music it is, and like enough to carry the name of some notable courtesan of the city of Bergamo, for no man will deny that the Justiniana is the name of a woman.

There be also many other kinds of songs which the Italians make, as Pastourelles and Passamezzos with a ditty, and such like, which it would be both tedious and superfluous to dilate unto you in words, therefore I will leave to speak any more of them and begin to declare unto you those kinds which they make without ditties.

The most principal and chiefest kind of music which is made without a ditty is the Fantasy, that is when a musician taketh a point at his pleasure and wresteth and turneth it as he list, making either much or little of it according as shall seem best in his own conceit. In this may more art be shown than in any other music because the composer is tied to nothing, but that he may add, diminish, and alter at his pleasure. And this kind will bear any allowances whatsoever tolerable in other music except changing the air and leaving the key, which in Fantasie may never be suffered. Other things you may use at your pleasure, bindings with discords, quick motions, slow motions, Proportions, and what you list. Likewise this kind of music is, with them who practise instruments of parts, in greatest use, but for voices it is but seldom used.

The next in gravity and goodness unto this is called a Pavan, a kind of staid music ordained for grave dancing and most commonly made of three strains, whereof every strain is played or sung twice; a strain they make to contain eight, twelve, or sixteen semibreves as they list, yet fewer than eight I have not seen in any Pavan. In this you may not so much insist in following the point as in a Fantasy, but it shall be enough to touch it once and so away to some close. Also in this you must cast your music by four, so that if you keep that rule it is no matter how many fours you put in your strain for it will fall out well enough in the end, the art of dancing being come to that perfection that every reasonable dancer will make measure of no measure, so that it is no great matter of what number you make your strain.

After every Pavan we usually set a Galliard (that is a kind of music made out of the other), causing it go by a measure which the learned call *trochaicam rationem*, consisting of a long and short stroke successively, for as the foot *trochaeus* consisteth of one syllable of two times and another of one time, so is the first of these two strokes double to the latter, the first being in time of a semibreve and the latter of a minim. This is a brighter and more stirring kind of dancing than the Pavan, consisting of the same number of strains; and look how many fours of semibreves you put in the strain of your Pavan, so many times six minims must you put in the strain of your Galliard. The Italians make their Galliards (which they term Saltarelli) plain, and frame ditties to them which in their masquerades they sing and dance, and many times without any instruments at all, but instead of instruments they have courtesans disguised in men's apparel who sing and dance to their own songs.

The Alman is a more heavy dance than this (fitly representing the nature of the people whose name it carrieth) so that no extraordinary motions are used in dancing of it. It is made of strains, sometimes two, sometimes three, and every strain is made by four; but you must mark that the four of the Pavan measure is in Dupla Proportion to the four of the Alman measure, so that as the usual Pavan containeth in a strain the time of sixteen semibreves, so the usual Alman containeth the time of eight, and most commonly in short notes.

Like unto this is the French Branle (which they call "Branle Simple") which goeth somewhat rounder in time than this, otherwise the measure is all one. The "Branle de Poictou" or "Branle Double" is more quick in time (being in a round Tripla) but the strain is longer, containing most usually twelve whole strokes.

Like unto this (but more light) be the Voltes and Courantes which being both of a measure are, notwithstanding, danced after sundry fashions, the Volte rising and leaping, the Courante travising [i.e., traversing] and running, in which measure also our Country Dance is made, though it be danced after another form than any of the former. All these be made in strains, either two or three as shall seem best to the maker, but the Courante hath twice so much in a strain as the English Country Dance.

There be also many other kinds of dances, as Hornpipes, Jigs, and infinite more which I cannot nominate unto you, but knowing these the rest cannot but be understood as being one with some of these which I have already told you. And as there are divers kinds of music so will some men's humours be more inclined to one kind than to another; as some will be good descanters and excel in descant and yet will be but bad composers, others will be good composers and but bad descanters extempore upon a plainsong; some will excel in composition of Motets and being set or enjoined to make a Madrigal will be very far from the nature of it; likewise some will be so possessed with the Madrigal humour as no man may be compared with them in that kind and yet being enjoined to compose a Motet or some sad and heavy music will be far from the excellency which they had in their own vein. Lastly some will be so excellent in points of voluntary upon an instrument as one would think it impossible for him not to be a good composer and yet being enjoined to make a song will do it so simply as one would think a scholar of one year's practice might easily compose a better. And I dare boldly affirm that look which is he who thinketh himself the best descanter of all his neighbours, enjoin him to make but a Scottish Jig, he will grossly err in the true nature and quality of it.

Thus you have briefly those precepts which I think necessary and sufficient for you whereby to understand the composition of three, four, five or more parts, whereof I might have spoken much more. . . .

Part III The Seventeenth Century

6. Music a Gentleman's Recreation

Henry Peacham (1576?–1643?), educated at Cambridge, was an author and man of varied talents. In 1606 he published a treatise on art, Graphice, *which went through numerous editions under the title* The Gentleman's Exercise. *During the years 1613–14 he traveled on the Continent, mainly in France, Italy, and the Netherlands. His best known work is* The Compleat Gentleman *of 1622 (reprinted 1626, 1634), a handbook and guide for young men of good birth. Music, in Peacham's view, was one of the truly important accomplishments for the well-bred gentleman, along with scholarly pursuits and manly arts. Peacham himself may very likely have had musical talent, for he was a friend of John Dowland and moved in musical circles. Like Castiglione a century earlier, he presents a good picture of the life of his period.*

SOURCE: *Henry Peacham,* The Compleat Gentleman *(Oxford: Clarendon Press, 1906; reprint of the 1634 edition), Ch. XI.*

HENRY PEACHAM

from *The Compleat Gentleman*

Music a sister to Poetry, next craveth your acquaintance (if your Genius be so disposed). . . .

The Physicians will tell you, that the exercise of Music is a great lengthener of the life, by stirring and reviving of the Spirits, holding a secret sympathy with them; besides, the exercise of singing openeth the breast and pipes: it is an enemy to melancholy and dejection of the mind, which S. Chrysostom truly calleth the *Divels Bath*. Yea, a curer of some diseases: in Apuglia, in Italy, and thereabouts, it is most certaine, that those who are stung with the Tarantula, are cured only by Music. Beside the aforesaid benefit of singing, it is a most ready help for a bad pronunciation, and distinct speaking, which I have heard confirmed by many great Divines. Yea, I my selfe have known many children to have bin holpen of their stammering in speech, only by it.

Plato calleth it *A divine and heavenly practice*, profitable for the seeking out of that which is good and honest.

Homer saith, Musicians are worthy of Honor, and regard of the whole world; and we know, albeit Lycurgus imposed most straight and sharp laws upon the Lacedemonians, yet he ever allowed them the exercise of Music.

Aristotle averreth Music to be the only disposer of the mind to Vertue and Goodness; wherefore he reckoneth it among those four principal exercises, wherein he would have children instructed.

Tully saith, there consisteth in the practice of singing and playing upon Instruments, great knowledge, and the most excellent instruction of the mind: and for the effect it worketh in the mind, he termeth it, *Stabilem Thesaurum, qui mores instituit, componitque, ac mollit irarum ardores, &c.* A lasting Treasure, which rectifieth and ordereth our manners, and allayeth the heate and fury of our anger, &c.

I might run into an infinite Sea of the praise and use of so excellent an Art, but I only shew it you with the finger, because I desire not that any Noble or Gentleman should (save at his private recreation and leisurable hours) prove a Master in the same or neglect his more weighty employments: though I avouch it a skill worthy the knowledge and exercise of the greatest Prince.

King Henry the eighth could not only sing his part sure, but of himself composed a Service of four, five and six parts; as Erasmus in a certain Epistle, testifieth of his own knowledge.

The Duke of Venosa, an Italian Prince, in like manner, of late years, hath given excellent proof of his knowledge and love to Music, having himself composed many rare songs, which I have seen.

But above others, who carryeth away the Palm for excellency, not only in Music, but in whatsoever is to be wished in a brave Prince, is the yet living *Maurice Landgrave of Hessen*, of whose own composition I have seen eight or ten several sets of Motets, and solemn Music, set purposely for his own Chapel; where for the great honor of some Festival, and many times for his recreation only, he is his own organist. . . .

I desire no more in you than to sing your part sure, and at the first sight, withal, to play the same upon your Viol, or the exercise of the Lute, privately to yourself.

To deliver you my opinion, whom among other Authors you should imitate and allow for the best, there being so many equally good, is somewhat difficult; yet as in the rest herein you shall have my opinion.

For Motets and Music of piety and devotion, as well for the honour of our Nation, as the merit of the man, I prefer above all others our Phoenix, M. William Byrd, whom in that kind, I know not whether any may equal, I am sure none excell, even by the judgment of France and Italy, who are very sparing in the commendation of strangers, in regard of that conceit they hold of themselves. His *Cantiones Sacrae*, as also his *Gradualia*, are mere Angelical and Divine; and being himself naturally disposed to Gravity and Piety, his vein is not so much disposed for light Madrigals or Canzonets, yet his *Virginella* and some others in his first Set, cannot be mended by the best Italian of them all.

For composition, I prefer next Ludovico de Victoria, a most judicious and a sweet composer: after him Orlando di Lasso, a very rare and excellent Author, who lived some forty years since in the court of the Duke of *Bavier* [Bavaria]. He hath published as well in Latin as French many Sets, his vein is grave and sweet: among his Latin Songs his seven penitential Psalmes are the best, and that French set of his wherein is *Susanna un jour:* upon which Ditty many others have since exercised their invention.

For delicious Aire and sweet Invention in Madrigals, Luca Marenzio excelleth all other whosoever, having published more Sets than any Author else whosoever; and to say truth, hath not an ill Song, though sometime an over-sight (which might be the printer's fault) of two *eights*, or *fiftes* escapt him; as between the Tenor and Base in the last close, of *I must depart all haplesse:* ending according to the Nature of the Ditty most artificially, with a Minim rest. His first, second, and third parts of *Thyrsis, Veggo dolce mio ben, Chi fa hoggi mio Sole, Cantava,* or *Sweet singing Amaryllis,* are Songs the Muses themselves might not have been ashamed to have had composed. Of stature and complexion, he was a little and black man; he was Organist in the Popes Chappel at Rome a good while, afterward he went into Poland, being in displeasure with the Pope for overmuch familiarity with a kinswoman of his, (whom the Queen of Poland sent for by Luca Marenzio afterward, she being one of the rarest women in Europe, for her voyce and the Lute:) but returning he found the affection of the Pope so estranged from him, that hereupon he took a conceit and died.

Alphonso Ferabosco the father, while he lived, for judgment and depth of skill, (as also his son yet living) was inferior to none; what he did was most elaborate and profound, and pleasing enough in Aire, though Master Thomas Morley censureth him otherwise. That of his, *I saw my Lady weeping,* and the *Nightingale* (upon which Ditty Master Bird and he in a friendly emulation, exercised their Invention) cannot be bettered for sweetness of Ayre or depth of judgment.

I bring you now mine owne Master, Horatio Vecchi of Modena: beside goodness of Aire most pleasing of all other for his conceit and variety, wherewith all his works are singularly beautified, as well his Madrigals of five and six, as those his Canzonets, printed in Norimberge: wherein for trial, sing his *Vivo in fuoco amoroso, Lucretia mia,* where upon *Io catenato moro,* with excellent judgment he driveth a Crotchet through many Minims, causing it to resemble a chain with the links. Again, in *S'io potessi raccor' i miei Sospiri,* the breaking of the word *Sospiri* with crotchet and crotchet rest into sighs: and that *Fa mi un Canzone,* &c. to make one sleep at noon, with sundry other of like conceit, and pleasant invention.

Then that great Master [Giovanni Croce], and Master not long since of S. Markes Chappell in Venice; second to none for a full, lofty, and sprightly vein, following none save his own humour: who while he lived was one of the most free and brave companions of the world. His Penitential Psalms are excellently composed, and for piety are his best.

Nor must I here forget our rare Country-man, Peter Philips, Organist to their *Altezza's* at *Bruxelles,* now one of the greatest Masters of Music in Europe. He hath sent us over many excellent Songs, as well Motets as Madrigals: he affecteth altogether the Italian vein.

There are many other Authors very excellent, as *Boschetto,* and *Claudio de Monte Verde,* equal to any before named; *Giovanni Ferretti, Stephano Felis, Giulio Rinaldi, Philippo de Monte, Andrea Gabrieli, Cyprian de Rore, Pallavicino, Geminiano,* with others yet living; whose several works for me here to examine, would be over tedious and needless; and for me, please your own care and fancy. Those whom I have before mentioned, have been ever (within thirty or forty years) held for the best.

I willingly, to avoid tediousness, forbear to speak of the worth and excellency of the rest of our English Composers, Master Doctor Dowland, Thomas Morley, M. Alphonso, M. Wilby, M. Kirby, M. Wilkes, Michael East, M. Bateson, M. Deering, with sundry others, inferior to none in the world (however much soever the Italian attributes to himself) for depth of skill and richness of conceit.

Infinite is the sweet variety that the Theorique of Music exersizeth the mind withall, as the contemplation of proportion, of Concords and Discords, diversity of Moods and Tones, infiniteness of Invention &c. But I dare to affirm, there is no one Science in the world, that so affecteth the free and generous Spirit, with a more delightfull and inoffensive recreation, or better disposeth the mind to what is commendable and virtuous. . . .

But to conclude, if all Arts hold their esteem and value according to their Effects, account this goodly Science not among the number of those which *Lucian* placeth without the gates of Hell, as vaine and unprofitable: but of such which are *pegai ton kalon,* the fountains of our lives good and happiness: since it is a principal means of glorifying our merciful Creator, it heightens our devotion, it gives delight and ease to our travails, it expelleth sadness and heaviness of Spirit, preserveth people in concord and amity, allayeth fierceness, and anger; and lastly, is the best Phisick for many melancholy diseases.

George Herbert (1593–1683), younger brother of the diplomat Lord Herbert of Cherbury, was educated at Cambridge and was something of a literary man. He took orders about 1628 and in 1630 accepted a living at Bemerton. His verse is chiefly found in The Temple *(1630), consisting of 160 poems of a religious character. His major prose work is* A Priest to the Temple *(1652), said by Izaak Walton to contain "plain, prudent, useful rules for the country parson." Walton, who is best known for his* Compleat Angler *(1653), was, however, friend of both Herbert and John Donne and wrote their biographies. Walton's delightful anecdote reflects the widespread practice of amateur music. Like so many men of letters and of the priesthood, Herbert loved music and played the viol regularly in an amateur consort.*

Source: *Izaak Walton,* The Lives of John Donne, Sir Henry Wotton, Richard Hooker, George Herbert, and Robert Sanderson *(London, 1670).*

IZAAK WALTON
from *The Life of George Herbert*

His chiefest recreation was Musick, in which heavenly Art he was a most excellent Master, and did himself compose many divine Hymns and Anthems, which he set and sung to his Lute or Viol; and, though he was a lover of retiredness, yet his love to Musick was such, that he went usually twice every week on certain appointed days, to the Cathedral Church in Salisbury; and at his return would say that "his time spent in Prayer, and Cathedral Musick, elevated his Soul, and was his Heaven upon Earth." But before his return thence to Bemerton, he would usually sing and play his part, at an appointed private Musick-meeting; and, to justifie this practice, he would often say, Religion does not Banish mirth, but only moderates, and sets rules to it. . . .

In another walk to Salisbury, he saw a poor man, with a poorer horse, that was fall'n under his Lead; they were both in distress, and needed present help; which, Mr. Herbert perceiving, put off his Canonical Coat and help'd the poor man to unload, and after to load his horse. The poor man blest him for it: and he blest the poor man; and was so like the good Samaritan, that he gave him money to refresh both himself and his horse; and told him, that if he loved himself, he should be merciful to his Beast.—Thus he left the poor man, and at his coming to his musical friends at Salisbury, they began to wonder that Mr. George Herbert which us'd to be so trim and clean, came into that company so soyl'd and discomposed; but he told them the occasion. And when one of the company told him he had disparaged himself by so dirty an employment, his answer was, That the thought of what he had done would prove Musick to him at Midnight, and that the omission of it, would have upbraided and made discord in his Conscience, whensoever he should pass by that place; for, "if I be bound to pray for all that be in distress, I am sure that I am bound so far as it is in my power to practise what I pray for. And though I do not wish for the like occasion every day, yet let me tell you, I would not willingly pass one day of my life without comforting a sad soul, or shewing mercy; and I praise God for this occasion. And now let's tune our Instruments."

Roger North (1653–1734) was a gentleman of good family, lawyer, writer, and amateur musician, as was his elder brother, Baron Francis North, also a lawyer and Keeper of the Great Seal of England. Roger North was not known in his lifetime as an author, although he had published two small books anonymously; but some fifty years after his death Dr. Burney brought North's musical memoirs to notice, drawing on them for material for his (Burney's) history of music. The most important of North's manuscripts are the "Musicall Grammarian" (first and second versions), the "Theory of Sounds," and "An Essay of Musicall Ayre." Although North wrote chiefly from his own "observation and experience," he ranges widely and provides a rich store of comment on music in the society of his day.

Memoirs of Music makes it clear that music was an important activity in the North family; both brothers played the viol and sang, and the younger sisters sang. North's description of music-making in his home and his comments on musical instruction paint a delightful picture of amateur music in the late seventeenth century.

Source: *British Museum, Add. MS 32,506, pp.69 et passim.*

ROGER NORTH

from *Memoirs of Music*

As to Musick, it was my fortune to be descended of a family where it was native. My Grandfather, Dudley the [3rd] Lord North, having travelled in Italy, where that music is queen, took a liking to it. . . . He play'd on that antiquated instrument called the treble viol, now abrogated wholly by the use of the violin; and not only his eldest son, my father, who for the most part resided with him, play'd, but *his* eldest son Charles, and yonger son the Lord Keeper, most exquisitely and judiciously. And he kept an organist in the house, which was seldom without a profes't musick master. And the servants of parade, as gentlemen ushers, and the steward, and clerck of the kitchen also play'd; which with the yong ladys my sisters singing, made a society of musick, such as was well esteemed in those times. And the course of the family was to have solemne musick 3 days in the week, and often every day, as masters supply'd noveltys for the enterteinement of the old lord. And on Sunday night, voices to the organ were a constant practice, and at other times symphonys intermixt with the instruments. . . .

The consorts were usually all viols to the organ or harpsichord. The violin came in late, and imperfectly. When the hands were well supply'd, then a whole chest went to work, that is 6 violls, musick being formed for it; which would seem a strange sort of musick now, being an interwoven hum-drum, compared with the brisk *battuta* derived from the French and Italian. But even that in its kind is well; and I must make a great difference when musick is [only] to fill vacant time, which lyes on hand. Then, that which hath moderate buissness in it, and being harmonious, will lett one sleep or drouse in the hearing of it, without exciting the ball or dance, is well enough. But where heads are brisk and airey hunting of enterteinements, and brought to musick as the best, where it is expected to be accordingly . . . then I confess this sort will not please. . . .

And nothing, of the unprofitable kind, can be so good as Music, who is a kind companion and admitts all to her graces, either men by themselves, or men and women together, or the latter single, with either instruments and voices, or either alone, as the capacitys are; and fail not to enterteine themselves, and their parents and friends, with pleasures sensible to those that have found the sweets of them. . . .

This letts me in to speak a little of Teaching, on which much of this depends. For men the viol, violin, and the thro-base instruments organ, harpsicord, and double base, are proper; for women the espinnett, or harpsicord, lute, and gittarr; for voices both. I cannot but comend the double base, or standing viol, for plaine bases, especially for accompanying voices, because of its softness joyned with such a force as helps the voice very much. And the harpsicord for ladys, rather than the lute; one reason is, it keeps their body in a better posture than the other, which tends to make them crooked. . . .

In music the materiall is sound, which may be made well, or ill, and that difference in the first formation of it is of the greatest importance. . . .

Therefore as to the *pratique*, I would have a voice or hand taught, first to prolate a long, true, steddy and strong sound, the louder and harsher the better; for that will obtein an habit, of filling and giving a body to the sound, which else will be faint and weak, as in those who come to sing at maturity of years, when the organs of voice are stiff and intractable. And so for a bow hand, to spend the whole bow at every stroke, long or short. These lay a good foundation, the roughness and harshness of which will soften in time. The loud may abate, but soft voices cannot be made loud at pleasure. Those must be formed early, as the limbs to arts, by much striving and continuall exercise, so as to grow, and settle into a forme, to fitt the use and practise of them.

Then next I would have them learn to fill, and soften a sound, as shades in needlework, *insensatim*, so as to be like also a gust of wind, which begins with a soft air, and fills by degrees to a strength as makes all bend, and then softens away againe into a temper, and so vanish. And after this to superinduce a gentle and slow wavering, not into a trill, upon the swelling the note; such as trumpetts use, as if the instrument were a little shaken with the wind of its owne sound, but not so as to vary the tone, which must be religiously held to its place, like a pillar on its base, without the least loss of the accord. . . .

The next thing to be taught is the transition of the voice or hand from one tone to another, or the practise of the Gamut. . . . Then next the grace of passing from one to another, which in some sort connects them, though severall, as if they were links in a chaine, very distinct, yet connected all together. . . . Then lastly, the art of mixing 2 sounds with the same prolation of breath should be learnt, which brings the trill, and being rightly used is a great beauty, but otherwise rediculous in music; and this ought to be strictly observed, that the trill give way to harmony. . . . But wise masters are to be aware of this and lead their scollars by fitt paths and stepps, whereby they may attaine a just perfection.

7. Travelers' Accounts of Musical Performances

Thomas Coryat (1577–1617), an Englishman by birth, traveled through Europe on two different occasions, in 1608 and again in 1612. The first time he limited his trip to western Europe, including France, Italy, Germany, Switzerland, and Holland, taking note of anything that struck his fancy. His description of his journey was published in two volumes, whimsically titled Coryat's Crudities *and* Coryat's Cramb. *Four years later he undertook a much more extensive trip, overland to India via Constantinople, Palestine, Mesopotamia, and Persia. He completed his journey as far as Agra in four years. He died at Surat in 1617.*

Coryat was interested in many things, which he set down in a strange, barbaric style, but he included much of interest about music and culture. His description of the music he heard in Venice is especially valuable because he described the numbers and kinds of instruments and voices.

SOURCE: *Thomas Coryat,* Coryat's Crudities hastily gobled up in five months travells in France, Savoy, Italy, Rhetia commonly called the Grisons country, Helvetia alias Switzerland, & some parts of high Germany, and the Netherlands; newly digested in the hungry aire of Odcombe in the county of Somerset, & now dispersed to the nourishment of the travelling members of this kingdom . . . *(London: W. S. [Stansby], 1611), pp.349ff.*

THOMAS CORYAT
from *Coryat's Crudities*

The Music of St. Roch's Feast

[Coryat mentions having heard the music of three feasts in Venice.] The first was in the church of certain nuns in St. Lawrence parish, which are dedicated to St. Lawrence. This was celebrated the one and thirtieth of July, being Sunday, where I heard much singular music. The second was on the day of our Lady's Assumption, which was the 5th of August, being Friday. At that time I heard much good music in Saint Mark's church but especially that of a treble viol which was so excellent that I think no man could surpass it. Also there were Sagbuts and Cornets as at St. Lawrence's feast which yielded passing good music. . . .

The third feast was upon Saint Roch's day, being Saturday and the 6th of August, where I heard the best music that ever I did in all my life, both in the morning and the afternoon, so good that I would willingly go an hundred miles afoot to hear the like. . . . The second room is the place where this festivity was solemnized to the honour of St. Roch, at one end whereof was an Altar garnished with many singular ornaments, in number 60, and candles in them of virgin wax. This feast consisted principally of music, which was both vocal and instrumental, so good, so delectable, so rare, so super excellent that it did even ravish and stupefy all those strangers that never heard the like. But how others were affected with it I know not; for mine owne part I can say this, that I was for the time even rapt up with St. Paul into the third heaven. Sometimes there sung 16 or 20 men together, having their master or moderator to keep them in order; and when they sung the instrumental musicians played also. Sometimes 16 played together upon their instruments, 10 sagbuts, 4 cornets, and 2 violdegamboes of an extraordinary greatness; sometimes 10—6 sagbuts and 4 cornets; sometimes 2, a cornet and a treble viol. Of these treble viols I heard three several there, whereof each was so good, especially one that I observed above the rest, that I never heard the like before. Those that played upon the treble viols sung and played together upon Theorboes, to which they sung also, who yielded admirable sweet music but so still that they could scarce be heard but by those that were very near them. These two Theorboes concluded that night's music, which continued three whole hours at least. For they began about five of the clock and ended not before eight. Also it continued as long in the morning: at every several time that every several music played, the organs, whereof there are seven fair pair in that room, standing all in a row, played with them. Of the singers there were three or four so excellent that I think none in Christendom do excell them, especially one, who had such a peerless and (as I may say) such a supernatural voice for sweetness, that I think there never was a better singer in all the world, insomuch that he did not only give the most pleasant contentment that could be imagined to all the hearers, but also did, as it were, astonish and amaze them. I always thought he was an Eunuch, which if he had been, it had taken away some part of my admiration, because they do most commonly sing passing well; but he was not, therefore it was much the more admirable. Again, it was the more worthy of admiration, because he was a middle-aged man, as about forty years old. For nature doth more commonly bestow such a singularity of voice upon boys and striplings than upon men of such years. Besides it was for the more excellent because it was nothing forced, strained, or affected, but come from him with the greatest exactitude that ever I heard. Truly I think that had a nightingale been in the same room, and contended with him for the superiority, something perhaps he might excell him, because God granted that little bird such a privilege for the sweetness of his voice, as to none other; but I think he could not much. To conclude, I attribute so much to this rare fellow for his singing that I think the country where he was born may be as proud for breeding so singular a person as Smyrna was of her Homer, Verona of her Catullus, or Mantua of Virgil. But exceeding happy may that city or town or person be that possesseth this miracle of nature. These musicians had bestowed upon them by that company of St. Roch six shilling, eight pence sterling. Thus much concerning the music to those famous feasts of St. Laurent, the Assumption of our Lady, and Saint Roch.

André Maugars (?–?) was a seventeenth-century French viol player of considerable prominence. He was not only a musician in Cardinal Richelieu's entourage but also "counselor, secretary, interpreter to the King for the English language," according to Thoinan. He spent four years in England at the court of James I; while there he translated Bacon's Advancement of Learning, which was published in Paris in 1624. On his return to Paris he entered the service of Cardinal Richelieu, where he remained until his death.

He was undoubtedly an exceptionally fine violist, and is mentioned as such by Mersenne in his Harmonie universelle *and praised by Jean Rousseau in his* Traité de la viole. *He composed works for viols, but they are no longer extant.*

Maugars' letter, published as a small pamphlet in 1640, shows him to have been very observant as to the musical practices and performances he witnessed while in Rome. His account provides an excellent picture of the Roman musical scene of that time.

SOURCE: *André Maugars,* Response faite à un curieux sur le Sentiment de la Musique d'Italie, Ecrite à Rome le premier Octobre 1639, *ed. Ernest Thoinan (Paris, 1640).*

ANDRÉ MAUGARS

Response to an Inquisitive Person on the Italian Feeling about Music

Well, to justify in a way the high opinion you have conceived about my knowledge of music, I resolved finally to write to you candidly about the feeling I have regarding Italian music, and the difference I find between it and ours; begging you, because of the desire I feel to please you, to judge sincerely this little Harmonic Reasoning. I hope to tell you today, without passion or disguise, what hope has brought to me during the twelve or fifteen months I have associated in Italy with the most excellent men in the art, and what I have listened to carefully at the most celebrated concerts in Rome.

In the first place, I find that their composers of church music have more artistry, more knowledge, and more variety than ours; but also that they have more freedom. And for me, since I could not disapprove of this freedom, when it is used discreetly and with skill, which insensibly deceives our feelings, so I cannot approve of the stubbornness of our composers who keep themselves religiously limited in pedantic categories and who feel that they would commit solecisms against the rules of the art if they wrote two successive fifths or if they departed even a little bit from their modes. No doubt it is in these very agreeable departures that the secret of the art consists—since music has figures of speech just like rhetoric, which all tend to charm the listener and deceive him insensibly. To tell the truth, it is not so necessary to amuse ourselves by observing the rules so rigorously that it makes us lose track of a fugue or the beauty of a song, in view of the fact these rules have been invented only to keep young schoolboys under control and prevent them from emancipating themselves before they have reached years of discretion. That is why a judicious man, with full knowledge of the science, is not condemned, by absolute fiat, to stay eternally in this narrow prison and can always soar according as his caprice carries him into some fine experiment, wherever the power of the words and the beauty of the parts shall lead him. This is what the Italians practice to perfection, and as they are much more refined than we in musical matters, they sneer at our musical regularity, and thus they write their Motets with more art, more knowledge, more variety, and more skill than we do ours.

In addition to the great advantage they have over us, what makes their music the more agreeable is that their concerts are much more orderly and they place their choirs much better than we do, giving each one a little organ, which makes them sing better in tune.

To enable you to understand this distribution better, I will give you an example by describing to you the most celebrated and most excellent concert, which I heard at Rome the eve and the day of Saint Dominic at the church of the *Minerva* [Santa Maria sopra Minerva]. This church is rather long and wide and there are two large elevated organs, one on each side of the main altar, where they had also placed two choirs. Along the nave there were eight other choirs, four on one side and four on the other, raised on platforms eight or nine feet high, an equal distance from one another and all facing one another. With each choir there was a portative organ, as is the custom. You must not be astonished, because one can find more than two hundred [organs] in Rome, while in Paris one could scarcely find two of the same tuning. The leading conductor beat the measure for the main choir, accompanied by the best voices. With each of the others there was a man who did nothing but keep his eyes on the leading conductor, to conform his own beat to the leader's; in this way all the chorus sang in the same time, without dragging. The counterpoint was decorated, full of fine chants, and many agreeable recitatives. Sometimes a high voice [*dessus*] in the first choir did a *récit*, then one of the 3rd, 4th, and 10th answered. Sometimes two, three, or four voices from the different choirs sang together, sometimes the parts of all the choirs recited, each in turn, in emulation of each other. Sometimes two choirs contended with each other, then two others answered. Another time three, four, and five solo voices sang together, and at the *Gloria Patri* all the choirs joined together. I must admit that I have never been so delighted; but especially in the Hymn and in the Prose, where ordinarily the conductor tries to do better, I heard singing that was perfectly beautiful: very elegant variety, very excellent inventions, and delightful different movements. In the Anthems they had also very lovely instrumental performances, with one, two, or three violins with the organ, and with archlutes playing certain dance tunes and answering each other.

Let us place our hands, Sir, on our consciences and let us judge sincerely if we have similar performances; and even if we should have them, it seems to me that we do not at present have the voices; they would need a long period of performing together, whereas the Italian musicians never practice but sing all their parts at sight. And what I find more admirable is, that they never miss, though the music is very difficult, and that a voice in one choir often sings with the voice of another choir, which perhaps has never been seen or heard. What I beg you to notice is that they never sing the same Motets twice, though scarcely a day passes that there is not a festival in some church where some good music is played, so that one is assured every day of some new composition. That is the most agreeable diversion I have in Rome.

There is still another kind of music which is not performed in France and which for this reason deserves my telling you about it separately. It is called *Stile recitativo*. The best that I have heard was in the Saint Marcel Chapel, where there is a congregation of the Brothers of the Holy Crucifix, composed of the greatest nobles of Rome, who as a consequence have the power to bring together every rarest thing in Italy; and, indeed, the most excellent musicians are proud of being there and the most excellent composers seek the honor of having their compositions heard there, and try to present what is best in their studios.

This admirable and ravishing music is heard only on Fridays during Lent, from three to six o'clock. The church is not nearly as big as the Sainte Chapelle in Paris. At the end is a spacious rood screen with a medium-sized organ, very sweet and very suitable for voices. At the two sides of the church there are two small galleries where were located the best musical instruments. The voices began with a Psalm in the form of a Motet and then the instruments played a very good Sinfonia. The voices after this sang a story from the Old Testament in the form of a *comédie spirituelle*, like that of Susanna, of Judith and Holofernes, of David and Goliath. Each singer represented a personage of the story and perfectly expressed the energy of the words. Then one of its most celebrated preachers recited the Exhortation. When this was finished, the music recited the Evangel of the day, like the story of the Good Samaritan, the feast at Canaan, the story of Lazarus, of Mary Magdalen, of Our Lord's Passion, the singers imitating to perfection the personages the Evangelist writes about. I cannot praise the Recitative Music enough; one must hear it to judge of its merit.

As to the instrumental music, it was composed of an organ, a large clavecin, two or three violins, and two or three archlutes. At times a single violin sounded with the organ, and then another answered; another time all three played different parts together; and then all the instruments repeated together. Sometimes an archlute performed a thousand variations on ten or twelve notes, each note five or six measures long; then another played the same passage differently, I remember one violin played purely chromatically, and though at first it seemed to me very hard on the ears, nevertheless I gradually grew accustomed to this manner and took great pleasure in it. But specially the great Frescobaldo brought out a thousand kinds of inventions on his clavier, the organ always holding firm.

It is not without reason that this famous organist has acquired such a reputation in Europe; because his printed works render sufficient evidence of his skill, to judge his profound knowledge adequately you must hear him as he improvises toccatas full of refinement and admirable inventions. That is why he deserves that you hold him up as a unique player to all our organists, to make them want to come to hear him in Rome. Since I have unwittingly begun the praises of this excellent man, it would not be bad for you to convey my feeling to other people.

The person who holds first place for the harp is that renowned Horatio, who, appearing at a time favorable for harmony and having found Cardinal Montalto favorable to his playing, found himself peerless without a rival, by more than five or six thousand *ecus* of income, which this Harmonious Spirit generously gave him for his enjoyment and well-being. I would not want to water down the praise that he deserves, since we cannot always remain what we once were, and age dulls our senses little by little, and robs us insensibly of grace and delicacy, and especially of that agility of the fingers which we possessed in our youth. The Ancients were right in depicting Apollo as always young and vigorous.

After these two I have seen no others in Italy that deserve to be rated with them. There are certainly ten or twelve that do marvels with the violin, and five or six others with the archlute, there being no difference between the archlute and the theorbo except they place the second [string] and the chanterelle at the top, using the theorbo to sing to and the archlute to accompany the organ, with a thousand variations and an incredible swiftness of hand.

The lyre is still acceptable among them, but I know of none of them to be compared with Ferrabosco in England.

There are many others excellent on the harp, like Signora Constancia, who plays perfectly. These are the persons, Sir, who excel on the instruments. It is true that I heard many others who can play a fugue on the organ, but they do not have the pleasing quality of our players. I do not know whether it is because their organs do not have as many registers and keys as those we have in Paris today; it seems to me that most of their organs are only to sustain the voices and to support the other instruments.

As for the spinet, they play it very differently from ours. I have seen some curious ones made with two keyboards, one to sound the Dorian mode, the other the Phrygian, dividing the tone into four strings to enable one to play the pure chromatic and enharmonic genera and to turn easily from one kind of half-tone to another. I assure you that it creates a very fine effect; but since these two genera have not yet been treated intelligibly enough in our language, I hope, if God grants me the favor of ever returning to Paris, to give you a lecture on this subject, drawn from the best ancient and modern writers, Italian and English, who have tried in their writings to reestablish the two genera, lost by the inundation of barbarians, who caused a discontinuation of music for so many centuries, so that of the three genera, which the Ancients used so efficiently, only the diatonic has remained and today has truly reached a high degree of perfection.

As for the viol, there is no one at present who excels in it, and it is even played very little in Rome. I am very surprised at this, in view of the fact that they once had a Horatio de Parme, who worked wonders with it, and who left very good compositions, which some of our players have used cleverly for other instruments, as well as for their own. And also the father of the great Ferrabosco taught their use to the English, who have surpassed all the other nations since that time.

You would scarcely believe, Sir, how greatly the Italians esteem those who excel on the instruments and how much more they prize instrumental music than vocal music, saying that a single man can produce more beautiful inventions than four voices together, and that it has a charm and freedom which the vocal music does not have. But I would not be entirely of this opinion if one could find four voices, just, equal, harmonious, which did not predominate one over another. To sustain their opinion they say it produces more powerful effects than the vocal, and that it is easy to prove from ancient stories celebrating the power and influence of the lyre of Pythagoras, "who moved souls with his lyre"; also about the harp of Timotheus, who moved the passions of Alexander in whatever way he pleased, and several other tales also. But because these other examples have been reported by poets, in whom I never believed, I leave them aside, to use only two or three instances from Holy Scripture, for fear of exceeding the limits of a letter. David drove out the evil spirits who possessed Saul and made his soul tranquil with the melodious sounds of the harp. And Saint Francis, in the fervor of his meditations, having asked God to let him hear one of the joys of the Blessed, heard a concert of angels playing on the viol as the sweetest and most charming of the instruments. This will be sufficient for the moment about instrumental music.

There remains, according to my plan to discourse with you about vocal music, the singers, and the Italian way of singing.

There are a large number of castrati for the Dessus and the Haute-Contre, very beautiful and natural Tenors, and very few deep Basses. They are very certain of their technique and sing the most difficult music at sight. In addition, they are almost all actors by nature, and it is for this reason that they succeed so perfectly in their musical comedies. I have seen them play three or four this last winter, but I must admit that in truth they are incomparable and inimitable in music for the stage, not only for their singing but also for the expression of the words, the postures, and the gestures of the characters they play naturally and very well.

As for their manner of singing, it is much more animated than ours; they have certain inflections of the voice that we do not possess. It is true that they perform their passages with more roughness, but today they are beginning to correct that.

Among the excellent castrati the Chevalier Loreto [Vittori] and Marco Antonio [Pasqualini] hold first place; but it seems to me that they do not sing the airs as agreeably as does Leonora [Baroni], daughter of that *Bella Adriana* of Mantua, who was a real miracle in her day and has produced an even greater one by bringing into the world the most perfect person for singing well.

I think I would wrong the excellence of this illustrious Leonora if I did not mention her to you as one of the marvels of this world, but I do not intend to outdo the powerful Italian geniuses who, to celebrate in a worthy fashion the merit of this incomparable lady, have produced a large volume of excellent writings in Latin, Greek, French, Italian, and Spanish, which they published in Rome under the title *Applausi poetiche alle glorie della Signora Leonora Baroni*. I shall content myself with saying that she is endowed with a fine mind, that she has good judgment in distinguishing bad from good music, that she understands it perfectly well and even composes; which means that she is in complete possession of what she sings and she pronounces and expresses perfectly well the sense of the words. She makes no pretence of being beautiful, but she is not ugly or coquettish. She sings with assured and generous modesty and with gentle gravity. Her voice has a wide range, is true, sonorous, harmonious; she softens it and makes it louder without any grimaces. Her exclamations and sighs are not lascivious, her glances have nothing immodest, and her gestures have all the modesty of a worthy young girl. When she passes from one note to another, she sometimes makes you feel the divisions between the enharmonic and the chromatic modes with such skill and artistry that there is no one who is not greatly pleased by this beautiful and diffcult method of singing. She does not need to ask the help of a theorbo player or a violinist, without one of which her singing would be imperfect, for she herself plays these instruments perfectly. Finally, I had the good fortune to hear her sing several times, more than thirty different songs, with second and third verses, which she had composed herself. I must tell you that she did me the special favor of singing with her mother and her sister, her mother playing the lyre, her sister the harp, and she the theorbo. This concert, composed of three beautiful voices and three different instruments, so affected my senses and so ravished my spirit that I forgot my mortal condition and thought I was among the angels enjoying the delights of the blessed. So to address you as a Christian, the purpose of music is, by touching our hearts, to raise them to God, because it is a sample in this world of the eternal joy, and its purpose is not by lascivious gestures to lead us to vice, toward which we are only too much inclined by nature.

It was in this virtuous house that I was first obliged at the request of these rare ladies to exhibit in Rome the talent which it has pleased God to grant me, in the presence of ten or twelve of the most intelligent persons in Italy, who after having listened attentively flattered me with some praise; but this was not without some jealousy. To test me further, they obliged Signora Leonora to keep my viol, and to ask me to return the next day, which I did; and having been warned by a friend that they said I played very well the pieces I had studied, I gave them all sorts of preludes and fantasies this second time, which they really esteemed more highly than they had the first time. Since then I have been visited by good people, since my viol wishes that I leave the room only for the Purple, which it has been accustomed to obey for many years. After the esteem of these good people, it was not yet enough to win absolutely that of the professionals, who are a little too refined and much too reluctant to applaud foreigners. I was informed that they admitted that I played very well alone and that they had never heard anyone play so many parts on the viol, but they had doubts, since I was French, that I was capable of treating and diversifying a subject impromptu. You know, Sir, that that is where I succeed best. Since these words were told to me on the eve of St. Louis's day in the French church, where I was listening to the fine music that was being played, it made me resolve the next morning, emboldened by the holy name of Louis, by national honor, and by the presence of twenty-three Cardinals who were present at the Mass, to mount a pulpit, where having been greeted with applause, they gave me fifteen or twenty notes on a small organ after the third *Kyrie eleison*, which I played with so many variations that they were eminently satisfied, and asked me on behalf of the Cardinals to play once more after the *Agnus Dei*. I counted myself lucky to render this small service to such an eminent company. They sent me another subject, gayer than the first one, which I diversified with so many inventions, with different movements and different speeds, that they were astonished, and came immediately to compliment me, but I retired to my room to rest.

This action brought me the greatest honor that I shall ever receive, for having spread throughout Rome, the rumor of it came to the ears of his Holiness, who a few days afterward did me the special grace of sending for me and among other words said to me, "noi abbiamo sentito che lei ha una Virtù singolare, la sentiremmo volentieri." ["We have heard that you have a special talent, we would like to hear it."] I shall not relate to you here the satisfaction that his Holiness expressed to me after having done me the honor of listening to me for more than two hours; you will some day encounter persons worthy of being believed, who will give you an ample account.

The friendship which you have for me, persuades me, Monsieur, that you will not accuse me of too much vanity in this digression, which I have made only to inform you that it is necessary for a Frenchman who wants to acquire a reputation in Rome to be very well versed in his subject, the more so because they do not think that we are capable of treating a subject impromptu. And certainly no man who plays an instrument deserves to be thought excellent unless he knows how to improvise, and especially on the viol, which being a different instrument because of the small number of strings and the difficulty that exists in fingering all the parts, its true talent is to play around with the given subject and to produce fine inventions and agreeable diminutions. But two essential and natural qualities are necessary for this result: to have a lively and strong imagination and quickness of the hand to execute one's ideas promptly; that is why people cold and slow by nature will never succeed well.

But to conclude this treatise, my feeling is that if our singers were willing to take more pains to study and to associate with foreigners, they would succeed as well as they in singing well. So we have an example in a French gentleman to whom the Muses have not denied their finest favors, who has adjusted the French and Italian methods so well that he has received wide applause from all right-thinking men, and has deserved, with the other fine qualities he possesses, to have the honor of serving the most just and intelligent King in the world.

As for our composers, if they were willing to emancipate themselves a little more from their pedantic rules and take a few journeys to observe foreign music, my feeling is that they would succeed much better than they are doing now. It is not because I am not aware that we have many [who are] very capable in France, and among others that illustrious Intendant of the King's music [Antoine Boësset], who can play such lovely chords in his charming motets, in his ravishing songs, and in his manner of singing. All the Italian music will never be powerful enough to make me lose the esteem that I have for his merit and his virtue.

In order that this discourse may have some usefulness, I have observed that, in general, we sin in omission and the Italians in commission. It seems to me that it would be easy for a smart man to write compositions that would have their variety without their extravagances; we should not despise them:

Nec verò terrae ferre omnes omnia possunt.[1]

There is no country that has nothing strange about it. We compose *airs de mouvement* admirably well, and the Italians compose church music marvelously. We play the lute well and the Italians the archlute. We play the organ agreeably and the Italians learnedly. We play the spinet admirably, and the English play the viol perfectly. I admit that I owe them something and that I have imitated them in their tunings, but not in other things; our French birth and training give us this advantage over all the other nations in that they will never be able to equal us in fine movements, in agreeable diminutions, and particularly in the natural airs of Courantes and Ballets.

I was about to end here when I became aware of a crime that my memory was about to cause me to commit, by forgetting the great Monteverdi, master composer at the church of Saint Mark. He has found a new, very admirable manner of composing both for instruments and for voices, which forces me to propose him to you as one of the first composers in the world; I will send you some new works of his, when God grants me the grace to go to Venice.

Here, Sir, is what you wanted so passionately to learn about Italian music; but I perceive that when I satisfy your curiosity I shall never satisfy the vanity of some of our presumptuous musicians, if you communicate this letter to them, and you will cause me to lose their good graces. Nonetheless, if they are willing to unseal their eyes and to get rid of passion, as I am detached from all sorts of prejudices, if they consider and weigh my reasoning by thinking over their too-regular music, unless they wish to be considered opinionated enemies of Reason, they will find that I have judged sincerely and justly, and they will doubtless profit from my observations. If this should happen, by chance,

1. "Nor indeed are all the lands capable to produce everything" (i.e., not everybody can do everything).

I would esteem myself very lucky to have opened some way to make greater progress in music; but if they persist in their obstinacy, it matters not to me; at least they cannot prevent my having this satisfaction in my soul: that I have rendered faithful witness to the truth and satisfied the duties of friendship. Thus I hope to content persons of merit and knowledge and to be not unworthy of the profession which I have always exercised without sham.

8. On Organ Playing

Adriano Banchieri (1567–1634), an Italian priest at the monastery of S. Michele near Bologna, was an organist, a very progressive composer and theorist, and an outstanding music educator. He was a pupil of Gioseffo Guami and may be said to have been educated in the Venetian musical style. He wrote a great deal of music, including a number of stage works, some of which are very amusing; a great many sacred and secular vocal pieces, most of which remain in manuscript; and organ and instrumental compositions. Among his important works is L'organo suonarino (1505), which was one of the first books to contain rules for figured bass. He also published a series of Cartella musicale, *which set forth rules for singing and counterpoint, from 1601 to 1623. His four books of* Nuovi Pensieri Ecclesiastici *(1613), pieces for one or two solo voices to be performed with accompaniment of organ, cembalo, theorbo, and chitarrone, are valuable as showing the style of solo vocal music performed in liturgical services.*

His delightful Conclusioni nel suono dell' organo, *which may be roughly translated as "Ideas about Playing the Organ," is one of Banchieri's earliest instructional works. It is designed to help young organists or those in small churches. In it he discusses kinds and styles of music suitable for various services or feasts, and offers precepts and advice, as well as some church history and information about organists and composers of the time. The entire book provides good insight for modern performers into the practices of Banchieri's day. The two chapters given here deal with the playing of fantasias and styles to be observed in compositions for church use.*

Source: *Adriano Banchieri,* Conclusioni nel suono dell' organo *(Bologna, 1609),* Sesta et Settima Conclusioni.

ADRIANO BANCHIERI

from *Conclusioni nel suono dell' organo*

Sixth Conclusion Explained

Kinds of Music to Be Preferred in Playing the Organ

For two reasons music, and the organ, were introduced into the holy Mother Church (*Cerimonale Romanum*, Ch. 8). First, to praise God; second, to attract the people from their servile tasks to devotion on feast days. This praise of the Lord was introduced as early as the Old Testament, as we read in Ch. 6 of Kings: *Et erant cum David septem chori, & immolabant Bovem, & Ovem, & Arietem, & David percutiebat in organis, & saltabat totis viribus ante Dominum:* signifying in these words that while the sacrifices were made before the Ark, while the musical choir sang, and the organs played, King David, overcome with joy, danced with all his might, From this the organist should understand that in the fantasia he should adopt a joyous style, beautiful and pleasing to the Divine Majesty and joyful to the faithful, as we see in the works of the *canzoni francesi* of Antonio Mortaro and Flaminio Tresti, both celebrated organists, and other such things that they may produce, attracting also with new compositions such as *Dialoghi ecclesiastici* and *Arie musicali;* in this respect observing the 22nd session of the Council of Trent, thus: *Ab ecclesiis verò Musicas eas ubi sive cantum sive Organo lascivum, aut impurum aliquid miscetur,* meaning that in music and the organ, lascivious melodies should not be heard, nor songs with vulgar words, dances, morescas, and the like. The organist will take care that they will not be of the kind spoken of in Job 21: *Et gaudent ad sonitum Organi,* for instead of exciting the people to devotion they move them to mundane pleasures.

The *stile allegro* should not always be used, only at certain times; and also at the Elevation of the Holy Sacrament some serious sonata that moves one to devotion should be used. Franchino [Gaffurio] in [*Practica musica*] Book 3, Ch. 13 writes in his discourse on Ambrosian chant: *Quum D. Ambrosius ecclesiastica describeret cantica, in sola dulcedine mirabiliter elaboravit (eccettuando) Cantum lugubrem, ac mortuorum sufragis.* From these words one should understand that sweetness should be used. In short, see that the faithful hear sweet and soave harmonies

(& *suavi modulatione*, says Rationale Diu. book 2). One can consider these to be celestial melodies, concerted by the Angels and Cherubim before the Divine Majesty—the divine melodies that we may all enjoy throughout eternity. And here, to fill out this page, do not forget those words cited above, *ac mortuorum sufragia*, for in the Mass for the Dead one must not play the organ (*Cer. Rom.* Ch. 28). It is, however, usual in the funerals of prelates or titled principals to play the organ, not as the organ but as Concerti, as a solemn filling to the devotions, using the Principal only, with the cover, or its louvers, closed.

Seventh Conclusion Explained

Musical Styles to Be Observed in the Composition of Organ Music
    The Masses, Psalms, Canticles, Motets, and Concerti to be performed with the Organ must be in the *affettuoso*, devout, attractive, and *recitativo* styles, imitating the words and employing gravity in concerting them. Be advised that the *Guide*, or fugues of eight, ten measures, more or less, do not at all succeed in such compositions. Likewise double fugues, *al rovescio*, involved, lacerated, or delayed, which at the same time appear to be great extravaganzas, are not suitable.
    It is also my opinion that, for example, while singing the *Dixit* verses as *cantus firmus*, to have one voice sing at the same time *Donec ponam*, another *Virgam*, the third *Tecum principio*, and so on, successively, would make, alas, great confusion.
    So in other music, if the soprano, alto, tenor, and bass sing different words in the same measure, is it not the same thing? In truth, yes. Not without reason Pope John the 20th in 1306 issued a decree (as Gioseffo Zarlino affirms in his *Supplimenti Musicale*, Ch. 3) that music in the church should be sung in consonances of octaves, fifths, and thirds; and from this came the origin of that kind of cantilena called vulgarly *Falsobordone*, an improper use and word, which, being a contest of sweet consonances, instead of using the name *Soavibordoni*, it was called *Falsibordoni*. It is true that with the passage of time this devout idea was abused by the composers; again (as Agostino Agazzari writes in his treatise on instruments), Pope Marcellus barely avoided forbidding all music of the church, thanks to Giovanni Palestrina, who showed it to be a vice of the composer and not of the art, he therefore on that occasion composed the Mass entitled *Pope Marcellus* and dedicated it to Pope Paul the Fourth, and again introduced music in consonances. In the organ concerti, a graceful invention was that of Ludovico Viadana (as he states in the introduction to his *Cento Concerti Ecclesiastici*) in which he

has one, two, and three voices sing in *stile recitativo*, and consonantly, in such a way that, being over a *Basso continuato*, one hears the words distinctly—something, in truth, of general satisfaction to the organist, singer, and audience. And since that style is so welcome, we see it in the [works of] modern composers, which from day to day are ornamented with the most beautiful ideas. I do not say that the double fugues and long pieces are not those that give proof of a good organist, but I say truly that where words enter, they are not suitable. One should there- fore use *ricercari*, as Annibale Padovano, Andrea Gabrieli, and other virtuosi have done; and though many compositions are printed by illustrious men in this style of the art, one should prize them, putting them into score to help the beginning organist become proficient in ideas; and play them in the churches in concert with instruments and organ, and in the Academies in any way as most pleases. In sum, avoid the lengthy and confused pieces, so that the devout faithful may participate in the Divine Offices with souls that are satisfied and consoled.

Agostino Agazzari (1578–1640), scion of a noble Sienese family, was an organist, composer, and Maestro di cappella of the German–Hungarian College in Rome from 1602 to 1606. He also served as Maestro di cappella of the Roman Seminary in 1606. In 1607, he returned to Siena, where he became organist of the cathedral of that city, a position he held until his death. He composed numerous sacred and secular composi- tions, most of which were provided with the new basso continuo. *In 1607 he published his essay* Del sonare sopra il basso con tutti li stromenti, *in which he takes up Viadana's rules for concerting voices and organ and amplifies them, introducing, in addition to organ or cembalo* basso con- tinuo, *other instruments. He also adopted the new monodic style for church use in place of the older choral polyphony.*

This letter of 1606, written to a Sienese gentleman, would appear to be a sketch for Agazzari's essay on playing over a bass with all the instruments, which he published the following year. It contains his basic ideas for combining organ, voices, and instruments and is a useful guide for the performance of both sacred and secular music in the early part of the seventeenth century.

SOURCE: *Adriano Banchieri,* Conclusioni nel suono dell' organo *(Bologna, 1609), pp.68–70.*

AGOSTINO AGAZZARI

Letter on Style in Organ Playing

Copy of a Letter written by Sig. Agostino Agazzari to a Sienese Virtuoso, his compatriot, from which we can gain knowledge of the style which should prevail in playing an organ together with voices and instruments.

Because I have understood in substance that you want me to send you a memorandum on the style that the Roman master musicians use when they arrange voices and stringed instruments with bows, and keyboard instruments together with the organ, to satisfy you I say this: that in concert (the organ serving as foundation) it should be played with great discretion, paying attention to the quantity and quality of the voices and the instruments. If these are few, one should use a light register and chords; if they are many, add and plan as the occasion demands. When two similar sounds appear together with the organ—as it were, two tenors, two basses, two sopranos, two lutes, two violins, or other instruments—they should be separated from each other, because such distance provides enjoyment and avoids confusion. The organist should also play the work exactly [as written], avoiding runs and passagework, playing sometimes gracefully with the pedals in the contrabass, above all else strictly and in the low register, for the high register harms the voices and other instruments. And what has been said about the organ applies to the harpsichord, the chittarone, and the lute when they are used as the fundamental harmony.

The voices, when they concert with the organ, should be governed by the ear and by good judgment, being careful that one does not overshadow the other but are sung equally, with sweetness and elegance.

The lute in a concert should be played with pleasing inventiveness and diversity, at times with firm strokes and with soft repercussions, at other times with broad passagework, and sometimes *stretti*; at still others with graceful figures on the low strings, repeating fugues in different places, and with *groppi*, trills, and accents to make it very attractive. And one should not play, as some people do who have quick hands and little training, nothing but *tio, tio, tio,* a thing really most hateful to the ear.

The chitarrone or theorbo, whichever you want to call it, should be played in a concert with full and suave consonance, striking and playing scales lightly on the *bourdon* strings. The particular excellence of these instruments is the use of trills and soft accents from time to time, made with the right hand.

The bass viol in concerts (as the lowest part) should proceed as the foundation, sustaining the harmony of the other parts in sweet consonance with the basses and contrabasses.

The viols should be played with full bowing, clear and sonorous, and in particular the lirone, or viola bastarda, should give out its notes with great judgment and a foundation of good counterpoint and technique.

The violin demands clear and lengthy runs, with scherzi, echoes, and responses, fughette, repetitions in different keys, chords, accents, lyrical passages, soft bowings, with *groppi* and varied trills.

And this is briefly as much as I can remember at this time about the subject, and to satisfy your lordship I hope with all my heart in a few days to put on paper a treatise on similar material, in which it will be treated more fully for the sake of better understanding.

Let it suffice for me to say to you that what is said here should be applied with prudence, warning the organists, the singers, and the ensemble to give each other room, not being offended by the multitude, but with ear and judgment waiting for the time and the place, and not act as though the passage at any one time belongs to the one who shouts the loudest.

And so, in ending, I hope you are happy and contented.

FROM ROME
APRIL 25, 1606

Girolamo Frescobaldi (1583–1643) was a brilliant musician—organist, trained singer, and composer—who enjoyed international fame during his lifetime. He was born in Ferrara, where he studied with the famous organist Luzzasco Luzzaschi. He was organist in a church in Rome in 1607, then for a time in Flanders. In 1608 he became organist in St. Peter's Cathedral in Rome, a post he held until 1628. It is said that at his first performance there he had an audience of 30,000 persons. During his tenure in Rome he appears to have concertized widely. He may have sung while he played, for a contemporary writes, "His voice was so beautiful and he sang with such taste, that music lovers followed him from city to city, in order not to be deprived of hearing him." It is probable that in his concerts he also played the cembalo and directed concerts of chamber music.

From 1628 to 1634 he served as organist to Ferdinand II de' Medici, then returned to St. Peter's and remained there until his death. During the years 1637–1641, Froberger, the virtuoso harpsichordist, studied with Frescobaldi.

Frescobaldi's output includes a book of five-part madrigals and a collection of Arie musicali for solo voice. His organ works, still known and used today, are of interest not only for their beauty but also for their prefaces. In these Frescobaldi set down instructions and suggestions for playing his pieces. In the three presented here Frescobaldi makes it clear that an artistic rendition is essential, requiring use of rubato, rolled or broken chords, ornaments, and dynamic and rhythmic changes, and gives directions for achieving it.

SOURCES: *Girolamo Frescobaldi,* Toccate e partite d'intavolatura, *Book 1 (Rome, 1614, 1637);* Il primo libro di Capricci fatti sopra diversi soggetti *. . . (Rome, 1624, 1626);* Fiori musicali di diversi compositioni *. . . (Venice, 1635).*

GIROLAMO FRESCOBALDI
from *Toccate e partite d'intavolatura*

Preface

1. The manner of playing, just as in the performance of modern madrigals, should not be subjected to strict time. Although such madrigals are difficult, they are facilitated if one takes the beat now languidly, now lively, or holding back, according to the affection of the music or the meaning of the word.

2. In the Toccatas I have attempted to offer not only a variety of passagework and expressive ornaments but also to make the various sections such that they can be played independently, so that the performer may stop wherever he wishes and not have to play the entire toccata.

3. The beginning of the toccatas should be played slowly and *arpeggiando;* similarly, syncopations and tied notes in the middle of the piece. Chordal harmonies should be broken with both hands so that the instrument may not sound hollow.

4. In trills and passages (either stepwise or by leaps) the last note should be held, even when these notes are eighths, sixteenths, or differ-

ent from the following ones. This pause eliminates confusion of the different sections.

5. In the cadences, even though written in notes of small values, one must sustain them. As the performer approaches the end of a passage, he must slow the tempo.

6. A passage should be separated, and marked off from another one, when one encounters a consonance that is written for both hands in quarter notes.

If there is a trill for the right or left hand, and the other plays a passage simultaneously, the trill must not be played note for note but rapidly, the accompanying passage being played less rapidly and expressively; otherwise there will be confusion.

7. If one finds passages in eighths and sixteenths in both hands together, one should not play them too fast. The hand that has sixteenths may play them somewhat dotted; of two notes, not the first but the second should be dotted and so on, the first not, the second dotted.

8. When playing passages in sixteenth notes in both hands, one should pause on the preceding note, even if it is black [short], then play the passage resolutely in order that the agility of the hands may appear.

9. In the Partitas, where runs and expressive passages occur, it will be advisable to play them broadly. The same applies to the Toccatas. On the other hand, in the Partitas without passagework one may play rather fast. It is left to the good taste and fine judgment of the performer to decide the tempo that best suits the spirit and perfection of the manner and style of interpretation.

(The Passacaglia sections can be played separately *a piacere*. The tempo of one may be adapted to that of other sections. The same holds true for the Chaconnes.)

from *Capricci fatti sopra diversi soggetti*

Capriccio sopra La Spagnoletta

To those who will study this work:

Because the performance of these works may appear very different to some, seeing them in divers rhythms and variations, and since it also seems that many may have neglected the practice of studying the score,

I wished to point out that in these things, which do not seem to be governed by the rules of counterpoint, one must first of all seek the feeling of the passage and the aim of the author concerning the effect on the ear, and the way in which one should try to play them.

In these compositions entitled Capricci, I have not employed a style as easy as in my Ricercari. But one should not, however, judge of their difficulty before having essayed them well on the instrument, where one will find, by study, the feeling which ought to prevail. Also I have paid attention to the facility of study together with that of beauty; it appearing to me somewhat more suitable to the performer that if the work should appear too fatiguing to play from beginning to end, one might begin a passage wherever he most pleases and end with a passage that finishes in the same mode.

The beginning should be played slowly to give greater spirit and beauty to the following passages; and in the cadences broaden them a little before beginning the next passage; and in the groups of three or six, if they are long values one should bring them out slowly; if in smaller values, a little faster; if of three semiminims, faster; if of six against four, one may give their rhythm by playing in a lively measure. It is suitable in certain dissonances to slow down by arpeggiating them in order that the following passage may produce a livelier effect.

from *Fiori musicali*

Preface

Having always been desirous (because of that talent God has granted me) to benefit by my labors studious persons of the [musical] profession, I have always shown to the world, through my printed tablatures and scores, all kinds of *capricci* and inventions, my earnest desire that each one, seeing and studying my work, may be pleased by it and profit from it. With this book I will say only that my chief aim is to help organists, having completed certain compositions in such a style of playing as to make them suitable for Mass or Vespers, and know them to be useful. The Verses may be used as one pleases; in the Canzoni and Ricercari [the organist] may finish at the cadences if the pieces appear too long.

I consider it a matter of great importance for the players to use the score; not only do I think it important, but necessary for those who wish to study such compositions, because this practice, like a touchstone, distinguishes and makes known the true gold of the *virtuosi* from the actions of the ignorant. Nothing else need be said except that practice is the master of all; let him who wishes to advance in this art experiment and put these things to proof. He will see how much he will profit by them.

1. In the Toccatas, when some trills or *affettuoso* passages are found, play them slowly; and in the eighth notes that follow in the several parts, make them somewhat faster. The trills should be played more slowly, with a slowing down of the tempo, although the Toccatas may be played according to the desire and taste of the performer.

2. The beginnings of the Toccatas may be played *adagio*, even if they are written in eighths, and then, according to their movement, make them faster.

3. In the Kyries some can be played with a lively tempo and others more slowly, according to the player's judgment.

4. Also, the aforesaid Verses, although written for the Kyrie, may serve for other *affetti* [expressions], as may be deemed most suitable.

5. In the *Canti fermi*, although the notes may be tied, in order not to impede the hands one can break them up for greater ease, after having used all the facility that one may command.

9. The Performance of Sacred Music

Matthias Hoe von Hoenegg's account of the musical program for the centennial celebration of the Reformation in 1617 provides an insight into the kind of music considered suitable for such a celebration at that time and the kinds of instruments that were deemed appropriate for use in divine service. Heinrich Schütz was in charge of the music for this occasion, an event that was undoubtedly an important one for him, as he was still relatively new in his position as Kapellmeister of the Dresden court church.

The program as reported by von Hoenegg, then the Dresden court preacher, reveals that Schütz had arranged splendid music for the occasion, undoubtedly employing the full forces of singers and instrumentalists available to him. Schütz's instrumental ensembles—resembling those recommended by Agazzari or Praetorius as suitable for festival performances—appear to have been modeled on the Italian practice of the time. The five or seven choirs von Hoenegg mentions refer of course to both vocal and instrumental groups. It is not possible to assume that all the compositions performed were by Schütz, but it is very likely that most of the works were his settings; surely Psalm 100 was the setting found in his Psalms of 1619.

SOURCE: Matthias Hoe von Hoenegg, Parasceve ad solemnitatem evangelicam, 1617; in Musik und Kirche III, Chr. Mahrenholz, ed. (Kassel: Bärenreiter, 1941), p. 149.

MATTHIAS HOE VON HOENEGG
from *Parasceve ad solemnitatem evangelicam*

**Schütz's Program for the Centennial Celebration
of the Reformation, 1617**

At noon, October 30, the festival was begun by the ringing of bells of all the churches in the city and surrounding areas. Vespers were held, and confessions heard.

The first day of the festival, October 31, began at six o'clock in the morning with the joyful firing of guns. Other salutes, as is the custom on high festival occasions, also were sounded. On this day, and also on the first and second of November, services were held in both morning and afternoon, with glorious music presented. And because the music, especially that of the court church, was magnificent, delightful, and impressive, I should not neglect, for the sake of future readers and also as a lasting record, here to recount fully what kinds of Masses, concerted works, and Psalms were performed, as well as the manner in which they were performed.

The First Festival Day
   Introit: O sing unto the Lord a new song (Ps. 98) followed by the *Kyrie, Christe, Kyrie, Gloria in excelsis*, etc., *Et in terra pax*, all performed by seven choirs, together with trumpets and kettledrums.
   After the Epistle: *Allein zu dir, Herr Jesu Christ*, in which the choir alternated with the congregation.
   After the Gospel: the *Credo*, the choir again alternating with the people. In the pulpit, before the Lord's Prayer preceding the sermon, was sung a portion of the *Te Deum laudamus*, from *Now help us Lord, Thy servants*, etc., to the end, by the choir with instruments, and also the congregation.
   After the Sermon: the German songs ordinarily sung at the Communion of His Electoral Grace: *Gott sei gelobet und gebenedeiet*, etc., and also *Jesus Christus unser Heiland*.

The Afternoon Sermon

Intonation before the altar: *Deus adjutorium meum intende.*

Response: *Domine ad adjuvandum,* etc. *Gloria.*

Introit: Jubilant hodie omnes gentes, accompanied by trumpets, and Psalm 100, *Jubilate Deo,* as an interlude between the trumpets in five choirs. *This is the day which the Lord hath made* followed, performed by the festival choir; also the *Credo* by the choir alternating with the congregation.

After the Sermon: a six-choir Magnificat with kettledrums and trumpets, and between every verse of the Magnificat was sung a verse from Luther's hymn *Erhalt uns, Herr, bei deinem Wort.* To conclude, the choir sang *Verleih uns Frieden gnädiglich,* etc., *Gib unserm Fürsten,* etc., all by the choir, *Benedicamus,* etc.

The musicians of the Elector of Saxony, our Gracious Lord, performed this music: eleven instrumental players, eleven singers, four organists, four lutenists, one theorbo player, three organ choir boys, five discant singers, alternating with various kinds of magnificent instruments, also with two organs, two regals, three clavicymbals, and in addition eighteen trumpeters and two kettledrums, all presented with appropriate solemnity under the direction of Heinrich Schütz from Weissenfels.

Heinrich Schütz (1585–1672), a native of Saxony, received an excellent education in music as well as in the liberal arts of his day; further, he studied law at the University of Marburg and earned distinction in that discipline. From 1599 he was a chorister in the chapel of the Landgrave Maurice of Hesse-Cassel, who, perceiving Schütz's outstanding musical talent, sent him to Venice in 1609 for further musical training under Giovanni Gabrieli. He remained there three years, and in 1611 he published a book of five-part madrigals in the Italian style, dedicated to his patron the Landgrave. In 1613, after Gabrieli's death, Schütz returned to Germany, where he continued his law studies for a while, then, turning again to music, became organist of the Landgrave's chapel. In 1615 Schütz held a temporary post in the chapel of the Elector of Saxony at Dresden, and in 1617 became director of the Elector's chapel. Here he reorganized the cappella *after the Italian usage, introducing the new concertato style for voices and instruments.*

Schütz's music for the chapel was a fusion of German and Italian styles, adding Italian brilliance to the warmth and sincerity of the German style. His Psalmen Davids, *of 1619, for eight voices, began the long series of splendid concerted works. In 1623 Schütz wrote* Historia der Auferstehung Jesu Christi *("Story of the Resurrection of Jesus Christ"), a setting of the Easter oratorio text often used in the Lutheran church at that time. He followed somewhat the plan of an earlier work by Scandello, set for voices only, but expanded it greatly and added instruments. Apart from the role of the Evangelist, which is for a solo voice, other characters may be sung as duos, and groups are represented by three- or six-part choruses. Schütz employs four viols da gamba to accompany the Evangelist, asking that they improvise ornamented passages in the manner of the then popular Italian* falsobordone.

In his title Schütz says that the work is intended not only for performance in church but also for chamber, and in his instructive preface he provides specific directions for its performance.

SOURCE: *Heinrich Schütz,* Historia fröhlichen und siegneichen Auferstehung unsers einigen Erlösers und Seligmachers Jesu Christi. In fürstlichen Capellen oder Zimmer um die Osterliche Zeit zu Geistlicher Recreation füglichen zu gebrauchen *(Dresden, 1623).*

HEINRICH SCHÜTZ

from *Historia der Auferstehung Jesu Christi*

TO MY READERS—GREETINGS AND SERVICE:

Who wishes to perform my composition—*The History of the Joyous and Victorious Resurrection of our Lord God, Redeemer and Savior, Jesus Christ*—must prepare two choirs, as follows

1. The choir of the Evangelist
2. The choir of other personages who speak

The choirs may be located together or separated, according to the place and the occasion.

About the Chorus of the Evangelist

1. The Evangelist's part may be accompanied by an organ, positif, or an instrument such as a lute or pandora, etc., as the case may be, which then, at the end of the Evangelist's words, will play together with the

Basso continuo. The organist who is to represent this character must remember that so long as the *Falsobordone* continues he must always play under it beautiful and appropriate runs or *passaggi* on the organ or other instrument, which will give to this work, as to all other *Falsobordoni,* the right style; otherwise it will not achieve its proper effect.

2. When it is possible, it is better that the organ and other [instruments] remain silent and instead only 4 viols da gamba (whose parts are here given) be used to accompany the person of the Evangelist.

3. It will be necessary that the 4 viols practice with the Evangelist carefully in the following way: the Evangelist takes his part as he wishes and recites freely without any strict measure, but he holds the syllables no longer than one ordinarily does in ordinary slow, clear speech.

In the viols also they must play not in strict rhythm but on the words that the Evangelist recites, as in their parts, which are written under the *Falsobordone,* taking care that no one make a mistake. There might also be an occasional viola *passaggio* under the frequent [vocal] ones, as is customary in *Falsobordone,* and this gives a good effect.

4. Also it should be noted that in the 4 parts of the viols, the *Basso continuo* of the other characters will be added, to the end that they may know when they must play again with the Evangelist, so that the parts of the work can follow each other in an orderly way without confusion.

5. At the end of the book for the 4 viols there is also a final chorus à 9 copied, in which, if they like, the viols can play.

About the Chorus of Other Personages

1. This chorus must be near the organ because all their actions must be played very quietly so that one can hear the singers' words clearly.

2. The Kapellmeister or whoever directs this work may also be placed beside this choir and give them a correct, slow, and appropriate *tactus* (which is the life and soul of all music).

3. In the large book in which this chorus is written will be found the text for the Evangelist, so that the other personages may see where they enter.

4. When sometimes in the *History* only one person speaks, as for example, Lord Jesus, Maria Magdalene, etc., I have written a duo. Here, in special instances the personage of the Lord Christ can be sung with both voices, an alto and a tenor, or only one part sung and the other played on an instrument, or if desired, it [the second part] may be omitted completely.

5. When the word "Chorus" stands before a Verse, it means that it may be sung with full chorus.

For information I specify thus the parts that belong to this *History*:
1. A large book in which are the parts of the other personages
2. A book for the Evangelist's part
3. Four books for the viols da gamba
4. The *Basso continuo*.

It should be kept in mind that this *History* will be performed with better grace or effect if only the Evangelist is seen, the other personages and others remaining hidden.

Meanwhile, let them mark these my few instructions, and let me commend myself to their favorable affection.

DRESDEN
ANNUNCIATION DAY, 1623

Michael Praetorius (1571–1621) was both composer and scholar. He served first as Kapellmeister *at Lüneburg, then in 1604 he became organist, then* Kapellmeister *and secretary to the Duke of Brunswick. He was most productive, producing multivolume sets of works:* Polyhymnia, *fifteen volumes, and* Musae Sionae, *sixteen volumes, both choral compositions;* Musae Aonia, *for instruments, which includes* Terpsichore, *two volumes;* Calliope, *two volumes;* Thalia, *two volumes;* Erato, *one volume;* Diana Teutonia, *one volume; and* Das Regensburgische Echo, *one volume; and many other works.*

Praetorius' Syntagma musicum *("Musical Treatise"), written between 1614 and 1619, is a work of great historical importance and musical interest, for it is a compendium of information on musical practice in the first quarter of the seventeenth century. The first volume, written in Latin, deals with church music exclusively and is divided into four parts: the first is on choral music and psalmody as practiced in antiquity; the second treats of music for the Mass; the third deals with the other forms of music for the Offices, Matins, and Vespers; and the fourth describes instrumental music of the synagogue and the early Christian church. The second volume, entitled* Organographia, *deals exclusively with instruments—their forms, nomenclature, construction—and includes a section of woodcuts illustrating the most important instruments discussed in the text.*

Volume III, also divided into three parts, includes discussions of various kinds of composition and theoretical matters, such as solmization, transposition, arrangements of choirs, and explanations of technical musical terms. There was to have been a fourth volume devoted to counterpoint, but apparently it was never completed.

In explaining the word Capella *and giving certain instructions for arranging choirs and* capellae, *the following extract provides a fairly comprehensive view of the usual practice c. 1615–1620.*

SOURCE: *Michael Praetorius,* Syntagma musicum, *III (Wolfenbüttel, 1619), Pt. III, Ch. 2; Pt. II, Ch. 12; Pt. III, Ch. 3.*

MICHAEL PRAETORIUS
from *Syntagma musicum*

Capella: Chorus pro capella. Palchetto.

The word *Capella* may be used in three ways: the first, in my opinion, is the meaning the Italians originally used when, in the imperial Austrian and other large Catholic chapels, several different choirs were brought together, so that another particular choir might be drawn from them. This choir is called *Chorus a capella,* for the whole *choralis vocalis,* or the entire capella, performs entirely separately from the other choirs, yet they likewise sing together, in the same way as the full *Werk* of an organ. This then provides an admirable ornament, splendor and sparkle in such music; this choir almost always joins in when the other choirs all come together.

And such harmony becomes fuller and richer if one adds a large bass pommer, double fagott, or large bass viol (Italian, violone); also other instruments, if they are available, added to the middle and upper voices. One, two, or three such *capellas* can be drawn from every *Concerto,* each with four or more persons if available, and placed in different parts of the church. If performers are lacking they can be omitted entirely, for this *capella* is like the *Ripieno,* only used to fill and strengthen the music; an additional chorus may be taken from the other choirs. Therefore the unisons and octaves are used without distinction between the choirs. . . .

Capellas of this kind I have seen in some of Giovanni Gabrieli's *Concerti* on many different occasions.

2. In the same *[concerti]* as well as in his first published *Sacre cantiones,* of 1597, one finds that the word *Capella* means to him *Chorus vocalis, Chorus vocum* in the same way as I employ it; that is, the chorus which is made up of singers; and in a concert the one choir is with

cornetts, another with viols, the third with trombones, bassoons, flutes, and similar instruments, so that with each choir there is at least a *Concertato*—that is, a man's voice added. Thus for the most part there is another choir in addition, in which all four parts are given to voices. This choir Giovanni Gabrieli calls *Capellam*. And such a choir or capella, because it belongs to the Principal Choir, must never be omitted. It can be recognized by the clefs assigned to the parts, and also often may be performed with viols da gamba or arm viols, as will be discussed in the eighth chapter.

In my *Concerti*, especially the Latin pieces but also in the German, where I do not use a *Chorus pro capellam*, for the most part I give the words *omnes* and *solus*, or voice, instrument, trombone, etc. Anyone can understand that and act accordingly. Then, where later voice and trombone, or voice and violin, etc., are placed, one must use a vocalist and an instrumentalist with either a trombone or viol. Where *Voice* alone is found, the vocalist sings alone; when *Trombone* is given, it plays alone; where *Omnes* appears both perform together. Similar procedures are used when other kinds of instruments are indicated. And so anyone can form one or two *capelle* of four parts not only from such *concerti* but also from others, if he has sufficient singers and instrumentalists. Then he can have those parts which have the words *Omnes* or *Chorus* marked at the beginning copied on separate pages (as shown in Part II in Ch. 12), and where the words *solus* or *voce, instruments*, etc., are found, an equivalent number of rests must be added [in the other parts]. And this *Chorus pro capella* will then be placed in a separate place in performance.

I began to use the words *Omnes* and *Solus* in my *Cantiones* several years ago; but now I find the Italians use the words *Ripieni* in their *concerti*.

3. Finally, some call it a *Capella* when one composes an instrumental choir and adds it to a vocal choir. The instrumental choir, being the secondary group, can be dispensed with if it lacks players, but it should be placed apart from the vocal choir, either opposite, or at a higher or lower place. The vocal choir, being the principal choir, can do without the instrumental players; however an organist with a positif or regal should be placed nearby.

In Italy such a choir is called a *Palchetto*, since they sometimes use more than one *Chorus pro capella*, always placing one above the other; just as the musicians in David's time were divided into higher and lower choirs and set apart. Therefore certain Psalms, as Psalms 120 through 134, are called *Songs in the Higher Choir* (as in Vol. I, Pt. One, Sec. i, Ch. II).

The word *Palchetto* [box at a theater, or shelf] can be better understood by the following short description: in some churches and princely chapels it is customary to erect on the ground floor or some other convenient place, a certain platform, like a stage, with joists and boards—or it may be over the width of several steps that will bear it—and to garnish it with tapestry and benches. One can also, if one wishes, make a special place, like a small Borkirche, where different choirs may be separated from each other. Such useful places are often found in old churches, especially in the rear of choir lofts. They may be used for the purpose as explained, and can be called *palchetto.* . . .

In arranging a Concerto . . . it is quite customary that in a low choir, where the cantus is to be sung by an alto with three trombones or three bassoons, one must double the alto with a violin; the instrumentalist must then put or (as some say) play the alto part an octave higher. Also in full choirs, as well as when only a few choirs join together, one can have the alto part of the vocal choir written in the instrumental choir

an octave higher. Thus instead of  a is used and now

marked alto. And then it frequently happens that instead of the alto standing a fourth below the cantus, it is now a fifth above. Some believe this manner to be acceptable, but I cannot as yet agree with this.

Such a choir is then written in this manner:

C. A. T. B.

In such a choir, lacking an instrument, one has the alto part sung by a discant singer, and the discant by an alto in the lower octave; this brings about the previous correct arrangement.

And for this reason the same thing may be done in all voices, and it is not unwelcome to the ears when the same part as that of the singer in an ensemble is played by the instrumentalist an octave higher or lower on cornetts, fiddles, flutes [recorders], trombones, or bassoons. On the other hand, some melody instruments, especially flutes . . . are always to be played one or two octaves higher than the song itself. In this case it is no different from the organist combining many different stops in unisons, octaves, super-octaves, and sub-octaves and (as some call them) contrabasses, into a concord.

A very splendid sound is possible in full choirs if one adds to a bass, from the group of instruments, an ordinary or a bass trombone, a *Chorist*-bassoon, or pommer bombard at the regular pitch; in addition a double bass trombone, double bassoon or large double bombard and double bass, which like the sub-basses or foundation on the organ, all sound an octave lower. This is very often used in present-day Italian *concerti* and can be sufficiently justified.

I have therefore in the *capella fidicinia* (an account of which will follow) not hesitated to arrange it so that two, three, or four discant singers or two tenors sing together, the parts played in the *capella fidicinia* on fiddles or other instruments to fill out the harmony, mixing and making music, sometimes also played in octaves with the voices, which any intelligent musician who reflects upon this will approve, and in this case agree with me.

In my *Urano-Chorodia* I have in several places put the chorale in discant and alto, which are to be sung by voices, in octaves; but I have introduced these intervals also for other reasons, because the entire church congregation usually joins in on the chorale, [singing] high and low, softly and loudly. However, this practice, apart from the chorales, I cannot permit.

It is now quite customary in Italian *concerti*, where there are high and low *bassetti*,* for the *bassetto* of the higher choir to move for the most part in parallel octaves with the bass of the lower, or second, choir, when the choirs are joined.

Although this practice in compositions for two or three choirs could sometimes be altered by letting one bass ascend and the other descend, and vice versa, it can be excused and justified thus:

1. That one usually assigns a tenor voice to the *bassetto* of the higher choir, and a bass trombone, pommer, or double bassoon to the bass of the lower choir.

2. Although in a concerto for three, four, or more choirs, where the basses are set two or three octaves apart, the *bassetto* must play likewise with the lowest or other basses in the different choirs, among which two or more are performed by voices. Thus I cannot disapprove of or reject this practice; rather, I find it necessary to make use of it myself and show my approval of everyone who does likewise. If one should have a concert in a church or large hall, using only two choirs, one high and one low, placed at opposite ends, if he remains in the midst of

* *Bassetto, Basset* is the diminutive of *bass*, and indicates the lowest voice; thus in the high choir it serves as foundation and likewise resembles the bass in its intervals. It is most often assigned the tenor clef, but occasionally an alto clef is used. (*Syntagma musicum*, Pt. III, Ch. 1, p.122.)

the high choir he will find, when the two choirs sing together, that he cannot hear the lowest choir well. He will find that with no foundation in the high choir, in place of the lowest fifth, which the foundation bass gives to the *bassetto* or tenor of the high choir, most often dissonances or fourths will be heard, especially if no foundation instrument, such as a positif or regal, is used.

Capella Fidicina vel Fidicinum

How to Arrange and Set Up the Same

This capella I have particularly observed to be not unnecessary; because some among us Germans are still not accustomed to the new Italian Invention, where only one *Concertato* voice, or two or three, sing with the organ or regal, and, still unaccustomed to it, think that it sounds too thin, and does not especially please or give pleasure to those who do not understand music. Therefore I have had to think of a means to add a choir or capella with four voices, which could join with either trombones or violins at all times.

And because such harmony, when used in church, fills the ear somewhat better, I have received popular acclaim because of it.

Now, in my opinion it also sounds well if, in such ensembles with one or two concerting voices (especially if lively and agile voices are used), a regal, or a reed stop on the organ is added. For because the organist (as will be shown in the sixth chapter, on Generalbass) must play very simply, with good harmonies and syncopations, without any diminutions or coloraturas; with flute stops alone this sounds too poor and lacks charm, but on the regal, or other reeds that sound like trombones, the harmony is more pleasing if one performs the piece elegantly, seriously, and slowly, without any diminutions.

Also this must be noted: 1. That I call this *capellam fidiciniam* because it is better to constitute it of stringed instruments, such as violins, lutes, harps, and all the others, particularly with viols de gamba, or, lacking them, one can have viols da braccia. Then the *Sonus* and harmony of the viols and violins is continuous, always playing one after another with singular charm, without having to breathe, which those who play trombones and other wind instruments cannot do without. However for variations one can occasionally use four trombones; but do not forget that the cantus part in some will be played an octave lower on the trombone, or three trombones and a tenor flute [recorder] or a cornett and a discant [recorder] or a fagotto; and three flutes can be used in exchange.

2. On these occasions I sometimes like to have commas or little strokes [placed in the music] so that for one Versicle a viol can be used, for another trombones; for the third, flute and fagotti; or where there is a lutenist, he can exchange with the violins, and occasionally the lute and violin can play together. In this way a director can arrange and write out two or more choirs as it may suit him.

This also is very attractive to hear: when one employs a full consort in the English manner for this *capellam Fidiciniam,* he should add to them a loud clavicembalo, two or three lutes, a theorbo, bandora, cittern, bass viol, block or traverse flutes, soft trombone, viola bastarda, and a small discant violin, all very purely and sweetly tuned together; the *Concertato* voices however should add to the others graceful and suitable harmonies.

3. From my observations I have found that it is better to place this *capella* or *chorus fidicinium* somewhat to the side, away from the organ and those who sing the *Concertato* parts, so that the vocalists will not be overshadowed or drowned by the instruments, but each separate group can be clearly heard and understood. . . .

4. It remains however for anyone to use this *capella* or omit it; for, as I said at the beginning, I have added it only because of the approbation of certain auditors, otherwise I would not have considered it of great importance.

5. And if one wished to compose and set up such a *capella fidicinia* in the form of these kinds of concert pieces to best please—as in the works of L. Viadana, A. Aggazzari, Antonio Cifra, and similar composers—one would attract audiences in Germany who still at this time do not know how to judge the new style, and further interest them, as it were, so that they would have great pleasure and contentment from such.

6. This *capella* would also be useful to organists who are not trained and inexperienced in composition, and therefore are lost in thoroughbass right at the start; sometimes then it would be easier to write out all the middle voices or parts (which usually are not provided in such *concerti*) in their tablatures, rather than that they should have to speculate whether or not fourths and fifths or thirds should be played. Therefore I have in several of these compositions called them *Capella pro Organo,* also *pro Testudine, Theorbo,* etc.

7. One should not take it as a mistake if in this *capella* the four voices of the stringed or wind instruments occasionally play in unison and octaves with the other *Concertato,* or vocal parts. It has been explained previously in Chapter Twelve of Part II why the unisons and octaves that occur when one voice is sung, the other played with instruments,

such as trombones, trumpets or violins, are perfectly acceptable. If any-one who has heard the music in princely and other *capellae,* as well as that played by musicians in town bands, stops to consider that he himself places a wind player with a cornett or trombone along with the students, which plays in unisons and octaves with them, he will not misunderstand this.

10. Tempo, Tactus, and Musical Terms

The following extract from Praetorius' famous Syntagma musicum *presents his views on the necessity of changing tempo and dynamics in performances of choral music. It is followed by a brief explanation of some musical terms. For biographical information see selections in Chapter 9.*

Source: *Michael Praetorius,* Syntagma musicum, *III (Wolfenbüttel, 1619), Pt. II, Ch. 8; Pt. III, Ch. 1.*

MICHAEL PRAETORIUS
from *Syntagma musicum*

How Variations and Changes Can Be Made in the Lowering and Raising of Voice and Tactus

Music should not be hastened, else the most delightful concert will sound confused. However with a moderate tactus the harmony will sound better and be more easily perceived. The mensuration likewise is to be observed, so that the harmony may not be deformed or disturbed; for to sing without law and measure is to offend God himself, who gave all things number, weight, and measure, as Plato says. Nevertheless, for reasons of the text, sometimes to use now a slower, now a faster, beat adds singular majesty and grace, and marvelously ornaments the melody.

Not a little charm is added to harmony and melody if the variation of human voices and instruments is sometimes lively, sometimes the singing voices relaxed. (This could be set forth in a treatise.)

Some people do not wish to allow a mixture of motet and madrigal styles in a single composition. But I cannot accept their opinion, since motets and concertos are given a particular charm and delight when at their beginning a number of measures are set pathetically and slow, then several quick phrases follow immediately, succeeded again by slow and grave ones, changing and mingling, so that it is not always moving in one key and sound; rather [using] such and similar changes with a slow and fast beat; likewise with the raising of the voices and then with a very quiet sound, done with all care and attention, as has been indicated before.

Further, it is not attractive or worthy of applause when singers, organists, and other instrumental players habitually hasten from the penultimate note of a composition directly into the final note without any retardation. I believe therefore I should admonish those who have not heretofore observed this as done in princely courts and other well-composed musical choirs, [that is,] to remain some time on the penultimate note, whatever it may be, lingering four, five, or six beats, and then at last moving to the final note.

When a work is brought to its close, all the remaining voices, at the will and nod of the conductor, should stop simultaneously. Nor should the tenors prolong their note, a fifth above the bass or fundamental part (where the tenor most often should finish), after the bass is silent. But should the bass continue for two or four beats longer, it adds grace to the Cantilena, which no one can deny.

On Musical Terms

Forte; Pian; Presto; Adagio; Lento: these words are occasionally used by the Italians in different places in the Concerto, and are indicated either above or below [the music] on account of the changes in the voices and choirs; this does not displease me, although there are some who think this usage, especially in churches, is not good. But I think such variations and changes, when they are moderate and graceful, used to express the affections and to move men, are not unpleasant or incorrect; rather do they affect the heart and spirit of the hearer, and add a certain kind of grace to the Concerto.

The composition, as well as the text and the meaning of the words, sometimes, but not too often, requires that the tactus be beaten now fast, now slow; also that the choir be allowed to sing now softly and quietly, now loud and vigorously. Although in such and similar exchanges a certain moderation will be more necessary in churches than at the table. Thus everyone knows what such words mean: *forte, elate, clarè, id est, summa seu intenta voce* when the instruments and voices are to be loud; *Pian, submisè,* when the voices are to moderate and softly intone the music. Sometimes *Pian* is the same as *placidè, pedententim, lento gradu,* so that the voices should not only be moderated but also sing slowly.

Marin Mersenne (1588–1648), most often referred to as Père Mersenne because he was a Jesuit priest, was born into a peasant family in the province of Maine. Showing intellectual promise, he was sent to school at the Jesuit College of Le Mans and then to the college at La Flèche for studies in mathematics, physics, the classics, and metaphysics. Here he was a fellow student of the philosopher René Descartes, with whom he founded a lifelong friendship. Mersenne then transferred to the Sorbonne, in Paris, for further training in theology, and in 1611 he became a member of the order of Minorite friars. From 1619 he taught Hebrew, philosophy, and theology at the Sorbonne, then a religious training school, and in the Convent of the Annunziata, but his main interest was music, not as a performing artist but from the historical and analytical viewpoint.

Père Mersenne soon had a wide reputation and many connections, mainly epistolary, with the foremost philosophers and musicians in Europe—in Italy, England, Germany, Holland, and Switzerland—including such notables as Galilei, Doni, and Huygens. In Paris, together with Descartes and other intellectual friends, he formed a discussion group, or "academy," to study the sciences. Mersenne constructed his own theory of music, based no longer on theology but on the physics of acoustics.

The result of Mersenne's interest and investigations in music was the publication of his Harmonie universelle *(1636), a massive work comprising studies on the nature of sound, mechanics, consonance and dissonance, modes, composition, the voice and singing, and especially instruments—their construction, range, musical possibilities. His great work remains a most important source of information on seventeenth-century musical thought and practice.*

This extract, taken from Mersenne's Fifth Book on Composition, is indicative of the interest then current in precise measurements of tempo, a problem that was nearly solved by Étienne Loulié in 1696 with his invention of the Chronomètre, and finally by J. N. Maelzel with his Metronome in 1816.

SOURCE: *Marin Mersenne,* Harmonie universelle, contenant la Théorie et la Pratique de la Musique *(Paris, Cramoisy, 1636). The Fifth Book on Composition, Proposition XI, vol. II. pp. 324ʳ–25ʳ.*

MARIN MERSENNE
from *Harmonie universelle*

Explanation of the Manner of Regulating, Denoting, Holding, or Beating the Measure in Music, Which the Spanish Call "Compás"

The beating of the measure, which St. Augustine and the other ancient Latins call *Plausus*, is nothing but the lowering and raising of the hand, which shows the [length of] time that is to be given to each note. For example, the semibreve ordinarily has the length of one raising and lowering of the hand, which can also be made with the foot or in any other way one may desire. The minim, which is usually called a white note, has the length of one raising or one lowering of the hand; and the black note, [semiminim] equals half a raising or lowering of the hand, because they always go four to a measure, which is composed of both a raising and a lowering [of the hand] and are equal in binary measure.

In ternary measure, however, the lowering or striking movement is twice [the duration] of the upward movement; in it one sings two minims in the duration of the downward beat and a single note in the upward gesture. For this reason one puts a 3, alone or with a 2 beneath it $[\frac{3}{2}]$, at the beginning of the staffs and ruled lines when singing in ternary measure; and the C, with or without a stroke through it [₵] when it is binary, or equal. No sign is used to show the measure is free. It seems to me that it would suffice to put the number 2 at the beginning of the staffs, or in any other place that one would wish, before the notes that are to be sung in binary measure, just as one is content with the number 3 to mark the ternary, in order to avoid the multitude of signs and to facilitate the practice of music.

As to the different signs of the *modus*, and perfect and imperfect *tempus*, and of *prolation*, perfect as well as imperfect, I will treat them most amply in the 30th Proposition of the VIth book, which follows and is particularly dedicated to the meters of music; in it one will find all he could desire here.

Now it should be remarked that the measure is one of the principal and most necessary parts of music, whether singing in parts of two, three, or more voices, or when one sings alone. That is why I devote this particular Proposition to it and say, first, that it seems that measure may have taken its time and regularity from the beating of the heart, and the raising to its *diastole,* or dilation and elevation. However, the musicians do not follow the rhythm of this *systole* and *diastole* ordinarily, and the beatings of the heart are more prompt than those of the hand, except when they hasten the measure or choose a very slow pulse, as that which beats only once a second, that is to say, 3600 times in an hour. And because a string of 3½ feet in length attached at one end to a nail and swinging free at the other, which has a piece of lead (for example, a musket ball) tied to it, marks the seconds as it moves from one side to the other—it can be used to beat, or mark, the time of binary, or equal measure, as I have shown in the 18th Proposition of the Third Book on Instruments. I have also given the correct experiments in the 13th through the 16th Propositions of the Second Book and the 20th Proposition of the Third Book on Movements.

If one wishes to use this method for ternary measure, the duration of which would equal that of binary, that is to say, that the measure lasts a second, it would be necessary to shorten the string so that it would make three movements in the same time it made two [for binary]. This is easy to do according to the method I have explained in the aforementioned propositions. The *maîtres* who teach singing could become accustomed to the use of the device to beat the measure evenly at whatever speed they might wish, since each of the swings [*tours ou retours*] lasts a second when the cord is 3½ feet long. They would find it very easy to make the movements slower or faster in any kind of proportion, since it is necessary only to lengthen or shorten the string, doubled or halved as the beat requires.

But because they change the measure many times, either binary or ternary, in performing a single piece of music, by hurrying or holding back the lowering and raising [of the hand] according to the character and the words, or the different passions of the text which they treat, it is difficult to apply any certain rule if they do not use as many different [lengths of] strings as they wish to have different meters.

One can also use many movements similar to those of the wheels of a clock to mark the measure, so that all see the movement of a torch at night, or of a fragment of wood or coal during the day. Those who conduct concerts at present mark the measure by the movement of the necks of their lutes to guide and regulate the singers and to keep to the key. It does not matter at all in what manner the [rhythm] is marked, provided that it suffices to make the singers sing with precision, as in the concert of Monsieur Ballard, where the five or six lutes playing together followed so well all the different kinds of rhythms and movements that he gives his airs, and all his compositions, that one would judge there to be only one lute, or a single man who played them all together. This happens likewise in the concerts of Sieur Maugars, Lazarin, la Barre, du Buisson, or others who play the viols and clavecins together, and in those of Monsieur Moulinié when he has the best voices of the court.

Those who have a sensitive and accurate ear and an orderly imagination keep to the measure very well, although they never mark it, as when one experiments with all those who play rhythmically on instruments, or who sing with such good conduct that, although one marks the measure without their perceiving it, one finds that they are not lacking in exactitude. After one has become accustomed to keeping the measure very exactly, and if one has a true voice, one can be assured of having two of the best qualities necessary for good singers, so that he need no longer be concerned except with the other necessary qualities of a perfect voice, of which I will speak more extensively in the VIth Book on the Art of Singing Well.

Henry Purcell (1659–1695), the most famous member of a family of prominent musicians, was the son of Thomas Purcell and the namesake of Henry Purcell, his uncle (d. 1664), both of whom served in the Chapel Royal. Henry followed in their footsteps, serving as organist in Westminster Abbey from 1679 until 1682, when he became organist of the Chapel Royal. His fame as an organist was great, but his renown as a composer was greater. His catalogue of works is extensive, including operas; incidental music and songs for plays; church music of all kinds (his anthems were especially famous); odes; and a small body of instrumental music, including fantasias for strings, three- and four-part sonatas for strings, and a handful of harpsichord music. This last category included a collection of pieces entitled Music's Handmaid *(1689); miscellaneous songs, dances, and arrangements of some of Purcell's theatrical songs; and* A Choice Collection of Lessons for the Harpsichord or Spinnet, *published posthumously in 1696 by Purcell's widow and dedicated to Princess Anne.* A Choice Collection *contains eight suites, a chaconne, a jig, and two trumpet tunes. These pieces were intended for instruction; nevertheless they are among Purcell's most important works, though uneven in quality. The introduction, for its time, is quite complete and informative. Here, in the section on time, fingering, and graces, Purcell relates different kinds of meter signs to tempos, something not usually done in such collections. He also explains clearly rests, note values, and ornaments.*

SOURCE: A Choice Collection of Lessons for the Harpsichord or Spinnet composed by ye late Mr. Henry Purcell, Organist of His Majesties Chappel Royal, & of St. Peters Westminster, London . . . *1696. Preface.*

HENRY PURCELL
from *A Choice Collection of Lessons*

Example of Time or Length of Notes

There being nothing more difficult in Musick than playing of true time, 'tis therefore necessary to be observ'd by all practitioners, of which there are two sorts: Common time, & Triple time; and is distinguish'd by this C, this ₵ or this Φ mark. The first is a very slow movement, the next a little faster, and the last a brisk & airy time; and each of them has always to the length of one Semibrief in a Bar, which is to be held in playing as long as you can moderately tell four, by saying, one, two, three, four. Two Minums [are] as long as one Semibrief, four Crotchets as long as two Minums, eight Quavers as long as four Crotchets, sixteen Semiquavers as long [as] eight Quavers.

Triple time consists of either three or six Crotchets in a bar, and is to be known by this $\frac{3}{2}$, this $\frac{3}{1}$, this 3 or this $\frac{6}{4}$ mark. To the first there is three Minums in a bar, and is commonly play'd very slow; the second has three Crotchets in a bar, and they are to be play'd slow; the third has the same as the former but is play'd faster; the last has six Crotchets in a bar & is commonly to brisk tunes as Jiggs and Paspys. When there is a prick or dot following any Note, it is to be held half as long again as the Note itself is, let it be Semibrief, Minum, Crotchet, or Quaver. When you see a Semibrief rest you are to leave off playing so long as you can be counting four; a Minum rest so long as you tell two; and a Crotchet one; and so in proportion a Quaver and Semiquaver. You may know how these rests are marked in the five lines under the example of time.

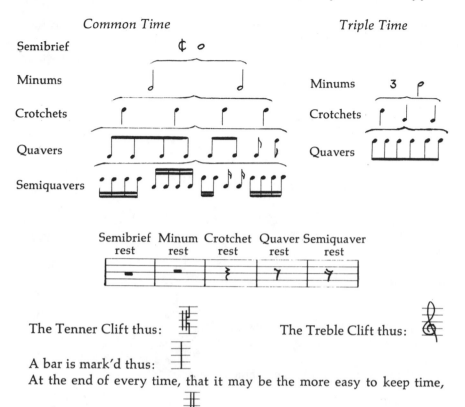

Common Time   *Triple Time*

Semibrief

Minums   Minums

Crotchets   Crotchets

Quavers   Quavers

Semiquavers

Semibrief Minum Crotchet Quaver Semiquaver
rest   rest   rest   rest   rest

The Tenner Clift thus: The Treble Clift thus:

A bar is mark'd thus:

At the end of every time, that it may be the more easy to keep time,

a Double bar is mark'd thus and set down at the end of every Strain, which imports you must play the strain twice.

A Repeat is mark'd thus ⸬S· and signifies you must repeat from the note to the end of the Strain or Lesson; to know what key a tune is in, observe the last note or Close of the tune, for by that note the key is nam'd. All Round O's [rondeaux] end with the first strain.

Right hand, the fingers to ascend are the 3rd & 4th, to descend the 3rd and 2nd.

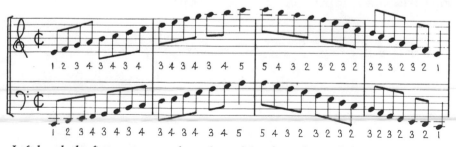

Left hand, the fingers to ascend are the 3rd & 4th, to descend the 3rd and 2nd.

Observe in the fingering of your right hand your Thumb is the first, so on to the fifth.

In the fingering of your left hand your little finger is the first, so on to the fifth.

Rules for Graces

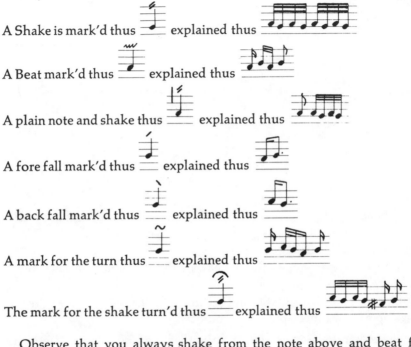

A Shake is mark'd thus ___ explained thus ___

A Beat mark'd thus ___ explained thus ___

A plain note and shake thus ___ explained thus ___

A fore fall mark'd thus ___ explained thus ___

A back fall mark'd thus ___ explained thus ___

A mark for the turn thus ___ explained thus ___

The mark for the shake turn'd thus ___ explained thus ___

Observe that you always shake from the note above and beat from the note below, according to the key you play in, for the plain note and shake, if it be a note without a point [dot], you are to hold half the quantity of it plain, and that upon the above what which is mark'd and shake the other half; but if it be a note with a point to it you are to hold all the note plain and shake only the point.

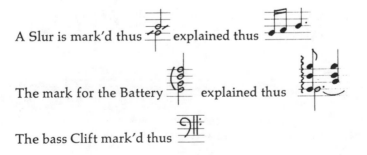

A Slur is mark'd thus ___ explained thus ___

The mark for the Battery ___ explained thus ___

The bass Clift mark'd thus ___

11. On Singing

Andreas Ornithoparcus His Micrologus or Introduction: containing The Art of Singing *is the title John Dowland gave to his translation of Ornithoparcus'* Musicae active micrologus *(1515), which he dedicated to the Earl of Salisbury in 1606. Andreas Vogelsang (who preferred the Greek form of his name) was well known for his treatise, and for many years it was considered a useful, basic work for music instruction. Dowland himself may have used it in his own teaching, and in his dedication to the Earl he speaks of Ornithoparcus as a "father of Musicke."*

Dowland (1562–1626) was born in Ireland but spent all of his life on the Continent and in England. A virtuoso lutenist and singer, he held appointments in the royal courts of Denmark, in various German courts, and finally in England as one of six lutenists at the court of Charles I.

Dowland was not only a performer but a composer as well, one of the greatest writers of songs. The English critic E. H. Fellows says, "He may reasonably be regarded as the greatest song writer this country has yet produced, not excepting even Purcell." Between 1597 and 1613 he composed five volumes of songs, many of them masterpieces.

SOURCE: Andreas Ornithoparcus His Micrologus . . . trans. John Dowland (London, 1609), Ch. 8, Book 4, pp. 88–90.

ANDREAS ORNITHOPARCUS/
JOHN DOWLAND

from *Andreas Ornithoparcus His Micrologus*

Of the Divers Fashions of Singing, and of the Ten Precepts for Singing

Every man lives after his owne humour; neither are all men governed by the same lawes, and divers Nations have divers fashions, and differ in habits, diet, studies, speech and song. Hence it is that the English doe carroll; the French sing; the Spaniards weepe; the Italians, which dwell about the coasts of Ianua, caper with their voyces; the others barke; but the Germanes (which I am ashamed to utter) doe howle like wolves. Now, because it is better to breake friendship than to determine anything against truth, I am forced by truth to say that which the love of my Country forbids me to publish. Germany nourisheth many Cantors, but few Musitians. For very few, excepting those which are or have been in the Chappels of Princes, doe truely know the Art of Singing. For those Magistrates to whom this charge is given, doe appoint for the government of the Service young Cantors, whom they choose by the shrillnesse of their Voyce, not for their cunning in the Art; thinking that God is pleased with bellowing and braying, of whom we read in the Scripture that he rejoyceth more in sweetness than in noyse, more in the affection, than in the Voice. For when Salomon in the Canticles writes that the voyce of the church doth sound in the eares of Christ, hee doth presently adjoyne the cause, because it is sweet. Therefore well did Baptista Mantuan (that moderne Virgil) inveigh every puffed up, ignorant, bellowing Cantor, saying:

> Cur tantis delubra Boum mugitibus imples,
> Tu ne Deum tali credis placare tumultu.

Whom the Prophet ordained should be praised in Cymbals, not simply, but well sounding.

Of the Ten precepts necessary for every Singer

Being that divers men doe diversely abuse themselves in Gods praise, some by moving their body undecently, some by gaping unseemely, some by changing the vowels, I thought good to teach all Cantors certaine Precepts, by which they may erre lesse.

1. When you desire to sing anything, above all things marke the Tone and his Repercussion. For he that sings a Song without knowing the Tone, doth like him that makes a syllogisme without Moode and Figure.

2. Let him diligently marke the Scale, under which the Song runneth, lest he make a Flat of a Sharpe or a Sharpe of a Flat.

3. Let every Singer conform his voice to the words, that as much as he can he make the *Concent* sad when the words are sad; and merry, when they are merry. Wherein I cannot but wonder at the Saxons (the most gallant people of all Germany, by whose furtherance I was both brought up and drawne to write of Musicke) in that they use in their

funerals an high, merry and joconde *Concent*, for no other cause (I think) than that either they hold death to be the greatest good that can befall a man (as Valerius in his first Book writes of Cleobis and Biton, two brothers) or in that they believe that the souls (as it is in Macrobius his second Book *De somnis Scipione*) after this body do return to the original sweetness of Musicke, that is, to heaven. Which if it be the cause, we may judge them to be valiant in contemning death, and worthy desirers of the glory to come.

4. Above all things keep the equality of measure. For to sing without law and measure, is an offence to God himself, who hath made all things well, in number, weight, and measure. Wherefore I would have masterly *Franci* (my country-men) to follow the best manner, and not as before they have done; sometime long, sometime to make short the notes in Plainsong; but take example of the noble church of Herbipolis, their head, wherein they sing excellently. Which would also much profit, and honour the Church of Prague, because in it also they make the notes sometimes longer, sometimes shorter than they should. Neither must this be omitted, which that love which we owe to the dead, doth require: whose Vigils (for so they are commonly called) are performed with such confusion, haste and mockery (I know not what fury possesseth the minds of those, to whom this charge is put over) that neither one Voice can be distinguished from another, nor one syllable from another, nor one verse sometimes throughout a whole Psalm from another. An impious fashion to be punished with the severest correction. Think you God is pleased with such howling, such noise, such mumbling, in which is no devotion, no expressing of words, no articulating of syllables?

5. The songs of Authenticall *Tones* must be [deemed] deep, of the sub-jugall Tones high, of the neutral, meanly.[1] For these goe deep, those high, the other both high and low.

6. The changing of Vowels is a sign of an unlearned singer. Now (though divers people doe diversely offend in this kind) yet doth not the multitude of offenders take away the fault. Here I would have the Francks to take heed they pronounce not *u* for *o*, as they are wont, saying *nuster* for *noster*. The country Churchmen are also to be censured for pronouncing *Aremus* instead of *Oremus*. In like sort, doe all the Renenses from Spyre Confluentia change the vowel *i* into the diphthong *ei*, saying *Mareia* for *Maria*. The Westphalians for the vowel *a* pronounce *a* and *e* together, to wit: *Aebs te* for *Abs te*. The lower Saxons, and all the *Suevians* [Suabians], for the vowel *e* read *e* and *i*, saying *Deius* for *Deus*. They of lower Germany do all express *u* and *e*

1. Here "middle."

instead of the vowel *u*. Which errors, though the German speech do often require, yet doth the Latin tongue, which hath the affinity with ours, exceedingly abhor them.

7. Let a singer take heed, lest he begin too loud, braying like an Ass, or when he hath begun with an uneven height, disgrace the song. For God is not pleased with loud cryes, but with lovely sounds; it is not (saith our Erasmus) the noise of the lips, but the ardent desire of the Heart, which like the loudest voice doth pierce Gods ears. Moses spake not, yet heard these words, *Why dost thou cry unto me?* But why the Saxons, and those that dwell upon the Baltic coast, should so delight in such clamouring, there is no reason but either because they have a deaf God, or because they think he is gone to the South side of Heaven, and therefore cannot so easily hear both the Easterlings, and the Southerlings.

8. Let every singer discerne the difference of one holiday from another, lest on a slight holiday he either make too solemn service, or too slight on a great.

9. The uncomely gaping of the mouth, and ungracefull motion of the body, is a sign of a mad singer.

10. Above all things, let the singer study to please God, and not men; (saith Guido) there are foolish singers, who contemn the devotion they seeke after, and affect the wantonness which they should shun, because they intend their singing to men, not to God; seeking for a little worldy fame, that so they may lose the eternal glory: pleasing men that thereby they may displease God: imparting to others that devotion which themselves want: seeking the favour of the creature, contemning the love of the Creator, to whom is due all honour, and reverence, and service. To whom I do devote myself, and all that is mine, to him will I sing as long as I have being, for he hath raised me (poor Wretch) from the earth, and from the meanest baseness. Therefore blesed be his Name world without end. Amen.

Here Michael Praetorius considers the necessary instruction for choir boys wishing to learn to sing in the new Italian style. He refers to Caccini and Bovicelli and, in fact, draws on their writings. Praetorius appears to have been very well informed on the new styles and quite familiar with the ornaments and diminutions then in fashion and to have used them in his music. For biographical information see the selections in Chapter 9.

SOURCE: *Michael Praetorius*, Syntagma musicum, *III (Wolfenbüttel, 1619), Pt. III, Ch. 9.*

MICHAEL PRAETORIUS
from *Syntagma musicum*

Instruction for Singers

How to teach and inform the choir boys to sing in the new
Italian style with particular pleasure and joy

Just as an Orator's concern is not only to adorn his oration with attractive, beautiful, and lively words and splendid figures, as well as to pronounce correctly and to move the emotions by his speech, now raising his voice, now allowing it to fall, now louder, now soft, now with full voice; so must a musician not only sing, but sing with art and grace, thereby moving the heart and affections of the auditors and permitting the song to accomplish its purpose. For a singer must not only possess a beautiful voice, given by Nature, but also have a good intellect and thorough knowledge of music, so that he executes the *accenti* [ornaments] with judgment, and the *modulos* or *coloratura* (called by Italians *passaggi*) not at every possible place in the song, but appositely, at the right time and in a certain way, so that the beauty of the voice as well as the artistry can be perceived and heard. Because they are not to be praised who, endowed by God and Nature with an especially beautiful, vibrant, and floating or quivering voice as well as a round neck and throat suitable for *diminution*, do not accept the laws of music but rather continue with their excessive ornamentation, which exceeds the limits of the song to such a degree that it is spoiled and obscured, so that one does not know what they are singing. Also neither the words nor the notes of the song (as the composer wrote it and gave it the best ornaments and grace) can be grasped or understood. This bad method (used particularly by instrumentalists) gives little pleasure to the auditors, especially those who have some knowledge of the art; instead, it annoys them and makes them sleepy. For that reason singing should not be spoiled by inappropriate diminutions of its natural power and grace, given it by the master; instead, each word and sentence should be properly understood by everyone. It is highly necessary that each cantor or singer from early youth practice diligently in singing and articulate enunciation and make himself proficient.

How this is to be done and in what manner one is to train one's self to sing with good taste in the new Italian style, how to express the accents, and affections, as well as the *trilli*, *groppi*, and other *coloratura* in the proper and suitable way, will be published very soon in a little treatise, with God's help (wherein the remarkable Giulio Romano, otherwise called Giulio Caccini of Rome, in his *Le nuove musiche*, and Giovanni Battista Bovicelli have been of help).

To sing in a pleasing, proper, and beautiful manner requires, as in all other arts, three things: namely, Nature, Art or Doctrine, and Practice.

1. Nature

First, a singer must have a [fine] natural voice; regarding which three requisites and three defects may be noted.

The requisites are these: first, the requirement that a singer must have a pleasantly vibrating voice (not, however, as some are trained to do in schools, but with particular moderation) and a smooth round throat for singing diminutions; second, he must be able to maintain a steady long tone, without taking too many breaths; third, he must choose one voice, such as cantus, altus, or tenor, etc., that he can sustain with a full and bright sound without falsetto (i.e., half and forced voice).

Here *Intonatio* and *Exclamatio* must be mentioned.

Intonatio is the way in which a song is started; and there are different opinions about this. Some want to start it on the proper note; others a second below the proper note, so that the voice climbs and rises gradually. Others say the third [below], others on the fourth [below]. Some begin with a graceful soft tone. All these different manners are included for the most part under the term *Accentus*.

Exclamatio is the correct means to move the affections and must be done by increasing the tone. It can be applied and used with all dotted minims and semiminims in descending motion; and in particular, to move the following note somewhat faster continues the affection more than the semibreve, which by increasing and decreasing of the voice without *exclamatio*, has more freedom, also greater grace. All this will be treated and thoroughly explained with examples in the aforementioned treatise.

The defects in the voice are: that some singers take too many breaths; some sing through the nose and hold the voice in the throat; others sing with the teeth closed. All these are not to be praised, rather they deform the harmony and do not please.

This ends the remarks on *Nature*. *Doctrine* follows.

2. Doctrine

Furthermore a singer must have a good knowledge of how to form the diminutions (usually called *coloratura*) attractively and appositely.

Diminutio is when a long note is broken and resolved into many other small and fast notes. These are of different kinds and manners. Of these some follow in order, such as *Accentus, Tremulo, Gruppi,* and *Tirata.*

Accentus is: when the following figures are drawn in the throat [see Ex. 1[1]].

N.B. The two flagged notes with 3 below, means that they should have three flags, 32 of which belong to a Tactus.

1. Note values in the examples have been halved in order to conform with modern usage.

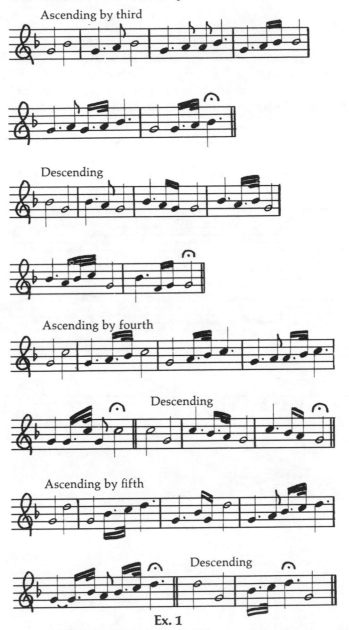

Ex. 1

Tremolo, or *Tremulo:* is nothing other than a trembling of the voice on one note; the organists call it *Mordanten* or *moderanten.* And this is used more on organs and quilled instruments than by human voices.

Ascending tremolo

Descending. This is not as good as the ascending.

Tremoletti

Ex. 2

Gruppo, or *Groppi:* These are used in cadence and formal *Clausulae*, and must be struck more sharply than the *Tremoli.*

Ex. 3

Tiratae: Are long, fast runs stepwise, and can be used on the clavier either ascending or descending. The faster and cleaner these little runs are made, so that one can hear each note clearly, the better and more attractive it will be.

Ex. 4

Diminutions that do not move by degree are *Trillo* and *Passaggi*.

Trillo: Is of two kinds: the one occurs in unison, either on a line or in a space, when many rapid notes are repeated one after another.

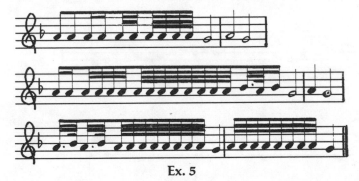

Ex. 5

The second *Trillo* is performed in a different way. And indeed it is impossible to learn to form a trill properly from the preceding [examples], for it is taught *Viva praeceptoris voce et ope*. The [trill] is sung and presented so that one may learn from another, just as a bird learns by observation of another. Since I have not found this kind of trill described or translated by any Italian author (even in the time of the aforementioned Caccini) except only a "t" or "tr" or "tri" over the note where a trill should be made, nevertheless I have considered it necessary to add here in passing several kinds so that ignorant tyros may see and know approximately what will be called a trill.

Ex. 6

Passaggi: These are swift runs, which move by degrees and also leaps of all kinds of intervals, both ascending and descending, over longer notes.

They are of two kinds: some are simple, formed with minims or semiminims, or minims and semiminims combined; others are broken, made up of fusas and semifusas, or fusas and semifusas combined.

(The semiminims are called *chromata* by the Italians; the fusas, *semichromata*; the semifusas, *bischromata*.)

Beginning students of this art should first start with simple passages, then gradually practice industriously the broken ones, with fusas, and continue until they finally come to those with semifusas, and can bring them off successfully.

3. Practice

So that one may better grasp what has been touched on briefly up to now, many and all kinds of musical examples of diminutions should be demonstrated (so that from the kind of diminution as indicated above the notes [as in Ex. 6], one may see what forms can be used for this or that note, also one can see what kind of intervals are used in ornamentation and coloration. Because this would go too far, it cannot be included in this volume. Let the well-intentioned musician and singer make use of what has been presented herewith until the complete treatise containing rules and examples will, with God's help, be brought to light by me. I will therefore refer the kind and eager musician who wishes to sing in the new style, to that work. . . .

In this extract Marin Mersenne discusses the training of voices in connection with the making of ornaments and gives some principles to be followed. He also directs some remarks to the teachers of singing and discusses Italian airs. For biographical information see selection in Chapter 10.

SOURCE: *Marin Mersenne,* Harmonie universelle, contenant la Theorie et la Pratique de la Musique *(Paris: Cramoisy, 1636). The Sixth Book on the Art of Singing Well, Proposition VI, vol. II, pp. 354–56.*

MARIN MERSENNE
from *Harmonie universelle*

How to Train Voices and Make Them Capable of
Singing All Kinds of Airs and Chansons, and
Particularly How to Sing Embellishments

There is no difficulty in teaching those who have good voices because they bring themselves to imitate and do everything that one wishes, as do all apprentices who need more use of the rein than of the spur, as was said of Aristotle when he was still a student. From this comes the Latin proverb *gaudeant bene nati*, because of the good qualities that Nature and birth give to some and deny to others; they may be related to the command of Divine Providence, who uses all kinds of conditions, just as of voices, to compose the great concerts of the universe, the beauties and charms of which we will perceive only in Heaven.

Now, after one has taught the singer to form the tone and adjust the voice to all kinds of sounds, one trains him to make embellishments, which consist of roulades of the throat, corresponding to the shakes and accents that are made on the keyboard of the organ and harpsichord, and on the lute and other stringed instruments. These ornaments are the most difficult of all things to do in singing, because it is necessary only to beat the air of the throat without the aid of the tongue to make a number of shakes. But they are, however, as delightful as they are difficult, for if the other movements are colors and nuances, one could say the embellishments are their brilliance and light.

Those who do not have a throat disposed to the aforesaid *cadences* and passages use movements of the tongue, which are not so pleasant, particularly when they are made with the tip; as to those made with the middle, they are necessary for certain passages that cannot be executed without the aid and trembling of the middle of the tongue, because of the vowels which must be pronounced and made clear to the audience.

As for shakes made by the lips, they are not attractive, nor permitted, any more than those that seem to be drawn from the stomach. One should also remark that the aforesaid shakes are not on a single note or string, like those sounds produced by strings, for they would be faulty, unless one wished to imitate the *Trillo* of the Italians; rather they descend and rise a semitone or a tone. For example, if the cadence is composed of the three notes, *la, sol, fa*, one should place the shake on the *sol*, making 4, 8, 16, or as many repercussions as one can or wishes on *la sol, la sol, la sol*, etc., as one sees in the following example [Ex. 1],

Ex. 1   **Ex. 2**

which has eight 32nds that should be made in the time equal to the half measure *sol*. And if one wants to make this ornament in all its perfection, one should increase the number of beats on the note marked with a dot above it with such delicacy that this doubling may be accompanied by an extraordinary sweetness, which may contain the greatest charms of the song.

After one has learned to make these ornaments, which can be used for all kinds of passages, he should learn to perform *ports de voix* [appoggiaturas], which make songs and recitatives most attractive, and which, alone, being well executed, make voices estimable even though they may not be able to execute the accented and unaccented trills, for the mind receives a singular pleasure when it considers a voice that is placed as it should be throughout all kinds of degrees and intervals, and which, holding firm on the principal notes of the mode that animates the song, seems to transport the spirit of its hearers.

But these *ports de voix* are not marked in the printed books; this one can do by putting a little dot after the note on which one begins the portamento and then adding a quarter or eighth, or sixteenth after the dot, which signifies that one must just touch the preceding tone to lead to the note following. This will be better understood from the three preceding examples [in Ex. 2], the first of which shows how the voice must be carried from *ut* to *re;* the second shows how it moves from *mi* to *fa*, and the third from *re* to *mi*, or *fa*. In short, the voice flows and passes from *re* to *mi* as if it drew the *re* after itself, and continues to fill out the interval, or degree *re–mi*, by an uninterrupted movement and renders these two sounds continuous. This should only be done where it is most suitable and in places where the *ports de voix* have some grace; and one can draw the same conclusion in regard to the trills, roulades, accents, shakes, and decrescendos of the throat and voice.

It should be noted that the Maîtres employ different characters to indicate the places and notes where shakes are to be used; for example, Le Baillif, Boësset, and Moulinié put a cross or half cross on the note where they want a simple ornament or two or three *tremblements*, and another character in the form of the letter *m*, or the *dièse* [♯], when one should lengthen the embellishment or multiply the beats.

One can use a number of other characters to signify the other embellishments in recitatives, as this little upright stroke|, or this accent', to show that one must make a plaintive accent on the accentuated note—raising the tone a little at the end of its enunciation and giving it a little dot, which passes so quickly that it is difficult to perceive; but it must be raised only a half step, which consists of a small effort of the voice.

As to the Italians, in their recitatives they observe many things of which ours are deprived, because they represent as much as they can the passions and affections of the soul and spirit, as, for example, anger, furor, disdain, rage, the frailties of the heart, and many other passions, with a violence so strange that one would almost say that they are touched by the same emotions they are representing in the song; whereas our French are content to tickle the ear, and have a perpetual sweetness in their songs, which deprives them of energy.

Notice for the Maîtres who Teach Singing, in Which Italian Airs Are Discussed

One of the great perfections of song consists of good pronunciation of the words and rendering them so distinctly that the auditors do not lose a single syllable, as one remarks in the recitatives of Baillif, who pronounces very distinctly and sounds all the syllables instead of stifling them in the throat, as do most of the others, who press them so strongly between the tongue, teeth, and lips that one understands almost nothing of what they are saying, either because they do not open their mouths sufficiently or do not move the tongue as they should. This is what the Maîtres ought to consider in order that their students may do them honor and that the pages and other children, who sing before the King and in churches, pronounce as well in singing as they do in speaking, and that their recitatives have the same effect as a speech distinctly pronounced. For this they should be taught the way to pronounce equally well the five vowels, *a, e, i, o, u* in performing embellishments and roulades. Now one of the things that most ordinary Maîtres lack is due to the fact that they do not themselves have good voices fit for recitative and for executing the beauties that embellish the airs, and that they do not pronounce each syllable sufficiently well to execute these things for their scholars, so that they are like those who would teach people to write well before they know how to write well themselves. In addition, they should have traveled in foreign countries, particularly in Italy, where they pride themselves on their fine singing and knowing music better than do the French. While all that they do cannot be approved, nevertheless it is certain that they display a certain excellence in their recitatives, which they animate more strongly than do our French, who surpass them in exquisiteness but not in vigor.

Those who are unable to travel can at least read Giulio Caccini, called the Roman, who published a book on the *Art of Singing Well* at Florence in 1621. In it he distinguishes the passages suitable to instruments from those which best serve the voice, and divides the principal beauties of song in *augmenting* and *diminishing* of the voice, which he calls *Crescere e scemare della voce;* in *exclamation;* and in two kinds of passages, which he calls *Trillo* and *Gruppi,* which correspond to our *passages, fredons, tremblements,* and beatings of the throat. He adds that one must make the passages and roulades of the voice on long syllables, and that the voice should be softened or reinforced on certain syllables to express the passions of the subject, which is what one does naturally without having learned it, however little judgment he has. But our singers think that the exclamations and accents the Italians use in singing smack too much of Tragedy or Comedy; therefore they do not want to employ them, although they should imitate those which are good or excellent, for it is easy to temper the exclamations and to accommodate them to the French sweetness, in order to add that which the Italians possess of greater pathos to the beauty, clarity, and gentleness of the *cadences* that our musicians make with good grace when, possessing a good voice, they have learned the method of singing well from good teachers.

The aforesaid Giulio joined his *chitarrone* to his voice in order to provide a perpetual bass, as they still do now in Italy, where almost always they have a little organ or theorbo in the recitatives that they perform in the theater when they present some comedy or celebrated action, as one saw in *La Flora* of Andrea Salvadori, which was performed in Florence for the wedding of the Duke of Parma to the Princess Marguerite, with such an apparatus that the spectators declared they had never heard nor seen anything like it, either for the beauty of the recitative that each actor gave in speaking and singing on the stage, or for the majesty of the poetry, or for the richness, and the machines that represented the thunders, lightnings, and other storms with such perfection that the spectators remained astounded and ravished.

Giacomo Peri, in the year 1600 in Florence during the festivities for the wedding of the Queen Mother, began to introduce the manner of reciting poetry in music on the stage; this was followed by *La Flora,* of which I have just spoken, in 1628. The musical drama of *Saint Alexis,* represented at Rome in 1634, was the last work of any consequence that was viewed with such great pleasure. But our musicians are, it seems, too timid to introduce this style of recitative in France, although they are just as capable of it as the Italians, if some persons who wished to go to the expense required by such a subject would push them into it.

I return to *cadences* and *exclamations*, which can be done in an infinity of ways, there being no rule as to what depends on the opinion and fantasy of men, so that one could always add to them. Now those who like a multitude of passages and diminutions can read those of Ignace Donat; the 156 passages or *glosados* of Cerone, in the fifth chapter of his Eighth Book; those of the Fontegara of Sylvestro Ganassi, which fills 120 pages with passages suitable for flutes and other instruments, and particularly the *Nuove musiche* of Giulio Caccini, of which I have spoken above. But it will suffice to consider those examples that we give at the end of this book because they will serve as a model for posterity, to demonstrate the manner of ornamenting or embellishing Airs; for no one, it seems, has ever proceeded with so much address and polish as is done today.

12. Music for the Theater

Claudio Monteverdi (1567–1643) was one of the most gifted and prolific composers of the Italian Renaissance. He was at the court of Mantua under the Gonzaga regime from 1589 until 1613. There he produced many madrigals (Books II–V), his Vespro della Beata Vergine, *the Magnificats à 6 and à 7 and various sacred works (1610), his opera* Orfeo *(1607),* L'Arianna *and* Il Ballo delle ingrate *(1608), and other works. In 1613 he was called to Venice to be Maestro di Cappella at the cathedral of San Marco, for which he produced much sacred music, continuing also to write madrigals, secular pieces for solo voices, and operas.*

In addition to being a composer of much magnificent music, Monteverdi was also a copious letter writer. Many of his communications are preserved and have been collected and edited. The four translated here show Monteverdi's method of working and his ideas on composing for the theater.

SOURCE: *G. P. Malipiero,* Claudio Monteverdi *(Milan, 1929), Letters 3, 23, 22, 25.*

CLAUDIO MONTEVERDI
Four Letters

YOUR HIGHNESS, MY LORD AND BENEVOLENT PATRON:
Ten days ago I received the most recent letter from your Highness, which commanded me to prepare two *entrate*—one for the stars that are to follow the moon, and the other for the shepherds that accompany Endymion; likewise, two *balletti:* one for the stars alone, and the other for the stars and shepherds together. Thus, with a most ardent desire to obey and fulfill as quickly as possible the commands of Your Highness, as I have always done and will always do until I die, I first began to work on that of the stars. But not receiving any instructions as to the number there will be to dance it, wishing to insert in it something I

thought would have been new, beautiful, tasteful—that is, first having all the instruments play a lively short air, danced by all the stars, then quickly change to the five viols *da braccia*, having them play an air different from the aforesaid while the other instruments are silent, with only two stars dancing, the others resting, and at the end of the score taking up the first air with all the instruments and stars, continuing this order until all the stars would have danced two by two—but not having had their number, and it being necessary to know this (providing, however, this plan of alternating as I have said pleases Your Highness), I have left off work on it until I am informed. In order to know about this I have written to Mons. Giovanni Battista *ballerino*, so that by means of my brother he may send me the exact number, and as soon as I have the scene of the shepherds and stars I will send them to Your Highness.

I have done this, my most Serene Lord, with my usual good will and ready desire to serve you that I have always had and always will have, but not yet with the obedience of my strength and readiness of my desire that I have had in the past, for they are still weak from past labors and duties, so that with neither medicine nor diet, nor leaving off my studies, have they returned to their former vigor, although to some degree, yes. Nevertheless, I hope in God to recuperate them if it pleases His Divine Majesty. I beg Your Highness, then, for the love of God, you will never again burden me with so much work at one time nor such a short time [to do it in], for certainly my great desire to serve you, and the great fatigue, would immediately shorten my life, during which, should I live longer, I will serve Your Highness and benefit my poor children.

If, Most Serene Highness, my lord, you find yourself not well served by me, nor with the beauty and swiftness that perhaps you expected and as it was my desire to serve, as I likewise have always desired to do, do not blame my good will nor my spirit, since both the one and the other will always receive the greatest grace and highest favor if Your Highness deigns to command them; to whom, bowing, I make the humblest reverence and pray Our Lord will give you all happiness.

FROM CREMONA
DECEMBER 1604

Most humble and devoted servitor
CLAUDIO MONTEVERDI

MY ILLUSTRIOUS LORD AND BENEVOLENT PATRON:
I have received, from Sig. Carlo de Torri, with greatest pleasure the letter from Your Illustrious Lordship together with the small libretto

containing the *favola maritima* of Thetis. Your Lordship writes that you sent it in order that I may examine it diligently and then write to you my opinion, since I must compose the music for it to be used in the future marriage of His Serene Highness [Duke Ferdinand]. Illustrious Signor, I desire nothing other than to be worthy in some way to serve His Serene Highness; I will say only in this first response that I promptly offer myself to undertake whatever His Serene Highness will deign to command me, and always, without repetition, to honor and revere all that Serene Highness will command; if Serene Highness approves of it, it in consequence would be most beautiful and much to my taste. But if you add that I should say [what I think], I must obey the order of Your Excellency with all respect and promptness, it being understood that my opinion would be nothing, as I am a person of little worth in every respect, and a person who honors every person of virtue, in particular the present poet, whose name I do not know, and even more because the profession of poetry is not mine.

I will say then, with all respect to obey you because I am thus commanded, I will say first in general, that the music should be the mistress of the air and not only of the water. I want to say in my language that the *concerti* described in this *favola* are all low and close to the earth, greatly lacking beautiful harmonies because the harmony will be placed in the largest winds in the aria of the Earth, placed so as to be heard by all and concerted behind the scene; and in this I leave the judgment to your exquisite and intelligent taste that for this defect, instead of one chitarrone three would be needed; instead of one harp, three, and so on. And instead of a delicate voice a powerful one would be needed. Besides that, the proper imitation of speech in my judgment should be founded on wind instruments rather than on delicate strings, so the harmonies of the Tritons and other marine gods, I would think, should be supported by trombones and cornetts and not by citharas or clavicembali and harps, since this action, being maritime, is in consequence outside the city; and Plato teaches that *cithara debet esse in civitati, et thibia in agris;* so that either the delicate ones are improper, or the proper ones not delicate.

Moreover, I have seen the interlocutors to be Winds, Cupids, Zephyrs, and Sirens; consequently there will be many sopranos needed. And it is added that the winds have to sing, that is, the Zephyrs and Boreal Winds. How, dear Signore, can I imitate the speech of the winds if they do not speak? and how can I move the affections by their means? Arianna moved [the audience] because she was a woman, and likewise Orfeo, being a man and not a wind; the harmonies imitate their own natures and not through words—the uproar of the winds and the bleating of the sheep, the neighing of the horses and so on—but they do not imitate the speech of the winds because there is none. The dances also that come into such a *favola* are few because they do not have the character of dances. The whole story, then, according to my not small ignorance, does not move me one bit, and also I understand it with difficulty, nor do I feel that it carries me in a natural way to an ending that moves me. *Arianna* led me to a true lament, and *Orfeo* to a true prayer; but this, to I don't know what kind of an ending. So what does Your Illustrious Highness wish the music to do in it? However, the work will be accepted by me with all respect and honor if His Serene Highness should command and approve it, for he is indeed my master. And should His Serene Highness command that it be put into music, seeing that in this [work] more deities speak than others, and since it pleases him to hear them sing with grace, I would say for the Sirens the three sisters, that is, Signora Adriana and the others could sing and also compose their songs; also Signor Rasi his part, likewise Signor D. Francesco, and so on for the other Signori, and in this imitate the Cardinal of Montalto, who wrote a comedy in which each actor in it composed his own part. If this were a work that tended to a single end, like *Arianna* and *Orfeo*, to be sure, it would also be necessary to have a single guiding precept; that is, that they should tend to speak in singing and not, like this one, to sing in speaking. And I consider also in this reflection that it is too long in each part of the speech of the Sirens and following, and in certain other harangues.

Excuse me, my dear Lord, if I have said too much, not to detract from anything but through desire to obey all your wishes; for having to compose it in music if I were to be commanded, your Serene Highness might be able to consider my ideas. I beg you with every devoted and humble affection to hold me servitor to your Most Serene Highness, to whom I make most humble reverence and kiss Your Highness's hands with affection, and pray that God will give you the utmost happiness.

FROM VENICE
DECEMBER 9, 1616

> From the most humble and obligated servitor of
> Your Serene Highness, to whom I wish with every affection
> joyous holidays.
>
> CLAUDIO MONTEVERDI

MY ILLUSTRIOUS LORD AND BENEVOLENT PATRON:

Your Excellency will pardon me if I have not tried to obtain by my letters the reply of your Illustrious Lordship to the letter that I sent twenty days ago to Your Lordship in reply to your most kind [letter], which was accompanied by the *favola maritima* of the *Marriage of Thetis and Peleus,* to learn from you what I must do about it, Your Excellency having written in your letter that before I did anything I was to write to you my opinion of it. Thus my delay is due to work on the Mass for Christmas Eve, on which, between composing it and rewriting it, I had to spend all the month of December almost without any interruption whatever. Now by the grace of God I am free, it having come off honorably, and I come again with this to Your Excellency, asking that you do me the honor to inform me of that which His Serene Highness desires me to do. Finding myself unengaged, after the fatigue of the Night and Day of Christmas, for a while I shall have nothing to do for St. Mark's. Therefore I will begin to do some little thing about the aforesaid *favola* if you so command me, but I will do nothing else until a new commission arrives from Your Illustrious Excellency.

I have returned to examine it more minutely and carefully and, as I see it, many sopranos are needed, and many tenors; very little dialogue and that little spoken and not sung with beauty; the only choral singing being the Argonauts in the ship, this will be the most beautiful and lively [piece] and will be resolved in six voices and six instruments. There are indeed the Zephyrs and the Boreal Winds, but I don't know how these are to sing, though I know that they blow and hiss, as Virgil remarks; speaking of the winds he uses the verb *sibillare,* which exactly imitates in pronunciation the effect of the wind. There are two other choruses, one of the Nereids and the other of Tritons; but these, in my opinion, should be concerted with wind instruments, which if that should be the case, I ask Your Excellency what delight of the senses will be the result? And so that Your Excellency may again (diligently) see this truth, I send Your Excellency on the piece of paper enclosed, the order of the scenes as they will be placed in the aforesaid *favola,* so that you will favor me with your opinion. The whole affair however will be excellent, depending on His Serene Highness, to whom I promptly bow and show myself to be his humble servitor. I will then be awaiting the reply of Your Excellency and whatever you deign soon to command me. I humbly kiss your hands and pray with heartfelt affection the completion of your most honored thoughts.

FROM VENICE
DECEMBER 29, 1616

Your Excellency's most obligated and devoted servitor,

CLAUDIO MONTEVERDI

My illustrious Lord and benevolent Patron:

The most welcome letter from Your Excellency, now received together with the sheet that gives the personages that are to be in the *favola* of Thetis, has brought much light in doing what may be apropos to the taste of Your Excellency, for I know it will also be the taste of His Serene Highness, for whom I desire with all my heart to do something that will please. I confess, Excellency, when I wrote the first letter in reply to your first, that the *favola* sent me, not having any other title than *The Marriage of Thetis, favola maritima,* I confess that I [thought] it to be something to be sung and represented in music as was *Arianna.* But having understood, from this last letter from Your Excellency, that it has to serve as *intermedi* for the great comedy, just as in that first sense I thought it to be a work of little worth, now, in the second sense, on the contrary I believe it is a worthy and most noble work. However, in my opinion it lacks a conclusion of the whole after the final line, which says *Torni sereno il ciel, tranquillo il mare.* Here, I say, there is lacking a canzonetta in praise of the Most Serene Princely couple. Its harmony could be heard in the sky and earth of the scene, where noble dancers could perform a noble dance; such a noble ending seems to me to be most suitable for the proposed noble vista. At the same time, if the verses that the Nereids are to sing could be accommodated to dance meters, to the tempo of which expert dancers could perform a dance in most graceful manner, it seems to me this would be something most appropriate.

I am somewhat opposed to the three songs of the three Sirens, for I fear that to have all three sing separately will make the work seem too long to the hearers and lacking variety, since between one and another [song] it will be necessary to have an instrumental interlude, passagework that supports the declamation, and trills, and in general there will be a certain similarity; therefore I consider also for variation of the whole [scene] that the two first madrigals be divided into three parts, to be sung now with one voice, now two together, and the third by all three.

The part of Venus, the principal part that comes after the lament of Peleus and the first piece to be heard in stylish singing, that is, with runs and trills, I have deemed best that Signora Adriana sing it, as she has a strong voice, and by her two sisters serving as Echoes, seeing that the text has an echo in this line: *E sfavellin d'Amor gli scogli e l'onde.* But first the minds of the auditors must be prepared by a sinfonia of instruments, filling half the stage if possible, because two lines of Peleus anticipate this, after his lament

Ma qual per aria sento
Celeste soavissimo concerto!

And I believe Signora Adriana would have time to disguise herself, or
even one of the three other ladies. Until now I thought it would be
about a hundred and fifty lines in length, perhaps more, and I think it
will not be ready until next week. If it pleases Your Excellency all the
soliloquies will be done, that is, those that are spoken; after them I will
do those that are in florid style. May it please God that I succeed in this
work inasmuch as I am most desirous to do something that will be to
the taste of His Serene Highness; also that the results will serve me
as true testimony in the appreciation of His Serene Highness, whom I
love and revere, and to whom always, in every condition and place, I
dedicate myself as a most humble servant. Nor do I remain any less a
most indebted servitor to Your Excellency, who deigns to support me
in this work by your customary kindness and most honorable manner.

And now, most humbly bowing to Your Excellency, I pray with warm-
est affection that God may bestow upon you the height of your true
aspirations.

From Venice
January 6, 1617

Most obligated and devoted servitor

Claudio Monteverdi

*Emilio de' Cavalieri (ca. 1550–1602) was born in Rome, where he spent
his early life and received his musical training. Though his contemporaries never granted him the title of* maestro, *he was well trained and
had some success as a composer before he moved to Florence in 1584. He
was drawn there by the possibility of giving vent to his talents for the
theater.*

Here he came in contact with the Florentine Camerata, *its patron
Giovanni de' Bardi, and the musicians Peri and Caccini. Apparently he
never joined the group but pursued his independent course and was
rewarded by being appointed controller in 1588 of all music and musicians at the Medicean court. He was very active as a composer and
producer of music, chiefly theatrical, for the next several years. He also
served as special envoy from the Florentine court to the Papal court in
Rome, going there often in the years after 1587.*

In spite of a busy life, de' Cavalieri continued to write music, but un-

fortunately very little remains of his extensive production, which we know only from references in contemporary documents. We do have, however, the score and text of his Rappresentazione di Anima, et di Corpo, *first produced at Rome in 1600. It is basically what might be called a sacred drama with solo passages and ensembles. The preface, written by Alessandro Guidotti, gives Cavalieri's specific instructions on how it is to be performed.*

SOURCE: Rappresentazione di Anima, et di Corpo, *Nuovamente posta in Musica dal Sig. Emilio del Cavalliere per recitar cantando (Rome, 1600); facs. ed. (Bologna: Forni, 1967), preface (unpaged).*

EMILIO DE' CAVALIERI
from *Rappresentazione di Anima, et di Corpo*

Preface

Wishing to perform on the stage the present work, or others like it, and to follow the instructions of Sig. Emilio del Cavalieri, in such a way that this kind of music renewed by him moves [the hearers] to different emotions, as pity, joy, tears, and laughter, and other similar emotions, as was done in a modern scene composed by him—*The Despair of Fileno,* in which Signora Vittoria Archilei, whose excellence in music is known to all, reciting, moved [all] most marvelously to tears, while in the same place the person of Fileno moved them to laughter: wishing, I say, to perform the work, it appears necessary for all things to be excellent. Let the singer have a beautiful voice with good intonation, and well supported, and let him sing with expression, soft and loud, and without passagework; and in particular he should express the words well, so that they may be understood, and accompany them with gestures and movements, not only of the hands but other gestures that are efficacious aids in moving the affections. The instruments also should be well played, and their numbers be more or less according to the place—theater or hall—which, to be proportionate to this recitation in music should not not seat more than a thousand persons, who can be comfortably seated for their greater satisfaction and silence. For if it is presented in very large halls it is not possible to hear all the words; and the singer would have to force his voice, which lessens the emotional effect; also, so much music with the words not being audible becomes tiresome.

The instruments, because they are not to be seen, must play behind the backdrop of the scene; and they must be persons who play without diminutions and with full tone, supporting the singers.

And to give some idea of the instruments which have served in a similar situation for rehearsal, a double lyre, a clavicembalo, a chitarrone, or theorbo as they say, all together make a good effect: as do likewise a sweet-toned organ with a chitarrone. And Sig. Emilio would approve of changing the instruments according to the *affetti* of the performer.

He also is of the opinion that similar representations in music should not exceed two hours in length and that they should be divided into acts, and the actors be attractively clothed and with variety.

Changing from one *affetto* to another that is contrasting—as from sadness to happiness, ferocity to gentleness, and the like, greatly moves [an audience]. When a soloist has sung for some time it is good to have the chorus sing, and to vary the key often. And let now the soprano, now the bass, then the contralto, and tenor sing; and see that the airs and music are not similar, but varied, with many [rhythmic] proportions, that is, triple, sextuple, and binary, and adorned with echoes and many inventions, in particular the dance. This enlivens as much as possible the representation, as has been the opinion of all the spectators. The dances will be more attractive and novel if they are a little out of the ordinary, as for example, the *moresca* as a battle, the *ballo* as a game; and let them be playful, as in the Pastoral of *Fileno*, where three satyrs come to do battle and sing while fighting and dancing to a *moresca* melody. And in the game of Blind Man's Buff [*Giuoco della Cieca*] four nymphs dance and sing while they play around the blindfolded Amarilli, obeying the rules of the game.

I do not say that a dance at the end should not be performed; on a suitable occasion a formal dance. But take note that the Ballo should have for it those who dance and sing, and if possible it should be more perfect and out of the ordinary, like that Sig. Emilio made in the great comedy recited at the time of the wedding of the Most Serene Grand Duchess of Tuscany in 1588.

When the composition is divided into three acts, which experience shows are sufficient, four *intermedii* can be added. These should be divided so that the first one will be before the Prologue, and one of the others at the end of each act. And this order should be observed: behind the scene there should be a full orchestra and harmonious symphony of instruments, to the sound of which the actions of the *intermedio* will be concerted. Care should be taken that there is no need for recitation, as there should not be, for instance, in representing the Giants when they wished to make war on Jove, or a similar theme.

And in each of them there should be a change of scene that would suit the occasion for the *intermedio*. It is to be noted, however, that it is not suitable to use the descent of clouds, it not being possible to make the movement conform with the tempo of the Sinfonia, as would properly occur where there were *morescas* or other dances.

The poem should not exceed 700 lines, and it is suitable that it be simple and full of short lines, not only of seven syllables but of five and eight, and at times *sdrucciole,* and with close rhymes, for the beauty of the music, as it makes a pretty effect.

And in the dialogues the proposals and responses should not be long; and narrative by a single person as short as possible. And the variety of the personages without doubt will enrich the scene with great beauty, as can be observed in the Pastoral of the *Satyrs* and of the *Desperation of Fileno,* which, conforming to the intention of Sig. Emilio, the most noble Laura Guidiccioni of the Luchesini was pleased to compose. She also extracted the Blind Man's Buff from the *Pastor fido* by Sig. Cavaliere Guarini, and by her own invention that noble spirit most beautifully arranged it.

Instructions for the Present Representation for
Those Who Wish to Recite It in Music

The words without music are placed at the end, and with the numbers conforming to their position in the music in order to facilitate the preparation. By these numbers the scenes will be distinguished, as well as the personages who will recite solo and together.

In the beginning, before the curtain falls, it will be suitable to have a full symphony with voices doubled and a large quantity of instruments. The madrigal no.86, *O Signor santo e vero* for six voices, will serve very well.

The curtain falling, the two youths who are to recite the Prologue will be seen on the stage. After their recitation Time will appear; and the instruments that are to accompany the singers must wait in giving the first consonance until he starts.

The chorus will remain on the stage, some seated, others standing, seeing to it that what is being represented is heard; and at times they should change places and make gestures. When they have to sing they should rise to their feet so that they can gesticulate, and then return to their places. The music being in four voices one can, if desired, double them, having now four sing alone and sometimes all of them together, the stage being large enough for eight.

It will be good if Pleasure, with his two companions, have instruments in their hands, playing while they sing, and also playing their Ritornelli. One can have a *chitarrone*, another a *chitarrina alla spagnuola,* and the third a small cymbal with bells in the Spanish style, which makes a little sound. They will go off while they are playing the last ritornello.

When Body speaks the words "Si che hormai Alma mia" and what follows, he may remove some vain ornament, such as a golden chain, a feather from his hat, or the like.

The World and Worldly Life should in particular be richly clothed. When their garments are removed, the clothes beneath, of one, should show great poverty and ugliness; the other should show a corpse.

The Sinfonie and Ritornelli can be played with a great number of instruments; and one violin, which plays the soprano, will make a fine effect.

The Finale can be done in two ways; either with or without a dance. If a dance is not used, one should end with verse no.91 (*recte* 90) for eight parts, doubling the voices and all the instruments. The final line is "Rispondono nel Ciel, Scettri e Corone."

To finish with the dance, omit the aforesaid verse for eight parts and begin to sing *Chiostri altissimi e stellati* [no.91]. The dance begins with a *Riverenza* and a *Continenza,* and then follow other slow steps with interweavings and crossings of all the couples with gravity. In the Ritornelli there are four dancers, who dance exquisitely a leaping dance with *caprioles* and without singing. And so continue through all the stanzas, always varying the dance. And the four *maestri* who dance may vary it one time with a Gagliard, another time a Canario, and another with a Corrente, which will suit the Ritornelli very well. If the stage is not large enough to accommodate four dancers, have at least two: and the dance should be devised by the best dancing master to be found.

The stanzas accompanying the dance are sung by all, both behind and on the stage, and all the instruments play the Ritornelli.

One of the most prolific and successful composers of the Italian seventeenth century was Marco da Gagliano (1575–1642), so called because he was from the village of Gagliano, a few miles from Florence, in Tuscany. He came of a musical family, and the career of his brother Giovanni Battista paralleled his own.

Marco was destined for the priesthood and early began his study of music in the capella of San Lorenzo in Florence, where he became maestro di capella in 1608. He soon was called to the same post at the court of the Grand Duke of Tuscany and headed the musical life of his city and state.

His reputation was great, and in 1607 he went to Mantua, where in that same year he produced his opera Dafne with great success. His preface to the printed edition of 1608 is important because of his ideas on the performance of opera and the functions of the actors and chorus in such a performance.

Marco remained at Mantua until 1608, when he returned to Florence to occupy his old post as court conductor, providing music for the various festivities at the Medicean court. Many of his musical scores have disappeared.

SOURCE: Marco da Gagliano, La Dafne (Mantua, 1608), preface as printed in A. Solerti, L'Origine del melodrama (Turin, 1903), pp.78–89.

MARCO DA GAGLIANO
Preface to *Dafne*

To the Reader

During the last carnival season I happened to be in Mantua, where I had been called by Your Highness, who honored me by using me for the music to be written for the royal wedding of the Most Serene Prince your son and the Most Serene Infanta of Savoy. Since the wedding had been deferred until May by the Duke, in order not to pass several days without some feast, he ordered among other things that the *Dafne* of Signor Ottavio Rinuccini should be staged, increased in length, and embellished by him for this occasion. I was charged with setting it to music, which I did in the way I now present to you. And although I used every diligence and satisfied the exquisite taste of the poet, I will not believe that the great delight taken in it not only by the general public but also by Princes and Cavalieri and the most intelligent people came from my art alone, but also from some suggestions that appeared in this performance. Therefore, together with the music, I have tried to take these into consideration so that, as best I can, I may show them to you in this writing, since in such affairs the music is not everything, but many other things are necessary, without which harmony, no matter how excellent, would be of little use. In this respect many persons are deceived, for they wear themselves out making *gruppi, trilli, passaggi,* and *exclamazioni* with no regard for their purpose or whether or not they are apropos. I certainly do not intend to deprive myself of these adornments, but I want them to be used in the right time and place, as in the choral songs such as the *ottava* stanza *Chi da' lacci d'amor vive disciolto,* which is put in this place so we can hear the grace and the disposition of the singers. It was fortunately assigned to Signorina Caterina Martinelli, who sang it so beautifully as to fill the whole theater with delight and wonder. To be recollected also is the exquisiteness of the singing of the last terzetti *Non curi la mia pianta o fiamma o gelo,* where a good singer can set forth all the best qualities that singing demands. They were all heard from the voice of Sig. Francesco Rasi, who, in addition to other fine qualities, stands alone in singing. But where the sense does not demand it, leave aside every ornament, so as not to act like that painter who knew how to paint cypress trees and therefore painted them everywhere. Instead, try to pronounce every syllable distinctly so the words are understood, and let this be the principal aim of every singer whenever he sings, especially in performing on the stage, and let him be persuaded that real pleasure is increased by understanding the words.

But before fulfilling my promise I think it would not be useless nor outside our subject to recall to mind how and when such spectacles had their origin, which without any doubt, since they were received with much applause at their beginning, will at some time or other reach much greater perfection, perhaps such that they will some day approach the celebrated Greek and Latin tragedies. And that could happen if more of the great masters of poetry and music set their hands to it; and if the Princes, without whose aid any art has difficulty in attaining perfection, should also be favorable.

After having many times discussed the way the Ancients presented their tragedies, how they introduced the choruses, if they used singing and what kind of singing, and such things, Sig. Ottavio Rinuccini began to write the story of *Dafne.* Sig. Jacopo Corsi, of honored memory, lover of all disciplines, especially music to such an extent he was rightfully called *Padre,* Sig. Corsi composed songs for some parts of the play which pleased him best. Very anxious to see what effect they would have on the stage, he together with Sig. Ottavio told his thoughts to Sig. Jacopo Peri, who was most expert in counterpoint and a singer of great discrimination. He, when he had heard their ideas and had approved that part of the music already composed, began to compose the rest. This pleased Sig. Corsi greatly, and on the occasion of the celebration of the carnival in 1597 he had it staged in the presence of His Excellency Don Giovanni Medici and several of the principal gentlemen of our city.

The pleasure and the astonishment which this new spectacle brought about in the minds of the spectators cannot be expressed; suffice it to say that on the many occasions when it was played, it generated the same admiration and the same pleasure. Signor Rinuccini, convinced by this evidence how appropriate singing is to express every sort of emotion, and that not only did it not cause tedium (as perhaps many people would have believed) but instead caused incredible delight—Signor Rinuccini composed his *Euridice*, giving more scope to his reasoning. When Jacopo Corsi had heard it and had been pleased by the story and the style, he decided to stage it at the wedding of the Most Christian Queen. Then Sig. Jacopo Peri revived that artistic manner of reciting in singing that all Italy admires. I shall not tire myself by praising him, since there is no one who fails to give him infinite praise, and no lover of music who does not have always before him the songs of Orpheus. I will say that no one can fully appreciate the sweetness and the power of his airs who has not heard them sung by Peri himself, because he gave them such a grace and style that he so impressed in others the emotion of the words that one was forced to weep or rejoice as the singer wished.

How well the performance of this story was received is superfluous to say, the testimony of so many Princes and Nobles being sufficient. One might say they were the flower of Italian nobility who had come to attend this magnificent wedding. Among those who praised it, the Serenissimo Sig. Duca di Mantova was so completely satisfied that among the many admirable festivities that his Highness ordered for the wedding of his son, the Prince, and the Infanta of Savoy, he wanted a play with music to be presented. This was *L'Arianna*, composed by Ottavio Rinuccini, whom the Duke brought to Mantua for that purpose. Sig. Claudio Monteverdi, the most celebrated musician, head musician to His Highness, composed the songs in so exquisite a way that one can truthfully say the excellence of ancient music was revived. It visibly moved the whole theater to tears.

Such is the origin of musical performances, a truly princely spectacle and very pleasing to other people also, being one in which are united every noble pleasure, such as the arrangement and invention of the plot, the opinions, the style, the sweetness of the rhyme, the expertness of the music, the agreement of the voices and instruments, the exquisiteness of the singing, the lightness of the dancing, and the gestures. One can also say that painting has a great part because of the scenery and the costumes. In such manner, together with the intellect, is flattered every noble feeling about the most delightful of the arts that human ingenuity has discovered.

There remains for me to discuss (as I promised) some things that took place during the performance of this story which might be useful in any other performance.

In the first place, make sure that the instruments that are to accompany the solo voices are located so that they can see the faces of the performers, in order that by hearing each other better they may perform together. Take care that the harmony is not too much or too little, but such that it supports the singing without obscuring the understanding of the words. Let the manner of playing be without ornament, taking care to repeat the notes that are sung, playing those that will support them, all the time maintaining a lovely harmony.

Before the falling of the curtain, in order to get the attention of the audience, a piece should be played by different instruments, which serve to accompany the choruses and play the ritornelli. At the fifteenth or twentieth measure the Prologue should enter, that is, Ovid, taking care to regulate his steps to the sound of the orchestra; not affectedly, as if he were dancing, but gravely, in such a way that his tread shall not be discordant with the sound. When he reaches the spot where it seems to him most appropriate to begin, without further ado let him begin. Above all, his singing and gestures should be full of majesty, more or less in accordance with the loftiness of the music. He must take care that every gesture and step follow the beat of the music and singing. When the first four lines are finished, let him take a breath, walking two or three steps during the ritornello, always observing the beat. He should be careful to begin his walking on the *tenuto* of the next to the last syllable, and should begin again in the place where he happens to be. He can sometimes join two quatrains together to show a certain liveliness [*sprezzatura*]. His dress should be suitable for a poet, with a laurel crown on his head, the lyre at his side, a bow in his hand.

When the last quatrain is ended and the Prologue is off-stage, the chorus enters, formed of nymphs and shepherds, their number more or less in conformity with the capacity of the stage. As the chorus enters, one at a time, they should show by facial expression and gestures that they are afraid of meeting the Python. When half the chorus has entered, which should consist of six or seven nymphs and shepherds (for the chorus should be made up of no fewer than sixteen or eighteen people), the first shepherd turns toward his companions and begins to speak. Singing and walking, he reaches the right place, where he stops, and when the chorus has formed a half-circle around him they go on singing their song, making the gestures that the plot requires. As they sing the hymn *Se là su tra gli aurei chiostri*, they go down on one knee, turning their eyes to heaven, pretending to direct their prayers to Jove. The hymn finished, they rise to their feet and continue, pretending as they sing *Ebra di sangue* to be sad or gay according to Echo's answers, which they show they are awaiting very attentively. After Echo's last answer the Python appears from one of the stage entrances, and at the same time, or a little later, Apollo appears from another direction with his bow—a large one—in his hand.

The chorus, showing fear sings, at the sight of the serpent, almost shouting, *Ohimè che veggio*. At that moment the shepherds and nymphs leave the stage by several exits, imitating flight and terror, without however turning their backs entirely to the audience or hiding themselves completely. Apollo remains, the chorus singing *O Divo, o Nume eterno*, trying to give the effect of praying with their facial expressions and gestures. Meanwhile Apollo moves toward the Python with light and proud step, shaking his bow, brandishing his arrows in his hand, regulating every step, every gesture to the singing of the chorus. He should be careful to let fly with his bow at the exact time when the words *O benedetto stral* occur. Thus, when he shoots his second arrow, he should take care in the same way that it be at the very moment the chorus continues *O glorioso Arciero*. The third arrow may be shot while *Vola, vola pungente* is being sung. At this blow the serpent, showing that he has been badly wounded, flees by one of the exits. Apollo follows and the chorus reappears at this flight, singing *Spezza l'orrido Tergo*, showing that they are watching him die.

When the song is ended they reenter the stage, forming a crescent. Apollo also reappears and strides up and down singing *Pur giacque estinto in fine*. When he has left the stage the chorus sings a song in honor of Apollo, moving successively to the left, to the right, and to the rear, avoiding the appearance of dancing. This same maneuver may serve for all the choruses.

But very often a singer is not capable of this attack on the serpent, needing for this effect agility, leaps, and wielding of the bow with the appropriate poses, traits that appear in a good fencer and dancer as well as a fine singer. So, finding himself having to combine both these aspects, it would be difficult to sing after the combat because of fatigue from the previous action. So let two Apollos be dressed alike, and the one who sings shall enter in the place of the other one after the death of the Python, with the same bow in his hand or another like it, and he sings as we have described above.

This exchange works so well that no one even perceived the deceit during the many times it was played. The character who plays the part of the Python should come to an agreement with Apollo so that the fight shall be in time with the music. The serpent should be large; and if the painter who makes it knows how to make the wings move and [the Python] to breathe fire, as I have seen, it will be a fine sight. Above all it must writhe; the wearer of the costume must go on all fours, with his hands on the ground.

In the scene that follows and the rest, make sure that the characters who speak do not mingle with the chorus but stand at least four or five paces forward, according to the size of the stage. The chorus should keep to a crescent formation. Make sure that the shepherd, who recounts the victory of Apollo to Daphne, steps forward two or three paces in front of the others and imitates with gestures the behavior of Apollo in the combat.

But when this shepherd comes to bring news of Daphne's transformation, the leaders of the chorus should all draw back to the part of the stage from which they can face the Messenger, standing a little in front of the others. And above all they should show pity and sorrow as they hear the sad news. The role of the Messenger is extremely important; it needs expressiveness in the words more than any other role.

At this point I wish I could portray to the life how the part was sung by Sig. Antonio Brandi, called *il Brandino*. He had been called in by His Serene Highness for the wedding, with no warning; and he sang the part in such a way that I do not think anyone could have desired more. His voice is a most exquisite contralto; his pronunciation and grace in singing wonderful, for not only does he make the words intelligible, but with his gestures and his movements he insinuates into your mind something very much more.

The following chorus, when they talk among themselves about the character and lament the loss of Daphne, is easy enough to understand as it progresses. When they sing together the duo *Sparse più non vedrem di quel fin oro*, looking at each other in this exclamation, the duo is very powerful. So also when they sing all together *Dove, dove è il bel viso*, not a little grace is produced by their mourning with the movement of the music, and when together they reply *Piangete, Ninfe, e con voi pianga Amore.*

The scene of Apollo's lament, which follows, should be sung with the greatest possible emotion; at the same time the singer should take care to make a crescendo when the words demand it. When he utters the line *Faran ghirlanda le tue fronde e rami,* winding around his head the branch of laurel over which he has been mourning, he makes a crown for himself. There may be some difficulty in this and I would like to make it easier to do this action in a pleasing way. Choose two laurel branches of the same length (the bay laurel would be best), no longer than half an arm's length, tie them together at the ends, and hold them at the butt end so that they appear to be one branch. In the act of crowning yourself spread them apart, circling your head, but keeping the ends together. I have wanted to describe these details because they are more important than some people think, and while it seems a trivial thing, it was not easily discovered; indeed, in rehearsal the action was omitted as impossible to accomplish neatly, though many persons had thought about it. Seeing a big branch in Apollo's hand was an ugly sight and also, since it is not pliable, it is difficult to make a crown of it. The short branches will not serve. These difficulties were solved by M. Cosimo del Bianco, a man most skillful at this trade, marvelously inventive in matters of costume, apparatus, and such like things.

I don't want to omit that when Apollo sings the terzetti *Non curi la mia pianta o fiamme, o gelo* he should hold his lyre against his chest (which should be done in a fine attitude). It is necessary that it should appear to the audience that the extraordinary melody comes from Apollo's lyre, so place four viol players (*a braccio* or *gamba,* it matters not) in one of the rear exits in a place where, unseen by the audience, they can see Apollo, and when he applies his bow to his lyre, they can play the three written notes, taking care to draw their bows together so it will seem to be only one bow. This trick cannot be detected except in the imagination of some hearer, and gives great pleasure.

There only remains for me to say (so as not to usurp praises due to others and, though a crow myself, to embellish myself with other people's plumage) that the melody of the octet *Chi da' lacci d'Amor vive disciolto* and the melody Apollo sings when he has defeated the Python, *Pur giacque estinto al fine,* together with that other one sung by Apollo in the last scene, *Un guardo, un guardo appena,* and finally *Non chiami mille volte il tuo bel nome*—which songs shine like stars among my own —all these are compositions of one of our principal Academicians, a great protector of music and a great expert in it.

Courteous readers, please receive this essay of mine not as that of a teacher who has the pretension to teach other people (I have no such presumption) but as the work of a person who has diligently observed every small detail in the performance of this play. I end it, so that with less fatigue you can open a path and reach that complete perfection, which is necessary in the performance of such compositions. Live happily!

Thomas Campion (1567–1620) is best known to the general public as a poet, but he was also an excellent musician, being a prominent composer of the English lutenist school, second only to John Dowland. Campion's gift for musical composition as well as poetry enabled him to create lyric songs of exceptional beauty and grace, although he was of the opinion that classical poetic meters were preferable to rhyming verse. Campion's musical production includes five books of Airs *(1601, 1613 [?], 1617 [?]); songs for a "Maske in honour of Lord Hayes and his Bride" (1607), songs for a "Maske at Caversham House" (1613), songs for a "Maske at the marriage of Princess Elizabeth" (1613), and songs for a "Maske at the marriage of Robert, Earl of Somerset." He also published a book on counterpoint in 1613, entitled* A new way of making Foure parts in Counterpoint by a most familiar and infallible Rule.

Campion held a degree in medicine, probably from a foreign university, for though he was educated at Cambridge, he took no degree there. He did at some time practice medicine, and it is certain that he visited Sir Thomas Monson as medical advisor during Monson's incarceration in the Tower of London in 1617.

The Discription of a Maske *was apparently written and caused to be printed by Campion himself. It is exceptionally complete and contains a fuller account of the music performed in the Maske than is usually found in such accounts. Campion gives the numbers and kinds of instruments used, the texts of the songs, and where and how the music was used. Five songs were printed at the end of the Maske; two of them are by Campion, two by Thos. Lupo, and one by Thos. Giles. This was by no means the total amount of music used in the Maske, and there are several pieces in British Museum Add. 10444 bearing the indications "The Lord Hayes his first Maske," "the Second," "the Third." There is also a "Lord Hayes Corant" in another manuscript, which may belong to this Maske or another.*

The Discription *exists in ten copies; one is held by the British Museum, and others are in the Bodleian Library at Oxford University, the Irish Academy of Music in Dublin, the Library of Congress and the Folger Shakespeare Library in Washington, D.C., the Widener Library at Harvard University, the Beinecke Library at Yale University, the Huntington Library, and the Lilly Library at Indiana University. The five songs have been edited by G. E. P. Arkwright,* Old English Edition

(London, 1899) and by A. J. Sabol, Songs and Dances for the Stuart
Maske (Providence, R. I., 1959).

SOURCE: The Discription of a Maske, Presented before the Kinges
Majestie at White Hall, on Twelfth Night last, in honour of the Lord
Hayes, and his Bride, Daughter and Heire to the honourable Lord
Dennye, their marriage having been the same day at Court solemnized
. . . Invented and set forth by Thomas Campion, Doctor of Phisicke, 1607.

THOMAS CAMPION

The Description of a Maske presented before the King's Majesty at White Hall, on twelfth night last, in honour of the Lord Hayes, and his Bride.

As in battles, so in all other actions that are to be reported, the first,
and most necessary part is the description of the place, with his opportunities and properties, whether they be natural, or artificial. The great
hall (wherein the Maske was presented) received this division and
order: The upper part where the cloth and chair of State were placed,
had scaffolds and seats on either side continued to the screen; right
before it was made a partition for the dancing place; on the right hand
whereof were consorted ten Musicians, with Bass and Meane Lutes, a
Bandora, a double Sack-Butt, and an Harpsichord, with two treble
Violins; on the other side somewhat nearer the screen were placed nine
Violins and three Lutes, and to answer both the Consorts (as it were in
a triangle) six Cornetts, and six Chapel voices were seated almost right
against them, in a place raised higher in respect of the piercing sound of
those instruments. Eighteen foot from the screen another Stage was
raised higher by a yard than that which was prepared for dancing. This
higher Stage was all enclosed with a double veil, so artificially painted,

that it seemed as if dark clouds had hung before it: within that shroud was concealed a green valley, with green trees around about it, and in the midst of them nine golden trees of fifteen foot high, with arms and branches very glorious to behold. From the which grove toward the State was made a broad descent to the dancing place, just in the midst of it. On either hand were two ascents, like the sides of two hills, dressed with shrubs and trees; that on the right hand leading to the bower of Flora; the other to the house of Night; which bower and house were placed opposite at either end of the screen, and between them both was raised a hill, hanging like a cliff over the grove below, and on the top of it a goodly large tree was set, supposed to be the tree of Diana; be-hind the which toward the window was a small descent, with another spreading hill that climbed up to the top of the window, with many trees on the height of it, whereby those that played on the Hoboys at the King's entrance into the hall were shadowed.

The bower of Flora was very spacious, garnished with all kind of flowers, and flowery branches with lights in them; the house of Night ample, and stately, with black pillars, whereon many stars of gold were fixed. Within it, when it was empty, appeared nothing but clouds and stars, and on the top of it stood three Turrets underpropped with small black starred pillars, the middlemost being highest and greatest, the other two of equal proportion. About it were placed on wire artificial Bats, and Owls, continually moving; with many other inventions, the which for brevity's sake I pass by with silence.

Thus much for the place, and now from thence let us come to the persons.

The Maskers' names were these, (whom both for order and honour I mention in the first place)

1. Lord Walden
2. Sir Thomas Howard
3. Sir Henry Carey, Master of the Jewel House
4. Sir Richard Preston } Gentlemen of the
5. Sir John Ashby   } King's Privy Chamber
6. Sir Thomas Jarret, Pentioner
7. Sir John Digby, one of the King's Carvers
8. Sir Thomas Badger, Master of the King's Harriers
9. Master Goringer

Their number Nine, the best and amplest of all numbers, for as in Music seven notes contain all variety, the eighth being in nature the same with the first, so in numbering after the ninth we begin again, the tenth being as it were the Diapason in Arithmetic. The number of 9 is famed by the Muses, and Worthies, and it is of all the most apt for change, and diversity of proportion. The chief habit which the Maskers did use, is set forth to your view in the first leaf: They presented in their feigned persons the Knights of Apollo, who is the father of heat, and youth, and consequently of amorous affections.

The Speakers were in number four.

Flora, the Queen of Flowers, attired in a changeable Taffeta Gown, with a large veil embroidered with flowers, a Crown of flowers, and white buskins painted with flowers.

Zephyrus in a loose robe of sky colored Taffeta, with a mantle of white silk propped with wire, still waving behind him as he moved; on his head he wore a wreath of Palm decked with Primroses and Violets, the hair of his head and beard were flaxen, and his buskins white, and painted with flowers.

Night in a close robe of black silk and gold, a black mantle embroidered with stars, a crown of stars on her head, her hair black and spangled with gold, her face black, her buskins black, and painted with stars; in her hand she bore a black wand wreathed with gold.

Hesperus in a close robe of deep crimson Taffeta mingled with sky color, and over that a large loose robe of a lighter crimson taffeta; on his head he wore a wreathed band of gold, with a star in the front thereof, his hair and beard red, and buskins yellow.

These are the principal persons that bear sway in this invention, others that are but seconders to these, I will describe in their proper places, discoursing the Maske in order as it was performed.

As soon as the King was entered the great Hall, the Hoboys (out of the wood on the top of the hill) entertained the time till his Majesty and his train were placed, and then after a little expectation the consort of ten began to play an Ayre, at the sound whereof the veil on the right was withdrawn, and the ascent of the hill with the bower of Flora were discovered, where Flora and Zephyrus were busily plucking flowers from the Bower, and throwing them into two baskets, which two Silvans held who were attired in changeable Taffeta, with wreaths of flowers on their heads. As soon as the baskets were filled, they came down in this order: first Zephyrus and Flora, then the two Silvans with baskets after them; four Silvans in green Taffeta, and wreaths, two bearing mean Lutes, the third a bass Lute, and the fourth a deep Bandora.

As soon as they came to the descent toward the dancing place, the consort of ten ceased, and the four Silvans played the same Ayre, to which Zephyrus and the two other Silvans did sing these words in a bass, tenor, and treble voice, and going up and down as they sung, they strewed flowers all about the place.

Song.   Now hath Flora robbed her bowers
          to befriend this place with flowers; *etc.*

[The music ceases, and Flora and Zephyrus speak, then the Silvans sing a "song in form of a dialogue."]

This song being ended the whole veil is suddenly drawn, the grove and trees of gold, and the hill with Diana's trees are at once discovered.

Night appears in her house with her 9 hours, apparelled in large robes of black Taffeta, painted thick with stars, their hair long, black, and spangled with gold; on their heads coronets of stars and their faces black; every hour bore in his hand a black torch, painted with stars, and lighted. Night presently descending from her house spake.

NIGHT.   Vanish dark vales, let night in glory shine, *etc.*

[Flora, then Zephyrus both speak, then Night. Hesperus descends during Night's speech and speaks after her, and so on. At the end of the dialogue with Zephyrus, Flora, and Hesperus, Night calls for dancing.]

Thus spoken, the four Silvans played on their instruments the first strain of this song following: and at the repetition thereof the voices fell in with the instruments which were thus divided; a treble and a bass were placed near his Majesty, and another treble and bass near the grove, that the words of the song might be heard of all, because the trees of gold instantly at the first sound of their voices began to move, and dance according to the measure of the time which the musicians kept in singing, and the nature of the words which they delivered.

Song.   Move now with measured sound
          You charmed grove of gold,
          Trace forth the sacred ground
          That shall your forms unfold. *etc.*

This dancing song being ended, the golden trees stood in ranks three by three, and Night ascended up to the grove, and spake thus, touching the first three severally with her wand.

NIGHT.   By virtue of this wand, and touch divine,
          These Silvan shadows back to earth resign, *etc.*

Presently the Silvans with their four instruments, and five voices, began to play and sing together the song following, at the beginning whereof that part of the stage whereon the first three trees stood began to yield, and the three foremost trees gently to sink, and this was effected by an Engine placed under the stage. When the trees had sunk a yard they cleft into three parts, and the Maskers appeared out of the tops of them, the trees were suddenly conveyed away, and the first three Maskers were raised again by the Engine. They appeared then in a false habit, yet very fair, and in form not much unlike their principal, and true robe. It was made of green Taffeta cut into leaves, and laid upon cloth of silver, and their hats were suitable to the same.

Song of trans-   Night, and Diana charge,
formation.   And th' Earth obeys
                        Opening large
                        Her secret ways, *etc.*

When those words were sung, the three maskers made an honour to the King, and so falling back, the other six trees, three by three, came forward, and when they were in their appointed places Night spake again thus:

NIGHT.   Thus can celestials work in human fate,
              Transform, and form as they do love or hate. *etc.*

Night touched the second three trees and . . . the third three trees and the same charm of Night and Diana was sung the third time, the last three trees were transformed, and the Maskers raised. When presently the first Musick began his full *Chorus.*

Again this song revive and sound it high,
Long live Apollo, Britain's glorious eye.

This chorus was in manner of an Echo, seconded by the Cornetts, then by the consort of ten, then by the consort of twelve, and by a double Chorus of voices standing on either side, the one against the other bearing five voices apiece, and sometimes every Chorus was heard severally, sometime mixed, but in the end all together: which kind of harmony so distinguished by the place and by the several nature of instruments, and changeable conveyance of the song, and performed by so many excellent masters, as were actors in that music, (their number in all amounting to forty-two voices and instruments) could not but yield great satisfaction to the hearers.

While this Chorus was repeated twice over, the Nine Maskers in their green habits solemnly descended to the dancing place, in such order as they were to begin their dance; and as soon as the Chorus ended, the violins, or consort of twelve began to play the second new dance, which was taken in form of an Echo by the cornetts, and then catched in like manner by the consort of ten, sometimes they mingled two musics together; sometimes played all at once; which kind of echoing music rarely became their Silvan attire, and was so truly mixed together, that no dance could ever be better graced than that, as (in such distraction of the music) it was performed by the Maskers. After this dance Night descended from the grove, and addressed her speech to the Maskers, as followeth.

> NIGHT.   Phoebus is pleased, and all rejoice to see
> His servants, from their golden prison free. *etc.*

At the end of this speech Night began to lead the way alone, and after her an Hour with his torch, and after the Hour a Masker, and so in order one by one, a torch-bearer and a Masker, they march towards Diana's tree. . . . So through the bower of Flora they came, where they joined two torch-bearers, and two Maskers, and when they passed down to the grove, the Hours parted on either side, and made way between them for the Maskers, who descended to the dancing place in such order as they were to begin their third new dance. All this time of procession the six Cornetts, and six Chapel voices sung a solemn motet of six parts made upon these words.

> With spotless minds now mount we to the tree
> Of single chastity. *etc.*

The motet being ended the Violins began the third new dance, which was lively performed by the Maskers, after which they took forth the Ladies and danced the Measures with them, which being finished the Maskers brought the Ladies back again to their places: and Hesperus with the rest descended from the grove into the dancing place, and spake to the Maskers.

[Hesperus addresses some lines to the bridal pair, Night then calls for a "musical farewell," which is a Dialogue of four voices, two basses and two trebles. At the end the Chorus joins in. Hesperus retires to the grove, and Night calls on Flora to join in departing that "th'eclipsed revels may shine forth again."]

Now the Maskers began their lighter dances as Currantoes, Levoltas and Galliards, wherein when they had spent as much time as they thought fit, Night spake [from the grove] . . .

> . . . with one quick dance sound up your delight,
> And with one song we'll bid you all good-Night.

At the end of these words, the violins began the fourth new dance, which was excellently discharged by the Maskers, and it ended with a light change of music and measure. After the dance followed [a] dialogue of voices, a bass and tenor, sung by a Silvan and an Hour. [At the end of the dialogue a short Chorus followed.]

Сно. Yet ere we vanish from this princely sight,
      Let us bid Phoebus and his states good-night.

This Chorus was performed with several Echoes of music, and voices, in manner as the great Chorus before. At the end whereof the Maskers putting off their visards, and helmets, made a low honour to the King, and attended his Majesty to the banquetting place.

Giovanni Battista Doni (1590–1647) was a versatile man such as the early Renaissance produced: lawyer, classical scholar, critic, and musical theorist. His Florentine father, a patrician, sent him to the best schools for training in classical languages and literatures at Florence, mathematics at Bologna and at Rome, and jurisprudence at Rome and at Bourges in France, where he worked with the famous legal scholar Cujas.

He served under two patrons, Cardinal Ottavio Corsini and Francesco Barberini, in whose trains he traveled widely in Europe, to Paris, to Madrid, and elsewhere, associating with artists, scholars, musicians, and scientists.

He applied himself to the study of musical theory of antiquity, a study that resulted in his invention of the Lira Barberina, a triple lyre with three sets of strings tuned to the Phrygian, the Dorian, and the Lydian modes. He is also said to have substituted the do *for* ut *as the first syllable of the scale,* do *being the first syllable of his last name.*

In 1640 Doni returned to Florence to occupy the Chair of Eloquence at the University. He was soon elected a member of the Accademia della Crusca, a gathering of savants highly regarded in its time; their dictionary of the Italian language is still useful. His works on musical theory and various aspects of music were chiefly concerned with the classic music of antiquity. Doni's writings on ancient music have been outdated by more recent scholarship, but his "Trattato della musica scenica" (Treatise on Music for the Theater), probably written between 1635 and 1639, is still of great importance in the history of early opera. Doni refers to the operas of Peri, Caccini, and Monteverdi and to their music—although he did not greatly admire the recitar cantando *of the Camerata—and he had many opinions about the operatic and theatrical practice in the early seventeenth century. In the following extract Doni sets forth his ideas about the kinds of voices to be used by different theatrical characters.*

SOURCE: *Giovanni Battista Doni, "Trattato della musica scenica," Ch. xxix in* Lyra Barberina *(Rome, 1640), vol. II.*

GIOVANNI BATTISTA DONI

from "Trattato della musica scenica"

About Assigning the Correct Voice and Tone to the Right Personage

By "tone" should not be understood the term used alternately for "mode," called in Greek *armonia*, but that part of the vocal system low or high, about which it can only do good to make a few observations, though they are not necessary for expert composers. When two or more actors appear together, all grown men and of equal condition (let us assume three shepherds), it would not be well to assign to each one the same pitch or tension of the voice. It would be better, since this is heard between men, who speak with great variety, to give to one of them a higher voice level and to another a lower level. For example, to the first a level between F and e, to the second, F and f, to the third, G and g; taking care however that cadences that are contrary by nature (like those of E la mi and F fa ut) do not follow one another immediately, if this is possible. This has been judiciously observed by Peri, who distinguishes the higher voice of Arcetro from the lower one of Tirsi, assigning to the former the clef of C sol fa ut in the middle line, and to the second the clef on the fourth line. So where three young shepherds might be talking, one could be given the voice of a baritone, another a tenor, and the third a contralto, separating the systems by at least a third. In the same way, if there are two nymphs, assign to one the high soprano and to the other, the lower. One may have some doubts as to what to do when deities, celestial spirits, virtues, vices, etc., come into the picture. I will point out one thing, first in talking of real beings, then of pretended and fabulous ones.

When Jesus, our Lord, is introduced both before he died and after he was revived in glory, I would make no difference between them; it seems right to give him the same voice, that is, a fine tenor (which should be smooth and clear, as is the voice of Sig. Francesco Bianchi) because this voice is more suitable than any other to a well-adjusted and perfectly organized body. As for God the Father, who is always presented in the shape of an old man, in my opinion a baritone suits him better than any other voice. To the Angels, who always appear in the shape of youths, according to the age they seem to be, I would give a soprano, more or less high, or even a contralto. As for the celestial and the infernal souls (who rightly have no voices), when they take on an astral or other body appearing as human beings, they should have the same qualities and actions. To the Prince of Demons, because ordinarily he appears in gross and bearded form, it is best to assign a basso profundo, which will suit him better when it is lower than the tuning note, when he sings to the accompaniment of some low instruments with an extravagant sound. To the other demons, according to the form, sex and age they represent, may be assigned different voices, but never sopranos, only some falsettos.

One should take care also when there are many voices that the clearest, most beautiful, and neatest be assigned to the good spirits and the Celestial Deities, and the gloomy, harsh, cracked, and rough ones to the evil spirits and the infernal gods. Saturn, Jove, Neptune, Vulcan, Janus, Hercules, and such fabulous gods should receive deep voices, that is, bass or baritone, with tones even below the tuning note when possible, as the Ancients did. They were also accustomed to assign to the heroes the Hypodorian or Hypophrgyian mode, the first of which was lower than the tuning note by a fourth and the second by a semitone. Mars likewise can be given a bass voice, or a broad and robust tenor.

Mercury, Apollo, Bacchus, and such characters, who usually appear as young men, should be tenors or contraltos unless you would rather assign a falsetto to Mercury, the better to convey his varied and fraudulent nature; in the same way Proteus (by the Latins called Vertumno) is portrayed; it would be a clever trick to have him use different voices, when that is possible.

For the good goddesses one could make differences in the same way —for those who are imagined as more elderly or more virile, a lower tone; as for Cybele, mother of the gods, or Bellona, goddess of War, a contralto; for Juno, Ceres, Minerva, and Venus, lower soprano; for Diana and Prooerpine, higher soprano.

Because the vain pagan gods were thought to have been born in different countries, where they were obstinately worshiped according as the different countries had different systems of music, it would be suitable to assign the different systems to these different gods, for example, the Dorian mode or Hypodorian to Jove of Cretan birth, a province of the Doric nation. But Bacchus would receive the Phrygian, though he was born at Thebes, city in Beoetia of the same Dorians in more ancient times, because he was especially venerated by the Phrygians; and the Greeks sang the music of the sacrifices to Bacchus in this mode. To Minerva the Iastrian or Ionic is appropriate, because the Athenians were of this race, and she was believed to have been born among them.

But much more attention should be paid to the quality and proper use of each mode, such as for Mars, god of War, the Hypophrygian would be suitable; for Venus, the Lydian; for Saturn, the Hypophrygian; for Neptune, the Hypophrygian; and the same process for others, to be left to the judgment of the erudite poet, or the judicious musician. Especially is this true of the gods to whom no birthplace has been assigned, like Fortune, Nemesis, etc. One can be doubtful as to what should be done with the Shades or Souls of the dead, who, according to legend, are introduced by the poets on the stage. From whatever place they may come, whether it be the Elysian Fields, or the Inferno—if they are presented in their usual human form they should be given the same voice as if they were alive. But if only their likenesses covered with a veil are introduced, there would be no difficulty in having them speak in a more subtle voice than their natural one, or by means of some trick their natural voice might be altered so as not to appear to be the voice of a living man; and with this difference, that the Blessed Souls should have (for example) a contralto and the Damned Souls a forced tenor, or some other similar voice, even if the personage of antiquity is of heroic and great stature, such as Polychorus in the *Hecuba* of Euripides, or Tantalus in the *Tieste* of Seneca.

To the Furies of Inferno some persons give a natural soprano, not with good reason in my opinion, because a falsetto would be more suitable, or even a contralto.

It would also be fitting for the Tritons, Nereids, and such gods and monsters of the sea to sing with strange and unusual voices; the Harpies also with shrill voices, and in like manner the other chimerical and fantastic figures of the Ancients.

Also for certain characters one should use a special kind of melody; for instance, one should have the Sirens sing with a special inflection of the voice: *strascini (portamenti)*, trilli, tremoli, passeggetti, and other very artistic ornaments, especially of the genere *Diatonico inspessate dalle corde Chromatici.*

13. On Ballet

Michel Depure (mid-seventeenth century) was in the service of Louis XIV, but nothing seems to be known about him. It appears from the dedication of his book to Louis that he must have held a fairly important post—perhaps intendant *or* sous-intendant *in charge of court entertainments. The king's* privilège *for printing the work refers to Depure as "notre cher et bien aimé M.D.," which would seem to indicate Depure had considerable status.*

Depure's Idées des Spectacles anciens et nouveaux *is a small volume in two parts: the first is an essay on spectacles and games in ancient Greece and Rome; the second is on spectacles and divertissements in the seventeenth century. In the second part Depure discusses the entertainments of his own time, very often pointing out their shortcomings. His views on the use of recitative in the ballet are interesting, and his remarks on the instruments used for the ballet music are informative.*

SOURCE: *Michel Depure,* Idées des Spectacles anciens et nouveaux *(Paris: Michel Brunet, 1668), Pt. II, Ch. XI, sec. 11, Du Ballet; sec. 12, Des Instruments.*

MICHEL DEPURE
from *Idées des Spectacles anciens et nouveaux*

On Récits

Dancers do not think that recitatives are in the least necessary to the ballet, and singers are persuaded that a ballet is imperfect if it lacks a symphony and some recitatives. . . .

The recitative is an ornament foreign to the ballet, but one that fashion has naturalized and made necessary. This taste is not inappropriate to provide relaxation by something that pleases the ear, and it is also the beauty of the spectacle to extend its pleasures to all the senses and to give the spectators as much diversion as they can gain from it. Indeed, the action of the ballet would appear more continuous, or at least the interruption of it is more disguised by the words, or the singers, than by the machines or a thousand other accessories. And it seems that the whole almost could not do without this part. The subject likewise may be rendered more intelligible, provided that he who is occupied with the words understands what he must do.

It is appropriate to know what a *récit* is. In church music or that of the Chapel, there is a singular idea that the silence of the large choir and the use of a single voice, or a very few voices from the small choir, like parts detached from a large mass that sustains them, make considerable *éclat* and display. Therefore the small choir and the most beautiful voices ordinarily are given the *récits* of a section of a motet or hymn or psalm, or of whatever can be sung separately from the large choir.

But with respect to the ballet, the *récit* has another sense. For although it may be sung by a single voice, or accompanied by a very few others, without relation to a large choir, it has not taken its name from the resemblance but rather because the action, of itself mute, and which has taken a vow to remain silent, borrows the voice of the Reciter, so that he may sing that which the dance would not dare to say, and to remove all the obstacles that the dance alone might cause in understanding the subject.

Therefore it is easy to see that the *récit* is only a supplement to truncated, imperfect, and ambiguous expressions of the dance and its steps; for its function is to recite what ought to occur in the actions— either in form of a prologue, or of that which is really happening, or the consequences that could arise if it is employed in the middle or at the end of the ballet.

It is a borrowed spokesman and a kind and courteous interpreter of the mysteries of the plan and the secret of the disguises. But also one can remark that *récits* are defective, and that they sin against their natural duty if they abandon themselves to singing of extravagant things, which do not relate to the subject. The beauty of their singing may cause the ear to excuse them; but there is nothing that may cause good judgment to excuse their extravagances.

. . . Also, singers ordinarily, whether because of a bad habit in their singing, or because of their ambition to show off their beautiful voices, or by their affectation of ornaments, or, finally, in order to follow the beat, will pronounce the words only halfway and do not make the words clear. In this case one can truly say that the *Récit* is not a recitation; that the voices are only organ pipes and concerts of instruments. I cannot stand a singer who mumbles; I would as soon see an actor who stammers, or a lame person who leaps about. Song is only an agreeable way of speaking, invented to add force to words by the pleasantness of the voice and by the pursuit of beautiful and suitable tones. Whoever therefore chews up his words or does not make that which he is singing intelligible acts against what he does, and against the intention of the poet and the demands of the subject.

Of Instruments

Although our principal object is to give all the kinds of instruments that can be used in the ballet, we do not intend to detail all those that could be used. . . .

It is a question of making a choice of the instrument that we judge to be most suitable to make one dance and, what is more, to dance well. The theorbo is suitable only to accompany a voice in concert, or to play Allemandes, Sarabandes, and other pieces where there is more majesty of melody than vigor of the dance. It is the same with the lute. Both are too solemn; and the great number of strings that are touched and the chords that are formed to charm the ear only hinder the feet. These are instruments of repose, designed for serious and tranquil pleasures, whose languishing harmony is enemy of all action and demands only sedentary auditors.

The musette is innocent and rustic; it has remained in favor a long while among shepherds, the echoes of the hills, and the ploughed fields of the hillsides and the plains. But it is too shrill and too coarse for the city manners which have now prevailed, or for the strange delicacy of the people of the court, ignorant or prejudiced.

The Oboe has a higher pitch, and the manner in which it is played at court and in Paris leaves little to be desired. They play just cadences and sweet ornaments and diminutions just as well as the best-trained voices or the most perfect instruments. We have even witnessed their success on the stage and in certain kinds of *entrées*. I have no doubt they will make a wonderful effect in a *Pastourelle*. But one can never be certain of the necessary breath; it fails, the lungs are empty, the abdomen grows tired, and finally one detects a notable difference between the end and the beginnings; there is no longer the right balance.

The organ and the clavecin are the most perfect instruments and are capable of everything; but the first seems consecrated to churches and the latter to dancing rooms, and neither of them is portable enough to be used in the various *divertissements* nor transported easily enough to the places that are used for theatrical performances. As for the harp, there are none among us; and as for the guitar, I can get on without it, and would use it only to ruin my ears or lacerate my insides. May that be said in passing and with no malice.

Generally speaking, only the violin is capable of the French movement, or of responding to the nimbleness of our genius and of sustaining with evenness and accuracy the whole length of a ballet. The pauses that occur successively become imperceptible, and of the three violins that may be playing, one who is resting can do it without any effect upon the harmony, or at least without affecting the harmony, while people are dancing. Discords are soon adjusted and the reasonable size of the *Dessus*, since it does less violence to the strings, keeps them in tune longer and makes them easier to adjust.

So I conclude absolutely in favor of the violins. They must be well chosen, however, work together, and be sensible. For when the hand has no guide, or when caprice directs it, immediately ability is ruined and disappears, and a thousand capricious and wild strokes of the bow cause forced ornaments and cause the dancer to make unforeseen mistakes, or to be thrown completely out of time. The poet or the person who is directing the ballet must take care to have the ballet music played note for note without allowing any variation or arpeggiations, for then there is no dancing. For when the *Entrée* has begun, the glory of the violin is henceforth to play exactly according to measure and movement, without adding passagework or diminutions, for you could not add or subtract a beat cleverly enough not to interrupt the time of the dancer, and without the missed beat causing a great indignation among those people who have the best ears for music. There are certain incorrigibles, dazzled by the velocity of their own fingers, who no longer care about the feet of the dancers nor the steps of the ballet. This should be one of the principal cares of the manager or the director, who should never relax in favor of a clever hand or a pretence of skill [on the part of the violinist].

Part IV The Eighteenth and Early Nineteenth Centuries

14. Instructions for Playing the Clavecin

Michel de Saint-Lambert lived and worked in Paris during the last half of the seventeenth century and into the first part of the eighteenth; his exact dates are not known. Further, nothing is known of his life except that he was a clavecinist and teacher of the clavecin and wrote two important didactic works. Traité de l'accompagnement du clavecin, de l'orgue, et de quelques autres instruments, *1680, is now lost. It was republished, presumably with additions, in 1707 as* Nouveau traité de l'accompagnement. *. . . More important was Saint-Lambert's general work on playing the clavecin, which appeared in 1702,* Principes du Clavecin. *. . . This book shows the author to have been a very able performer and teacher, who developed a good and very modern method of teaching. In his* Principes *he sets forth the basic rules of music, and his method of playing is practically and clearly explained. Of particular importance and interest is his chapter on ornaments, in which he gives those of the three leading French master clavecinists—Chambonnières, d'Anglebert, and Le Bègue—along with his own set of ornaments.*

An extract from the chapter on the Position of the Fingers and one from that on Ornaments are exemplary of his clear and careful instruction.

Source: *Michel de Saint-Lambert,* Les Principes du Clavecin, contenant une Explication exacte de tout ce qui concerne la tablature et le Clavier. Avec les remarques nécessaire pour l'intelligence de plusieurs difficultés de la Musique *(Paris, 1702), preface, Ch. XIX, XX, XXI, XXVII, XXVIII.*

MICHEL DE SAINT-LAMBERT
from *Les Principes du Clavecin*

NOTE TO THE READER

People who want to learn to play the clavecin must have two principal aptitudes to succeed. These aptitudes are Ear and Hand. "Ear" consists in hearing the different tones in music and the different rhythms in the tunes with all imaginable accuracy. Though this at first sight may appear a large order, it is nevertheless sure that this extreme accuracy in intonation and rhythm is a gift given to almost all men, like sight and speech. There are very few who do not sing and dance naturally; if it is not with the delicacy and correctness that Art has sought, it is at least with the correctness which Art dictates and which Art itself has derived from Nature. It is already a great asset for those who want to learn music or to play some instrument that they know they have discernment of the ear by nature, that is to say, the first and most important of these aptitudes. But if they wish to assure themselves further, let them try the experiments I am going to teach them. Let them see if when they hear a fine piece of music they enter into all the movements it attempts to inspire; if they are moved by the touching passages, and are aroused by the gay passages; if they sing to themselves what they hear other people singing; if it does not seem to them that had they been taught they could do just as well without difficulty. For if the thing appears easy to them, it is a mark that they might succeed; but if it appears surprising and difficult, they would do well to renounce it. Let them see if they enjoy the melody and the harmony of the pieces; if they feel the rhythms of the Airs; if they feel brought, in spite of themselves, to follow the measure; if they without thinking beat it with their head or otherwise: these are the true dispositions that make the musician, and without which they work in vain to become one.

In regard to the disposition of the hand, there is no one who cannot develop it if he begins early to practice. This disposition being nothing other than a great suppleness in the nerves that allows the fingers to move subtly, childhood is the best time to acquire it. It is an established fact that those who began in their childhood have become expert and that those who started later have not succeeded. One cannot tell precisely the age beyond which it is no longer time to begin, because abilities differ in different people. However, one can say in respect to ladies that because of the natural delicacy of their sex, they still have better aptitude in their hands at the age of thirty than men have at fifteen or sixteen; but the best time for both is early childhood, that is, before ten years of age, and even at five or six.

People who possess both the aptitudes must take care of another thing; it is to choose a good teacher. Upon this choice as much as upon his aptitudes depends the success of a pupil's studies. One person who would have become skillful if he had been well trained, remained ignorant because his teacher was ignorant; another person profited greatly, though with less natural talent, because his teacher had been able to teach him to make good use of the small talent he possessed.

A teacher to be good must have two qualities: *knowledge* and *probity*; because to make a good pupil the master must absolutely have two rules: *he can* and *he will*.

By the "knowledge" of a teacher is not meant simply that he is a very expert player on the clavecin and an excellent composer of music; it must be demonstrated that he joins to those two advantages the talent of expounding clearly, which is a quality completely apart from that of being a celebrated musician.

A good teacher knows to the bottom the abilities of those who put themselves in his hands, and accommodating himself to the range and capacity of each of them, he teaches each in the way that suits their talent. He devises as many methods as he has different talents to bring along. He speaks childishly to children, reasonably to reasonable persons: to both he speaks intelligently and tersely. He expounds his principles in an orderly way and always presents them as simple and separate ideas. He does not embarrass the memory of those he is teaching with useless fine distinctions. He teaches a general rule as if it had no exceptions, waiting for the time when this exception arises to talk about it, because he knows that it is better understood at this point, and he knows that if he had talked about it earlier it would have confused the general rule. He gives his first rule as if it were the only one he would ever have to talk about, and when he passes to the second he never mentions those which are about to follow.

Passing from theory to practice, the good teacher is able to choose for each pupil the pieces best suited to the abilities of their hands. He even composes some expressly for those who may need them. But after having given some easy piece to his pupils to assure them at the beginning, he then gives them some that are directly opposed to the abilities of their hands in order to correct the faults.

The good teacher brings far along the road to perfection the scholar who has much facility in this practice and even further the one who has more facility. He causes the male and female scholars who may have more talent than he has to play better than he does. And because he knows that one cannot profit unless one really likes playing, he has a special secret to cause his pupils to like learning. This talent is the most necessary when he has children to teach, for the natural fickleness of young children often, after having desired ardently to play the clavecin, makes them take a distaste for it after the third or fourth lesson because of the difficulty they have found; and their distaste goes so far at times that an exercise which is really a game and should really be learned as a game becomes for them a cause for sadness and tears. So it is up to the teacher to relieve his young pupils of the difficulties that annoy them and to act so that they give themselves over to their exercises, if not with pleasure at least with courage and perserverance.

After having talked about the good qualities of the clavecin teacher a word must be said about the faults he may have.

Leaving aside the dishonesty of not showing conscientiously what he really knows, a piece of cowardice that I cannot imagine any teacher whatever having, I know no greater fault in a clavecin teacher than that of not knowing how to position the hand of his pupils to allow them to make use of the fingers. The bad principles and the false rules he may teach are errors easy to correct when they are recognized, but the fault of using the fingers wrongly is the one that is the most difficult to correct when it is once acquired; it remains sometimes during a whole lifetime, as it were, an eternal obstacle to the perfection of playing. Since this fault never comes except from the teacher who started us off, it is important to choose one who knows how to avoid it.

But this fault is scarcely to be feared by people who learn in Paris, where there are now such clever teachers of the clavecin that I must admit without flattering them that it is they who gave me the idea of the perfect teacher I have described in this discourse.

The Position of the Fingers

There is nothing more free in playing the clavecin than the position of the fingers. Each player should see only convenience and grace. But since there are times when everyone who plays uses his fingers in the same manner, because that has been recognized as the best, a sort of rule has been established that one is almost obliged to follow, and that at least the beginners cannot afford to do without.

This rule regards less the passages where the hand must play only one note at a time than those where it must play several.

Several notes to be played at the same time by one hand, in terms of the clavecin, are called a chord. There are chords of two, three, and four notes. A chord of two notes may be a third, a fourth, a fifth, a sixth, or an octave. One calls a third a chord of the extent of three degrees, a fourth, that which extends over four degrees; a fifth, one that goes as far as five, and so forth, as the following examples will explain.

A chord of three notes may be composed of two thirds, or of a third and a fourth or of a fifth and a fourth.

A chord of four notes is ordinarily composed of two thirds and a fourth, sometimes it is of three thirds, but more rarely. Chords are used preferably in the bass than in the treble, but in the right hand they are not played with the same fingers as those of the left hand.

In both hands, in clavecin terms, the thumb is the first finger. The one after that is the second finger, the middle finger is the third, the following one the fourth, and the little finger the fifth. [Ex. 1 is an] example or demonstration of the nature of chords, and of the fingers to be used in playing them.

1a

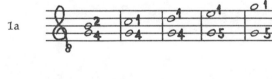

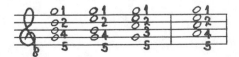

1b

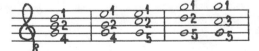

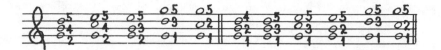

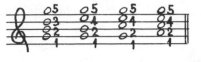

Ex. 1

When there is an accidental, that is a sharp or a flat, to the top note of some chords of the left hand, and to the bottom notes of some others of the right hand, that changes the position of the fingers.

Ex. 2

But when the high note and the low note of the chords each have an accidental, they are played in the way we have already taught, that is to say, as if there were no accidentals.

When there are accidentals in the middle of chords, that does not change the position of the fingers either.

There are passages which are not chords, but which become chords because of the way the notes are arranged, and by the rule that you must hold some of them until others are played, as was taught in the chapter on Liaisons. On these occasions, the position of the fingers is the same as the others.

3a

3b

Ex. 3

I shall not multiply these examples further; that would be useless. Common sense is sufficient to recognize such passages when they appear in compositions, and to understand that they may exist in as many different ways as there are different kinds of chords.

As for the passages where the hand has to play only one note at a time, there is only one instance in which the fingers must observe a rule. That is when there are many successive and uninterrupted steps. Then one uses the fingers as they are indicated in the following example.

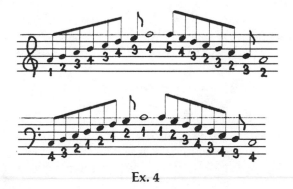

Ex. 4

On every other occasion one uses his fingers as he judges best. Good or bad, according as one has judgment and taste in this matter. Convenience of the player is the first rule to follow, and grace is the second. This consists in holding the hands straight on the keyboard; that is, leaning neither inward nor outward, the fingers bent and arranged on the same level as the elbow, which depends on the seat one uses; not raising the fingers too high when you play, and also not pressing too hard on the keys.

On Adornments in General

If the choice of the fingers is arbitrary in playing the clavecin, that of adornment is no less so. Good taste is the only rule to be followed. There are ornaments that are essential in the music and that it would be hard to do without. The most important of these is the trill; the others are the mordant, the arpeggio, and the falling tone. But though those we shall talk about later are not so necessary nor so much used, they lend much grace to compositions and one would be wrong to neglect them.

Chapter XXI

The trill is the agitation of two notes, struck alternately, as equally and as rapidly as you can. It is marked in the tablature with a figure made like this ₩, which is placed above or below the note that is to be trilled, as is shown in the following example [Ex. 5]. The figure which marks the trill is called trill also, just as all the other figures which indicate the various ornaments have the names of the ornaments they designate.

Since the trill is the striking of two notes or keys alternately, one must always use a second note to play it, since it is always marked on one note only. The note one borrows is always the neighboring one higher than the one marked with the sign. For example, if it is the note *ut* that is marked, borrow the note *re*, and strike alternately and rapidly the two keys *re* and *ut*.

The trill is begun with the borrowed note and ends with the marked one.

As the keys to be struck are neighboring, so the striking fingers are neighboring.

The fingers used in the trill are, for the right hand, the third and the second, or the fourth and the third; and for the left hand the first and the second or the second and the third.

Persons who are beginning have more trouble playing the trill with the fourth and third fingers, than with the third and second of the right hand. In the same way, with the left hand they play it better with the second and third than with the first and second, and for this reason they ordinarily neglect the fingers that give them trouble and use only the ones that they can move easily. But one should exercise both equally, because there are occasions when one is obliged to play trills with different fingers, just as there are others where one can do without them. However, we will not talk about these occasions at this point, since our method cannot predetermine them exactly, and since only common sense can make the judgment.

The length of the note upon which the trill is marked determines its length. It is longer on a whole note than on a half note, longer on a half note than on a quarter note, etc.

When the trill is to be long, it is more beautiful to start it slowly at first, and only increase the speed toward the end; and when it is short, it should always be rapid.

The fingers that play the trill should not remain on the two notes they have played. The one on the borrowed note should remain in the air, and the one on the main note should remain on it as long as the value allows it. *I use the words "note" and "key" equally to indicate the same thing, when I speak of ornaments.*

Ex. 5

When with a trilled note there are other notes to be played, either in the hand that is making the trill or in the other hand, one must strike those other notes exactly when one begins the trill, that is, as soon as one touches the borrowed note for the first time.

Ex. 6

When a note marked with a trill is preceded or followed in the score by a note one degree higher, accompanied by an accidental, either a sharp or a flat, you must borrow on the clavier the neighboring accidental, going upward from the one that is marked [Ex. 7].

Ex. 7

Although there may be a note or two between the note dominated by an accidental and the trill, which follows or precedes it a degree lower [Ex. 8 A, B, C, D], one still uses the accidental to make the trill, because the ear could not endure it without the accidental a moment after having heard it or a moment before starting it.

Ex. 8

One can play the trill with a sharp or a flat independently of what precedes or follows if the figure that marks it is accompanied by an accidental.

Ex. 9

It is rare that the figures which indicate a trill have above them an accidental, but when that occurs it is more often a flat than a sharp. . . .

So that the reader can clear his mind of all that has just been said about the trill, I am going to sum up the substance in two rules which will include everything that can be taught about them.

1. The trill, as regards the borrowed notes, is regulated by the next note higher. If by the laws of the key this note is a sharp, the trill is made with a sharp. If it is a flat, it is made with a flat, and if it is a natural it is made with a natural note. This is the great and infallible rule of the trill. The second is no less important, though it is only an exception to the first general rule.

2. On any occasion whatsoever in pieces transposed by flats or by sharps, or where there is no transposition, the trill in respect to the borrowed note is always governed by the nature of the note which precedes or follows in the tablature, provided that the note which follows or precedes is one degree higher than the note to be trilled.

It is sufficient to understand these two rules to know everything about trills; but remember that the first is the general rule and the second is the special rule and the exception to the general rule. . . .

The other ornaments are made like the trill, by adding to the note indicated for it, other notes that are not given in the tablature. So it will be enough to mark here all the signs which designate the ornaments and to explain with the aid of notes how they must be played. But before starting this enumeration I will speak first about the different kinds of trills that one can make.

M. d'Anglebert distinguished five, which are explained together with the other ornaments he has invented in the book of pieces he has published. I have collected here all these ornaments, as well as those of other teachers who have had their works engraved. Here are the five trills of M. d'Anglebert: the simple trill, which is the one whose rules I gave at the beginning of this chapter; the supported or leaning trill (*tremblement appuyé*), which consists in playing the borrowed note once, to make it sound before beginning the trill; he calls the third and fourth *Cadence*, and gives to the fifth the name of "trill and mordent" at the same time.

Ex. 10

M. Nivers mentions three different trills. He names the first an orna-ment (*agrément*), the second *cadence*, and the third *double cadence*.

The trill which M. Nivers calls "agrément" is the same thing the other masters call "mordent," as will be seen from what follows, except that he begins with the borrowed note and the others begin with the essential note.

What he calls "double cadence" is the same ornament M. d'Anglebert calls "trill and mordent." So there is no difference between the orna-ments of these two teachers except the names and the way of noting them on paper.

Ex. 11

M. de Chambonnières and M. Le Bègue know only one kind of trill, which is the one we first discussed and which M. d'Anglebert calls "simple." They both mark the figure.

On the Détaché

The last ornament M. d'Anglebert refers to is the *détaché*. It occurs before a trill or a mordent and consists in giving a small silence be-tween the trill or mordent and the note that precedes them, which is done by diminishing the length of the preceding note.

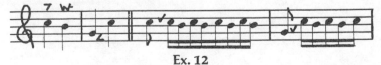

Ex. 12

The practice of the separation is very necessary in certain pieces with a lively movement, particularly when the note preceding the trill is a step higher and the one that precedes the mordent a step lower. It is not inapplicable in other pieces and on other occasions, but it is a matter of taste to judge the places where it must be used.

On the Aspiration

To this last ornament I would add another, which I call *aspiration,* which consists in playing very rapidly one note that one borrows only once. It is noted and played in this manner.

Ex. 13

The mark for *aspiration* is always put after the note to be aspirated. When this mark has the point up ∧ , one borrows from the next note above, as for the trill; when the point is down ∨, from the next note below, as for the mordent. The example shows this.

There you have the ornaments in use among those persons who play the clavecin best.

After having learned to recognize them here, one should practice them every time one feels they are suitable, for, as I have said many times, one is entirely free in his choice of ornaments, and in the pieces you study you can play them in places where they are not marked, if you find they are not suitable in the music, and add others at your pleasure.

You can even, if you want, neglect all those that I have indicated here (except only the essential ones) and make up new ones according to your taste, if you think you are able to invent better ones; but you must be on your guard and not take too many liberties in this regard, especially at the start, for fear that when you want to embellish too soon you will spoil what you are trying to embellish. That is why it is well and even necessary to use embellishments devised by other people at the beginning and to play them only in pieces where they are marked until the time you feel you can judge without making a mistake. You should be convinced, whatever talent you have for the clavecin, that if you have studied only six months, you cannot discern what lends grace to the playing as well as those who have practiced the art for twenty or thirty years, and so have acquired by long experience a surer knowledge of what may embellish their art. . . .

The ornaments should never alter the melody nor the pace of the piece. Thus in the pieces with gay movements the runs and arpeggios should go faster than in slow movements. You must never hurry in making an ornament, however fast it should be played. You must take your time, prepare your fingers, then execute it boldly and freely.

But all this, nor anything I could say in addition, will never make you understand a thing of which good taste alone is the arbiter. It is important however to know how to play the ornaments well, for without that, they would disfigure the pieces instead of increasing their beauty, and it would be better not to do them at all, than to do them badly.

François Couperin ("le Grand") (1668–1733) was the most brilliant and famous of an outstanding family of musicians. He was the son of Charles Couperin, violinist, organist, and composer, and nephew of Louis Couperin, the well-known clavecinist. François—organist, clavecinist, composer, and teacher—became organist at St. Gervais in 1685, where he became renowned for his motets, masses, and other church music. In 1692 he published his first set of Sonatas for Violin in the Italian style. In 1693 Louis XIV appointed him as one of the four organists serving the Chapel Royal, and in 1694 Couperin became Maître de Clavecin *to the royal children. The king ennobled Couperin in 1696, and a few years later he was made Chevalier of the Lateran order. Couperin's position at court during the early years of the eighteenth century is not entirely clear; d'Anglebert the younger still held the position of* Ordinaire de la musique, *but as his health and eyesight were failing, it would appear that Couperin was actually in charge of the court music from 1700 on.*

Couperin's musical output is varied: church music, chamber music, music for court functions, organ pieces, and, chiefly, harpsichord compositions. His L'Art de toucher le Clavecin, *published in 1717, is his one didactic work. Although somewhat poorly organized, it is one of the most important treatises on the playing and interpretation of French music of the period. The following extracts deal with the position of the player at the keyboard, fingering, and ornaments.*

SOURCE: *François Couperin, L'art de toucher le Clavecin (Paris, 1717); in Oeuvres complètes, Vol. I, ed. P. Brunold (Paris: L'Oiseau Lyre, 1930), pp.14–16, 22–23.*

FRANÇOIS COUPERIN
from *L'Art de toucher le Clavecin*

Plan of This Method

The position of the body, of the hands, the ornaments used in performing, some little preliminary exercises, and essentials for enabling one to play well, some remarks on good fingering, relative to many places in my two books of pieces, eight preludes of different kinds, proportionate to the progress I think one ought to make, in which the fingering is noted and some remarks are added about playing with taste, are the parts of this work. . . .

The proper age for children to begin [study of the harpsichord] is six or seven years old; this however should not exclude persons of more advanced age. But, naturally, to mold and form the hands to play the harpsichord the earlier the better; and as gracefulness is necessary, one must begin with the position of the body.

In order to be seated at the proper height, the underside of the elbows, the wrists, and the fingers should be on the same level; therefore one should have a chair that will agree with this rule.

One should put something additional, more or less high, under the feet of young people as they continue to grow, so that their feet do not dangle in the air and that their bodies may be maintained in proper balance.

The distance an adult should be seated from the keyboard is about nine inches, measured from the waist; this should be less in proportion for young people.

The center of the body and that of the keyboard should correspond.

One should turn the body slightly to the right when seated at the harpsichord, with the knees not too close together. The feet should be side by side, with the right foot well advanced.

In regard to making grimaces, one may correct this habit by putting a mirror on the music rack of the spinet or harpsichord.

If a person holds the wrist too high in playing, the only remedy that I have found is to have someone hold a little flexible wand, which is passed over the defective wrist and under the other wrist. If the defect is the reverse, one will do the contrary. This wand must absolutely not constrain the person who is playing. This defect can be corrected little by little, and this invention has been very useful to me.

It is better and more seemly not to beat time with the head, the body, or the feet. One should have an easy posture at the keyboard, not gazing fixedly at any one object nor looking about vaguely; rather, look at the audience, if there is one, as if one were not concerned with anything else. This advice is only for those who play without the aid of their books.

For very young persons one should use at first only a spinet, or a single keyboard of the harpsichord, and the one or the other should be very lightly quilled. This point is of infinite importance, fine execution depending more on suppleness and great freedom of the fingers than on force; for if from the beginning one allows the child to play on two claviers he will of necessity stretch his little hands to make the keys sound, and from that comes badly placed hands and hardness of touch in playing.

Delicacy of touch depends alone on holding the fingers as close to the keys as possible. It is reasonable to believe (aside from experience) that a hand that falls from above gives a harder stroke than if it touches the keys from quite close; and that the quill draws a harder sound from the string.

It is better, during the first lessons given to children, to advise them not to practice in the absence of their teacher. Children are too readily distracted to force themselves to hold their hands in the position prescribed for them. For my part, in the earliest lessons given to children, I take away the key to the instrument on which I have been teaching them, so that during my absence they cannot destroy in one moment all that I have carefully taught them in three-quarters of an hour.

Apart from the most used graces, such as shakes, mordents, appoggiaturas, etc., I have always made my pupils do little finger exercises, such as passages or different kinds of arpeggios, beginning with the simplest and in the easiest keys; and gradually I have brought them to the greatest dexterity and the most difficult keys. These little exercises, which cannot be too often repeated, likewise provide material ready to put in place and can serve on many occasions.

Persons who begin late, or who have been badly taught should be careful, as the tendons may be hardened or may have taken on bad habits; they should be cleared up, or have someone loosen their fingers before sitting down at the harpsichord: this is to say, they should pull or have someone pull their fingers in all directions. That will also set their minds to work and they will find greater freedom. . . .

Graces Used in Playing

It is the value of the notes that, in general, should determine the length of the double mordent, the double *ports-de-voix* (appoggiaturas), and the shakes.

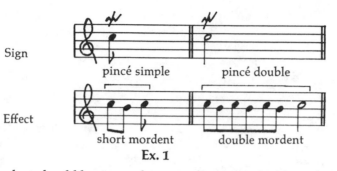

Sign   pincé simple   pincé double

Effect   short mordent   double mordent

Ex. 1

Each mordent should begin on the note where it is placed; and in order to make myself clear, I use the term *point d'arrêt* (stopping point), which is marked by a small star: thus the repercussions and the note where one stops should all be included in the value of the principal note.

double mordent

Ex. 2

The double mordent, in playing the organ and the harpsichord, takes the place of the *martèlement* (tremolo) in the stringed instruments. . . .

The *port-de-voix*, being composed of two notes of value and a little "lost note," I have found that there are two ways of fingering, one of which, in my opinion, is preferable to the other.

The notes of value of the *ports-de-voix* are marked by a little x in the following examples.

First progression   new style   old style   Third progression

Second progression   Fourth progression

Ex. 3

Reasons for Preferring the New Style in Ports-de-voix

The finger marked 3 in the third progression and that marked 4 in the fourth, being obliged to leave the last eighth note of value, where there is a little x, in order to restrike the little lost note, permit less legato than the first progression, where the finger marked 3 is preferably replaced by the second finger, and in the second progression by the finger marked 4; this is also replaced by the finger marked 3. I have found that, without seeing the hands of the person who is playing, I can distinguish whether the two notes in question have been made by the same fingers or by two different fingers. My students hear it as I do; from that I conclude there is some truth in it, which I relate to the majority of opinions.

The little lost note of a *port-de-voix,* or *coulé* (descending appoggiatura) strikes with the harmony; that is, in the time that one should strike the note of value which follows it.

The most used shakes are made in the right hand by the third finger with the second, and the fourth with the third. Those of the left hand use the thumb and the second finger, and the second and third.

Although the shakes are marked as being equal in the table of ornaments in my first book, they should nevertheless begin slower than they finish; but this gradation should be imperceptible.

On any note where a shake is marked, one must always begin on the note or on the half-step above.

The shakes of considerable length include three parts, which in their execution appear to be a single thing: 1. The stress *(appuy),* which should be made on the note above the essential one. 2. The beats. 3. The stopping point.

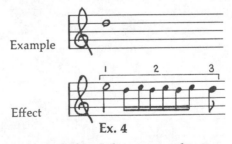

Example

Effect

Ex. 4

In regard to other shakes, they are arbitrary. Some have the opening stressed note, others so short that they have neither stress nor stopping point. One can even make them aspirated (cut extremely short).

Jean Philippe Rameau (1683–1764) was a French theorist, organist, harpsichordist, and composer. His father was an organist in Dijon, and Rameau received instruction in the keyboard instruments and musical theory as a child. After his early training he spent some time in Italy, but he seems not to have been influenced by Italian music. In 1705 he went to Paris, unknown, and in 1706 he published his first book of clavecin pieces. Not being able to establish himself there, he returned to Dijon in 1708 and became organist of the church in which his father had served. From there he moved to Clermont-Ferrand in 1715. Returning to Paris in 1722, he published his Traité de l'harmonie, *on which he had worked during his seven years in Clermont-Ferrand. In 1724 he published his second book of clavecin pieces, which established his reputation. His fortunes improved further after he became associated with La Riche de la Pouplinière, a high official, and at that time he turned to opera, in which he had considerable success. During this period he wrote a* Nouvelle Suite de pièces de Clavecin, *the preface of which was devoted largely to a discussion of a problem in music theory. In 1741 Rameau published his single collection of chamber music works, five suites for harpsichord and two melody instruments.*

While Rameau is best known for his Traité de l'harmonie *and his theatrical works, his compositions for harpsichord are not inconsiderable. There are many features in them that are quite progressive, and his approach to playing is a modern one, leading to a sound technique. The* Pièces de clavecin *of 1724 contains an important little treatise on "The Technique of Playing the Harpsichord" as well as many of Rameau's finest compositions for that instrument. The treatise, here translated, explains Rameau's method of training the fingers and is profitable even today in forming finger technique on keyboard instruments of any kind.*

Rameau's explanations are clear and to the point. The words roulement *and* batterie *do not, however, correspond to any specific terms in English.* Roulement *means very rapid legato playing of connected notes or scale passages; whereas* batterie *always indicates notes that are disjunct.* Roulement *may also mean an arpeggio as well as scale passages, as Rameau indicates in* Les Tourbillons. Batterie *can also mean the hands crossing over one another, and sometimes alternating notes in each hand ("like that of two drumsticks"), as in* The Cyclops.

SOURCE: *Jean Phillippe Rameau,* Pièces de clavessin *avec une méthode pour la mécanique des doigts, ou l'on enseigne les moyens de se procurer une parfaite exécution sur cet instrument, et avec une table pour les agréments (Paris, 1724; 1731), preface.*

JEAN PHILIPPE RAMEAU
from *Pièces de clavecin*

The Technique of Playing the Harpsichord

Perfection of playing the harpsichord consists chiefly in a well-controlled movement of the fingers.

The movement can be acquired by simple mechanics, but one must know how to do it.

This technique is nothing but a frequent use of a regular movement; the aptitudes it demands are natural to everyone; it is like those one needs to walk, or if you prefer, to run.

The faculty of walking or running comes from the suppleness of the leg muscles; that of playing the clavecin depends on the suppleness of the fingers at their base.

The continual exercise of walking makes the movement of the leg almost equally free for everybody. On the contrary, the little exercise we have of the movement of the fingers necessary in playing the clavecin does not allow them to develop freely; besides, our special habits cause the fingers to acquire habits so contrary to those the clavecin demands, that this liberty is constantly balked; it even develops obstacles in the natural talents for music which we think we possess; however little appreciative we may be to the effects of this art, we try to express what we feel, and this can be only by a certain constraint injurious to the performance. All the measures we ought to take to acquire suppleness are denied to us by the impression our senses have received; and because we have not been able to reconcile the performance with the rapidity of our imagination, we become convinced that it is Nature that has refused to us what we have taken from ourselves by bad habits.

It is certainly true that aptitudes are better in some people than in others; nevertheless as long as no perceptible incapacity affects the natural movement of the fingers, it depends entirely on ourselves to use them in the way they are intended to be used; and that to a degree quite sufficient to be pleasing. I dare to say that assiduous and well-conducted work, that the necessary pains and a little time, will inevitably loosen the least adaptable fingers.

I will admit however that what presupposed much practice to many people may perhaps be only a lucky chance in others; but who would dare wait for the natural aptitudes? How can one hope to discover them without having gone through the work necessary to reach the point of making the test? And to what can one attribute the success that is attained if it is not to the work itself?

The result of all these remarks is that frequent and well-planned practice is the infallible cause of perfect playing on the clavecin; and it is from that fact that I have devised a special method to renew in the fingers that movement with which Nature has endowed them and to increase their liberty.

This method is the simple mechanics of which I have already spoken; I am about to propose the laws, and I think that one can scarcely avoid following them exactly and by degrees; for in addition to the fact that they will be found to be based on reason, recent experiment has assured me of their efficacy.

The numbers 1, 2, 3, 4, 5 will designate the fingers about which I wish to speak and which must be used in those places where they are joined to the notes; so that 1 will designate the thumb, 5 the little finger, and 2, 3, 4 the other fingers in the same way.

First, one must take a seat before the clavecin so that the elbows are raised higher than the keyboard and the hand can fall upon the keyboard by the natural movement of the joints of the hand.

This is so that the hand may drop of itself on the keyboard and that the elbows should be above its level and never too high; and they are never too high as soon as 1 and 5 can be placed on the end of the keys.

At the same time that 1 and 5 are placed on the end of the keys, the elbows must fall nonchalantly to the player's side in their natural position, a position which one should note carefully and from which one should move only when absolutely necessary, as when one is obliged to move the hand from one end of the keyboard to the other.

The natural position of the elbows, together with correct placement of 1 and 5, gives the correct position where every person, of any height, should be placed at the clavecin, and it only remains to put the bench in the right place.

Since the 1st and 5th fingers are placed on the edge of the keys, the other fingers must be bent so they may also be on the ends of the keys; but if you allow the hand to fall, as has been said, the fingers curve naturally to the right place; after this one should never straighten them nor curve them any more, except in certain cases where nothing better can be done.

The joints of the wrist should always be supple: this suppleness, which then extends to the whole hand, gives them all the freedom and all the necessary lightness; and the hand, which is now dead, so to speak, is used only to support the fingers which are attached to it and to convey them to the places on the keyboard which they could not reach by the movement they are fitted for.

The movement of the fingers begins at their base, that is to say at the joint by which they are attached to the hand, and never anywhere else; that of the hand begins at the joining with the wrist; that of the arm, supposing it is neccessary, starts at the elbow joint.

The greater movement should occur only when a lesser one does not suffice, and even when a finger can reach a key without moving the hand but only by extending it or opening it, one must take good care not to make too many more movements than are necessary.

Each finger must have its own special movement independent of all others, so that even when one is required to move the hand to a certain place on the keyboard, the finger one is using at that moment must fall on the keys and not strike them; also they must, so to speak, flow from one to another successively, which ought to warn about the gentleness with which one ought to go about beginning.

Now you must arrange the five fingers of the hand on the five notes of consecutive keys; there is an example of this in the first lesson, in the first illustration that follows this chapter.

When the five fingers are arranged on the five notes, presupposing that the hand is placed as we have said, you press with number 1 or number 5 the key on which it is resting, without any other finger nor the whole hand making the slightest movement.

From the fingers with which you have begun, proceed to their neighbors, and so from one to another, making certain that the finger that has just pressed a note leaves it at the instant that its neighbor presses another; for raising one finger and pressing with another should be performed at the same instant.

Remember to move each finger with its own special movement, and observe that the finger that leaves one key to press another should be close enough to it so as to seem to touch it.

Do not weigh down the touch on the keys with the weight of the hand; it should be just the contrary. Your hand, by supporting your fingers makes their touch lighter; this has important results. Observe an evenness of movement between the fingers, and especially never hurry your movements, for lightness and speed are acquired only by this evenness of movement, and often because of too much hurrying one loses what one is seeking.

One must try to acquire the movement necessary for the fingers and give to each one its own physical movement before testing their strength; so that what I propose is to put them at first on the keyboard only to make the distance from one to the other proportionate to that of the keys of the clavier. But since at first one has difficulty in making them move separately, the difficulty one has in making them press the keys might be capable of destroying that perfection which should exist in their movement. One must take good care that the resistance of the keys does not affect the movement of the fingers, and so the clavecin on which one practices should not be too soft; but as the fingers grow stronger in their movements, one can oppose a less soft keyboard so as to reach gradually the ability to press down the hardest keys.

The lesson is practiced at first by each hand separately, and when one feels that he can control his fingers separately in conformity with the preceding explanations, one can practice both hands together. You must start one hand before the other by as many notes as you wish, sometimes more, sometimes less, so that it can be done in all possible ways, until one knows that the hands have acquired such good habits that they will not spoil the passages. This is not acquired in one day, but it shortens immensely the period of study needed to reach the desirable point of perfection.

This lesson, though very simple, leads gradually to the most perfect playing on the clavecin. First of all, you must make the hand accustomed to supporting the fingers; make the distance between them the same as that between the keys; one acquires a different movement for each of them; one grows accustomed to raising one while another is lowered; their weight and their movement become equal to each other after a certain time; the equal and contrary motion of the two hands is acquired also; finally, however attentive a teacher may be to having all these remarks observed in other passages and in the ornaments, one must practice after this lesson; [by these means] it is almost certain, to speak in general, that one can scarcely fail to attain good execution.

Without knowing any more than what is given in this lesson, one can learn the little menuet which is on the same Plate, taking care to mark the fingering and to omit the ornaments.

When one plays the notes of this lesson quickly, that is called a *roulement*, and if the notes of this lesson were separated, that would be called a *batterie*. To continue a *roulement* more extended than those in this lesson, one has only to accustom one's self to passing finger 1 under any other finger, and passing one of the other fingers over number 1. This manner is excellent especially when there are sharps and flats to play; it facilitates the execution of certain *batteries*, an example of which is in the following illustration.

Observe that the finger which passes over or under another reaches by its own movement the key which you want to play at that time.

As much as possible avoid touching a sharp or a flat with finger number 1, especially in the *roulements*, and make sure that finger number 1 falls on the key that precedes this sharp or flat, because that can facilitate your execution. Often one plays a single *roulement* with both hands, the fingers of which follow one another consecutively. An example is to be found in the piece called *Tourbillons*, where the letter D indicates the right hand [main droite] and the letter G the left hand [main gauche].

In this kind of *roulements* [arpeggios and scales] the hands pass one over the other, but you must be certain that the sound of the first note over which one hand passes should be just as much joined to the preceding note as if they were played by the fingers of the same hand. Here the fingers follow the order of the lesson, and no. 5 should be used as little as possible.

There are certain *batteries* where the hands pass equally one over the other, which is not difficult to do provided one observes what has just been said about the liaison of the sounds.

There are two other kinds of *batteries*, examples of which will be found in the piece called *The Cyclops*; in one of these *batteries* the hands between them make the consecutive movements of the two sticks of a drum, and in the other the left hand crosses over the right hand to touch alternately the bass and the treble.

I think that these two kinds of *batteries* are peculiar to me, at least no others of this kind have appeared, and I will say in their favor that the eye shares the pleasure that the ear receives.

The performance of these different *batteries* and the different *roulements* depends mostly on the suppleness of the wrist, which performs them with a light and gentle movement, keeping a fixed point at the elbow joint when the chord exceeds the limit of the hand.

When you feel your hand is trained, diminish the height of the bench little by little until you feel that your elbows are slightly below the level of the keyboard, which forces the hands to be held as though they were glued to the keyboard, and which gives the player's touch the greatest amount of contact.

When you practice trills or shakes you must raise as much as possible only the fingers you use for that purpose; but as the movement becomes familiar you raise the fingers less; and the wide movement finally becomes a quick and light one.

You must take care not to speed up the trill toward the end; it ends naturally once you have acquired the habit.

I leave to the teachers the care of teaching the rest verbally, since everything derives from the first principles I have just laid down. But remember to persevere in first principles the further you advance in your career, because the person who is bored by these is almost always the victim of his impatience.

There are a few pieces in this book that can be transposed; for example the Musette can be played in C *sol ut*, especially to be played on the viol, and the Rigaudon in D *la re*.

You can omit, if you want, the *doubles* and the *reprises* of a Rondeau that you find difficult.

When the hand cannot reach over two keys easily, one can omit the one that is not absolutely essential to the melody, for one should not be held to what is impossible.

This method serves as an introduction to a complete system of the mechanics of the fingers on the clavecin, which I hope to publish soon; the usefulness of the mechanics has not yet become fully known, and it is in accompaniment that its influence will be felt most of all; in it I have relieved the memory of a lot of rules that one can use only when they have passed from the judgment to the ends of the fingers.

What I have said above about the clavecin is to be observed in the same way on the organ.

Table of Ornaments
[1724 and 1731 editions]

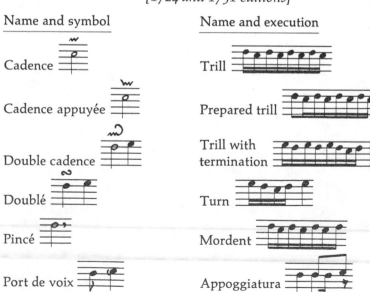

Name and symbol   Name and execution

Coulez   Slide, descending
                          appoggiatura

Pincé et port de voix   Mordent and ascending
                          appoggiatura

Son coupé   Staccato

Suspension   Suspension

Arpègement simple   Arpeggio

Arpègement figuré   Figured arpeggio

Liaison   Execution

A *slur* that embraces two different notes, like shows that the finger must not be raised from the first note until after the second note has been played.

The note tied to one that carries a Cadence or a Pincé serves as the beginning of each of its ornaments.

Example   Execution

A *slur* that embraces several notes, shows that one must hold them all down from one end of the *liaison* to the other, as they are struck.

Example   Execution

The thumb should be placed in the middle of this *batterie*.

First Lesson

Right hand

This is to be repeated over and over without stopping, and with equality of movement.

Left hand

Menuet en Rondeau

15. *Opera: Pro and Con*

Jacques Bonnet-Bourdelot (d. 1724) was a nephew of Pierre Bourdelot, a French musical historian who died before he was able to finish his history of music. Jacques' brother, Pierre (1675–1708) then undertook to finish his uncle's work, but he, too, died before he was able to complete it. It fell to Jacques to finish the work, in which he included notes made by his brother and also his own observations. Histoire de la musique et de ses effets *appeared in 1715. It was reprinted in 1726 and again in 1743; both of these later editions included Lecerf de La Viéville's famous* Comparaison de la musique italienne et de la musique française, *which had first appeared in 1704.*

Unlike earlier historians, Bonnet-Bourdelot takes a more modern point of view, not neglecting the music of the Ancients but also showing concern for the music and musical activities of his own time, and he writes in a style more reportorial than learned. This extract from "Dissertation on Good Taste" concerns the merits of French and Italian music, a subject that often led to heated argument. As might be expected, Bonnet tries to examine both sides fairly but finds it very difficult to be objective when it comes to Italian music. His discussion is representative of the attitudes of the partisans of French music (see also Charles de Brosses, "On Spectacles and Music" at the end of Chapter 15).

SOURCE: *Jacques Bonnet-Bourdelot,* Histoire de la musique et de ses effets depuis son origine, et les progrès successifs de cet art jusqu'à présent *(Paris, 1715) Ch. XII.*

JACQUES BONNET-BOURDELOT

from *Histoire de la musique et de ses effets*

Dissertation on Good Taste in Italian and French Music, and on Operas

In a previous chapter I have given an account of the origin of the antipathy between the Italian and French musicians, which existed from the time of Charlemagne over the subject of a solemn Mass.[1] It would be surprising that this disagreement should have lasted so many centuries had not the Italians been considered to be an irreconcilable nation. It appears that one would attempt in vain to agree on the perfection of their art through treatises on the music and opera of Italy parallel to those on the music and opera of the French. I will nevertheless not fail to bring up one more of them in the form of letters sent to me in 1712 by one of my friends, to which I have made additions I thought necessary to the subject in order to include it in the body of this history. In it will be found as many partisans for French music as in that which was written in 1702 in favor of Italian music;[2] besides, one must change opinions from time to time in order

1. According to the sixteenth-century historian Fauchet, the origin of enmity between French and Italian singers is said to have been a quarrel that arose between Charlemagne's musicians and those of the Pope, each claiming to have the right to direct the Mass music in St. Peter's Basilica on Easter Sunday morning. The French musicans won out, because of their relations with the first Emperor of the West, but after the ceremony Charlemagne inquired as to what the musicians had been arguing about. The Roman music director claimed that Rome was the source of music because of its connection with Gregorian chant. The French music master replied that their Emperor's glory would be diminished if he yielded the music to others than those of his chapel, and, as to the source of music, "the more a stream becomes distant from its source the greater force it has," meaning that he had not only the knowledge of Italian music but also that of other nations connected with French music.

The Emperor, to content the Pope, commanded his musicians to wait at "the source of music," that is to say, at the French frontier. Charlemagne, upon leaving Rome, brought with him a group of Italian musicians, which he established at Tours to sing the Offices according to Gregorian use, greatly displeasing the French musicians. From that time forth the animosity between the two continued.

2. Bonnet is referring to Abbé Raguenet's *Parallèle des Italiens et des Français* (1702); see translation by O. Strunk, *Musical Quarterly* XXXII (1946): 411–36.

to yield to sound experiences that are stronger and more convincing than all the lines of argument.

Apparently, Monsieur, it is to find out what I may know about music that you ask for my opinion on the Italian style that reigns today in Paris, since there is no one who could determine it more exactly than you; however, I obey. But it will not at all be as a musician committed in favor of one or the other that I write, for I will tell you what I think about it according to my natural taste for this science as fell to my lot at birth. I shall not use terms of art with which the musicians are obliged to load their musical treatises, which only serve to confuse the reader's ideas rather than to instruct. I will try to make myself clear to those who will read, so that they may understand me without knowing music.

You know then, as I do, Monsieur, that there are presently two parties formed on the subject of music; one, the rabid admirers of Italian music, sustained by a small sect of *demi-savants* in this art; nevertheless they are persons of fairly high standing who royally decide and proscribe absolutely French music as being stale and tasteless or entirely insipid. The other party, faithful to the taste of the country and better grounded in the art of music, are unable to suffer without indignation that the good taste of French music is scorned in the capital city of the kingdom, and they treat Italian music as bizarre and capricious and as a rebel against the rules of the art. Nevertheless, there should be a middle course in the midst of all that in order to reconcile the parties, thus rendering justice to both kinds of music by accepting each in its own character.

One would have to be deprived of good taste and knowledge not to admit that good Italian music in general contains whatever is most learned and refined, and that we owe to it a great part of the ornaments we use in ours; that the Italians are our masters in cantatas and sonatas, although those of Sieur Bernier and Morin[3] appear to be capable of being compared with theirs. I admire in their works the new designs of their figures, so well conceived and so skillfully exe-

3. Nicolas Bernier (1664–1734) was *Maître de Chapelle* at Chartres, then in 1704 succeeded M.-A. Charpentier at the Sainte-Chapelle. In 1723 he was *sous-maître* at the Chapelle de Versailles and also Master of Music and Councilor on Music to the Regent. His motets and sacred music are his most important work, but his seven books of Cantatas were also held in high esteem and important in the development of the French secular cantata.

J.-B. Morin (1677–1740) was a leading figure in the field of the eighteenth-century French cantata, along with Campra, Monteclair, and Clérambault. He was a musician at the court of the Duc d'Orléans, then *Maître de Chapelle* to the Abbesse de Chelles. His most celebrated cantata is *La Chasse du Cerf*, performed in 1708 at Fontainebleau in honor of Louis XIV.

cuted; the sparkling vivacity of their accelerated imitations; the variety of their songs; the diversity of their keys and their modes, so well linked to one another; and their harmony, as elegant as it is learned.

But if we cede to them science and invention, should they not cede to us with the same impartiality the good natural taste we possess, and the tender and noble execution in which we excel; above all, the harmony of our instruments? The enrichments we have added from our own store, should they not be accepted? And are we not among those scholars who, having profited greatly from the lessons of our masters, at the end have become more expert than they? Can one not say without offending the partisans of Italian music that their too frequent and misplaced ornaments stifle expression, that they do not sufficiently distinguish their works, being in that like to Gothic architecture, which, too heavily adorned with ornaments, is obscured by them, so that one can no longer distinguish the body of the work?

One can say also that Italian music resembles an amiable coquette, although somewhat painted, full of vivacity, always rushing about, seeking to sparkle everywhere without reason, and not knowing why; like a scatterbrain who shows her passions in everything she does; when it is a question of tender affection she makes it dance the gavotte or gigue. Would not one say that serious matters become comical in her hands, and that she is more suited to *ariettes* and *chansonettes* than to deal with noble subjects? In that, is she not like to those comedians who having talent only for the comic, succeed very badly, turning tragedy to ridicule when they wish to have a hand in it? One must admit that the majesty of French music treats heroic subjects with greater nobility and is more appropriate to the cothurnus and to the theater; whereas in Italian music all the passions appear alike: joy, anger, sorrow, happy love, the lover who fears or hopes—all seem to be painted with the same features and the same character; it is a continual gigue, always sparkling or leaping.

If the voice begins alone, the instrument echoes the melody; this pattern, often unusual, moves not only through all the notes of the key but also through those of foreign keys, where they may be more or less suitable; thus their compositions ramble through all the keys and change the mode at each moment, and at the end one is not able to say which key they are in. After having completed this long promenade, during which the same melody is repeated twenty times, both by the voice and the instrument, one must still return to the da capo, a transition often very harsh to the ear, being frequently made of only two neighboring chords; but ordinarily it happens that they continue, in order to avoid prolixity and to relieve boredom. It is a great fault in all works of the human mind, and principally in music, not to be able to finish; one should know how to restrain one's self, for a good work loses half its value if it is too diffuse.

We have difficulty also to accustom ourselves to the strange intervals in the recitatives of their songs, which sometimes exceed an octave, in which even the most skillful find difficulty with just intonation. Above all, the long *tenutos* make the hearer impatient because they are misplaced; these holds, which we also use and which are rarely suitable except on words of repose, they make indifferently on all the words that end with vowels. I do not say there may not be a great deal of art in having a violin and a bass frolic below one of these long fermatas, but what has liberty to do with this sound that lasts a quarter of an hour? Where is the taste and expression in all of that? It very often happens that Italian music expresses something quite different from the words. I hear a Prelude that is fast and furious: I then think that some lover, repelled by the coldness of his lady, is going to give way to spite and abuse Love; not at all: it is a tender lover who praises the price of his constancy, who calls Hope to his aid, or who makes a declaration of love to his mistress.

Let us return to those who write music for the violin, who give themselves completely to the fire of their imagination in their sonatas and lead their fugues through all the modes, those who are not hindered by the expression of words, which ought to be the rule for composers. We are indebted to Italy for these kinds of pieces, to the Corellis, the Albinonis, the Miquels, and many other great musicians who have produced pieces of this type that will become immortal. Where few men can attain, a thousand others wish to imitate them. I have seen some pieces of such a singular melody and of such extraordinary composition that one would have thought the composer had thrown drops of ink haphazardly on the ruled paper, to which they seem to have later added some tails with four flags and divided the piece into measures.

The music of their cantatas would be more suitable to chamber concerts than to our spectacles. Their sonatas à 2 ought to be played by a single violin, which can embroider and fingle-fangle as much as it pleases; it would become very confused if the same part were executed by several instruments, which would make different diminutions, and therefore should be banished from a large orchestra.

In general one hears in Italian music only a *Basso continuo* always ornamented, which is often a kind of *batterie*, with chords and arpeggios, which casts dust in the eyes of those who are not connoisseurs, and which, reduced to its simplest form, is equivalent to ours. These *B. C.* are only good to show off the swiftness of hand of those who accompany, either the clavecin or the viol. Also, to outdo these basses already too much ornamented, they vary them again, and the one who ornaments the most wins. Thus one no longer hears the subject, which appears all too naked in the midst of this great brilliance and remains buried under a jolting of very fast and sparkling sounds, which, passing too lightly, cannot make any harmony against the subject. It would be better then, that one of the two instruments shoud play the simple bass line and the other an ornamented line. These *B. C.* would pass for viol pieces rather than for an accompaniment which ought to be subordinate to the subject and not stand out at all. The voice should dominate and attract the chief attention, but the contrary happens here: one hears only the *B. C.*, which bubbles so loudly that the voice is smothered. There is also a disadvantage in having the basses in *batteries* and ornamenting *ad lib.*, for it is difficult for a clavecin, a viol, and a theorbo to be able to play together accurately in the same style of ornamentation, no more than can many string instruments or winds; one takes one passage, another the next, which causes an extraordinary cacophony, such that a composer no longer recognizes his work, which appears disfigured; and in the midst of it all, one contents one's self with admiring the rapidity of the hand that is executing the passage! However, there you have the style of execution of the Italian music that is so much extolled.

But this was not the case with Sieur de Lully, great disciple of the beautiful and the true, who would have banished from his orchestra a violin who had spoiled his harmony by some diminution, or a cat's cry badly placed, in imitation of those rigid Grecian inspectors of public spectacles. Can one not compel himself to play music the way it is written? Is it the Italian style to make false harmonies at every turn?

I have seen some musicians so enamored of the *allegros*, and of the figured basses, that they cannot suffer *adagios*, those places of slow recitatives, and consider them boring; however, it is in such places that the harmony can best be heard, rather than in those *vivacities* where, as I just said, the bass moving too lightly and only brushing the upper part, pleasing harmony cannot be produced.

If this figured music is suitable to Italian and Latin words, why does one wish to subject the French language to it? Does an Italian control his affairs like a Frenchman? Their tastes, their dress, their customs, their manners, their pleasures, are they not all different? Why does one not wish them to be so in their vocal music as well, and in the playing of instruments? Does an Italian sing like a Frenchman? Why does one want the Frenchman to sing like the Italian? Each nation has different customs; why wish to dress French music in disguise and make her extravagant, she whose language is so wise and so unaffected and cannot bear the least violence, being an enemy of the frequent repetitions and the long fermatas that one tolerates in Italian, or Latin, music, which do not suit ours at all?

Here one can compare French music to a beautiful woman whose simple natural beauty, without art, draws to her the hearts of all who see her, who has only to appear to please, without fearing defeat by the affected airs of an extravagant coquette who seeks to draw people to her side at any price.

I could also adduce the authority of the fair sex, which has scarcely bestowed its grace on Italian music, being bored by fifteen minutes of a sonata and would much prefer to hear sung *Sangaride ce jour est un grand jour pour vous* or to hear the pleasant dreams of *Atys* than all the *batteries* and arpeggios of a violin played learnedly, about which they know nothing and hear only what attracts them. In vain one can tell them it is sublime, beautiful, learned, and that such and such an author has written it: "It is very pretty," say the ladies, "but it bores us and we don't want any more of it." There are, however, women who decide the merit and destiny of works in the spectacles, and whom we must seek to please, above all in that art which seems to be made for them.

It must be admitted however that some of our clever masters have found the secret of allying most skillfully the natural taste of the French with the brilliant and learned style of the Italians in the cantatas, which are in everybody's hands and which are *chef d'oeuvres* of their kind, both in the music and in the poetry. Let it suffice, then, to have shown the Italians that the French can carry genius and knowledge just as far as they, both in cantatas and sonatas. This was shown to them by Abbé de la Loüette in Rome in 1689, by a concert that he composed in the Italian style, performed at the residence of the Princess Colonne. In this Francisci, one of the most famous musicians of Italy in those days, stumbled twice, confessing that its execution was difficult. This makes it clear that they are not infallible, as they pretend, when they play or sing pieces from the score. But these trials should not cause one to scorn the simple and natural grace of the French, since the Italians themselves begin to imitate it in order to perfect themselves.

Such works have produced an infinity of others; cantatas and sonatas spring up beneath one's feet. A musician may have no more than one or two pieces in his pocket, yet he wishes to compile a volume and have it engraved; he pretends to vie with the Italians and to outdo the bravest; the poet scarcely suffices for him; there are even some texts that have suffered more than once the torture of Italian music; in short, cantatas smother us here. I have heard some that last an hour by the clock, so that one was obliged to cry for quarter or leave the place. What has become of good taste? Must it expire beneath the lumber of all these cantatas? What would the Lamberts, Boessets, Camus, and Batistes say, if they returned to this world, to see French songs so changed, abased, and disfigured?

I am persuaded that our illustrious masters have too much taste, and too much science to abandon it, as may be seen from their own works, in which the most graceful passages and those that most please are treated in the French style, where they have known how to mingle the best of the Italian style and have avoided the worst. Let them render justice to heroes and to the Cicero of French music—that is, to Lully. Let them admire the grandeur and greatness of his genius, in the midst of his unaffected simplicity free of all foreign ornaments, which must be obvious to all the world. . . .

One might say that like an expert painter he was able to paint with his sounds the movement of all the passions; for that had he had recourse to all the false sparkle and misplaced ornaments of Italian music? Nothing is more direct and more natural than his composition, which is within the reach of everyone and at the same time so elevated, so noble, so lively in its expression. Although he was a learned musician, taste and genius appear to have been his guides; capable of prescribing new rules to those who would follow them, he seemed at times to have neglected the old ones and to have placed himself above them. It must be acknowledged that what makes the best part of a musician is genius. . . .

We must also show in what way Italian opera differs from the opera of France. The sincerity of the French causes them to agree, as the author of *Theatrical Practice*, Books 1 and 4, has said, that the magnificence of the Roman spectacle has bestowed on all Italy an admirable taste that is seen in Rome, Milan, Venice, etc., for operatic presentations that seem to surpass those of other nations.

To introduce these musical actions, it has been necessary to give them all the ornaments of other theatrical pieces: the selection of a good plot, a pleasing disposition of poetic verse, tender sentiments, excellent voices, the music of various instruments, and ballets, in order to capture the imagination and to satisfy the eye and ear entirely.

But to arrive at perfection in such a fine spectacle, it is necessary to have persons of talent who understand perfectly the principles on which St. Augustine placed the perfection of harmony, arranged in nine degrees: the first in the mind, the second in good judgment, the third in the imagination, the fourth in the emotions, the fifth in the word, the sixth in the melody, the seventh in the sound, the eighth in desire, and the ninth in the composition.

These principles embody also the perfection of the nine Muses, whom the Ancients considered divinities. Thus, to compose a perfect opera it takes at least a poet, a musician, a mathematician, a ballet master, a painter—all of whom excel in their art—and a superintendent of great perception to oversee the construction and execution of the work. Also a great prince, or a republic as powerful as that of Venice, should pay the expenses *à discrétion*, for it is necessary that everything be suitable to such a great subject, which is ordinarily drawn from a fable or history, or is allegorical. I shall give a description of each, in order that one can have an idea of them and can judge the difference that exists between the representations of the Italian opera and those of French opera, which also has beauties that the others do not.

One of the most beautiful, particularly for its scenery, is that created by Beverin on the subject of Darius, King of Persia. One saw the camp of Darius appear, with elephants carrying towers filled with soldiers on their backs; these formed a band of musicians. Next, the tents of Darius' camp and a portion of the army with all the machines of war. Then followed a great valley between two mountains, a plaza in Baby-lon, the tower of a superb palace, a royal salon in the palace of Babylon furnished with great magnificence; the mausoleum of *Ninus;* the cavalry and infantry arrayed for battle; the royal garden of Babylon; the ruins of an old castle with a horrid prison; and each scene had different music, with *entrées* and excellent voices accompanied by an infinity of instruments.

When the opera of the great *Pompey* was represented on the stage of the San Salvador theater in Venice, the first scene was the triumphal place in Rome with the Arch of Triumph, and the windows of the palace were filled with people, while Pompey, in his chariot drawn by two lions, was accompanied by a great number of soldiers, several Princes, and a troop of slaves, together with an *entrée* of gladiators, who fought to the sound of all the military instruments. This scene was succeeded by one of a great court, with a stairway on which a number of people ascended to a superb apartment; after this one saw a magnificent garden with *allées*, flower beds, arbors, and fountains. Thereafter a temple of amazing architecture appeared, followed by a treasury full of all kinds of vases of gold and silver and other riches; all of it was supported by accompaniments suitable to the grandeur of the spectacle.

But one of the most extraordinary of such representations was that presented at Turin in 1628, on the occasion of the birth of the Prince of Savoy: the theme was taken from the *Metamorphoses*. A great machine which represented the Ship of Happiness was constructed; all the divinities propitious to men appeared in the heavens and each recited to music, to which the chorus responded. At the same time one saw appearing in the four corners of the hall four machines representing the four elements: a *montgibel* for Fire, a rainbow for Air, a theater for Earth, and a vessel for Water. Suddenly the hall filled with water like a sea, and the vessel, advancing, showed a magnificent throne on its prow, prepared to receive the Princes and Princesses. Within the ship there was a huge table prepared for forty persons. The God of the Sea invited the entire court to enter this ship, which was served by Tritons, who brought the refreshments on the backs of various marine monsters.

On a reef somewhat distant from the ship the fable of Arion thrown into the sea and rescued on the back of a dolphin was represented; the band played the Prologue. The first part was the departure of Arion; the second showed him singing on the back of the dolphin; the third part transported him to Corinth, where Periander made him recount his adventures and confronted him with the mariners who had thrown him into the sea. The Sirens performed a grand ballet that ended this superb representation.

The French still say that all the Italian operas are composed of great events from Greek history, the empires of Asia, and Roman history, which include the heroic deeds and most virtuous actions of the great men of Antiquity and the most dazzling passions, like those of Marc Antony and Cleopatra. Sometimes they represent the greatest stories from the *Metamorphoses*, in which the machinists have the art to make all the elements appear—the conflagrations of the earth caused by Phaëton's fall, that of the city of Troy, of Rome, like the real thing; the battle of Pharsala between Caesar and Pompey. There are others where one sees the sea filled with ships besieging the maritime cities, tempests, shipwrecks, the destruction of Jerusalem by Titus, etc.

All these great events truly hold the spectators in admiration. Further, the Venetian nobility spare no expense for the grandeur of these spectacles during the Carnival of Venice, because the more beautiful they are the more they are lucrative and uphold the glory this superb republic has acquired in surpassing all Italy in such things. At such times nations of all kinds are drawn to Venice, and there are as many as four or five representations at different operas, all of which perform each day at the same hour; the one with the greatest reputation is the most crowded. There are certain singers, male and female, and *castrati*, who earn as much as a thousand *pistoles* for singing in a single opera during the Carnival.

But whatever ideas that one might have of these grand operas, if the Italians were sincere they would admit in their turn that they have powerful rivals in France. These are the operas *Cadmus, Thésée, Atys, Bellérophon, Phaëton, Amadis, Roland,* and *Armide,* composed by the famous Lully, whose extraordinary genius has almost effaced that which Italian musicians had acquired before he had given proof of his great genius in the establishment of operas in France, the taste for which has been perfected by French musicians, such as Sieur Quinault for the poetry, Berrin for the machines and scenery, and Beauchamps for the ballet *entrées.* The cost of these operas to be performed at Versailles was borne by the King, and exceeds others, because the machines and scenery were as astonishing as they were magnificent, the beauty of the costumes, even those of the orchestra, appeared with all the sumptuousness imaginable, such that these spectacles left nothing to be desired; in short, everything was in accordance with the grandeur of the most magnificent King of all the kings.

One can say also without ostentation that the French operas outdid those of Italy by the size and beauty of the choruses, by the *agréments* of the recitative, or declamation, as well as by the authority of execution by the instruments of the orchestra, whose symphony is inimitable, as well as by the magnificence of the ballet *entrées* and the *danses élevées, danses basses,* or *danses figurés* composed by Sieur Pécour and executed by dancers who know the art of characterizing the passions through movements of the dance with grace and a nobility worthy of admiration that is not found in Italy.

Therefore one can agree without prejudice that if one joined all these great perfections to those of the Italian opera, they would form a spectacle whose performance would be comparable to a Roman triumph.

Finally, the prodigious number of musical performances that have been given in the course of two centuries in all the courts of Europe could furnish an infinity of ideas, as ingenious as diverse, to those who wish to apply themselves to the composition of spectacles. The Ancients prescribed no rules for these actions in music, and abandoned them, so to speak, to the genius and experience of those who invent them, because they judged that the mind acts more successfully when it is without fear. Inspiration and caprice reign there as much as one wishes, provided there is some proportion or correspondence of propriety with the subject that is being treated, and to the diversity of scenes, to make them more attractive. But one must admit that all these representations are at least as indebted for their perfections to the magnificence and generosity of sovereigns who have paid for them as to those who composed them; otherwise music would still be limited to the chant of the church, and bounded by private concerts, as may be seen in states where spectacles are not yet enjoyed.

Charles de Marguetel de Saint-Denis, seigneur de Saint-Évremond (1613–1703) was a great noble and a literary man. He was a defender of the royal cause, called le Fronde, *during the civil disturbances in France in the 1660s. When his party was defeated in the civil strife, he took refuge in England and spent the remaining years of his life there.*

Saint-Évremond is one of the really free spirits of his time, a true libertin. *He was not interested in being an author, although his writings are extensive, and his works did not appear until 1705, after his death. His letter on the opera therefore deals with the operas of the second half of the seventeenth century.*

Saint-Évremond was not a musician, but he was an educated man and appreciated the arts. His views reflect those of a good many intelligent amateurs and men of taste and discrimination. The idea of the classic theater of the Ancients as a model for theatrical representations was still strong in the late seventeenth century; hence the often harsh criticism of the new development, opera. Unlike such men as the Abbé Raguenet or Le Cerf de La Viéville, both of whom had a parti pris, *Saint-Évremond presents a reasonable point of view and criticizes both French and Italian opera.*

SOURCE: *"Lettre sur les Opera," in* Oeuvres de Monsieur de Saint-Évremond *(Amsterdam, 1739), Vol. II, pp. 282–98.*

CHARLES DE SAINT-ÉVREMOND
Letter on the Opera

TO THE DUKE OF BUCKINGHAM:

For a long time, Milord, I have wanted to tell you my feelings about opera and to speak of the difference I find between the Italian and the French manners of singing. The chance that I had to speak about it at the home of Madame Mazarin has increased rather than satisfied my desire, and I am fulfilling it today in the discourse I am sending to you.

I shall begin by being very frank and telling you that I do not admire very much the *Comédies en Musique* as we see them at present. I admit that their magnificence pleases me, that the machines are really surprising, that the music is touching in places, that the *tout ensemble* seems marvelous; but you must admit that these marvels soon become tiresome because where the mind comes so little into play the senses necessarily languish after the first pleasure that surprise affords us; our eyes are busied and finally become tired from long-continued looking at objects. At the beginning of the concerts the rightness of the harmonies is noticed, none of all the diversities escape us; a little while later the instruments stir us, the music is now only a confused noise in our ears, where nothing can be distinguished. But who can resist being bored by recitative that has neither the charm of song nor the agreeable power of the spoken word? The soul, fatigued by long concentration where it finds nothing to be felt emotionally, tries to find within itself some secret movement which might touch it; the mind, which has given itself over in vain to outside impressions, turns to revery or is annoyed by its own weakness; finally the weakness is so great that one thinks only of leaving, and the only pleasure left to the languishing spectators is the hope of seeing a speedy end to the spectacle they have been given.

The fatigue which I ordinarily feel at the opera comes from the fact that I have never seen one which did not appear to me as despicable in the conduct of the plot and in its verse. Well, it is in vain that the ear is pleased and the eyes charmed if the mind is not satisfied. My spirit agreeing with my intelligence more than with my senses secretly resists the impressions it might receive, or at least it fails to give its glad consent, without which the most voluptuous objects can give me no great pleasure. A piece of stupidity loaded with music, dance, machines, and decorations is a magnificent piece of stupidity, but still stupid; an ugly base under a fine decoration that I encounter with great displeasure!

There is something else in the opera so unnatural that my imagination is hurt by it. That is, having the whole play sung from beginning to end as if the characters presented had ridiculously been adapted to express in music both the commonest and the most important events in their lives. Can you imagine a master calling his valet or giving him a task to do by singing; that a friend sing a confidence to a friend; that one should deliberate in a council by singing; that one express his orders in song, or kill men in combat melodiously with sword strokes or spear thrusts? That is to lose the spirit of the play, which is doubtless preferable to that of harmony; for harmony should be only a simple accompaniment, and the great masters of the theater have added it as agreeable, not as necessary, after having regulated everything that concerns the subject and the speech. However the idea of the musician precedes that of the hero in operas. It is Luigi, it is Cavallo, it is Cesti[1] who present themselves to the imagination. The mind cannot conceive a singing hero but attaches itself to the person who causes him to sing. One cannot deny that at the performances in the Palais Royal one thinks a hundred times more of Lully than of Theseus or Cadmus.

I do not pretend to exclude all kinds of singing from the theater. Some things should be sung; there are some that should be done without shocking propriety or reason. Vows, prayers, sacrifices, and generally anything involving service to the gods have been sung in all nations and at all times. Tender and tragic passions are expressed naturally by a kind of singing; the expression of a beginning love, the irresolution of a soul torn in different directions—these are matters for stanzas, and stanzas are suited to singing. Everyone knows that choruses were introduced in the Greek theater and it must be admitted that they could be introduced just as reasonably in ours. This is the function of singing in my opinion. Everything that is only conversation or speech making, having to do with intrigue and business which pertain to the council chamber and to action, belongs to the actors who speak and is ridiculous in the mouth of musicians who sing. The Greeks wrote fine tragedies in which they sang some things. The Italians and the French write bad tragedies in which everything is sung.

If you want to know what an opera is, I will tell you it is *a bizarre work of verse and music where the Poet and the Musician, each hampered by the other, take a lot of trouble to create a bad work.* It is not that you cannot find agreeable words and very beautiful tunes, but you will surely find in the end disgust with the verses where the genius of the poet has been constrained, and boredom with the singing where the musician has exhausted himself on music that is too long. If I felt capable of giving advice to the good people who like the theater, I would advise them to acquire again the taste for our fine comedies, where dancing and music could be introduced that would not in any way do harm to the performance. One could sing a prologue with agreeable accompaniment. In the *intermedi*, singing would give animation to the words, which would be, as it were, the spirit of what was being played. When the performance was ended an epilogue would be sung, or some reflection on the great beauties of the work. One would fortify its main idea and would make the spectators cherish more dearly the impression they had received. It is thus that you will find things to satisfy the senses and the

1. Luigi Rossi, Francesco Cavalli, M.-A. Cesti.

mind, since you are not forced to desire the charms of singing in a simple performance in prose, nor the power of the performance in the boredom of continual music.

There remains for me to give you a warning for all the comedies where there is singing: that is, to leave the authority to the poet for the direction of the play. The music must be made for the verse more than the verse for the music. The musician must follow the lead of the poet. Lully alone should be exempt because he knows the passions and penetrates deeper into the heart of man than the authors. Cambert[2] has a fine talent, suitable to a hundred different musics and all well arranged with a nice economy of voices and instruments. No recitative is better organized or better varied than his, but for the nature of the passions, for the quality of the sentiments which must here be expressed, he must receive from the authors the enlightenment that Lully affords them, and subject himself to direction, when Lully, because of the breadth of his knowledge, can justly become their director.

I do not wish to end my discussion without describing to you the little esteem the Italians have for our opera, and the great disgust we have for the Italian ones.

The Italians who are devoted to performance cannot endure our calling "opera" a series of dances and music which have no real connection or natural association with the plots. The French, accustomed to the beauty of their overture, the agreeableness of their tunes, the charm of their symphonies, can scarcely endure the ignorance or the bad use of the instruments in the operas at Venice, and refuse their attention to a long recitative which becomes boring because of the little variety to be found in it. I cannot explain to you clearly what one of their recitatives is, but I know that it is neither singing nor reciting; it is something unknown to the Ancients, which one might define as *bad usage of the singing and the words*. I admit that I have found admirable things in the operas of Luigi [Rossi], both as to the expression of sentiments and the charm of the music; but the ordinary recitative was very boring, so that the Italians themselves waited impatiently for the beautiful places, which, in their opinion, occurred too rarely. I shall sum up the defects of our opera in a few words. One expects to attend a representation and nothing is presented; one wants to see a comedy and finds no comic spirit at all.

Here is what I thought I could say about the different constitution of operas. As to the manner of singing, what we call the *execution* in France, I think with no partiality that no nation can rival ours. The

2. Robert Cambert, composer of *Pomone* (1671).

Spanish have admirable throats; but with their graces [*fredons*] and their roulades they seem in their singing to be thinking of rivaling the nightingale in the facility of their throats. The expressiveness of the Italians is false or at least exaggerated, because they do not know exactly the nature and degree of the passions. It is bursting out laughing rather than singing when they express some joyous feeling. If they try to sigh one can hear sobs that are formed violently in the throat, not the sighs with which a loving heart gives vent to its passion in secret. Of a sad reflection they make the most powerful exclamations; tears of absence become funereal weeping; sad things become lugubrious in their mouths; they utter cries of pain instead of laments; and sometimes they express the languor due to passion as a weakness of nature. Perhaps there is some change now in their way of singing and they have profited by their contact with us to acquire a clear-cut, polished execution, just as we have profited from them to acquire the beauties of a greater and bolder composition.

I have seen comedies in England where there was much music. But to speak discreetly, I have never been able to grow accustomed to English singing. I came too late to acquire a taste so different from any other. There is no nation which shows more courage in the men, and more beauty in the women, more wit in both sexes. But you cannot have everything. Where so many good qualities are common it is no great loss that good taste is so rare. It is certain that one meets it there very rarely, but in the people in whom it is found it is as delicate as in men of the world. They escape from the taste of the rest of the nation by exquisite art or by a very lucky constitution.

Solus Gallus cantat, only the French sing. I do not want to insult other nations and maintain what one author has suggested, "the Spanish sob, the Italian wails, the German moos, the Fleming howls, only the Frenchman sings." I leave to him all these fine distinctions and am content to base my feeling on the authority of Luigi, who could not endure to hear the Italians singing songs after he had heard them sung by M. Nyert, by Hilaire, by the little La Varenne. Upon his return to Italy he made all the musicians of that nation his enemies by saying aloud in Rome, as he had said in Paris, that to make music agreeable you had to have Italian airs in French mouths. He did not think much of our songs except for those of Boësset, which drew his admiration. He admired our concert of violins, he admired our lutes, our clavecins, our organs; and how charming would he have found our flutes if they had been in usage at that time? What is certain is that he remained greatly repelled by the coarseness and hardness of the greatest Italian masters after he had tasted the gentleness of touch and the clear playing of our French.

I would be too partial if I talked only about our advantages. There is no one slower in understanding the sense of the words and entering into the spirit of the composer than the French; there are few who understand quantity less, and who have so much trouble with the pronunciation; but when long study has enabled them to really understand what they are singing, nothing approaches their pleasantness. The same is true for instruments and especially in concerts, where nothing is sure or correct until after an infinity of rehearsals; but nothing is so proper nor so polished when the rehearsals are finished. The Italians, very learned in music, bring their knowledge to our ears with no sweetness whatsoever; the French are not content to rid knowledge of its first roughness, which smacks of the hard work of composing; they find in the secrets of performing something to charm the soul, a *je ne sais quoi* very touching, which they can bring to our very hearts.

I was forgetting to talk to you about the machines; it is so easy to forget those things that one would like to see curtailed. The machines may satisfy the curiosity of people ingenious at mathematical inventions but they will not be pleasing to people of good taste in the theater. The more they surprise you, the more they divert the mind from attention to the speech; and the more admirable they are the less impression these marvels make upon the soul of tenderness and exquisite feeling, which it needs to be touched by the charm of the music. The Ancients used machines only under the necessity of bringing on some god, and the poets were nearly always found to be ridiculous because they had been reduced to this necessity. If you want to spend a lot of money, spend it on fine decorations whose use is more natural than that of the machines. Antiquity, which exhibited its gods at doors and even in its hall—this antiquity, I say, ever vain and credulous, nevertheless only showed its gods in the theater very rarely. After belief in them had died out, the Italians reestablished in opera those very gods who had vanished from the world and have not been afraid to show men these ridiculous vanities, provided they gave the plays greater glory by the introduction of dazzling things and false marvels. Those theatrical divinities took the Italians in for a long time. Undeceived at last, we see them renounce the very gods that they had recalled and come back to things which, if they are not completely true, are at least less fabulous, and which with a slight indulgence common sense does not reject completely.

The same thing has happened to us in regard to the gods and machines as always happens to the Germans in regard to our fashions. We have just taken up what the Italians have abandoned, and as if we were trying to make up for the mistake of having been forestalled in invention, we are carrying it to excess, a usage which they had introduced *mal à propos* but which they had carried on discreetly. Indeed, we cover the earth with divinities and have them dance in crowds, whereas they have them descend with some sort of discretion on the most important occasions. Just as Ariosto had gone beyond the marvelous in his poems as far as the unbelievable fabulous, we go beyond the fabulous with a confused assemblage of gods, shepherds, heroes, magicians, ghosts, furies, and demons. I admire Lully as much for his conduct of the dancing as for what is related to the voice and the instruments; but the construction of our operas must seem very strange to persons who have good taste in matters of plausibility and the marvelous.

However, one runs the risk of being discredited by this good taste if one dares to show it in public, and I advise other people, when the subject of the opera is brought up, to keep secret their enlightenment. As for me, who has passed the time and the age of distinguishing myself by fashionable opinion and by the merits of my imaginings, I have resolved to take the part of common sense, even if it has been abandoned. I will follow reason in its disgrace with just as much ardor as if it were still the first consideration. What annoys me the most about this infatuation with the opera is that it is about to ruin tragedy, which has been the finest thing we possess, and the one most capable of forming the mind.

Let us conclude, after such a long discussion, that the construction of our operas could not be worse. But one must admit at the same time that no one will ever work as well as Lully on an ill-conceived subject, and that it is hard to be better than Quinault, no matter what is demanded of him.

Georg Frideric Handel is most often thought of as the creator of the Messiah, *the splendid* Water Music, *and the instrumental concertos Op. III and Op. VI, and one forgets that he first became known as the great genius he was through his operas. Opera in his day was a very different matter from opera as we know it; Handel's orchestra was small, although it displayed a wide range of instrumental color, occasionally using such obsolescent instruments as the viola da gamba or the theorbo. His basic orchestra consisted of the usual strings, oboes, bassoons, and harpsichord continuo, with occasional trumpets, horns, flutes, and tympani as needed; he even used recorders in several works. At most he would have had no more than 24 or 26 musicians. The format of his opera also was different from that of an opera by Verdi or Wagner; and the singers were supreme.*

Dr. Charles Burney's description of the music of Handel's Pastor fido casts considerable light on the kinds of instrumentation Handel used to accompany the arias in this work and occasionally in others, and also provides a good overview of the format of opera generally in the early part of the eighteenth century: literally one aria after another, with infrequent ensembles and chorus numbers. It was, in short, a vehicle that served as a showcase for the singers, the darlings of the public. The use of violins in unison or a single bass line as accompaniment may seem a bit strange today; nevertheless it was quite usual in Handel's time and employed by all composers.

Dr. Burney's eyewitness accounts of the famous opera singers provide an excellent source for information about their voices, their styles of singing (and therefore musical styles as well), and their place in the musical scene. Lacking such modern devices as records and tapes, persons today interested in studying the art of another age can only turn to such indefatigable witnesses as Dr. Burney, Sir John Hawkins, and others to gain an impression of musical performances and critical views.

Here are Dr. Burney's accounts of the singing of four extremely famous virtuosi, two castrati and two women. Farinelli was very likely the most famous male singer who ever lived, for all accounts speak of his phenomenal powers. Cuzzoni and Faustina, the two rival songstresses, were his contemporaries and very nearly equaled his fame. Pachierrotti, who belonged to a later generation, was also one of the true virtuoso sopranos; and if Dr. Burney is to be believed, he, too, must have possessed extraordinary powers, a voice of great sweetness and exceptional range.

SOURCE: *Charles Burney, A General History of Music, II (London, 1789), pp. 682, 736–39, 745, 789, 886.*

CHARLES BURNEY

from *A General History of Music*

Handel's Il Pastor fido

[In November, 1712] Mr. Handel was again in England, where he furnished our stage with a second opera, entitled *Il Pastor Fido*, or the Faithful Shepherd. This drama, written by Rossi, author of *Rinaldo*, and performed by the Cavalier Valeriano, a new singer, successor to Nicolini, Valentini Urbani, just returned to England, La Pilotti Schiavonetti, Margarita [Durastanti], Mrs. Barbier, and Leveridge. The overture, one of the most masterly and pleasing of the kind, is well known; but the opera itself having never been printed, I shall be somewhat minute in my account of it. The first air for a *soprano*, lets us know what kind of voice the Cavalier Valeriano was possessed of; and the pathetic style of the first part of his song, as well as the agility necessary to the execution of the second, seem to imply abilities in that performer, of no mean kind. This air, and many other airs in the opera, are only accompanied by a violoncello in the old cantata style; but Handel always contrives to make this single accompaniment interesting without overwhelming the voice part, or depriving it of attention. The next air, for the same singer, has not even a bass to accompany the voice part, which is doubled by the violins in unison. This purity and simplicity, when the melody and the voice which delivers it, are exquisite, would be always pleasing to an audience, as a contrast to rich harmony and contrivance; but some of these airs are now too trivial and far advanced in years to support themselves totally without harmony. The following air for the Pilotti Schiavonetti, has no accompaniment but a busy bass; which, however, if doubled and not kept under, would be as much as a voice not uncommonly powerful could penetrate. In the ritornel, which is in the style of the first opera songs of the last century, Handel has enriched the harmony by ingenious and admirable parts for two violins, tenor, and bass. The air, No.4, in this act is natural and pleasing, with only a violoncello accompaniment, except in the ritornello. This air, in the year 1732, was introduced in the opera of *Ezio* to different words, as appears from a pencilled memorandum made by Handel himself in the score. The air No. 5, which was originally composed for the Margarita, and is accompanied by two violins, tenor, and bass, requires more execution than any other in the first act. No.6, sung by Valentini, is an air in jig time, of which, at present the passages would be thought trivial and common. No.7, for Mrs. Barbier, is a simple air of a pathetic kind, with no other accompaniment than a bass, in almost plain counterpoint. No.8 and the last air in the first act, for Valentini, though it has some pretty passages, yet little of Handel's fire, or true vocal grace, is discoverable in it.

Act second contains nine songs, three of which are short and inconsiderable; one of these, however, is very pathetic, and accompanied in a singular manner by the violins and violoncellos in unisons and octaves pizzicati, and by the harpsichord arpeggiato throughout. The fourth air, *Finte labbia*, has a solo part for the hautbois, and is written in Handel's best manner. It was sung by Margarita, as were almost all the best songs of this drama. The next air, *Sol nel mezzo*, written for Valentini, is of a very original and gay cast; French horns, which it seems to want, had now not been introduced into the opera orchestra. This air is in jig time, *alla Caccia*, and was perfectly adapted to the character by whom it was sung in the opera, a gay and frolicksome swain, much fonder of field-sports than the society of females. The next air, No.14, *Se in ombre nascosto*, sung by Mrs. Barbier, has in it much of Handel's spirit; but the passages are now somewhat antiquated. No.15, *Nel mio core*, the sixth air of this act is very pleasing, and a great part of it still remains elegant and graceful. The divisions and embellishments, which, when a song is new, are its most striking and refined parts, soonest lose their favour and fashion. There is a passage, often repeated in this air, of which Handel made frequent use afterwards in other things.

No.16, *Nò, non basta*, has a great deal of Handel's fire and grandeur; and No.17, the last of the act, *Ritorno adesso amor*, with solo parts for two hautbois, is strictly *fugata* upon two subjects, and a very masterly composition. This style of writing, which was so much admired at the beginning of the present century, has, however, been long banished from the opera, as undramatic: for the voice-part is so much overpowered and rendered so insignificant by the complicated business of the accompaniments that she loses her sovereignty. Such ingenious contrivances seem best calculated for instruments, where narration and poetry are out of the question: but in a drama where instruments are, or ought to be, the humble attendants on the voice, riot and noise should not be encouraged. Most of the hautbois passages and the division in the voice part of this air were afterwards used in the overture of *Esther*.

Act third, the first air, *Se m'ama, o caro*, No.18, though short, simple and unaccompanied, except by a bass, is extremely plaintive and elegant. Time has robbed the next of some of its beauties. The subsequent air, which is to express joy and exultation, is truly gay and festal. Handel has been accused of crowding some of his songs with too much harmony; but that is so far from being the case in this opera, that he not only often leaves the voice without any other accompaniment than a violoncello, but sometimes even silences that. In the present air, and in an additional song to the beginning of the third act, the singer is frequently left alone, or with only a violin in unison; and when the voice is good and the performer knows how to use it, this is always acceptable to the undepraved part of an audience. No.22, is a short light air resembling one in the same key, but differing in measure, in his lessons. This air is followed by a solemn and fine symphony chiefly for two hautbois and a bassoon, accompanied by the rest of the orchestra. After which is an accompanied recitative and an admirable duet in the style of the times, which, though not dramatic, admits of great beauties of composition. No.23, is a spirited bass song which was sung by Leveridge; this was preceded by a short introductory symphony that is truly characteristic and Handelian. The usual short and light theatrical chorus terminates the opera; which, upon the whole, is inferior in solidity and invention to almost all his other dramatic productions, yet there are in it many proofs of genius and abilities which must strike every real judge of the art, who is acquainted with the state of dramatic Music at the time it was composed. In the first place, it was a *pastoral* drama, in which simplicity was propriety. Besides, Handel had at this period no real *great* singer to write for. Valeriano was only of the second class; and Valentini, with little voice when he arrived in this country, if that little had remained undiminished, having been five years among us, must have lost the charms of novelty, as was the case with Margarita, who had been a playhouse singer now for more than twelve years. Nothing but *miraculous powers* in the performers can long support an opera, be the composition ever so excellent. Plain sense and good poetry are equally injured by singing, unless it is so exquisite as to make us forget every thing else. If the performer is of the first class, and very miraculous and enchanting, an audience seems to care very little about the Music or the poetry. This opera was performed but four [six] times: November 22d, 29th, December 3d and 6th.

Farinelli

[Farinelli] was born at Naples 1705; he learned the rudiments of Music of his father, and singing of Porpora, as he informed me himself. In 1722, at the age of seventeen, he went from Naples to Rome, with his master, then engaged to compose for the Aliberti theatre in that city, where he contended with a famous performer on the trumpet. Here he continued with Porpora till 1724, when he first went to Vienna. In 1725 he performed at Venice in Metastasio's first opera of *Didone abbandonata*, set by Albinoni. After this he returned to Naples, where he performed with the celebrated female singer, Tesi, in a serenata composed by Hasse. In 1726 he sung at Milan, in *Ciro*, an opera set by the elder Ciampi. In 1727 he performed at Bologna, with Bernacchi, in an opera set by Orlandini. In 1728, he went to Vienna a second time; and afterwards returning to Venice in autumn, he sung with Faustina, just returned from England, in Matastasio's *Ezio*, set by Porpora. Here he continued two years, performing in 1729 with Gizzi and Nicolini, in *Semiramide Riconosciuta*, set likewise by Porpora, and in *Cato*, by Leo; and in 1730, with Nicolini and Cuzzoni in Hasse's celebrated opera of *Artaserse*, in which he first appeared in England. . . .

As general praise would convey to the mind of a musical reader no distinct ideas of the powers of this extraordinary singer, it will be necessary to discriminate the specific excellencies of which he seems to have been possessed.

No vocal performer of the present century has been more unanimously allowed by professional critics, as well as general celebrity to have been gifted with a voice of such uncommon power, sweetness, extent, and agility, as Carlo Broschi detto Farinelli. Nicolini, Senesino, and Carestini gratified the eye as much by the dignity, grace and propriety of their action and deportment, as the ear by the judicious use of a few notes within the limits of a small compass of voice; but Farinelli without the assistance of significant gestures or graceful attitudes, enchanted and astonished his hearers by the force, extent, and mellifluous tones of the mere organ, when he had nothing to execute, articulate or express. But though during the time of his singing he was as motionless as a statue, his voice was so active, that no intervals were too close, too wide, or too rapid for his execution. It seems as if the composers of these times were unable to invent passages sufficiently difficult to display his powers, or the orchestras to accompany him in many of those which had been composed for his peculiar talent. And yet, so great were his forbearance and delicacy, that he was never known, while he was in England, to exclaim, or manifest discontent at the inability of the band, or mistakes of individuals by whom he was accompanied. He was so judicious in proportioning the force of his voice to the space through which it was to pass to the ears of his audience, that in a small theatre at Venice, though it was then most powerful, one of the managers of the opera complained that he did not sufficiently exert himself—"let me then," says Farinelli, "have a larger theatre, or I shall lose my reputation, without your being a gainer by it."

On his arrival here, at the first private rehearsal at Cuzzoni's apartments, Lord Cooper, then the principal manager of the opera under Porpora, observing that the band did not follow him, but were all gaping with wonder, as if thunder-struck, desired them to be attentive; when they all confessed, that they were unable to keep pace with him: having not only been disabled by astonishment but overpowered by his talents. This band was small, consisting only of Carbonelli, Mich. Christ. Festing, Valentine Snow, afterwards sergeant-trumpet, and Mr. Vezan, a dancing-master, who was likewise a steady and excellent concert-player on the violin, and constantly employed whenever Carbonelli or Festing was the leader; it was from this man that I had this anecdote.

There was none of Farinelli's excellencies by which he so far surpassed all other singers, and astonished the public, as his *messa di voce* or swell; which, by the natural formation of his lungs, and artificial economy of breath, he was able to protract to such a length as to excite incredibility even in those who heard him; who, though unable to detect the artifice, imagined him to have had the latent help of some instrument by which the tone was continued, while he renewed his powers by respiration.

Of his execution the musical reader will be enabled to judge by a view of the most difficult division of his bravura songs. Of his taste and embellishment we shall now be able to form but an imperfect idea, even if they had been preserved in writing, as mere notes would only show his invention and science, without enabling us to discover that expression and neatness which rendered his execution so perfect and surprising. Of his shake, great use seems to have been made in the melodies and divisions assigned to him; and his taste and fancy in varying passages were thought by his cotemporaries inexhaustible.

The opera of *Artaxerxes*, in which he first appeared on our stage, had an uninterrupted run of eleven nights, and was afterwards so frequently revived, that the whole number of its representations, during Farinelli's residence in England, amounted to no less than forty.

Cuzzoni

Francesca Cuzzoni (c. 1700–1770) was born in Parma, and had her instructions from Lanzi, an eminent professor of his time, under whose tuition she became a most exquisite performer, having been endowed by nature with a voice that was equally clear, sweet, and flexible. It was difficult for the hearer to determine whether she most excelled in slow or rapid airs. A native warble enabled her to execute divisions with such facility as to conceal every appearance of difficulty; and so grateful and touching was the natural tone of her voice, that she rendered pathetic whatever she sung, in which she had leisure to unfold its whole volume. The art of conducting, sustaining, increasing, and diminishing her tones by minute degrees, acquired her, among professors, the title of complete mistress of her art. In a cantabile air, though the notes she added were few, she never lost a favourable opportunity of enriching the cantilena with all the refinements and embellishments of the time. Her shake was perfect, she had a creative fancy, and the power of occasionally accelerating and retarding the measure in the most artificial and able manner, by what the Italians call *tempo rubato*. Her high notes were unrivalled in clearness and sweetness; and her intonations were so just and fixed that it seemed as if it was not in her power to sing out of tune.

The first time that she appeared on the stage as a public singer, seems to have been with her rival Faustina in the opera of *Lamano*, set by Michel Angelo Gasparini, at Venice, 1719. She is called in the *dramatis personae* of this opera, Virtuosa di Camera of the Grand Duchess of Tuscany. After this, she sung in most of the great theatres of Italy, before her arrival in England, 1723, where she continued in undiminished favour till 1729, when she returned to Italy, where she frequently met her rival Faustina, particularly at Venice, in the carnivals of 1729 and 1730; but never on the same stage: Cuzzoni generally singing at one theatre with Farinelli, and Faustina at another with Bernacchi or Pasi. In 1734, she came to England a second time, and sung in the operas composed by Porpora, under the patronage of the nobility, against Handel, in whose service Strada was engaged. Cuzzoni on her arrival in England married Sandoni, a harpsichord master and composer of some eminence. She came to London a third time, in 1750 just after Giardini's arrival, who performed at her benefit, at the little theatre in the Haymarket, the first time he was heard here in public. I was at this concert myself, and found her voice reduced to a mere thread; indeed, her throat was so nearly ossified by age, that all the soft and mellifluous qualities, which had before rendered it so enchanting, were nearly annihilated, in her public performance; though I have been assured by a very good judge, who frequently accompanied her in private, that in a room fine remains of her former grace and sweetness in singing Handel's most celebrated songs, by which she had acquired the greatest reputation, were still discoverable.

Many stories are related of her extravagance and caprice. She survived, however, not only her talents and powers of pleasing, but even those of procuring a subsistence; being long imprisoned in Holland for her debts, and at last ending her days in extreme indigence at Bologna.

Faustina

Faustina Bordoni Hasse (1693–1783), of Venice, wife of the celebrated composer Hasse, was a scholar of Michel Angelo Gasparini of Lucca. She in a manner invented a new kind of singing, by running divisions with a neatness and velocity which astonished all who heard her. She had the art of sustaining a note longer, in the opinion of the public, than any other singer, by taking her breath imperceptibly. Her beats and trills were strong and rapid; her intonation perfect; and her professional perfections were enhanced by a beautiful face, a symmetric figure, though of small stature, and a countenance and gesture on the stage, which indicated an entire intelligence and possession of the several parts she had to represent. She first appeared as a theatrical singer at Venice in 1716, when she performed in the opera of *Ariodante*, composed by Carlo Francesco Pollarolo. In 1719, she appeared on the same stage with Cuzzoni and Bernacchi, in an opera composed by her master Gasparini. Here she is called Virtuosa di Camera of the Elector Palatine. In 1722, she sung in Leo's opera of *Bajazet* at Naples; and in 1725, we find her at Vienna, where, according to Apostolo Zeno, she received great honours, as well as presents. At the palace of Prince Lichtenstein, singing to a great assembly, she was presented with a purse containing a hundred pieces of gold, and near as much more at the French ambassador's. . . . The same author speaks *della bravura di Faustina*, and the *bella musica di Porsile*, in an opera by the Abate Pasquini, performed at Vienna, 1725; and of the regret expressed by the whole court at her quitting that city to go to London [1726]. She remained here but two seasons, and then returned to Venice, where, in 1732, she was married to Hasse, and soon after went to Dresden, in the service of which court she remained till the year 1756 [*recte* 1763]. At the bombardment of that city by the late King of Prussia, Hasse, her husband had all his manuscripts burned, which were to have been printed at the expence of his master and patron, the Elector [1760].

During the war they went to Vienna, and remained there until the year 1775; then retiring to Venice, the place of Faustina's nativity, they ended their days in that city, she in 1783, at the great age of ninety, and he soon after, at nearly the same age.

A late writer upon Music, of considerable merit with respect to the present times, though frequently erroneous as to the past, speaking of Faustina, says that her agility of voice has seldom been equalled; a matchless facility and rapidity in her execution; dexterity in taking her breath, exquisite shake, new and brilliant passages of embellishment, and a thousand other qualities contributed to inscribe her among the first singers in Europe.

Such were the two performers [Cuzzoni and Faustina] who in the opera of *Alessandro* began to kindle the flames of discord among the frequenters of the opera and patrons of the art, which increased to a more violent degree of enmity than even the theological and political parties of high church and low, of Whig and Tory, which then raged in this country. And yet, according to Tosi, their contemporary, and a most excellent judge of their several merits, their talents, and styles of singing, were so different, that the praise of one was no reproach to the other. "Indeed, their merit," says he, "is superior to all praise; for with equal force, in a different style, they help to keep up the tottering profession from immediately falling into ruin. The one is inimitable for a privileged gift of singing, and enchanting the world with a prodigious felicity in executing difficulties with a brilliancy, I know not whether from nature or art, which pleases to excess. The delightful soothing *cantabile* of the other, joined with the sweetness of a fine voice, a perfect intonation, strictness of time, and the rarest productions of genius in her embellishments, are qualifications as peculiar and uncommon as they are difficult to be imitated. The *pathetic* of the one, and the *rapidity* of the other, are distinctly characteristic. What a beautiful mixture it would be, if the excellences of these two angelic beings could be united in a single individual!". . . .

To enable my readers to form an idea of the comparative merit of these celebrated rival singers, I shall insert here the character drawn of them by an excellent and unprejudiced judge, the late Mr. Quantz, who was frequently present at the performance of [*Lucio Vero*] in London, during its first run, 1727.

"Cuzzoni had a very agreeable and clear *soprano* voice; a pure intonation, and a fine shake; her compass extended two octaves, from C to c in alt. Her style of singing was innocent and affecting: her graces did not seem artificial, from the easy and neat manner in which she executed them: however, they took possession of the soul of every auditor, by her tender and touching expression. She had no great rapidity of execution, in *allegros*; but there was a roundness and smoothness, which were neat and pleasing. Yet with all these advantages, it must be owned that she was rather cold in her action, and her figure was not advantageous for the stage.

"Faustina had a *mezzo-soprano* voice, that was less clear than penetrating. Her compass was only from B flat to G in alt; but after this time, she extended its limits downwards. She possessed what the Italians call *un cantar granito*: her execution was articulate and brilliant. She had a fluent tongue for pronouncing words rapidly and distinctly, and a flexible throat for divisions, with so beautiful and quick a shake that she could put it in motion upon short notice, just when she would. The passages might be smooth, or by leaps, or consisting of iterations of the same tone, their execution was equally easy to her as to any instrument whatever. She was doubtless the first who introduced, with success, a swift repetition of the same tone. She sung *adagios* with great passion and expression, but was not equally successful, if such deep sorrow were to be impressed on the hearer, as might require dragging, sliding, or notes of syncopation, and *tempo rubato*.

"She had a very happy memory in arbitrary changes and embellishments, and a clear and quick judgment in giving to words their full power and expression. In her action she was very happy; and as she perfectly possessed that flexibility of muscles and features, which constitutes face-playing, she succeeded equally well in furious, amorous, and tender parts: in short, she was born for singing and acting.

"The violence of party," says M. Quantz, "for the two singers, Cuzzoni and Faustina, was so great, that when the admirers of one began to applaud, those of the other were sure to hiss; on which account operas ceased for some time in London."

Pacchierotti

Gasparo Pacchierotti (1744–1821), born in Roman state, seems to have begun his career in 1770, at Palermo in Sicily, where he continued during 1771. In 1772, he was the principal singer in the great theatre of San Carlo at Naples, with the De Amicis. In 1773, at Bologna; 1774, at Naples again. In 1775 at Milan, with the Taiber; 1776, at Forlì; 1777, at Genoa and Milan; and in 1778, at Lucca and Turin, previous to his arrival in England, where his reputation had penetrated a considerable time. . . . I eagerly attended the first general rehearsal, in which though he sung *sotto voce* under a bad cold in extreme severe weather, my pleasure was such as I had never experienced before. The natural tone of his voice is so interesting, sweet, and pathetic, that when he had a long note, or *messa di voce*, I never wished him to change it, or to do anything but swell, diminish, or prolong it in whatever way he pleased, to the utmost limits of his lungs. A great compass of voice downwards, with an ascent up to B♭ and sometimes to C *in alt*, with an unbounded fancy, and a power not only of executing the most refined and difficult passages of other singers, but of inventing new embellishments, which, as far as my musical reading and experience extended, had never then been on paper, made him, during his long residence here, a new singer to me every time I heard him. If the different degrees of sweetness in musical tones to the ear might be compared to the effects of different flavours on the palate, it would perhaps convey my idea of its perfection by saying that it is as superior to the generality of vocal sweetness as that of the pine apple is, not only to other fruits, but to sugar or treacle. Many voices, though clear and well in tune, are yet insipid and uninteresting, for want of piquancy and flavour. A more perfect shake on short notice, and in every degree of velocity, I never heard. His execution of rapid divisions was so true and distinct, that, with a loud and vulgar-toned voice, he would have been admired as a bravura singer; but the natural tone, and, if I may so call it, sentimental expression, and character of his voice, is such as to make many hearers lament his condescending to rival the lark, or ever, even in pathetic songs, quitting simplicity in order to change or embellish a passage in the most new, artful, or ingenious manner possible. . . .

That Pacchierotti's feeling and sensibility are uncommon, is not only discoverable by his voice and performance, but countenance, in which, through a benign and benevolent general expression, there is a constant play of features, which manifests the sudden workings and agitations of his soul. He is an enthusiast in his art, and feels the merit of a composition and performance with true Italian energy. Nice and fastidious in criticising himself, he consequently does not gratify frivolous and doubtful claims upon his admiration or applause; but to *real* and intrinsic merit, I never met with more candour, or heard more judicious and zealous panegyric bestowed from one professor to another. . . .

He is not gifted with a very robust constitution, nor was his chest proof against the rude and sudden attacks of our climate; so that though he was never obliged by indisposition to be absent from the stage when his duty called him thither, about once or twice during four years residence among us, yet his voice was sometimes affected by slight colds, from which the stoutest natives are not exempt; but when it was quite in order and obedient to his will, there was a perfection so exquisite in tone, taste, knowledge, sensibility, and expression, that my conceptions in the art could not imagine it possible to be surpassed.

The low notes of his voice were so full and flexible, that in private, among his particular friends and admirers, I have often heard him sing Ansani's and David's *tenor* songs in their original pitch, in a most perfect and admirable manner, going down sometimes as low as B♭ on the second line in the bass.

Charles de Brosses (1707–1777), magistrate and French writer, was the first president of the Parliament of Dijon, from which he was twice exiled for having shown too much independence in dealing with matters of state. He was a highly educated man, an antiquarian scholar, and a connoisseur of art, literature, and music, and let somewhat of an epicurean life. Stendhal said, "He had a feeling for the arts and music as well as for painting and architecture." He was also an astute financier.

In short, he was one of those extraordinary men who appear occasionally in history. He was also a member of the Académie des Inscriptions, but not of the Académie française, Voltaire having vetoed his nomination because of some arguments about sales of wood.

De Brosses published among other things Lettres sur Herculaneum, Histoire de la République Romaine dans le cours du VIIe siècle, *and* Histoire des navigations aux terres australes, *but he is best known for his delightful* Lettres familières, *written during his travels in Italy in 1739 and 1740. De Brosses was a remarkable observer and very perceptive critic. His letter on spectacles and music shows his keen observance of the Italian musical scene and his discriminating comparison of the Italian and French styles of performance.*

Source: *Charles de Brosses,* Lettres familières écrites en Italie en 1739 et 1740, *ed. Romain Colomb (Paris, 1835; 4th ed., 1885), vol. II, Ch. L.*

CHARLES DE BROSSES
from *Lettres familières*

On Spectacles and Music

In spite of what you say, M. de Maleteste, you will not persuade me; and in the state of concern we are both in about the preference for the two musics, we could dispute for a whole century without convincing each other. First, it is only up to me to challenge you as an incompetent judge, as every Frenchman would be who tries to pass judgment on Italian music without having heard it in its native country. The French cannot know better the effect that *Artaxerxes* can produce on the stage than the Italians can feel the effects of *Armide*. I have heard the second and last act of this French opera sung in Rome, at the house of Cardinal Ottoboni; it was the best possible choice of Lully's music; the Italians yawned and we shrugged our shoulders.

Nothing could be more ridiculous; then too, we felt that no voice is capable of singing well any other music than that of its own country. Italian music which we sing in France should not appear more ridiculous than ours does in Rome; be careful not to pass any judgment on it, and certainly, to judge it, almost as much as to sing it, you must know the language perfectly and penetrate the feeling of the words.

I will add here what I have always maintained, that the stage at the opera should not be separated from the theatrical action, which gives it much of its power and expression, and that it was not at all suitable for chamber concerts.

In Paris we can hear pretty Italian minuets or great songs loaded down with roulades; on this point, after doing justice to the beauty of the harmony and the singing, we say that Italian music can only trifle with the syllables, that it lacks that expressiveness which characterizes real feeling. That is not at all the case; it excels, as much as ours, at rendering according to the genius of the language, at expressing feelings in a strong and pathetic way. It is these simple and touching places which here are the most admired in the operas; but it is these sorts of airs that our French singers never choose to let us hear, because they could never sing them themselves, and they do not feel their power; because, being simple and lacking songs more than other people, we cannot enjoy them; because the merit of these scraps, torn from a tragedy, consists in the correctness of the expression, which one cannot feel without being acquainted with what has preceded and the real position of the actor.

The other day in the Paglianini bookstore I found a treatise on the two musics written by a Frenchman named Bonnet. In spite of the paradoxes into which he is forced by his stubborn desire for simplicity in musical declamation, and the desire that he probably had to maintain that music is not written to sing, one can discern in his book an intelligent man of taste, an admirer of Lully, who almost always thinks straight as long as it is a question of French music.

As soon as he comes to Italian music, nothing could be more absurd than everything he says; there is not a shadow of truth nor any appearance of common sense; he cannot endure it; he reveals in a moment that he has never been in Italy, that he does not know a word of the language, and what is worse, that he has never heard real Italian songs.

He gives us as a masterpiece of Italian music, an old song pretending to be Italian, *Io provo nel cuore un lieto ardore,* manufactured in France, my guess is, and repeated for the last fifty years. It is the basis of comparison to judge all the rest.

The musician Menicuccio, having found this book on my table, began to read a few pages, and was astounded at this height of unreason. I took the occasion to remonstrate with him that he was himself unjust in his antipathy for our French music, which he scarcely knows better in spite of the short stay he has made in France; for the Italians are more unjust toward us than the greatest partisans of French music can be toward Italian music.

Nothing can make them change their prejudice against our music;

they are so infatuated with theirs that they cannot imagine that it is endurable to hear any other talked about.

The famous composer Hasse, called *il Sassone,* thought he was going to strangle one time in Venice in my presence, *à propos* of some mild remarks I tried to make to him about his unconquerable prejudice. "But," I was saying to him, "do you know what our operas by Lully are like, or those of Campra or Destouches? Have you cast your eyes on the *Hippolyte* of Rameau?" "I," he answered, "no! God preserve me from ever seeing or hearing any other music than Italian, because there is no language other than Italian." "But Latin," I said to him, "this language is so noble, so sonorous; what has it done to you? What have the Psalms of David done to you? They are so poetic, so full of lyrical images. Do you not know that we have a Lalande who is superior in church music to all of your composers of that same music?" Whereupon I saw my man about to suffocate with anger against Lalande and his partisans: and if Faustina, his wife, had not come between us, he was about to hook me with a double crotchet and overwhelm me with sharps.

I found that Tartini alone was reasonable on this point. Though he has never left Padua, he feels perfectly well that each nation must have its own music in conformity with the genius of its language and the kind of voices which the country produces; consequently they are different from that of other countries and not enjoyed by foreigners until they begin to become naturalized in the country. It is the same with comedy, which can be very amusing to the people in whose country it is written, because each person has his own ridiculous situations as well as his own songs, and both are appreciated only by those to whom they are familiar.

The comedies of Aristophanes and of Congreve are suitable to make only the Greeks and the English laugh, or at least only those who are beginning to be familiar with the language and the manners of the two peoples. But perhaps singing, natural as it seems to us to be for man, has something ridiculous about it, as well as the accentuation and inflection of voice, which differs from the simple words. No one can hear a foreign song for the first time without wanting to laugh; little by little one becomes accustomed to it and one has two kinds of pleasure of the same kind instead of one. This is a real gain.

The European courts, where the French language is still more used than Italian, have only Italian operas and never French operas; it is a pleasure of which they deprive themselves willingly. I see people among us who would like us to italianize our music. I cannot share their opinion for a thousand reasons, and among others because I prefer that they have two musics rather than only one. . . .

The number and size of the theaters in Italy are a good indication of the taste of the nation for this sort of amusement. The ordinary towns have handsomer ones than does Paris. In their large cities like Milan, Naples, Rome, etc., they are really vast and magnificent, built with fine architecture, beautiful, noble, and well designed.

The royal house at Naples is prodigiously wide and deep, with seven stories, served by corridors, with a wide and deep stage, capable of holding huge scenes in perspective. At Rome the theater called *Alle Dame*, built by Count Aliberti, a French gentleman in the service of Queen Christina, is the largest and passes for the most beautiful; it is there that the great tragedies are ordinarily played. The second, the Argentina, square at one end and round at the other, less large than the preceding one but better designed, contains almost as many people in a smaller space. The Tordinona, of about the same shape, is also very pretty.

In some theaters they have taken care to construct the loges on the same floor, projecting somewhat from one another as they get farther from the stage, so that those in the front do not interfere with those farther back. The spectators never go on the stage, neither at the comedy nor at the opera; only in France is there this ridiculous habit of occupying space that is only fit for the actors and the sets; but in France a thousand people go to the comedy more for the spectators than for the spectacle.

There are some theaters in which a space has been constructed (*La Ringhiera*) at the front of and the whole length of the loges, above the parterre. This seems to me a very good invention. The men go there, and when they stand during the entr'actes, they are in a position to converse with the ladies seated in the loges. The parterre is filled with benches, like a church, where people sit. It is no less noisy for that reason; it is a clam shell of cabals in favor of the artists, of applause when the favorite of one faction is singing, sometimes even before he begins echoes answer from the highest loges, verses are thrown down or yelled in praise of a singer; in a word, a racket so disturbing, so indecent, that the first row of loges becomes uninhabitable. It is turned over to the disreputable women because it is too close to the parterre, whose first row is raised almost not at all.

Respectable people rent the second, third, and even, if the hall is crowded, the fourth row of loges; the highest ones are for the common people. The custom for the nobles is not, in Italy, as it is in France, to take a ticket at the door and sit where one pleases. Only tickets to the parterre are sold at the door, at a very moderate price, and everyone must have his seat in a loge rented for the season.

Here and in the principal cities the operas begin in the month of November, or about Christmas and the festival of Kings, and last until Lent. There aren't any during the rest of the year. The musicians do nothing then, or gather in small bands to go to Reggio, to the fair at Alexandria, or other small-sized towns, sometimes to the country during the autumn, when there are many nobles vacationing in the surrounding castles.

As soon as the theaters open here assemblies are stopped at Princess Borghese's home, at the Casa Bolognetti, etc. The general meeting place is now at the opera, which is very long and lasts from eight or nine o'clock until midnight. The ladies have, so to speak, "conversazioni" in their loges, where the spectators of their acquaintance go to pay short visits. I told you that each one has to have her loge already rented. As there are four theaters open this winter we entered society by having four loges rented, at a price of twenty sequins each. I come there as I would to my own house. You use your lorgnette to see who of your acquaintance is there, and you visit each other if you want to. The taste that those people have for spectacles and music is shown more by their presence than by the attention they pay. When the first performances are over, when the silence is rather modest, even on the parterre, it is not good manners to listen except in the interesting passages. The loges are neatly furnished and lighted with chandeliers. Sometimes they gamble but more often they chat, seated in a circle around the loge; that is the way they sit and not, as in France, where the ladies dress up the performance by sitting lined up in the front of the loge. From this you may conclude that, in spite of the magnificence of the room and the ornaments of each loge, the total scene is much less beautiful than with us.

I took it into my head to play chess one time when I was almost alone in the La Valle theater with Rochement, at the charming *Dangerous Liberty*, which is not very close-knit and which amuses me much more than their great tragedies. Chess is wonderfully suited to fill in the emptiness of those long recitations, and the music to interrupt one's too great attention to chess.

When the Duke of Saint-Aignan goes to a play, he does something very gallant and much less expensive than you might think, according to what he told me. He sends his servants to serve ices and refreshments to all the loges where there are ladies.

Italian opera differs greatly from French opera in the choice of subjects, in the construction of the plot, in the number and the kinds of actors, as well as in the manner of bringing them together. It is not as it is here, a fixed repertoire composed of the same subjects, which are reused as needed. Here an entrepreneur who wants to stage a new opera for the season gets permission from the governor, rents a theater, brings together from different places voices and instruments, bargains with the workmen and the decorators, and often winds up by going bankrupt, like our directors of country comedies. For more security the workmen often have the income from certain loges turned over to them. In every theater they perform two operas each winter, sometimes three; so that we can count on eight during our stay. There are new operas each year and new singers. They do not want to see again old plays, a ballet, a stage set, nor an actor they have already seen another year unless it be some excellent opera by Vinci or some especially famous voice. When the famous Senesino appeared at Naples last year, people cried out "What's this! Here's an actor we've already seen! He's going to sing in an old-fashioned way." His voice is a little worn, but in my opinion it is the best that I have heard from the point of view of taste.

Here is how they are able to provide for so many novelties, either with voices or with plays. A lyric poem once set to music is common property; composer musicians are not rare; whenever one of them wants to work he seizes upon a poem already published, already set to music by several others; for this he makes new music to the same words. They especially take the operas of Metastasio; there are scarcely any of them that the famous masters have not worked on by turns. This method is useful and easy; one should use the same method in France, where operas often fail through the fault of the poet, it being impossible to compose good music to bad words.

In addition, although in the dramatic genre the words are subordinate to the music, they contribute infinitely in making the play succeed, for they are really the basis and the interest. Just look at our best operas and see if they are not those with the best words: *Armide, Thesée, Atys, Roland, Thétis, Tancrède, Iphigénie, L'Europe galante, Issé, Les Eléments, Les Fêtes Vénetiennes*, etc. I could wish that Rameau would take only the poems of Quinault or de Lamotte; he would make operas different from those of Lully or Campra, his genius being quite different from theirs. He could not equal them in the recitative part, but he would be superior in other respects; I advised him more than once; he said that he had had the same thought more than once, but was held back by fear of being accused of vanity and of trying to surpass the old masters; but it is even more, as I believe, by the fear of the adverse cabal and of its comparisons. This is less to be feared here, where one does not see a score again and the music is not printed or engraved; so that one retains in his memory only the most famous bits; the rest is soon forgotten. Nevertheless, the composers must be enormously fertile to work at so many shops on the same poem without meeting one another too much. Their facility is just as great; a master from whom an entrepreneur requests a play composes it entirely in a month or six weeks. "Should one be astonished," Tartini said to me one day, "if most of the time the recitative of our operas is worthless, when the musician gives all of his time to composing the airs and hastily scrawls everything that is only declamation?" As for me, I pardon them today, when the spectators have acquired the habit of not listening to the recitative. Tartini also complained about another abuse, that the composers of instrumental music try to compose vocal music and vice versa. "These two kinds," he said to me, "are so different that what is right for one is not at all right for the other; everyone must remain within his talent." "I have," he said, "been begged to write for the theaters of Venice, and I have never been willing, knowing full well that a throat is not the fingerboard of a violin. Vivaldi, who tried to compose in both genres, was always hissed in one, while he succeeded in the other." These composers are badly paid; the entrepreneur gives them thirty or forty pistoles; that is all they get, along with the price of the first copies of the tunes, which they sell dear as novelties, and get nothing more when they have once appeared and it is then easy to get copies.

I told you that in Italy they didn't know what it was to engrave or or print any music at all, either vocal or instrumental. There would be too much work; concertos, symphonies with large choruses rain from all sides. As for voices, you do not need a great number; the Italian opera is composed ordinarily of only half a dozen characters without that great apparatus of choruses, of festivals with songs and dances, such are found in our operas.

The orchestra here is large and more varied, but the instruments are neither rare nor costly; but fine voices are paid an exorbitant price, and in addition they must be brought from a distance at great cost.

The castrati are dandies, very pretty, very conceited, who do not give their accomplishments for nothing. There are in an opera company three or four high voices, and a *contralto* or *haute-contre* male or female, and a tenor or *taille* for the roles of kings. The bass voice is not widely used; they are rare and not highly thought of. They are used only in farces, where the comic role is usually for the bass.

These first three kinds of voice are a third or a fourth higher than with us. The countertenors are rare and greatly prized; they range as high as B-mi [high B] and are not of the same kind as ours. There are women's voices in *bas-dessus* lower than any of ours; they sing not an octave higher than the men, but in unison with the men. Sometimes the voice of the castrato changes at the time of breaking, or lowers as he grows older, and becomes *contralto* instead of the *soprano* it had been. It is not rare that they lose it completely at the usual time when it breaks, so that nothing at all is left in place of it. The operation is performed about the age of seven or eight years of age; the child must ask for it himself; the police have imposed this condition to render tolerance of it a little less intolerable. They usually become large and fat like capons, with thighs, buttocks, arms, breast, and neck round and plump like women. When one meets them in a crowd one is astonished when they speak to hear such a tiny child's voice from these colossi. Some of them are very pretty. They are stupid and forward with women, who, as the scandalous gossips pretend, seek them out for their talents, which are endless, for they have many talents. It is even said that one of these *demivir* presented a request to Pope Innocent XI, asking permission to be married, setting forth that the operation had been badly performed. To this the Pope wrote in the margin "che si castri meglio."

One must grow accustomed to these castrato voices to enjoy them. Their timbre is as clear and piercing as that of choir boys, and much stronger. It seems to me that they sing an octave above the natural women's voice. Their voices always have a dry and thin quality, far distant from the young and velvety quality of women's voices; but they are brilliant, light, full of *éclat*, very strong, and with a wide range. The voices of the Italian women are also of similar quality, light and flexible in the last degree; in a word, with the same character as their music. As for roundness, don't ask for it; they don't know what it is. Do not talk to them of the admirable tones of our French music, spun out, sustained tones gradually increased or diminished on the same degree; they would not be capable of understanding you any more than they could provide such sounds. The Italians nevertheless distinguish two kinds of voices: one they call *voce di testa*, which is quite light and suited to the charming little turns they can give to the musical ornaments; the other the chest voice, *voce di petto*, which has sounds more open, more natural, and fuller. In a word, the voices of this country are agreeable, flexible, seductive to the *n*th degree, but, if all them were put into the beaker, one would not get from all their voices joined together any voice comparable to or approaching that of [Catherine-Nicole] Lemaure. Though I am a zealous partisan of Italian music, I agree with you that this kind of voice, so round, so full and velvety, so sonorous, is preferable to all others.

The best that I have heard are la Faustina, la Tesi, la Baratti; among castrati, Senesino, Lorenzino, Marianini, Appianino, excellent contralto, Egiziello, Monticelli, Salimbeni, Porporino—a young pupil of Porpora, pretty as the prettiest girl; as to tenors, Babbi, the most beautiful tenor voice possible, going as high as Jellyot and a very good actor. The sexes are all mingled at Naples, la Baratti playing a man's role; here women are not allowed on the stage; *la bienséance* does not permit it and one sees only pretty little boys dressed like girls; and, God pardon me, in view of the passion that exists throughout the world for the women of the theater, I greatly fear that fornication slips in once in a while. Sometimes these disguised beauties are not too small. Marianini, six feet tall, plays a woman's part on the stage of the Argentina; he is the largest princess I shall ever see.

As for the good taste of the singing, no one can better give you an idea than the charming Vanloo, if you have heard her in Paris. Her voice is not very extensive, there are many more beautiful in this country, but no one surpasses her in delicacy and in exquisite taste in singing.

You see that almost all the roles, whether the personage is a man or a woman, are for high voices; they are always noted in the C-clef on the first line; the G-clef on the second line serves only for the instruments. They never make use of the G-clef on the first line, which we use.

Let us come to the difference between the construction of their poems and ours. The French poems are made abnormal and strange, as it seems they should be for this dramatic genre, which has nothing that is not strange, if you consider it according to the rules; but in it people have agreed to sacrifice *vraisemblance* and natural qualities to the bringing together of a great number of diverse amusements and the perpetual amusement of the senses. For that we have done well to choose fables, enchantments, magic, which leans toward the marvelous, machines, the intrusion of divinities, varieties of festivals, dances, and spectacles; where heaven, earth, and hell can appear successively, where unreality, being the very essence of the subject, will no longer be shocking.

We have another kind of spectacle, less grand and less noble, but nearer to Nature: these are our pastorals and our ballets, where each act, forming in itself a special and complete action, unites in a single general idea, to which all may contribute. We frequently mix with a simple action duets, trios, large choruses, various dances, which produce magnificence and that diversity which is sought in this sort of spectacle. Here there is none of that; their operas have purely historical subjects. One would say that the Italians have looked on this drama as a means of making, by singing, the action stronger and more interesting than it would be if simply recited. This idea would be good if it were correct; but it has only a first appearance of truth. Indeed, in the violent movements of the soul, song, which is a kind of exaggerated voice, becomes quite natural, and it is very true that a strongly passionate sentiment will move the hearers more strongly when it is joined to music than it does with simple declamation; but except for these great movements, song becomes ridiculous in a tragedy. It seems, in the first place, that one should sing or speak according to the situation, just as the English write the strong scenes of their tragedies in verse and the rest in prose; but one feels at once that this medley of song and declaiming would not be bearable.

So the Italian operas are real tragedies, utterly tragic, in the manner of Corneille or Crébillon; *Atrée* would not seem to them to be too strong. The plays are in three very long acts, the scene of the action changing two or three times in each act, so as to be able to show a greater number of sets. All the scenes are in recitative, they end regularly with a great aria. The actor leaves the stage because he has sung his aria; another remains because he is to sing one; in a word, I find that they do not understand at all the principle of the connection of the scenes. There are, in these long acts, no trios, no vocal choruses except perhaps a bad little chorus at the end of the last act. There are no dances; there are eternal scenes of recitative, followed by an air. This monotonous construction is, without contradiction, very inferior to ours. I admit that our fêtes are often badly wrought and with no regard for the time and place where they are used; but then it is the fault of the poet and not of the poem. Another and greater fault of our best musical tragedies is that, at the moment when the action has moved you the most, you are diverted from your emotion because your eyes are occupied by a dance and your ears by a song, each of which forms an amusement of another kind and lets the sentiment grow cold, which the action must reheat when it returns to the stage. The opera, because it tries to present too many pleasures at one time, decreases the enjoyment: also, with many agreeable moments, there are moments of boredom, which the good French tragedies do not have, where the interest produces its effect without diversion; it grows by degrees, and from act to act finds the heart stirred by the preceding act.

The partisans of opera will say that one does not go to the opera for the subject, but for the accessories of the music, the spectacle, and the dance; that is true: it is also what makes me prefer comedy and tragedy, because the pleasures of the mind are more lively than those of the eyes or ears. If the Italians thought they could avoid the difficulties which I have noted in our operas by the choice of the subject of theirs, and by stripping them of that apparatus which impedes the principal action, they are very much mistaken. In truth, their poems (I mean those of Metastasio) are admirable and very interesting; but the airs tacked on to the end of scenes, not always being linked strongly enough to the subject, these exquisite airs, which place Italian music so high above ours, make the same effect of diversion, by letting the interest grow cold while they delight the ears. So, since this fault has become an intrinsic vice of the poems in music, I still prefer the variety of ours to the uniform construction of theirs.

The songs are in lyric verse and the whole narration is in unrhymed free verse, which scarcely differs from prose. I told you that these verses could often be cut from the work without altering the sense; then the plays of Metastasio become very beautiful tragedies. But this poet, full of intelligence and taste, feels that it is more fitting to connect his airs to the subject, and does it as much as he can, especially in the interesting places. If he does not do this everywhere, I have to admit that he is right within his operatic system; singing is the capital part; so the music must be all important.

The Italians like to have all kinds of songs, which create the many different pictures of which music is capable. They have some very noisy ones, full of music and harmony, for brilliant voices; others have agreeable singing with delicate turns of phrase for fine and flexible voices; others are passionate, tender, touching, true in their expression of feelings, which are of a nature suitable for theatrical expression and for enhancing the play of the actor. Those of the first kind are portrayals of a rough sea, or an impetuous gale, of a wild torrent, of lightning, of a lion pursued by hunters, of a horse that hears the warlike trumpet, the horror of a silent night, etc. These images so suited to music are not always naturally found in a tragedy. It is necessary to bring them in by comparisons drawn from the connection that may be made between physical images and the spiritual situation in which the poet has placed his character. I know that such comparisons are completely out of place in the mouth of a man stirred by passion, who should express himself only in a lively, but natural, way. Music would be ill suited to this; here it plays the principal part. This simplicity would furnish perhaps only two words and would not furnish an image; and this music is so beautiful, so astonishing, it paints objects with such art and such truth, that one is quite willing to pardon still greater faults, like that of making a character stay on the stage to sing a very long aria at a time when danger urges him to flee. These kinds of arias of great effect are nearly always accompanied by wind instruments, oboes, trumpets, and horns, which give an excellent impression; a hundred stringed instruments and wind instruments can play at the same time without covering the voice. . . .

It is a rule in Italy never to shed blood on the stage nor show a catastrophe by the murder of one of the principal characters, even when the play contains the most atrocious deeds in the world; in this way one can be certain in advance that the greatest crimes will go unpunished at the dénouement. The people who are killed are completely subordinate, or they do not die. This custom, so well established that in *Caton d'Utique,* whose plot is so well known, Metastasio, wanting to depart from it by bringing the dying Caton on the stage, was obliged to make a change at this point in his play. Nevertheless, I have seen in *Hypsipyle* a Léarchus throw himself into the sea; but this is a gentle way to kill yourself, without striking a blow. One should give us, for the end of the Carnival, the *Caton d'Utique,* a fine opera by Leo, at the Aliberti theater. . . .

Italian recitative is highly displeasing to those who are not used to it. It is said that you enjoy it when you become accustomed to it: it is true that I am beginning to enjoy it. But the natives perhaps are not in that position, for as soon as they know the work they do not listen any more except to the interesting scenes. I was interested at first in how [the opera] could be both so baroque and so monotonous. One day I asked an Englishman, who should be without prejudice on this subject, if it were possible that the recitative of our operas was as flat and as ridiculous as that of the Italians. "Just as ridiculous," he told me, "I assure you that both are equally boring and insupportable in the highest degree." However, we love ours to the point of not doubting that it is good, at least for us. The Italians say the same thing about theirs; I even feel already that certain well-constructed places are beginning to please me; it is simpler and even less sing-song than ours; it is almost merely a simple recitation scanned according to the taste of the tragic actors who sing as they declaim. I imagine that it is almost like the manner that tragedy was performed in France before Baron and Mlle. Lecouvreur had given it the true tone; the basso continuo of the accompaniment is very simple, only providing one note during the rests between the phrases to sustain the tone; the clavecin plays in a rough way and never plays arpeggios. It is not that there are no recitatives with obligato accompaniments by the violin; those are even the finest, but they are rare. When they are perfectly played, like some of Jomelli's I have heard, I must admit that by the power of declamation and the harmonious and sublime variety of the accompaniment, it is the most dramatic thing that one can see or imagine, much above the best French recitative and the most beautiful Italian airs. The performance of these accompanied recitatives is very difficult, especially for the instrumental parts, because of the bizarre quality of the movements, which are not conducted at any fixed tempo.

The time is beaten in church for the Latin music, but never at the opera, however numerous the orchestra may be, however many parts the air has that is being played; these people have notions of precision much different from ours and they say much worse things about our playing than about our music. Zuccaroni said to me, "I have heard at the French Opera only one good piece of music; that is, the chorus from *Jephté* and it was miserably crippled." They are not wrong about the opera, but at the King's Chapel and at the sacred concerts they play rather well, though it is not with the same precision as here. The Italian orchestra, either because of the number or the variety of instruments, is in a position to make the big noise that certain pieces require. In a sacred concert performed on Christmas Eve in the Papal chamber of Monte Cavallo, I judged that there were about two hundred instruments; I expected a prodigious noise. In the performance the effect did not seem to me any greater than if there had been only fifty; from this I conjecture that a certain number of violins suffices to give to the air all the sound it is capable of enduring, and that a thousand additional ones would not make it louder. As the entire orchestra plays accompaniments, it must take care not to drown out the voices. While the parts of the *ripieno* play harmonic chords, the first violin almost everywhere plays the same melody as the voice; this unison sustains and accompanies it very well. I do not know why we do not play the same way. They have a method of accompanying that we do not understand, which it would be easy for us to introduce into our playing and which greatly increases the power of their music; it is the art of augmenting or diminishing the sound, which I might call the art of shadings or of *chiaroscuro*. This is applied either gradually by degrees, or all at once. In addition to loud and soft, they use also a *mezzo piano* and a *mezzo forte*. These are reflections, half-tints, which give incredible pleasure to the sound color. (Damn! what a pretty expression; Père Castel could not do better.) Sometimes while the orchestra is accompanying *piano*, all the instruments begin to force the tone at the same time for one or two notes, covering the voice completely, then they suddenly fall back into the *en sourdine*; it is an excellent effect.

Another variety comes from the way they use modulations. They rarely compose in the minor mode; almost all their tunes are written in the major mode; but they mix in minor phrases without anyone's expecting it, surprise and satisfy the ear to the point of affecting the heart. They have beautiful tones which we hardly ever use; among others *mi* major with three flats, of singular beauty.

They understand also how to vary the sound by the variety of the instruments they use, violins, horns, trumpets, oboes, flutes, harps, viols d'amore, archlutes, mandolins, etc. We do not have sufficient diversity in our instruments, which contributes to the monotony of which our music is accused. Their ritornellos are ravishing, and the chorus that follows them is so prettily turned out, so flattering and so surprising, that beside them our French airs are only sing-song; it is madness to want to compare them. I will say only a word about this to combat your opinion, to wit, that the essence of music being to be sung, that which is nearest to singing ought to have preference. The most unified of their pieces are on the level of the most singing ones of ours; and if ours are uniform, theirs seem repetitious, too, especially to the ears of foreigners, who are not used to their appoggiaturas, their way of slurring the notes, their passing notes, very different from ours; they are at first surprised by them, then afterwards they distinguish the repeats more easily.

The fault of their music, which they admit themselves, is that it is suitable only for stage performance and for concerts, since it must be accompanied. If you ask a singer to sing a drawing room song, she will not sing without going to the piano to accompany herself, playing the bass with her left hand and the melody, not the chords, with her right hand; they all know enough for that. So in spite of the small esteem they have for our songs, they praise our gay vaudevilles, our duets and *chansonettes de table*; that is all they like of our music.

Almost all their airs are for solo voice; there are scarcely ever more than two or three duets in an opera and almost never any trios. The duets are devoted to tender and touching subjects, to the most pathetic situations of the play; they are marvelously beautiful and move the hearers to very tender feelings. It is in them that the voices as well as the violins use that *chiaroscuro*, that imperceptible swelling of the sound which increases the power from note to note to the greatest degree, and then returns to a very soft and tender shading. They admire the cadences or organ-points that occur in the finale of every solo air. As for me, they do not please me at all; in addition to being very frequent they always say the same thing. I want to laugh when I see a fat eunuch blow himself up like a balloon, to show the range of his voice for a quarter of an hour without taking a breath in twenty elaborate passages, one after the other. Also I do not like, as in our cantatas, having every song divided into two parts, the first of which is repeated after the second. This is even shocking, because of the way the words are constructed; for there are two quatrains in which the strongest part of the thought is in the second quatrain and is greatly weakened by the repetition of the first.

Sometimes if there is dancing on the stage of the opera, it is not because the ballets are part of the plot; they are not brought about by the festival nor connected with the subject. Since every opera has three acts, each lasting about an hour, the length of the opera is relieved by length of the *entr'actes*, either by dancing or *intermedi*. These dances are a kind of pantomime, very ridiculously placed in the intervals of a tragedy. The dancers, women and men, are lively, light, jumping higher than La Camargo and as high as the bird Maltère; they have good legs and in addition a certain pleasing sweetness, and are not lacking in precision; but they have neither arms, grace, nor nobility. In a word, Italian dancing is much inferior to ours; they admit this themselves. When they try to dance at a ball, they don't use their own music; they play French or German minuets.

Italian music is not as danceable as it is singable; their beautiful symphonies, so harmonious, do not lend themselves to dance steps. They are not able to compose with dancing in view, since they have only a few tunes suitable to theatrical ballets. I have heard it said a thousand times in France that Italian instrumental music is better than ours, but that we excel in vocal music. It seems to me to be just the contrary and that these people think just as I do. In the first place, for vocal music no comparison at all; I will never endure it. For instrumental, they have concerts, with large choirs, or mixed concerts of choirs and solo violins much better than anything we can do in this genre; they arrange their instruments better; harmony is more familiar to them. They take care to have only one group work at a time and quite simply keep the others quiet, so that the theme of the subject will stand out in a clear line so that the chords may be correct, placed one apart from another, without getting mixed up, as happens when the treble and the bass work too much at the same time. They understand all of this better than we. On the other hand, our operas are full of an infinity of dance tunes, of movements of different kinds, of natural singing, agreeable, easy to remember, and when you leave the theater are on everybody's lips. This is our real symphony, but with songs more lively and gay.

As for the sonata for solo violin, in plain words, they have none that are equal to those of Leclair; besides, either because they do not think much of their riches in this kind of music or because the orchestra does not please them unless it is very large, they play only a few sonatas. Not long ago I took a rather good violinist to a concert at Cardinal Bichi's house, and I had him play the sixth sonata in *ut* minor from Leclair's third book, to see if those people would have the nerve not to find it beautiful; they were not so stupid, but they did not care much for the performer, who really did not play badly. I do not know, but I find French playing dull and insipid compared with theirs; it is not that our hands are not as good on the fingerboard of the violin, we lack the bow hand; they have a thousand delicate turns, a thousand sallies, in a word, an articulation that we are not able to acquire. Pascalini da Roma is exquisite in this brilliant part; he played like a God the other day at Saint Cecilia. He is the Guignon of Italy, as Tartini of Padua is its Leclair. For grandeur of execution, for being first violin at the head of an orchestra, I think that the Venetian girl yields to no one.

If you are shocked to see the *entr'actes* of a serious tragedy filled with ballet-pantomimes, you will be much more shocked to see it cut up by *intermedi*. We call *intermezzi* the little farces in two acts, of low comedy, their tone about the same as those that are played on the stages in the Place Royale.

Judge now if such plays make any sense in the *entr'actes* of a tragedy; but please pardon them, for they are delightful if the music is perfectly good and perfectly played; mediocrity in this genre is only low and trivial. These little farces have only two or three comic chacacters; the music is simple, gay, natural, comic in its expression, lively, and laughable in the highest degree. I would like to be able to get you to listen to a husband imitating his wife who has just lost all his money playing faro, the regrets of some poor devil who is about to be hanged, or the duet of a bizarre quarrel, or of the reconciliation between a gallant and his mistress; there is nothing jollier in the world. Add to that the air of truth with which it is presented by the musicians and the actors, and the strange precision of the execution. These *bouffons* weep, laugh loudly, work hard, do all kinds of pantomime, without missing the tempo by an eighth of a second. I admit that these kinds of plays, when they are like the *Maître de Musique* by Scarlatti, the *Serva padrona, Livietta e Tracollo* by my charming Pergolesi, give me more pleasure than any of the others. The intellectuals of this country who esteem only their serious plays laugh at me for my infatuation for these farces. But I stick to my opinion that the less serious the music is, the better Italian music succeeds. Indeed, one feels that it breathes gaiety and is in its element. I like their comedies also, half serious, with some comic roles. We were given a very nice one by Rinaldo di Capua at the theater *della Valle*, and I saw a charming one in Naples, by Leonardo Leo. I do not believe that we can succeed in creating laughable music, though we have excellent comedies of a slightly more elevated kind, witness the *Fêtes vénitiennes*, where the tone is really that of comedy; and God grant that we be often given others like it!

The best music schools, or to use their term, seminaries, for *maîtres de chapelle*, are in Naples. From there came Scarlatti, Porpora, Domenico Sarri, Porta, Leo, Vinci, Pergolesi, Gaëtan Latilla, Rinaldo di Capua, and several other celebrated composers. For voices the best school is at Bologna; Lombardy excels in instrumental music. It seems to me that

Italian music was at its highest period six or seven years ago; taste changes frequently here. Latilla is now in fashion at Rome. The opera *Siroës*, now being given at the Aliberti theater, was composed by him; but neither he nor Terradellas and others are as powerful as those who were working a few years ago; and these had surpassed their predecessors, like Buononcini, Porta, the elder Scarlatti, Sarri, a composer learned and sad, Porpora, natural, but not very inventive. Vinci, Hasse, commonly called the Saxon, and Leo are the ones whose music has the most reputation. Vinci is the Lully of Italy, true, simple, natural, expressive, and [wrote] the finest songs in the world, without being too refined; he produced much though he died young. They say that he was insolent, and, after being punished more than once for an affair he carried on too publicly with a woman, he ended by being poisoned. *Artaxerxes* passes for his best work; it was at the same time one of the best works of Metastasio, who took it partly from the *Stilicon* of Thomas Corneille and partly from the *Xerxes* of Crébillon. It is the most famous Italian opera. I have not seen it played, but I know it from having heard nearly all of it at concerts, and I was charmed. Excellent as this work by Vinci is, the scene of Artaban's despair, added by the poet and set to music by the Saxon, probably surpasses all the others. The recitative *Eccomi al fine in libertà del mio dolor* is admirable, as is the air which follows: *Pallido il sole*. This bit is not easily found; it is Prince Edward who had the kindness to give it to me; I look upon it as the most beautiful among the seven or eight hundred airs that I had copied from various pieces. The Saxon is very learned; his operas are worked out with great taste in their expression and their harmony.

Leo is an uncommon genius; he draws pictures well; his harmony is very certain, his melodies have an agreeable and delicate turn, full of subtle invention. They are not easy to follow, although in general Italian music is easier to read and to sing than ours, except that it requires so many voices. I had already had this experience, with surprise, with the young girls of Geneva, who were taught two at a time, and who learned three Italian airs in the time it takes for one French air.

Pergolesi, Bernasconi, Scarlatti, Jomelli are almost equal to the three I have talked to you about. Among all these musicians my favorite is Pergolesi. Ah! what a pretty talent, simple and natural. No one can write with greater facility, grace, and taste. Console me in my affliction; I need it greatly; my poor favorite has just died of pneumonia at the age of twenty-three years, already enjoying a considerable reputation, which soon would have equaled that of Vinci, his teacher. He died amid applause for his excellent opera *Olympiade*, which gave me so much pleasure. His small intermedi are charming, so gay, so pleasing. His cantata *Orphée* is looked upon as the best Italian cantata; his *Stabat mater* as the masterpiece of Latin music. There is no piece of music more praised than this for the profound knowledge of its harmonies. They say wonderful things also about his *De Profundis*, which is in the hands of the Duke de Monteleone; they have promised to give it to me, but it is yet to come. Jomelli has given us finally the opera *Ricimer* at the Argentina theater, and some other pieces. This young man promises to go far and to equal everything that has been said about great masters. He has no less power than delicacy and taste; he possesses harmony completely and uses it with surprising richness. I should not forget, in the catalogue of composers that I know, neither Jacomelli nor Lampugnani, who has written such touching airs, nor a Frenchman, by name Antoine Gay, who has succeeded quite well in this country. I pass over the many others in silence. Handel has a great reputation in England; his works are not much known in Italy, and, from what I have seen of his vocal music, I would think him to be inferior to all those whom I have named to you.

The magnificence of decoration in the Italian operas is such, especially in comparison with the shabbiness ordinarily found in ours, that I can give you only a feeble idea; one would have to see it. The art of painting is lost today in Italy; there remain only some clever men in the areas of perspective ornamentation. The immense grandeur of the theaters permits them to display their ability in a suitable space, which we do not have in our wretched halls in Paris; you would not believe with how much truth they render the place represented, in detail and in the whole; it is indeed a gallery, a vaulted prison, a forest, a field, a barn, a library, etc. Instead of placing the decorative columns in two rows as we do, they spread them across the stage; if they are galleries or colonnades, they dispose them obliquely on several diagonal lines, which increases the effect of perspective; if the place is to have little space, they restrict the stage and enclose it so well on all sides that one would say one was in a cave, in a tent, or beneath a vault. There are two or three changes per act; they change without much skill, with less teamwork and speed than we do. But also, when they are done, their truth is such that my whole attention is drawn to recognize, once they have changed the scene, where the junction of these pieces I have just seen put in place, one after the other, is to be found.

Instead of the vocal choruses and dancers that people and adorn our stages, they fill and decorate theirs with a great series of all kinds of marches, of sacrifices, of all kinds of ceremonies, which they present with true detail, curious and amusing. The silent spectacles which Servandoni is starting to give at the Tuileries are almost of the same kind. As for machines, properly so-called, I have not seen any of them; their poems having no marvels, no divinities, no magic, are not suited to these things. The marches are many, sometimes a hundred to a hundred and fifty personages. At first glance, the sight of these triumphal chariots, of this crowd, of all this apparatus has something full of pomp and magnificence; but it does not break the eternal monotony of scenes ending with an air as well as could have been done by a variety of choruses and intervening dances. In addition, the people in the suite of the many actors are not costumed like our groups of choristers, like our gallant companies of dancers. They are tramps, badly shod and dressed in a long coat painted in garish colors and with some sort of a cap.

The audience especially loves combats, mêlées; to please the groundlings there must be similar pomp in every opera: "When there occurs some frightful row in which there is a lot of noise, the parterre is content." These combats are pretty well performed. They amuse me too. I have seen captains enter at the head of their troops mounted on very fine horses; but these horses appear to have very little taste for the music, and are not pleased to trot on the boards of the theater.

To sum up the unheard-of length into which your letter has made me go, much beyond my expectations and yours, Italian music is certainly better than ours; but our opera is as good as theirs, everything being considered, unless that it would be easier to give their opera the form of ours, than for us to give French singing the brilliant turns and ornamentation of Italian singing.

I might add a couple of words on church music; we hear it often, for every time there is a service in a church there is music, and there are so many churches here, each of which has so many feasts! They perform not only motets but also concertos, sometimes with two choirs, which answer each other from two lofts, from one side of the church to the other.

There was a superb instance of this sort of music at the Gesù on New Year's Day, but still inferior than that at Saint Cecilia, where a Spaniard gave a motet of his own composition, the most beautiful I have heard in Italy. The choirs of their motets are admirable, but the chants are lacking in the nobility and gravity suitable to their subjects. I would praise their knowledge and their harmony but not their taste. Our motets by Lalande are more beautiful and better constructed than theirs. The music in Latin does not have the same popularity as that in the vulgar tongue; little of it is performed outside the church. I would have trouble in telling you which are the most celebrated composers. As to the old Carissimi, whom you have mentioned to me, for heaven's sake, do not speak of him here for fear of being looked upon as a sugarloaf hat; those who succeeded him have gone out of fashion a long while ago. For a long time at Venice they praised the psalms in the vulgar tongue of a certain Benedetto Marcello; they are in three or four voices with basso continuo, without an orchestra. Those that I have heard appeared learned to me, but sad and devoid of a singing quality.

Here, my dear Maleteste, is all that I can tell you about Italian music. A thousand embraces to all of our friends; tell little Potot about my letter; he is a dilettante, almost a virtuoso.

16. The Violin

These extracts from Roger North's Musicall Grammarian *and other memoirs, written from the point of view of an accomplished musical amateur who had studied with the famous John Jenkins and had played consort music, reflect the recent appearance and rapid acceptance of the violin, still something of a novelty in the 1720s, and the decline of the viol, especially the bass viol. North also comments on Italian bowing and ornaments and makes reference to Nicola Matteis, the first Italian virtuoso to work in England. His brief essay "The Noble Base Viol" seems to be a last, nostalgic look at an instrument that was greatly appreciated in the earlier decades of the seventeenth century. For biographical information see the selection by North in Chapter 6.*

SOURCES: *Roger North, "Some Usages of the Violin," Br. Mus, MS. Add. MS 32,353, pp.128–29; "On Bowing," Br. Mus. MS. Add. MS 32, 532, p.1; "On the Trill," Br. Mus. MS. Add. MS 32,533, p.108ᵛ ff., Add. MS 32,536, pp.38–39; "On the Stoccata, and the Concussion of Notes," Br. Mus. MS. Add. MS 32,536, pp.114–15; "On Double Notes," Br. Mus. MS Add. MS 32,536, pp.128–29; "The Noble Base Viol," Br. Mus. MS. Add. MS 32,537, pp.107ᵛ–108.*

ROGER NORTH
from *Musicall Grammarian* and Other Memoirs

Some Usages of the Violin

Consort Musick doth not succeed well, unless the master perfectly understands the capacity and extent of the instruments, as well as the dexterity that belongs to them. For now the musick is not ordered for plain sounds, as formerly, when the composition and mixture was the *summa totalis* of the ornamental part, and it was almost indifferent by what means or hands the sounds were excited, provided they were strong and true. But beautys now, in the upper parts at least (or those who imitate them), as well as sound, are required. And this hath made the usages of the Violin of very great moment to be considered in the fabrick of a good consort. Besides the very good tone that instrument commands, there are certain late manners of touch introduced—the result of the nicest skill and ability—of which some are of admirable efficacy and improvement, and others commonly overdone; and there are those also, which are better spared than used.

Of the first sort the chief is the sounding all the notes under the touch, and none with the strings open; for those are a harder sound than when stopped, and not always in tune, which the stop (assisted by the ear) effects with utmost niceness; so that upon instruments so handled, all the semitones, whatever the keys are or however they change, are in tune to the most scrupulous test of the ear. And besides all this, the power of the finger in giving temper and commixture to the notes, hath a superlative effect of sweetness; and by that means the violin hath grown upon the voice, whose prerogative that excellence, as well as the former hath been esteemed. To perform this [finger-stopping] well is sovereign skill, but seems more abstruse than really it is; for among us the old way of using the open strings hath been a prepossession, and it is not easy to leave it off. But in time, beginners will take into it, and then common practice will make it familiar.

On Bowing

The Italians have brought the bow to an high perfection, so that nothing of their playing is so difficult as the *arcata* or long bow, with which they will begin a long note, clear, without rub, and draw it forth swelling louder and louder, and at the acme take a slow waver; not a trill to break the sound or mix two notes, but as if the bird sat at the end of a spring, [and] as she sang the spring waved her up and down, or as if the wind that brought the sound shaked, or a small bell were struck and the sound continuing waved to and again—so would I express what is justly not to be shewn but to the ear by an exquisite hand.

On the Trill

When any [two] notes are of accord so nearly allied, that they will be heard together plain, but a little hard perhaps, then sounding them alternately, but so swift that they are *quasi* mixed, softens the sound and makes it more elegant; and this is the shake or trill. And accordingly there is the beat-up trill (f♯–g) and the backfall trill (a–b). And both going together, which I have seldom known exactly done, make the double trill, being the notes of the cadence broke by a devision.

And it seems a rule in all shaking graces, that if the alternated notes in their circumstances will not sound tolerably well together the shake is not proper. . . .

One great failure of [shaking graces] is the neglect of time, which much deforms them. The triller's aim is to make a strong spring shake, as fast as possible, and (if endeavors fail not) like a squirrel scratching her ear, but swifter or slower, without government as to measure. Now it seems that a trill is but a species of devision, and ought to keep time, and fall in with that of the consort. This I have heard done, but it was in a slow, and not a swift manner, which will by no means admit that decorum. . . .

Nothing is more expressly taught, and less correctly, than [the trill] is; which may be perceived by observing the manner of the several performers upon the same notes. For some trill with spring, and very swift, and on all occasions the same: which must be wrong, for the trill ought to be a just devision of the time used; and such a spring must needs be out of command, so whether the measures are swift or slow, the spring works all alike. Others that have or use not that spring, but stay or accelerate their trill according to occasion, conform much better to the musick, of which an uninterrupted measure is a chief perfection. This difference was seen in the two great violin masters, Signor Nicolai Matteis, and his son. The former had an absolute power of his trill, and used always in time; and so slow, as permitted the ingredients in his shakes to be distinctly heard sounding; which made some, that understood no better, say that he had not a good shake. But the other [i.e., the son] had a spring so active, that during his trill the sound was stopped, because the notes had not time to sound. And that is an objection to all prolonged trilling, so strong that the Italians have omitted it wholly rather than corrupt the sonorousness of the parts. And the late invention they call a wrist-shake is intended to that end, *vizt* that the sound may wave, but not stop or vary its tone, for all interruption of the sound where it ought to be heard is a fault; and such a fault as the neatest players are perpetually guilty of. All this is not to impeach the short touches of the finger, and slides, that give a spirit to the notes, which for elegance are taught by the masters; and scholars are wonderfully delighted to imitate.

Of the Stoccata, and the Concussion of Notes

Another grace, or rather manner, is the *Stoccata* or stab, which is a peculiar art of the hand upon instruments of the bow. And as it is an occasional imitation, so hath it a due acceptance; but to use it at all turns, whensoever the movement will allow it, creates a *fastidium*. For it doth not, as the other, mend the harmony, but rather by an affected snatching deprive it. And it appears manifestly so, when some consideration doth not go along with it; for though [a harmony] be short, it ought to sound full, else it is lost. Old Signor Nicola Matteis used this manner to set off a rage, and then a repentance; for after a violent *stoccata*, he entered at once with the bipedalian bow,[1] as speaking no less in a passion, but of the contrary temper. Therefore these artful manners of sounding are not to be used but to set off one and the other, and to bring Musick to Nature as a picture is to the life, (*quasi alter idem*).

On Double Notes

The use of double notes is too much affected, and done as if a consort of 3 or 4 parts might be obtained that way; but at best it proves hard and uncouth, and is not worth the pains and difficulty that belongs to it. But masters must do (seeming) wonders, as tumblers shew tricks which none else can perform, to obtain esteem by pleasing the ignorant.

Another practice upon the violin is much courted and admired, which is dealing in the hyper-superior octave which they call high notes, and with which is commonly joined the *arpeggio*. All this may also be called humour, any thing rather than musick. For the naturalists say that musical sounds are confined within limits: too low ceaseth to be sound, and too high loseth all effective force, and is rather squeak than tone, and at a distance is no better than a whistle. If the extreme sharpness hath a virtue in musick, a 4-inch flageolet would do very well in a consort. Therefor laying aside the trick, and the regular clinking, which may be perceived and wondered at by those whose ears are near, it hath no engaging effect upon any one's spirits, as may be perceived to

1. Two feet long?

come from full-bodied music. And certainly the best use that can be made of any instrument is drawn from the compass of its native force, where the tone is free, loud, and well-conditioned; and that for the most part proves to be about the middle of the instrument.

The Noble Base Viol

There is an instrument which, tho' very excellent in its kind, yet hath engross't all people's fancy to learne, and very few will touch upon any other, and that is the violin. That this is a prime part in a consort, true; but without its attendant harmony it is a bauble. And the ill effect is that all affecting the upper part, none apply to the base, and so no consort can be had, but by means of some hireling drudge, on the harsh violon, to serve as a tambour to vamp out the noise. And the noble Base Viol is not thought an instrument for a christiall to handle, and indeed it lyes under this disadvantage, that so few understand the bow, and regular fingering, with the proper gracing of the notes upon it, as one seldome hears it well used or rather not abused. Whereas in truth all the sublimitys of the violin—the swelling, *tremolo*, tempering, and what else can be thought admirable—have place in the use of the Base Viol, as well as drawing a mean and lower parts, and in a lute way toucheth the accords, and is no less swift than the violin itself, but wonderfully more copious. This I must say in vindication of the Base Viol, and for the encouragement to use it; and lett those that know it less, despise it as they please. It is from this chance, art hath an enemy called Ignorance.

Francesco Geminiani (1687–1762) was born in Lucca, in northern Italy. He studied with Carlo Ambrogio Lonati in Milan, and later with Corelli in Rome. He was a fiery player, with a lively temperament that some called "eccentric." He was a great solo player but apparently was not successful as a leader or conductor. Dr. Burney says that Geminiani lost his position as leader of the San Carlo opera orchestra at Naples because "none of the performers were able to follow him in his tempo rubato and other unexpected accelerations and relaxations of measure."

The Art of Playing on the Violin is a famous violin method, a most valuable addition to violin literature of the period. The treatise was written in English and was the first work of its kind ever published in any country previous to Leopold Mozart's Violinschule. It is said that in this work Corelli's principles of violin playing are handed down to posterity. Geminiani's rules for holding the violin and the bow are basic and the same as are used today; the same is true for the use of the left hand and the right arm.

As in most books of instruction of the eighteenth century, the importance of expression of emotions is stressed. In Geminiani's short treatise it is set forth clearly, and the necessary ornaments to heighten expression and add grace and beauty are explained in section XVIII.

SOURCE: *Francesco Geminiani,* The Art of Playing on the Violin *(London, 1751; facs. ed., Oxford University Press, [n.d.]).*

FRANCESCO GEMINIANI
from *The Art of Playing on the Violin*

Example XVIII

Contains all the Ornaments of Expression, necessary to the playing in a good Taste.

What is commonly call'd good Taste in singing and playing, has been thought for some years past to destroy the true Melody, and the Intention of their Composers. It is supposed by many that a real good Taste cannot possibly be acquired by any Rules of Art; it being a peculiar Gift of Nature, indulged only to those who have naturally a good Ear: And as most flatter themselves to have this Perfection, hence it happens that he who sings or plays, thinks of nothing so much as to make continually some favourite Passages, or Graces, believing that by this Means he shall be thought to be a good Performer, not perceiving that playing in good Taste doth not consist of frequent Passages, but in expressing with Strength and Delicacy the Intention of the Composer. This Expression is what every one should endeavour to acquire, and it may be easily obtained by any Person, who is not too fond of his own Opinion, and doth not obstinately resist the Force of true Evidence. I would not however have it supposed that I deny the powerful Effects of a good Ear; as I have found in several Instances how great its Force is: I only assert that certain Rules of Art are necessary for a moderate Genius, and may improve and perfect a good one. To the End therefore that those who are Lovers of Musick may with more Ease and Certainty arrive at Perfection, I recommend the Study and Practice of the following Ornaments of Expression, which are fourteen in number; namely, 1st A plain Shake (tr) 2ᵈ A turn'd Shake (✦) 3ᵈ A superior Apogiatura (♪) 4ᵗʰ An inferior Apogiatura (♪) 5ᵗʰ Holding the Note (—) 6ᵗʰ Staccato (|) 7ᵗʰ Swelling the Sound (✓) 8ᵗʰ Diminishing the Sound (◥) 9ᵗʰ Piano (p.) 10ᵗʰ Forte (f.) 11ᵗʰ Anticipation (♪) 12ᵗʰ Separation (♪) 13ᵗʰ A Beat (//) 14ᵗʰ A close Shake (*m*). From the following explanation we may comprehend the nature of each element in particular.

(First) Of the Plain Shake

The plain Shake is proper for quick Movements; and it may be made upon any Note, observing after it to pass immediately to the ensuing Note.

(Second) Of the Turned Shake

The turn'd Shake being made quick and long is fit to express Gaiety; but if you make it short, and continue the Length of the Note plain and soft, it may then express some of the more tender Passions.

(Third) Of the Superior Apogiatura

The Superior Apogiatura is supposed to express Love, Affection, Pleasure, &c. It should be made pretty long, giving it more than half the Length or Time of the Note it belongs to, observing to swell the Sound by Degrees, and towards the End to force the Bow a little: If it be made short, it will lose much of the aforesaid Qualities; but will always have a pleasing Effect, and it may be added to any Note you will.

(Fourth) Of the Inferior Apogiatura

The Inferior Apogiatura has the same Qualities with the preceding, except that it is much more confin'd, as it can only be made when the Melody rises the Interval of a second or third, observing to make a Beat on the following Note.

(Fifth) Of Holding a Note

It is necessary to use this often; for were we to make Beats and Shakes continually without sometimes suffering the pure Note to be heard, the Melody would be too much diversified.

(Sixth) Of the Staccato

This expresses Rest, taking Breath, or changing a Word; and for this Reason Singers should be careful to take Breath in a Place where it may not interrupt the Sense.

(7th and 8th) Of Swelling and Softening the Sound

These two Elements may be used after each other; they produce great Beauty and Variety in the Melody, and employ'd alternately, they are proper for any Expression or Measure.

(9th and 10th) Of Piano and Forte

They are both extremely necessary to express the Intention of the Melody; and as all good Musick should be composed in Imitation of a Discourse, these two Ornaments are designed to produce the same Effects that an Orator does by raising and falling his Voice.

(Eleventh) Of Anticipation

Anticipation was invented, with a view to vary the Melody, without altering its Intention: When it is made with a Beat or Shake, and swelling the Sound, it will have a greater Effect, especially if you observe to make use of it when the Melody rises or descends the Interval of a Second.

(Twelfth) Of the Separation

The Separation is only designed to give a Variety to the Melody, and takes place most properly when the Note rises a Second or Third; as also when it descends a Second, and then it will not be amiss to add a Beat, and to swell the Note, and then make the *Apogiatura* to the following Note. By this Tenderness is express'd.

(Thirteenth) Of the Beat

This is proper to express several Passions; as for Example, if it be perform'd with Strength, and continued long, it expresses Fury, Anger, Resolution, &c. If it be play'd less strong and shorter, it expresses Mirth, Satisfaction, &c. But if you play it quite soft, and swell the Note, it may then denote Horror, Fear, Grief, Lamentation, &c. By making it short and swelling the Note gently, it may express Affection and Pleasure.

(Fourteenth) Of the Close Shake

This cannot possibly be described by Notes as in former Examples. To perform it, you must press the Finger strongly upon the String of the Instrument, and move the Wrist in and out slowly and equally, when it is long continued swelling the Sound by Degrees, drawing the Bow nearer to the Bridge, and ending it very strong may express Majesty, Dignity, &c. But making it shorter, lower and softer, it may denote Affliction, Fear, &c. And when it is made on short Notes, it only contributes to make their Sound more agreeable and for this reason it should be made use of as often as possible.

Men of purblind Understandings, and half Ideas may perhaps ask, is it possible to give Meaning and Expression to Wood and Wire; or to bestow upon the Power of raising and soothing the Passions of rational Beings? But whenever I hear such a Question put, whether for the Sake of Information, or to convey Ridicule, I shall make no Difficulty to answer in the Affirmative, and without searching over-deeply into the Cause, shall think it sufficient to appeal to the Effect. Even in common Speech a Difference of Tone gives the same Word a different Meaning. And with regard to musical Performance, Experience has shown that the Imagination of the Hearer is in general so much at the Disposal of the Master, that by the Help of Variations, Movements, Intervals and Modulation he may almost stamp what Impression on the Mind he pleases.

These extraordinary Emotions are indeed most easily excited when accompany'd with Words; and I would besides advise, as well the Composer as the Performer, who is ambitious to inspire his Audience, to be first inspired himself; which he cannot fail to be if he chooses a Work of Genius, if he makes himself thoroughly acquainted with all its Beauties; and if while his Imagination is warm and glowing he pours the same exalted Spirit into his own Performance.

Eſsemp. XVIII

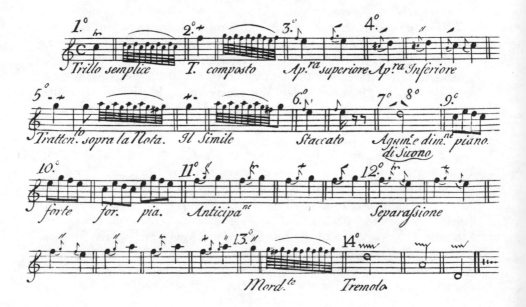

Georg Muffat (1653–1704), German organist and composer, studied in Paris from 1663 to 1669, where he was trained in the French style. He is said to have studied Lully's style for six years and undoubtedly had occasion to observe Lully's orchestral practice and to become thoroughly versed in it. His account may be considered that of an eyewitness. From 1678 he served in a Jesuit school in Alsace as a teacher of rhetoric; in 1678 he was appointed organist and valet-de-chambre *to the Archbishop of Salzburg. A few years later he went to Rome, where he worked with Corelli and Pasquini. He returned to Salzburg in 1682. In 1690 Muffat became* Kappellmeister *and Supervisor of the Pages to the Bishop of Passau, where he spent the remainder of his life.*

Muffat was an industrious composer and published a number of works; his first, Armonico tributo *(1682), a set of* sonate da camera, *was well received. His* Apparatus musico-organisticus *(1690), a collection of organ works, was dedicated to Leopold I. Most important are his two collections of dance music for strings,* Florilegium I *(1695) and* Florilegium II *(1698).*

The Florilegium secundum *contains a short treatise in four languages, as a preface to the collection, in which Muffat expounds Lully's manner of playing the violin. The first two parts of the treatise are presented here; the other three are "Tempo," "Certain Customs of the Lullists," and "How to Perform the Agréments." The principles Muffat sets forth are still valid for Lully's music and that of his contemporaries, and for compositions written during the next two or three decades; much of his teaching may also be valid for the orchestral music of Handel and Bach.*

SOURCE: *Georg Muffat,* Florilegium secundum *(Passau, 1698); also in* Denkmäler der Tonkunst in Oesterreich, *ed. H. Rietsch (Vienna, 1895), vol. 2, pp. 44–47, 52–53.*

GEORG MUFFAT

from *Florilegium secundum*

First observations of the author, on the manner of playing the *Airs de Ballets* in the French style according to the method of the late M. de Lully: of which the examples, that should be referred to from time to time together with what will be said in this discourse, will be found separately. . . .

The manner of playing the ballet airs on the violin according to the invention of the late Monsieur Baptiste de Lully, here taken in its purity, and thus worthy, due to the approbation of the best musicians of Europe, is a piece of investigation so exquisite that one could not be able to find anything more exact, more beautiful, nor more pleasing. Thus, to reveal to you here in a few words the principal secrets, you must know, dear reader, that it accomplishes at the same time two functions admirably linked together; that is, to please the ear and at the same time to mark the movements of the dance so well that one recognizes immediately the type of each air and feels inspired, in spite of one's self, a desire to dance. To come to the point, it appears to me that five things are necessary: 1st, to play in time, 2nd, that the entire orchestra observe the same manner of bowing; in third place, to maintain constantly the true movement of each piece. A fourth requirement is to take notice of certain usages with respect to repetitions, the interpretation of certain notes, and the propriety of the style and of the dance. And finally, to understand how to make use with judgment of the pretty manners and suitable ornaments that show off the harmony of now one, now another part, like so many precious stones. These five points are set forth in these lines. . . .

I. Contactus: On Playing in Tune

There is no difference of opinion among the good masters of any nation whatsoever regarding the accuracy of pitch. It is only the weak apprentices or the ignorant and spoilers who, in all countries, disobey the rules. Nothing is more able to help one avoid false notes than the instruction and correction of a good teacher, from whom one will have learned the first principles of this art, which it is not my intention to deal with in this place. I will say only that after having had good instruction to acquire and maintain a delicate ear, frequent exercise with persons of an exquisite taste will be of great help; just as one should not play with those who would be more likely to deprave, rather than to perfect, one's ear. Beyond that, I have noticed that the faults of those who play out of tune come, for the most part, from the two stops that together compose the semitone (for example, the *mi* and *fa*; a and b-flat, b-natural and c, or f-sharp and g, c-sharp and d, g-sharp and a, etc.). They never take the *mi* or the sharp high enough, nor the *fa* or the flat low enough. They err tremendously who, when, against the true proportion of the sounds and the structure of the keys or modes, or against harmonic relations, which ought to be surmised from what comes before or after, they also use trills on improper notes. Finally the ear is offended, even when playing in tune, when one does not touch the strings firmly nor assiduously, whence comes a whistle or scratch that is very disagreeable.

II. Plectrum: The Manner of Using the Bow

Most of the violinists of Germany, in playing the upper part or the middle parts, hold the bow like the French, pressing the hair with the thumb and resting the other fingers on the back of the bow. The French hold it the same way to play the bass; but the Italians differ in playing the upper parts, that is, they never touch the hair; and the gamba players also, like those who interlace their fingers between the hair and the wood of the bow, such as the basses.

Further, although all the best teachers of any nation hold by common agreement that the more the bow-stroke is long, firm, even, and soft, the more it is to be esteemed; nevertheless, we have observed that as far as the rules of down- and up-bow are concerned, neither the Germans nor the Italians are scarcely agreed up to now, and only rarely agree with the French on a few aspects.

However it is established that those who follow the method of the late Mons. Baptiste, such as the French, the English, those of the Low Countries, and others, all observe the same way of handling the bow on the principal notes of the measure, above all, in regard to those that end the cadences and those that must mark the movement of the dance. This uniformity, so suited to stress the rhythm, not being found among our violins in Germany, has caused a number of persons of quality, who, returning from the aforesaid countries and remarking such a great difference in harmony, have often been surprised and complain of the changes that occurred from it [i.e., lack of uniformity] in the dance.

To obviate this kind of inconvenience, and at the risk of some confusion in a similar circumstance, I thought it would please those who are interested, for me to set down here some of the principal rules of the French method regarding the bow. This mark | (as seen in the examples) over a note signifies drawing the bow downward; and this *v*, the pushing of the bow upward.

I. The first note of each measure, when it begins without a half or quarter rest, should always be bowed downward, no matter what value the note may have. Here is the principal, and so to speak, indispensable, rule of the Lullists, on which almost the entire secret of the bow stroke, and the difference between those and others, depend, and which all the other rules obey. Now, to understand how the other notes are accommodated and played, one must observe the following rule.

II. In ordinary measure, called *Tempus imperfectum* by the theoreticians, of all the notes that divide the measure into equal parts, those which have *uneven* numbers should be bowed downward; and those of even numbers should be bowed upwards. The uneven numbers are 1, 3, 5, 7, 9, 11, etc.; the even ones are 2, 4, 6, 8, 10, 12, etc. Now look at the examples.

(A.) This rule is also observed in triple meters and other proportions of measure as to diminishing equal notes (*notes égales diminuants*). I call those notes which move faster than those indicated by the sign or number of the measure *diminishing*.[1]

(B.) This manner of counting equal parts is observed in such a way that pauses or rests of the same value [as notes] take the place of notes.

(C.) All the best masters agree readily with the French on this rule.

III. Since by virtue of the first rule, the first note of the measure is played with a down-bow, of the three equal notes that make a full measure in triple meter, the second is bowed upward and the third is immediately bowed downward, at least when the movement is rather slow. Therefore, to begin the following measure one must use the down-bow twice in succession (D). Nevertheless, most often one pushes the

1. E.g., $\frac{2}{4}$ would indicate ♩ as the unit of measure, so ♪ or ♪ would be *diminishing* notes.

second bow upward, and the third as well, dividing the up-bow distinctly in half (E), which is called "to snap" (*craquer*), and is done with greater facility, especially when the tempo moves somewhat faster.

IV. In the proportion of six [$^6_4$, $^6_8$] the measure is divided into two essential parts (F); in that of nine, it divides into three (G), and that of twelve in four (H), which one attributes to each three of those denominated by the number of the measure. The first of these three notes is played almost always down-bow, even when it does not begin the measure, and the two others snap upward, by the up-bow divided in two (F, G, H). If there is a rest in place of the first note, the next note, either in triple meter (J) or in proportions (L), should be played with a down-bow without question.

V. When several notes of a full measure's length follow in succession, each one is to be played downwards (M). In the proportions of six or twelve, several successive notes equal to the value of an essential part are played downward and upward alternately, according as they fall on the even or uneven numbers, as in the second rule (N). But those in nine follow the first manner of the 3. (Rule for triple meter, O.)

VI. Several successive notes of equal length which are tied are bowed down and up ordinarily in alternation (P). This suffices for equal notes.

VII. As to the unequal notes (*notes inégales*), the first of the smallest ones that follow the largest is counted as unequal; that is why it is either played down-bow in order (Q) or in resuming the bow, in this case (R), or the first two small notes with up-bow dividing the stroke (S). Then the others of equal value following are bowed down and up alternately (Q, R, S). As to quarter and eighth rests, one counts them in place of notes of their value (T).

VIII. Of three notes which make an essential part of the measure in proportions, if the first has a dot after it, it should ordinarily be played down-bow (V).

IX. Several notes in succession, each filling a measure or one of its essential parts after a rest, may be played with alternate down- and up-bow when the aforesaid rests begin the measure or its essential part (X).

X. The little anticipation [neglected note] before the beginning of a measure (Y), or that which passes quickly after a dot, or a brief rest (Z), as well as the small note that follows a longer syncope (AA), should always be played up-bow. This is why, if the preceding note should, without it, also be bowed upwards, one must divide the up-bow in two, in order to add the following note (BB).

In the Courantes, because of the swiftness of the movement, one excepts the notes that begin the 2d, 4th, 6th, or similar even number (wishing to relate pieces of this kind to triple meters). By a kind of license, these may sometimes be bowed upwards for better arrangement and facility, provided those that begin the measure with uneven numbers and that mark most clearly the dance movement be played always with a down-bow stroke (CC). Beyond that, provided that the first rule regarding the first note of the measure is always rigorously observed, as to others that begin an essential part, or, touching the little residues of the measure in Airs of Gigues, Canaries, or others like them, one must often dispense with the proportions of the 4th, 8th, and 10th rule because of the speed. Ex. DD will show how it is to be done due to frequent dots mingled with the notes. Likewise, due to speed, one often ignores the 8th rule in Bourées and other similar airs, where one employs the bow according to Ex. EE without scruple, always maintaining in effect the First Rule. In these last three examples I have marked the licenses by asterisks below the notes. Finally, when there are two small notes such as two sixteenths joined only as ornament to another note, one sometimes plays them separated (FF), and sometimes, for greater sweetness, one slurs them with the preceding eighth or sixteenth (GG).

It is evident that to play an up-bow on any note that begins the measure is a mistake. This happens often among the Germans and the Italians in triple meters, especially when the first note is shorter than the second. From this contrariety of opinion and from the transgression of the aforesaid First Rule, comes this very great difference regarding the bow, both in the aforesaid first notes as well as others following that depend on them. To make this diversity more comprehensible, I have indicated a succession of notes played in two ways, that is, according to some Germans or Italians (HH) and according to the French method (II). Furthermore, it is repugnant to the vivacity of the Lullists and works against rule VII to slur the little note after a dot or a rest with the following one in a single stroke, as Ex. LL shows. Here, in the French style, they should be played according to Ex. MM, although on the contrary, it would be permitted, according to the situation, to join the aforementioned short note to the preceding in snapping it (NN).

These are the principal rules of the Lullyian method regarding the bow, which are ordinarily observed as much for the dessus as for the middle parts, and even for the bass. The greatest skill of the true Lullists consists in the fact that among so many repetitions of the down-bow, one never hears the least thing that is disagreeable or rough; on the contrary, one finds a marvelous connection of great speed with the length of the bow strokes, an admirable equality of measure with the diversity of movements, and a tender sweetness with the liveliness of playing.

17. The New Instruction Methods

Carl Philipp Emanuel Bach (1714–1788), second son of Johann Sebastian Bach, early showed his talent as a musician and was of course taught by his father. He became a brilliant clavier player and fine composer; Dr. Burney called him "the greatest composer and performer on keyed instruments in Europe." Most of his career was spent at the court of Frederick the Great. He was appointed cembalist in the king's musical chapel in 1740, and he remained in this post until 1767, when he became Kantor of the Johanneum in Hamburg, serving as director of music in the five principal churches of that city. He remained in that post until his death.

The publication of his treatise on playing the clavier—Essay on the True Art of Playing Keyboard Instruments—in 1753 (Part I) and 1762 (Part II) established Emanuel's reputation, and his book soon became a standard work. It is the first systematic treatment of the subject and may be said to have stemmed from J. S. Bach's principle, becoming the basis for principles developed by later keyboard players such as Clementi and Cramer. Haydn called Bach's Essay "the school of all schools." Mozart gave his approval to Bach's teachings, as did numerous other, later pianists. Beethoven, on the occasion when he accepted the young Czerny as a pupil, told Czerny's father to be sure to obtain Emanuel Bach's instruction book so that the youth might bring it to his first lesson. Czerny himself has said that Beethoven's teaching followed Emanuel's method very closely.

The Essay became extremely influential. Its practical advice was taken and followed by most clavier players well into the nineteenth century, and it is clear that a modern school of clavier and fortepiano playing soon came into existence. All contemporary writers on keyboard techniques are indebted to Emanuel's work, with the exception of Quantz and Marpurg, whose instructive writings appeared before Emanuel's treatise.

The first extract, taken from the chapter on fingering, shows how carefully and systematically Bach set forth his subject. The second, "On Recitative," offers good practical advice for a clavier player of his time.

SOURCE: *Carl Philipp Emanuel Bach*, Versuch über die wahre Art das Clavier zu Spielen. Erster und zweiter Teil *(Berlin, 1753, 1762), Ch. I, pt. I, Ch. XXXVIII, Pt. II.*

CARL PHILIPP EMANUEL BACH

from *Essay on the True Art of Playing the Clavier*

On the Placement of the Fingers

1. The placement of the fingers on most instruments is determined to a certain degree by the nature of the instrument. For the clavier, however, it appears to be quite arbitrary, because the keyboard is arranged so that any one of the keys may be depressed by any finger.

2. Nevertheless, there is only one good system of fingering for the clavier, and in only a few instances can more than one fingering be permitted; also, each new idea almost calls for a new and individual fingering, which, often by the mere connection of one idea with another, will again be altered, and the completeness of the clavier offers an inexhaustible number of possibilities. Finally, the correct use of the finger has up to now been so unknown, and remained a kind of secret for only a few, that most persons could not but fail to stray on this slippery and misleading road.

3. This error is the more considerable the less one has perceived it, since on the keyboard most things can be expressed even with a false fingering, although only with great trouble and awkwardness, because false fingering cannot be revealed, as in the case of the other instruments, merely by the simple impossibility of being able to play what is written. It has been thought, therefore, that all the difficulties of the instrument and its music must be due to the nature of the instrument and cannot be otherwise.

4. From this it can be seen that the correct use of the finger has a direct and inseparable connection with the entire art of playing; thus one loses more by incorrect finger placement than art and good taste can compensate for. Facility depends on it and experience shows that an average performer with well-trained fingers will always surpass the

greatest musician in performing if the latter is forced to play with bad fingering against his better judgment.

5. On the basis of each new idea having its own fingering, it follows that the present way of thinking has introduced a new manner of fingering, inasmuch as it is quite different from that of earlier times.

6. Our ancestors, who were more concerned with harmony than melody, consequently played in four parts most of the time. We will see, therefore, that because of this idea, in which one can play in only one style, with few changes, each finger is assigned its place; consequently such works are not so treacherous as are the melodic passages, because the use of the fingers in the former is more arbitrary than in the latter. Before today the clavier was not so well tempered; as a consequence not all the twenty-four keys were needed, as they are today, and therefore there was not such a variety of passages.

7. Generally we see from this that today one cannot progress in skillful playing without the correct fingers, as was done in the past. My blessed father told me that in his youth he had heard great men who never used the thumb except when it was necessary for a large stretch. Since he lived in a period in which a very special change in musical taste was occurring, it was necessary for him to devise a more perfect system of fingering, particularly for the thumb, which, apart from other good services, is indispensable chiefly in the difficult keys, and to use it in the way Nature intended. By this it became elevated from its former inactivity to the position of the principal fingers.

8. Because this new fingering is so constituted that one can easily perform anything at the proper time, I will set forth its basic principles.

9. It is necessary, before I proceed to the precepts of fingering, to recall certain things, some of which should be known in advance, some of which are so important that without them even the best rules would remain ineffectual.

10. A clavier player must sit at the middle of the keyboard, so that he may strike both the lowest and the highest notes with equal ease.

11. If the forearms hang somewhat close to the keyboard, the performer is [sitting] at the proper height.

12. One plays with arched fingers and relaxed muscles; the more these conditions are lacking, the more necessary it is to pay atttention to them. Stiffness hinders all movement, particularly the possibility of rapidly expanding and contracting the hands, which is necessary every moment. All stretches, the omission of certain fingers, the placing of two fingers one after another on a note, even the indispensable crossing and passing under [of the thumb] require this elastic power. Whoever

plays with stretched out fingers and tight nerves experiences, besides the naturally consequent clumsiness, a principal error as well, namely, that he spreads out the other fingers, on account of their length, too far from the thumb, which should always be close to the hand; this principal finger, as we shall see later, is thus robbed of all possibility of doing its duty. Therefore it is clear that he who rarely uses the thumb will play stiffly for the most part; on the contrary, he who has correct usage cannot do this even once, even if he wished to. Everything becomes easy for him; one can see this immediately in a performer. If he understands correct practice and has not acquired the habit of unnecessary gestures, he will play the most difficult things in such a way that one can scarcely see the movement of his hands, and especially one will also hear that it comes easy to him. On the contrary, another will often play the easiest pieces with a great deal of clumsy puffing and grimacing.

13. Those who do not use the thumb allow it to hang so that it is not in the way. Such a position causes even the most moderate stretch to be uncomfortable, because the fingers become extended and stiff in order to accomplish it. What can be done well in this way? The use of the thumb gives the hand not only another finger, but at the same time the key to all possible fingering. This principal finger serves in another capacity, because it keeps the other fingers supple, since they must always be curved if the thumb encroaches upon first one finger, then another. What one must jump to with stiff and stretched nerves without the thumb, is played by another with its help, round, clear, with a natural stretch and consequent lightness.

14. It is clear that through the stretching and leaping, relaxation of the nerves and arched fingers cannot be maintained; even the "snap" calls at times for brief tension.[1] Because these occur only rarely, and are taught by Nature herself, the rest remains as in the previous 12th section. Particularly one accustoms the not-yet-mature hands of children so that, instead of leaping back and forth with the entire hand, in which the fingers are pulled together in a lump, the hands are extended in necessary cases as far as possible. By this means they will learn to strike the keys more surely and easily, and bring the hands to not easily leave their proper and horizontal-floating position over the keyboard; for hands, through leaps, tend to twist first to one side and then to another.

15. One must not take offense if occasionally the teacher finds it

1. "Snap" refers to the use of alternate fingers in very fast repetitions of the same tone (see sec. 90, Ch. I).

necessary to try out for himself a particular idea as to the best fingering in order to show it to his student with certainty. Occasionally doubtful cases occur, in which one will play the correct fingering at first sight without having reflected on it so that he can show it to another person. In teaching, one rarely has more than one instrument, so that the teacher cannot play along with the pupil. We thus see, first, that without regard to the infinite variety of fingerings, only a few good principles are sufficient to solve all problems that arise; second, by means of industrious practice the use of the fingers finally becomes, and must become, so mechanical that one, without further concern, is enabled to think freely of the expression of more important things.

16. In playing one must continually think of the notes to follow, for these are often the reason that we must employ a finger other than the usual one.

17. Because the fingers on each hand are in opposing order, I am obliged to give examples of particular cases in contrary motion, in order that they may be useful for both hands. For that reason I have figured the examples with consideration for each hand, so that they can be used with both hands. As recommended in the Introduction, one cannot apply himself too often to practice with hands in unison. The clef signatures indicate the figures for each hand; when the figures appear above and below the notes, the top ones are for the right hand, the bottom ones for the left hand.

18. After these basic points, all grounded in Nature, I will turn to the precepts of fingering. I will base this, too, on Nature, because the finger arrangement is best when it is not related to unnecessary constraint and stretching.

19. The shape of our hands and of the keyboard likewise teach the use of the fingers. The first shows us that three fingers on each hand are considerably longer than the thumb and little finger. From the second we find that some keys lie lower and are longer than the rest.

20. I will indicate in the usual manner the thumb by the figure 1, the little finger by 5, the middle finger by 3, the finger next to the thumb by 2, and that next to the little finger by 4.

21. The raised and short keys [i.e., black keys] I will call by their more usual than correct names, the half-steps, to differentiate them from the others.

22. From the 19th paragraph it follows naturally that the half-steps properly belong to the three longest fingers. From this comes the first principal rule: that the little finger seldom and the thumb only by necessity should touch the half-steps.

23. Because of the variety of ideas, some of which may be in one

voice, some in several voices, some running, some leaping, I am obliged to give examples of all kinds.

24. The single voice examples will be arranged according to keys because I must present them in all twenty-four keys, both ascending and descending. Thereafter I will go through the examples in several parts; these will follow examples with leaps and stretches, because one can easily gauge them or can lead back to harmonic progression; last, I will give a number of difficult examples and expedients for tied notes and some licenses contrary to rules. At the end the *Probe-Stücken* will make up for others, through whose addition I will establish more profit in related ideas of all kinds, and more desire to acquire the hard study of fingering, than if I added many isolated examples that would have been intolerable and too detailed.

25. The changing of fingers is the chief subject of technique. We can with our five fingers strike only five notes, one after another; consequently one will observe mainly two means by which we can comfortably and instantly use as many fingers as we need. These two means are the *passing under* and the *crossing over* [of fingers].

26. Since Nature has made none of the fingers so capable of bending under the others as the thumb, so this flexibility works together with its advantageous shortness in its passing under the fingers in their proper time and place when they do not suffice.

27. Crossing over is used only with the other fingers and will therefore be easier if a large finger will strike over a smaller finger or the thumb if there is likewise a shortage of fingers. This crossing over must be done without interference as the result of skillful practice.

28. The turning under of the thumb after the little finger, the crossing of the second finger over the thumb, the third over the second, the fourth over the little finger, and similarly of the little fingers over the thumb are objectionable.

29. The correct use of these devices will be seen most clearly in the arrangement of the scales. This is the chief advantage of this introduction. In running passages through the scales that do not begin and end as are seen here, it is evident that on account of the fingers being distributed in such a way one comes out correctly, without being bound in any way to place each finger on one key only and no other.

30. In [Ex. 1] the scale of C major is depicted in ascending form. We see here three kinds of finger placement for each hand. None of them is objectionable, notwithstanding those in which the third finger crosses over the fourth in the right hand, and in the left the second finger over the thumb; and that where the thumb is put on F may perhaps be more usual than the third way.

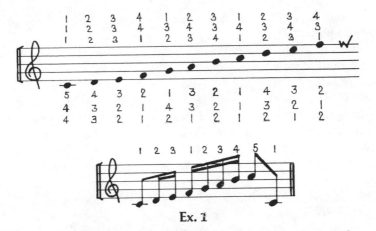

Ex. 1

31. [Ex. 2] shows us C major descending. There are three more kinds of fingering, all three of which can be used in certain situations, as we see in the exercises in [Ex. 3]; although apart from these cases, where they alone must be used, a fingering that is more usual than the others can be used.

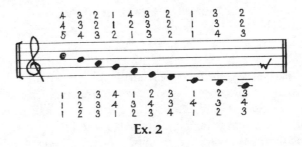

Ex. 2

Ex. 3

32. We learn from the [exercises in Exx. 3 and 4] that apart from the continual necessity to regard the notes that follow, the little finger is held apart in running passages, and thus not often used except at the beginning or when the passage ends correctly with it. This is also

seen in the scales, where it is often used. Outside of these cases, its place is taken by the thumb. In order to avoid confusion about the little finger, I have extended the scales beyond the octave, so that one can see the succession of fingers more readily. . . .

Ex. 4

On Recitative

Recitative [accompaniment] was until recently merely crammed with changes of harmony, resolutions, and enharmonic chords. One sought in these harmonic rarities a particular beauty without more than the merest basis, and considered the natural harmonic changes too meager for recitative. Thanks to sensible taste, one hears this today only rarely, and harmonic exceptions are introduced into recitatives only with sufficient reason. The accompanist must thus no longer sweat as formerly in preparation of recitative in the present style. However, in it today an exact figuring is necessary, even though the principal melodic line is given above the bass.

2. Certain recitatives, in which the bass or the other required instruments have either a definite subject or a certain movement in notes which continue throughout and do not share the pauses of the voice, must be executed strictly in time on account of maintaining good order. The other recitatives may be sung slowly or quickly, according to their content, without reference to meter, even though the music is barred. An accompanist must in both cases be extremely attentive, especially in the latter. He must continually listen to the performer of the principal voice, and if there is action with the recitative, he must also observe it so that he has the accompaniment under his hand; and he must never abandon the singer.

3. When the singer's declamation is rapid, the harmony must be instantly ready, particularly when it must be struck in the pauses of the voice. The beginning of a new harmony must occur as rapidly as possible as soon as the preceding harmony ends. The singer will thus not be disturbed in his *affects* and in the necessary rapid delivery, because

he will always know in advance the modulation and constitution of the harmony. If one must choose between two evils, it would be better to hurry than to delay. Indeed, better [faster?] is always better. In rapid declamation the player should abstain from arpeggios, especially if the harmony changes frequently. Here, one has no time for them, and even if one had, the clavier player himself, the singer, and the audience would fall into confusion. Also, this arpeggiation is not necessary, because it is not used in this style, and is used only in slow-moving recitatives and sustained harmonies to help the singer remember that he should remain in one harmony; failing which he might depart from the key because of the length of the chord or he could get into a change of harmony. Should there be fiery recitatives in the opera, where the orchestra ranges widely and where the singer must declaim apart and the basses are divided, then the first harpsichordist, if there are two, must not wait for the end of the singer's cadences but strike on the first syllable the correct harmony to follow, so that the basses or other instruments may be prepared to come in on time.

4. The rapidity or slowness of arpeggios in accompaniment depends on the tempo and content of the recitative. The slower and more effective the latter is, the slower the arpeggio. The recitative with sustaining instruments sustain the arpeggio particularly well. But as soon as the accompaniment turns to short and disconnected notes instead of sustained ones, the clavier player must then play chords, short and firm, in both hands, without arpeggio. Even if tied long notes appear, one should continue to play them sharply detached. A strong attack is necessary in the theater with its memorized recitatives because of the distance. The accompanist must, of course, at times play quite softly in the theater—but most often in the church and chamber, where noisy and furious recitatives are not even heard—because the harmony must likewise be adapted in the proper loudness to the recitative.

5. In a recitative with sustaining accompanying instruments one should play on the organ only the bass note in the pedal, while the chords are played by the hands and released soon after they are struck. Organs are not often purely tuned, consequently the harmony for the aforesaid recitatives, which are often chromatic, sounds out of tune and is not compatible with the instrumental accompaniment. In such a case one often has to deal with an orchestra, which is not the worst, to make it sound in tune. The arpeggio is not used on the organ. Apart from broken chords, no other ornaments or embellishments are used in recitative accompaniment on the other keyboard instruments.

6. In an intermezzo and a comic opera, in which there is much noisy action, as well as in other theatrical pieces where action occasionally

occurs at the rear of the stage, one must continually, or at least frequently, play arpeggios, so that the singers and the accompanist can hear each other clearly. When the sense of the words, or an intervening action, causes the singer not to enter promptly, after the preparatory chord the accompanist must repeat the chord, rolling it slowly from the bottom until he perceives that the declamation has recommenced. One must above all, when it is not essential, leave neither too much nor too little empty space in the accompaniment. When certain recitatives are accompanied with several instruments, except the bass, without pause, the clavier player must play the incidental small changes in the harmony, such as 8 ♭7 or 6♭5, if they are only in the bass part and at times appear in succession. These should be played either very softly or omitted, so that the principal voice will not have too thick an accompaniment and so that the other instruments will hear the singer clearly, and consequently give better atttention to their next entrances. The noise of the harpsichord, which appears very loud to the neighboring instruments, can sometimes, if its tone is penetrating, easily destroy good order. Sometimes the emphasis on certain words that the composer wants to be repeated for good reasons is achieved by the inactivity of the clavier player and the silence of all the instruments. If there is a vehement action upstage, this precaution is even more necessary, because then the notes of the singers are not heard over the orchestra, which for good reason is on a lower level than the *parterre*.

7. If the singer is not entirely secure in pitch, it is better if one plays the chords several times, one after another, than to play one interval after another. In recitative everything depends on correct harmony, and one should not demand that the singer, often in indifferent places, sing only the written notes and nothing else. It is sufficient if he declaims within the proper harmony. In a foreign modulation one can of course strike the difficult interval alone. If one can depend sufficiently on the skill of the singer, one must not be startled when, as in [Ex. 5a], he chooses the rendering of (1) and (2) instead of that of the score. Often this can be blamed on a desire for a more comfortable range on account of the highness or lowness. Often it is merely forgetfulness, because the singer, when learning by heart, easily changes similar recitative modulations, and imprints the basic harmony on his memory rather than the written notes. I would rather forgive an accompanist who would be surprised by the occasional occurrence of [Ex. 5a], if the figures were lacking, the tempo rapid, and half of the example written on a new line, than if he were startled by the mistaken rendering of [Ex. 5b].

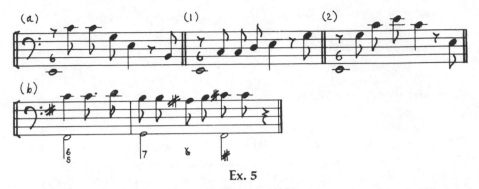

Ex. 5

8. The accompanist will do well if generally, at the last break in the previous harmony, he plays the singer's first interval in order to help him. It should be placed in the uppermost voice, because there it is heard most clearly. Rather than abstain from this expedient, one should permit some irregularities if they cannot be avoided and arise from the preparation of a dissonance, or take the resolution in a wrong voice, so that one may arrive quickly at the place where it is necessary. This last, however, can be done very easily by a rapid arpeggio, without making use of such liberties.

9. If in a recitative with accompanying instruments, the bass enters after a cadence or a pause and the other instruments follow, then the clavier player must strike his note with its harmony strongly and surely, when it is time, especially if the orchestra is large [Ex. 6a]. If all the accompanying instruments attack together, the clavier player must not anticipate, but with his head or body give a clear sign so that all can enter together [see Ex. 6b]. [Ex. 6c] calls for the f of the $^6_4$ chord, which one should preferably take at the octave in the upper voice. At the rest the 7th and 5th from the f should be played. . . .

Ex. 6

Johann Joachim Quantz (1697-1773), flutist and composer, became one of the most famous musicians of the eighteenth century. As a youth he showed musical talent and was given training in several instruments, notably the violin and the harpsichord. After his apprenticeship with the Stadtmusikus of Merseburg, he went to Dresden, where he became assistant to Schalle, Stadtmusikus of Pirna, not far from Dresden. There he was able to hear excellent music performed by great artists. In 1717 he went to Vienna, where he studied counterpoint with Zelenka, a pupil of Fux; the following year he became a member of the chapel of the King of Poland, who resided part of the year in Dresden, part in Warsaw. At that time Quantz began to study the flute with Buffardin, the virtuoso French flutist then in the chapel at Dresden.

From time to time Quantz made journeys to other capitals and countries in order to study or become acquainted with outstanding men: in 1724 he studied with Gasparini in Rome; in 1725 he visited Naples and met such personages as Scarlatti and Hasse; in 1726 he spent seven months in Paris, where he worked on improving the flute and added a second key to it; he also visited London for three months during the time Handel's opera was at its height.

In 1728 Frederick the Great, then crown prince, heard Quantz play the flute in Berlin and, liking his performance greatly, decided to learn to play the flute himself; thereafter Quantz went to Berlin twice a year to give him lessons. In 1741, after Frederick became king, Quantz was appointed court flutist and composer, in which post he remained until his death.

Quantz was an industrious and prolific composer, writing over 300 flute concertos for the king alone, and other works such as trios and quartets, few of which have been published. But his Anweisung die Flöte zu spielen of 1752 is his most famous work. Besides instruction on flute playing, it contains excellent advice on general performance practice; musical styles of the day; and questions of tempo, interpretation, and the like; it is in an invaluable compendium of practical musical knowledge pertaining to Quantz's period.

SOURCE: *Johann Joachim Quantz,* Versuch einer Anweisung die Flöte traversière zu spielen *(Berlin, 1752), Ch. XI, nos.11, 12; Ch. XVII, sec. vii, nos.1–8; Ch. XVII, sec. vi, nos.35–38, 40, 41; Ch. XVII, sec. vii, nos.46–51, 56–58.*

JOHANN JOACHIM QUANTZ

from *Versuch einer Anweisung die Flöte . . .*

On Good Execution in General

11. Good execution must be rounded and complete. Each note must be set forth in its true value and correct tempo. If properly performed, the notes will sound as the composer intended them to be, for he, too, is bound by rule. In this respect many players are not observant. Either because of ignorance or a corrupt taste, they often give a following note a portion of the time value of the preceding one. Sustained and caressing notes must be slurred together, but lively notes and those that leap must be separated and detached from each other. The tremolos and small ornaments should all be performed accurately and in a spirited manner.

12. Here it is necessary to comment on the length of time that is given to each note. You must be able to make a difference in execution between the main notes, which are usually called *frappantes* (accented) or, as the Italians say, *good* notes, and those that *pass*, which are called *bad* notes by some foreigners. If it is possible, the main notes should always be emphasized more than the passing notes. Therefore according to this rule, in every piece of moderate speed and even in an *Adagio*, the quarter notes are to be played somewhat unequally, even though they appear to have the same value, so that the strong notes of each figure, i.e., the first, third, fifth, and seventh, must be held a little longer than those that pass, or the second, fourth, sixth, and eighth; but this lengthening should not be as much as if they were dotted. Among these very quick notes I include the quarters in three-two time, the eighths in three-four time, and the sixteenths or thirty-seconds in two-four or common time. But this rule does not hold as soon

as these notes are mixed with notes still more rapid or half as long in the same meter, for then these latter must be played in the manner described above. For example, if the eight sixteenths shown under the letters (k), (m), and (n) are played slowly and evenly, they will not be as attractive as if the first and third of a group of four are held a little longer, and with a stronger tone, than the second and fourth.

However, we except from the rule, first, quick passages in a very fast movement, in which one can only stress and lengthen the first note of four, for time does not permit unequal execution. We also except all rapid passagework for the voice, unless it should be slurred; for since each note of this kind of vocal passage should be made distinct and stressed by a little supporting thrust from the chest, there is no possibility of inequality. Further exceptions are the notes that have strokes or dots above them. We must make the same exception when several notes follow each other on the same pitch; or when a slur is over four, six, or eight notes; and finally, eighths in Gigues. All these notes should be executed equally, one no longer than another.

On the Duties of Those who Accompany

35. If a composition is to be performed effectively, it must be played not only in the proper tempo but also in the same tempo from beginning to end, now sometimes fast, sometimes slow. However, daily experience shows that often this is not the case. To end slower or faster than one began is incorrect in both cases, but the latter is not so bad as the former. The former, particularly in an *Adagio*, often makes it impossible for one to know whether a piece is in duple or triple meter. By this the melody is gradually effaced and one hears in its place almost nothing but harmony. This not only affords the hearer little pleasure but also does the composition the greatest disservice if it is not performed in the correct tempo. Sometimes the soloist is to blame if he hurries the easy passages in a fast piece and then cannot succeed in the more difficult ones, or, when in a sad piece, he becomes so deeply absorbed in the *Affect* that he forgets about the tempo. Often the accompanists are at fault in changing the tempo, either when, in

mournful pieces or also in *Andante cantabiles* or *Allegrettos*, they fall asleep and thereby yield too much to the soloist; or when in a fast piece they play in too fiery a manner, which leads them to hurry. It will be easy for a good leader, if he has the necessary alertness, to avoid these errors, and keep the soloists who are not secure in the rhythm, as well as the ripienists, in order.

36. The accompanists must not, however, ask that the soloist adjust to them in regard to the rapidity or slowness in which he takes the tempo of a piece; rather they should allow him complete freedom to set his tempo as he sees fit. At the time they are only accompanists. It would be a mark of unreasonable pride if at any time one of the least among the accompanists should assume authority as to tempo, and, even though he had no more desire to play, wished, in defiance of the soloist, to override the tempo. If one perceives that the tempo should be faster or slower, and that a change is necessary, one must do it gradually and not all at once or violently, else disorder can easily arise.

37. Because the style of playing an *Adagio* requires that the soloist must often allow himself to be carried along by the accompanying parts rather than to lead them, it often appears as if he wanted the piece to move more slowly; therefore the accompanying parts must not be misled, but must keep the tempo going strictly, and not give way unless the soloist gives a sign to do so. Otherwise they will lapse into drowsiness.

38. If in an *Allegro* a ritornello has been played with vivacity, so must the same vivacity be continually maintained in the accompaniment. Likewise one need not pay attention to the soloist in case he delivers the same subject in a cantabile and caressing manner. . . .

40. That the fastest notes in any piece in *moderate tempo* must be played somewhat unequally, has been explained in no.12 of the Eleventh Chapter [see p. 316 above]. Thus the accented, or principal notes in a figure, namely the first, third, fifth, and seventh are held a little longer than the passing notes, namely the second, fourth, sixth, and eighth. I have also added some exceptions to this rule [in Ch. 11] and refer the reader to them there.

41. If in a ritornello the last note is a half note, and a half-note rest follows it, with the solo beginning on the following beat, the ending note of the ritornello must not be broken off too quickly. If the ritornello begins with a downbeat, and the following solo enters on an upbeat with a new idea, it should begin on a quarter or an eighth note, of which the accompanist cannot always be sure. It will therefore be well for the soloist to begin in strict time, and mark the downbeat, to avoid any confusion arizing.

On Keyboard Players in Particular

1. Not all who understand thoroughbass are, for that reason alone, at the same time good accompanists. One must learn learn through rules, through experience, and finally through one's own perception.

2. It is not my intention to deal with the first, because instructions are not lacking for it. But for the latter, however, because it is a part of my goal, I wish, with permission of my lords the clavier players, to make a few short remarks; the rest I leave to the consideration of each skilled and able clavier player.

3. As stated above, it is possible that a person who has a thorough knowledge of *Generalbass* may nevertheless be a poor accompanist. Thoroughbass demands that the voices, which the player adds extemporaneously, be played according to the figures and the rules as if they had been written down on paper. The art of accompanying calls not only for this but for much more.

4. The general rule of thoroughbass is that one should always play four parts; but if one is to provide a good accompaniment, it often gives a better result if one does not hold so closely to this rule, if one often leaves out some voices or doubles the bass in the right hand. For if a composer is not always able nor obliged to set a three-, four-, or five-voiced instrumental accompaniment to all melodies, which would avoid making them unintelligible or obscured, in the same way every melody cannot suffer a continual full-voiced accompaniment on the clavier; the accompanist must therefore conform more to the musical material itself than to the general rules of thoroughbass.

5. A full-voiced piece, accompanied by many instruments, calls for a full-voiced and strong accompaniment. A concerto performed by a few instruments certainly requires some moderation in this piece, particularly in the concerting passages. One must then pay attention to whether these same places should be played by the bass alone or be accompanied by other instruments; whether the *concertante* parts play softly or loudly, in the low or high register; whether they have to play suspensions and singing or leaping notes or passages; whether the passages are to be played deliberately or with fire; whether the passages are consonant or whether they are dissonant, modulating to a foreign key; whether the bass has a slow or rapid movement under the passages; whether the fast notes of the bass move stepwise or by leaps; whether four or eight notes are placed on each pitch; whether rests, or long and short notes are intermixed; whether the piece is an *Allegretto*, *Allegro*, or *Presto*, the first of which should be played seriously in instrumental works, the second lively, the third, however,

should be played in a fleeting and playful manner; whether it is an *Adagio assai, Grave, Mesto, Cantabile, Arioso, Andante, Larghetto, Siciliano, Spiritoso,* etc., each of which requires, both in the principal voice and in the accompaniment, a particular kind of execution. If each one observes these things properly, the compositions will have the desired effect on the hearers.

6. In a trio the clavier player must adjust to the instrumentalists that he is to accompany; whether they play loud or soft; whether the cello plays with the clavier or not; whether the composition is *galant* or learned; whether the harpsichord is loud or soft, open or closed; and whether the audience is close by or at a distance. The harpsichord rustles and tinkles loudly close by; but at a distance it is not as loud as other instruments. If the clavier player has a violoncello with him and is accompanying soft instruments, he may use some moderation in the right hand, especially in *galant* compositions, and even more if one part rests and the other plays alone; but with loud instruments and if the piece is very harmonious and elaborate, even when both parts play together, he may play with much fuller sound.

7. In accompanying a solo, the greatest discretion or knowledge is also required; and if the soloist is to play his part with composure, without anxiety, and with a certain satisfaction, much depends on the accompanist, because he can provide a [good] state of mind for the soloist as well as destroy it. If the accompanist is not secure in the tempo and drags, either by the *tempo rubato* or because of distortion of the ornaments, which are a grace in execution, or if instead of a rest he anticipates the next note, allowing himself to hasten, he then not only disturbs the soloist's interpretation but causes him to mistrust the accompanist, and makes him afraid to attempt anything further with boldness and freedom. In the same way the accompanist is to blame if he makes too much movement in the right hand; or if he plays melodies with it in the wrong places, or arpeggiates, or otherwise inserts things that are in opposition to the principal part; or if he does not express the *piano* and *forte* at the same time as the soloist, but plays everything without expression and always with the same volume.

8. What has been said here about the accompaniment of instrumental pieces can for the most part be applied to the accompaniment of vocal compositions.

On Tempo

46. For a long time a serviceable means of definitely establishing a tempo has been sought. Loulié, in his *Éléments ou Principes de Musique,*

mis dans un nouvel ordre, etc. à Paris, 1698, has communicated the draft of a machine which he has called Chronometer. I have not been able to see this plan and cannot therefore give my thoughts about it. However, this machine would be difficult for anyone to carry about; not to mention that it has generally fallen into oblivion, since, as far as one knows, no one has ever made use of it and suspicions are aroused about its soundness and adequacy.

47. The means I find most serviceable as a guide to establish the tempo, are more convenient and cost so little effort to possess, for everyone always has it with him. *It is the pulse beat of the hand of a healthy person.* I will try to give some instructions as to how one who is guided by it can find for himself without great difficulty any particular one of the different kinds of tempo. I cannot, indeed, claim to be the first person who has hit upon this method; it is certain however that no one has taken the trouble to describe its application clearly and fully, and to accommodate its use to the music of today. I do this last with greater confidence since, with regard to the essentials, I am not, as I have recently learned, the only one who has hit upon these ideas.

48. I do not claim that one should measure off a whole piece according to the pulse beat, for that would be absurd and impossible. Rather my intention is only to show how, in at least two or four, six or eight pulse beats, any tempo one desires can be comprehended by one's self and one can attain a knowledge of the different kinds of tempo and be able therefore to take the opportunity for further investigation. After having had some practice, an idea of tempo will gradually be impressed on the mind, so that one will no longer find it necessary to consult the pulse beat.

49. Before I go further I must examine more closely these various kinds of tempo. There are so many kinds of them in music that it would not be possible to name them all. However, there are certain main kinds from which the others may be derived. I will divide these into four classes, as they appear in concertos, trios, and solos, and use them as a basis. They are drawn from the ordinary, or four-beat, measure, and are as follows: (1) the *Allegro assai*, (2) the *Allegretto*, (3) the *Adagio cantabile*, (4) the *Adagio assai*. In the first class I place: the *Allegro di molto*, *Presto*, etc. In the second: the *Allegro ma non tanto*, *non troppo*, *non presto*, *moderato*, etc. In the third class I count: the *Cantabile, Arioso, Larghetto, Soave, Dolce, Poco andante, Affettuoso, Pomposo, Maestoso, alla Siciliana, Adagio spiritoso*, and the like. To the fourth belong: *Adagio pesante, Lento, Largo assai, Mesto, Grave,* etc. To be sure, these terms each have their own particular distinction; however it refers more to the expression of passion that predominantly

governs each piece than to the tempo itself. If one only understands correctly the four stated categories of tempo, one will in time readily learn the others, because the differences amount to very little.

50. The *Allegro assai* is, then, the fastest of the four principal kinds of tempo. The *Allegretto* is once again as slow as the *Allegro assai*. The *Adagio cantabile* is once again as slow as the *Allegretto* and the *Adagio assai* once again as slow as the *Adagio cantabile*. . . .

51. To come now to the principal matter, namely, how each of the [above discussed] meters can be placed in its proper tempo by means of the pulse beat, one must note first of all the word at the beginning of the piece that indicates the tempo, and also consider the fastest notes in the passages. Since one cannot execute more than eight extremely fast notes in a pulse beat, either by double-tonguing or bow strokes, it follows that:

In ordinary four-four time:
In an *Allegro assai*, on each half note, one pulse beat;
In an *Allegretto*, on each quarter note, one pulse beat;
In an *Adagio cantabile*, on each eighth note, one pulse beat;
In an *Adagio assai*, on each eighth note, two pulse beats.

In *Alla breve* time, there is:
In an *Allegro*, a pulse beat for each whole note;
In an *Allegretto*, a pulse beat for each half note;
In an *Adagio cantabile*, a pulse beat for each quarter note;
In an *Adagio assai*, two pulse beats for each quarter note.

There is, chiefly in common time, a kind of moderate *Allegro*, which falls between the *Allegro assai* and the *Allegretto*. It often occurs in vocal music, and in music for certain instruments which cannot maintain great speed in the passagework. It is usually indicated by *Poco allegro, Vivace*, or, most often, by *Allegro* alone. In this there is a pulse beat for each group of three eighth notes, and the second pulse beat falls on the fourth eighth note.

In an *Allegro* in two-four time or quick six-eight time, a pulse beat falls on each measure.

In an *Allegro* in twelve-eight time, where there are sixteenth notes, two pulse beats fall in each measure.

In three-four time, when the piece goes quickly (*Allegro*) and the passages in it consists of sixteenths or eighth-note triplets, one cannot set a definite tempo by the pulse beat in a single measure. However, if one takes two measures together, it can be done; then a pulse beat comes on the first and third quarter notes of the first measure and on the second quarter note of the second measure. Thus there are three pulse beats for six quarter notes. It is the same in the case of nine-eight time.

Likewise, in very fast three-quarter or three-eight time, where only six fast notes appear in the passagework in each measure, there is one pulse beat for each measure. However this should not be used in a piece that is to be taken *Presto*, because the beat would be too slow by two fast notes. If you want to know how fast these three quarters or eights should be in a *Presto*, take the tempo according to the fast two-four tempo, where four eighths are taken in one pulse beat, and play these three quarters or eighths as fast as the eighths in the afore-mentioned two-four tempo. The fast notes, then, in both the above-mentioned meters will fall into their proper tempo.

In an *Adagio cantabile* in three-four time where the lowest voice moves in eighth notes, a pulse beat should occur on each eighth note. Should the movement be only in quarter notes, however, and the melody more *Arioso* than sad, there should be a pulse beat on each quarter. Nevertheless, in this one must adjust [the tempo] according to the key as well as to the words marked at the beginning; for if there is an *Adagio assai*, *Mesto*, or *Lento* [marked], here also two pulse beats should come in each quarter.

In an *Arioso* in three-four time, there should be a pulse beat on each eighth note.

An *alla Siciliana* in twelve-eight time would be too slow if one counted a pulse beat to every eighth note. If, however, one divided two pulse beats into three parts, then a pulse beat comes on the first and third eighth. Once these three notes are divided, one must not continue to heed the movement of the pulse, for the third eighth would then become too long.

If in a fast piece the passages consist only of triplets, and there are no two- or three-flagged notes intermixed, the piece can be played somewhat faster than the pulse beat. This is to be observed particularly in the fast six-eight, nine-eight, and twelve-eight meters. . . .

56. I will now seek to apply the method of the pulse beats to the tempo of French dance music, about which I find it necessary to say a few words. This kind of music possesses for the most part certain characteristics; each character calls for its proper tempo, because this kind of music is not as arbitrary as the Italian, rather it is very limited. If the dancers as well as the orchestra are always able to arrive at one tempo they will be able to avoid many vexations, especially if it is not as well executed as that of the Italians. . . .

It cannot be denied that French dance music is not as easy to play as many think, and that its performance must be differentiated from the Italian style, insofar as it may be suitable to each character. Dance music must be played seriously for the most part, with a heavy, though short and sharp bow stroke, more detached than slurred. Tenderness or *cantabile* style are rarely found in it. The dotted notes will be played heavily, the following notes short and crisp. The fast pieces must be performed gaily, skipping, and with accent, with a very short bow stroke, always marked by a pressure; by this the dancers are continually helped and encouraged to leap, but it also makes the spectator perceive and understand what the dancer wishes to convey; for dance without music has the same effect as a meal that is only a painting.

57. Just as the correct tempo in all kinds of music is very important, so must it also be observed most strictly in dance music. The dancers must adjust to it not only by means of their hearing but also with their feet and bodily movements. Thus it is easy to imagine how unpleasant it must be for them if an orchestra plays a piece now slowly, now fast. They must strain every nerve, particularly if they venture on high leaps. Therefore fairness demands that the orchestra should accommodate itself to them as much as possible, which is easily done if one now and again pays attention to the fall of their feet.

58. It would take much too long to describe all the types that may be found in dances and to note their tempos. I will therefore adduce only a few, from which the others can be easily understood. . . .

The *Entrée*, the *Loure*, and the *Courante* should be played in a stately and elevated manner, and the bow should be lifted at each quarter, whether dotted or not. A pulse beat comes on each quarter note.

A *Saraband* has the same movement, but is played with a somewhat more agreeable manner.

A *Chaconne* is likewise played with stateliness. In it a pulse beat takes two quarters.

A *Passecaille* is similar to the preceding, but is played just a little faster.

A *Musette* is played in a very ingratiating way. A pulse beat comes on each quarter in three-four time or on each eighth in three-eight time. Sometimes, however, it will be taken so fast, according to the dancer's fantasy, that a pulse beat comes on every measure.

A *Fury* is played with much fire. A pulse beat falls on two quarter notes in duple or three-four time; in the case of the latter, when sixteenth notes appear.

A *Bourrée* and a *Rigaudon* are played jovially, and with a short and light bow stroke. A pulse beat comes on each measure.

A *Rondeau* is played somewhat calmly, and a pulse beat comes about every two quarters; it may be in Allabreve or three-four time.

The *Gigue* and the *Canarie* have the same tempo. If they are in six-eight time, a pulse beat comes on every measure. The *Gigue* is played with a short and light bow stroke, the *Canarie*, however, which is always written in dotted notes, with a short and sharp one.

The *Menuet* is played liltingly, the quarter notes marked with a somewhat heavy, though short, bow stroke. A pulse beat comes on two quarters.

A *Passepied* will be played somewhat lighter, somewhat faster than the preceding. It often happens in this that two bars are written in one, with two strokes over the middle note in the second bar. . . . Some leave these two bars separated from one another and write, instead of the quarters with the stroke, two eighths with a tie over them, and place the bar line between them. In playing, these notes are performed in the same way; namely, the two quarters short and with a detached bow, and in the same tempo as if it were in three-four time.

A *Tambourin* is played like a *Bourrée* or a *Rigaudon*, only a little faster.

A *March* is played seriously. If it is written in Allabreve or *Bourrée* measure, then two pulse beats come in every measure, etc.

Leopold Mozart (1717–1787), father of Wolfgang Amadeus Mozart, was himself a musician of considerable renown. An excellent violinist and a good composer, he produced music in a number of genres: symphonies, divertimenti, concertos, keyboard sonatas, church music, and various light pieces, practically all of which are forgotten today.

Leopold's important work, which became a standard method of instruction, was his Versuch einer gründlichen Violinschule. It was widely known and published in several editions, even translated into other languages. The instructions are thorough and carefully presented; and from the book one can readily grasp the technical principles for performance of the music of his time. It is therefore valuable for the performer, violinist or not, who wishes to play music of that period in the correct style.

SOURCE: *Leopold Mozart, Versuch einer gründliche Violinschule (1756; facs. ed., 1787; Leipzig; Breitkopf & Härtel, 1956), Ch. I, sec. 3; Ch. XI.*

LEOPOLD MOZART

from *Versuch einer gründliche Violinschule*

Musical Terms*

Prestissimo indicates the fastest tempo, and *Presto assai* means about the same. In these very fast tempos one should use a lighter and somewhat shorter bow stroke.

Presto means fast, and *Allegro assai* is little different from it.

Molto allegro is a little slower than *Allegro assai,* but it is still faster than

Allegro, which indicates a lively but not overly fast tempo, especially when modified by adjectives and adverbs such as:

Allegro, ma non tanto, or *non troppo,* or *moderato,* which indicate that one should not exaggerate the speed. In these cases a lighter and livelier, however broader and not so short bow-stroke as in the fastest tempos is required.

Allegretto is somewhat slower than *Allegro,* most often having something pleasant sounding, something graceful and playful, and has much in common with *Andante.* It must thus be played in an artful and playful manner; a clear idea of this pleasing and joking manner, in this and other tempos, can be given by the word *Gustoso.*

Vivace means lively, and *Spiritoso* indicates that one must play with understanding and spirit; and *Animoso* means about the same. All these kinds are the mean between fast and slow, and a musical work before which these words stand must show us the same in different degrees.

Moderato—temperately, moderately: not too fast and not too slow. This likewise is shown by the piece itself, which gives us the tempo from its movement.

Tempo Commodo and *Tempo giusto* lead us back to the work itself. They tell us that we should play the piece neither too fast nor too slow, but in the proper, suitable, and natural tempo. We must therefore seek the correct movement in such a piece itself. . . .

---

* One should really use these terms in one's own language; one can use *Slow* just as well as *Adagio* to describe the movement of a musical work. Am I alone to be the first to do this?

Sostenuto means to *sustain,* or rather to hold back and not exaggerate the melody. In such a case one must use a serious, slow, and sustained bowing, and the melody should be very legato.

Maestoso—with majesty, deliberately, not precipitately.

Stoccato or *Staccato,* thrust, indicates that one must separate the notes from one another and play them with a short bow stroke without dragging.

Andante, going. This word alone tells us that one must let the piece take its natural pace; especially if the words *un poco Allegretto* are added.

Lente or *Lentement*—very moderately; comfortably.

Adagio—slowly.

Adagio pesante—a melancholy *Adagio;* it must be played somewhat slower and reserved.

Largo—an even slower tempo; it should be played with long bow strokes and great calmness.

Grave—melancholy and serious, consequently very slow. One must also, in fact, by means of a long, somewhat heavy and earnest bowing, and through the steady continuing and maintaining of the changing tones, express the character of a piece before which the word *Grave* is placed.

To slow pieces are added also some other words to those given, in order to clarify even more the composer's intention; such as:

Cantabile, singing. That is: one must try not to play affectedly and should imitate with the instrument, insofar as possible, the art of singing. This is the most beautiful thing in music.*

Arioso, like an Aria. It may also mean the same thing as *Cantabile.*

Amabile, Dolce, Soave, all require a pleasing, sweet, tender, and gentle execution, in which one moderates the tone and does not tear it with the bow; rather one must give proper adornment to the piece by varying the soft and moderately loud tones.

Mesto, sad. This word reminds us that in performance we should place

---

* Many think they are giving something exquisite to the world when they thoroughly decorate the notes in an *Adagio,* and make out of one note several dozen. Such note-stranglers thereby bring their bad judgment to light, and tremble if they must hold out a long note or play a couple of notes slightly without adding their usual and clumsy ornaments.

ourselves in an attitude of sadness in order to arouse in the hearer the melancholy that the composer seeks to express in the work.

Affettuoso, affectingly, requires that we seek the *affect* in the piece and therefore play it movingly, in an expressive and touching style.

Piano means *quiet;* and *Forte*, loud or strong.

Mezzo means *half*, and is used for moderation of *Forte* and *Piano*. For example, *mezzo forte*, half strong; *mezzo piano*, half weak or quiet.

Più means *more*, so that *più forte* means a little stronger; *più piano*, a little softer.

Crescendo, growing, tells us that in successive notes where this word stands, the loudness of the notes must always be increased.

Decrescendo, on the contrary, the loudness of the tone must decrease gradually.

If *Pizzicato* stands before a piece or several notes, this piece or passage is to be played without using the bow. The string will be plucked, or pinched, as some say, with the first finger, or also with the thumb of the right hand. One must never pluck the strings from below, but always sideways, else they will strike the fingerboard on the rebound and rattle or then lose the tone. The thumb should be placed against the saddle at the end of the fingerboard, and with the tip of the first finger the string should be plucked; also the thumb can only be used if one must play full chords. Many pluck always with the thumb, but the first finger is better for this, because the thumb damps the tone of the string because of its thickness. You yourself may make the experiment.

Col Arco—with the bow. It reminds one that one must again use the bow.

Da capo—from the beginning. It shows one that the piece must be repeated from the beginning. But if

Dal Segno is written, that is, "from the Sign," one must find a sign, which then leads us to the place where one must begin the repeat.

The two letters V.S.—*Vertetur Subito*—or also only the word *Volti*, which ordinarily stands at the end of a page, and it means: One must turn the page quickly to the other side.

Con sordini, with mutes. That is: when these words are written in a piece of music, certain little attachments of wood, steel, clay, tin, or brass are placed on the bridge in order to express qualities of emotion and sadness better. They damp the tone; one calls them therefore "dampers"; more generally one calls them *Sordini*, from the Latin *Surdus*, or Italian *Sordo* = muted. It is best if one avoids playing on the open strings when using the *Sordini*, for they are too shrill in contrast with the stopped tones, and consequently cause a marked inequality of the tones.

From all these technical items here explained one sees, as clear as sunlight, that every effort must be made by the player to enter the mood which rules the piece itself, in order to penetrate the minds of the audience and to arouse their emotions. One must therefore, before beginning to play, consider well all things necessary to a reasonable and correct rendition of a well-written musical composition.

On the Tremolo, Mordente, and Several Other Optional Embellishments

1. The Tremolo* is an ornament that originates in Nature herself, and can be applied elegantly on a long note not only by good instrumentalists but also by skillful singers. Nature is the preceptress hereof. For if we touch a slack string or a bell vigorously, we hear after the stroke a certain wavelike beat (*ondeggiamento*) of the note that is touched; and this trembling reverberation is called Tremolo, or Tremoleto.

2. One should endeavor to imitate this natural trembling on the violin when one presses the finger strongly on the string and makes a little movement with the whole hand; which, however, should not move to the side but must go forward toward the bridge and backward toward the scroll. . . . For just as the remaining trembling sound of a struck string or bell continues to sound impurely on a note, swinging now too high, then too low, one must likewise by the movement of the hand, forward and backward, take pains to imitate exactly the rising and falling of intermediate tones.

3. Because now the Tremolo is not purely on one note but sounds floating, one would err if one wished to play every note with the Tremolo. There are such performers, who continuously shake on each note, as if they had a perpetual fever. One must, then, apply the Tremolo only in such places where Nature herself would produce it: namely, as if the touched note were the striking of an open string. For at the end of a piece, or even at the end of a passage, which closes on a long note, the last note would, if, for example, it were struck on a grand piano, infallibly continue to hum for some time. Thus one can ornament a final note, or other long-held note, with the Tremoleto.

---

* I do not mean here Tremulant, as is used in organ pieces, rather a *tremoleto*, or shaking.

4. But there is a slow, an increasing, and a fast shake. One can differentiate them in this way [Ex. 17]. The larger strokes represent

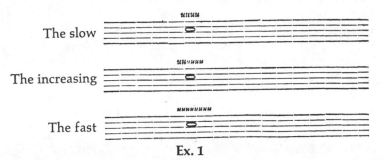

The slow

The increasing

The fast

Ex. 1

eighths, the smaller ones, on the contrary, sixteenths; and as many lines as there are shown, so often must one move the hand.

5. One must make the movement with a strong pressure of the finger, and the pressure must always be made on the first note of each group of quarters; but in the fast movement, on the first note of each half-group of quarters. For example, I will set down a few notes [see Ex. 2], which one can easily play with the Tremolo, indeed which truly require this movement. One must play these in all the fingerings. In the two examples, No. 1, the strong part of the movement always falls on the note with the number 2 because it is the first note of the whole or half quarter. In example No. 2, on the contrary, the stress falls on the note indicated with 1 for the same reason.

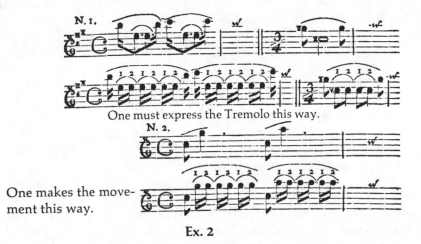

Ex. 2

6. One can make the Tremolo also on two strings, and thus with two fingers at the same time.

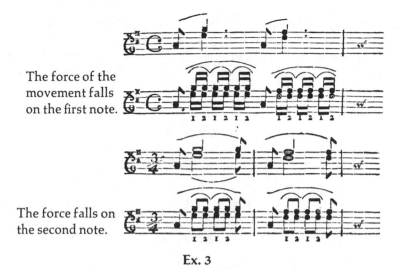

The force of the movement falls on the first note.

The force falls on the second note.

Ex. 3

7. Before one begins a cadenza of one's own invention, which is to be made at the end of a solo, it is usual to prolong a note either on the tonic or on the dominant. On such a long-held note one can always apply an increasing Tremolo. For example, one can play thus at the end of an Adagio [Ex. 4]. One must however begin the passage softly, toward the middle increase the strength, so that the greatest power falls on the beginning of the faster movement; and finally one must end the passage again softly.

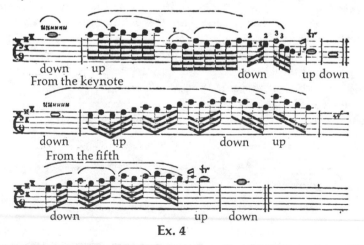

down · up
From the keynote

down up

down up

down up down

down up down

From the fifth

down up down

Ex. 4

8. Now we come to the Mordente. One calls a Mordente the 2nd, 3rd, and more small notes which very quickly and quietly surround the main note, so to speak, and disappear in an instant, so that one hears only the

main note sound strongly.* In ordinary usage it is called *Mordant*, the Italians call it *Mordente*, but the French, *pincé*.

9. The Mordant is made in three ways. First, it comes on the main note itself. Second, on the two next higher and lower tones. Third, it is made with three notes: where the main note is touched between the two neighboring notes. Here are the three.

Ex. 5

I know perfectly well that as a rule only the first type, or the so-called French *pincé*, has the right properly to be called Mordente; but as these, my second and third kinds are also "biters" and consequently have the properties of a Mordente, why should one not allow them to go with the Mordentes? Can there not be polite and impolite "biters"? My second kind appears to be very similar to the double appoggiatura, and the third seems like a slide. But the execution makes it entirely different. There are dotted and undotted double appoggiaturas, and the appoggiatura as well as the slide belong to the singing kind of execution and will be used only variously in slow or moderate tempos as filling out and binding of the song together. The second and third kinds of Mordentes, on the contrary, are unchangeable, are performed with utmost speed, and the stress always falls on the principal note.

10. The third kind of Mordant can be used in two ways, namely, ascending and descending. If the last note before the Mordente is lower than the following note where the Mordant will be used, then one makes it upward; if the note stands above, then it is made downward.

Ex. 6

* If others make fun of these Mordants, or Mordentes, according to etymology, from *mordere* (to bite), and call it a "biter," I may say of the French *pincé*, which means twitch, tug, or pinch, that the Mordant or so-called *Pincé* very quietly and quickly surrounds the main note, almost bites, twitches, or pinches it, but immediately lets go.

11. One must not, however, overload the notes with this type of Mordente. And there are only a few special places where an up-stroke can begin with a Mordente.

Here it is good.   But here, bad.

Ex. 7

12. Also in a series of Mordentes descending stepwise one plays the note of the up-stroke much better without Mordentes. For after the up-stroke the accent must first flow to the following note.

Ex. 8

13. Above all, one must only use the Mordente if one wants to give a note a certain expression. For the stress of the tone falls on the note itself; the Mordant, on the contrary, will be attached to the principal note very delicately and swiftly; otherwise it could no longer be called a Mordant. It makes the note lively; it distinguishes it from others, and gives the entire delivery a different appearance. One uses it also for un-equal notes, adding it mainly at the beginning of a quarter note, for there the stress properly belongs.

Ex. 9

14. Finally I must recall again that just as the appoggiatura, here also the descending Mordant is better than the ascending; and certainly for the same reasons. Moreover, the good execution of a Mordente de-pends on its speed; the faster it is, the better. But one must not carry speed to unintelligibility. Also, in the fastest performance one must ex-press the notes clearly and well delineated.

15. There are several other kinds of ornaments, most of which have Italian names. Only the *Batement* [*Battement*] is of French origin; the

Ribattuta, Groppo, Tirata, Mezzo Circolo, and the like are of foreign birth. And even though one rarely hears them spoken of, I will nevertheless put them down, for they are not without usefulness; one can still apply them. Indeed, who knows whether they may not rescue many from confusion and kindle at least a little light to enable him to play in the future with more method? It is indeed distressing always to play so haphazardly without understanding what one does.

16. The Battement (Batement) is a beating of two neighboring halfsteps, which is repeated several times from the lower note to the upper note, one after another, with the greatest rapidity. The Battement, or beating, must not be confused with the Tremolo or Trill, nor with the Mordente issuing from the main note. The Tremolo appears somewhat similar to the Battement, but the Battement is much faster, and is made with two fingers, and does not rise above the main note; on the contrary, the shaking of the Tremolo goes above the main note. The Trill comes from above the main note, but the Battement from below and is always only a half-step. The Mordente starts on the main note, whereas the Battement begins on the next lower semitone. The Battement looks like this [Ex. 10]. One uses this beating in lively pieces instead of the Appoggiatura and Mordente in order to perform certain notes that are empty [unornamented] in other respects with more spirit and vivacity. But one must not use the Battement often, indeed only rarely, and only to provide variety.

Ex. 10

17. The *Zurückschlag* (Ribattuta) is employed to sustain a fairly long note, and ordinarily before a Trill. See the fifth paragraph of the previous chapter, where I have written a *Ribattuta* before each double Trill. One can also use the *Zurückschlag* very prettily in an Adagio [Ex. 11]. One must begin the *Ribattuta* with a strong note, diminishing thereafter by degrees. [Ex. 12] is another example.

It is written this way.   And one can play it with
                                a Ribattuta, thus.

Ex. 11

One can embellish it with the Ribattuta, thus.

Ex. 12

18. The ornament called *Groppo* is a joining of notes that stand close together, which is done by combining a few very fast notes. If one uses these rapid notes always turned back before an ascending or descending passage, in order to delay reaching the principal note too soon, they have the appearance of a bunchy figure, so that some derive the word *Groppo* from the French and English *Grape*, which means a bunch, and figuratively after the old German *Kluster* (cluster); others however derive this designation from the Italian *groppo*, a knot, or button, *groppare*, to button. This embellishment appears thus [Ex. 13]. This ornament must be used only when one plays solo, and only for variation if the same passage is immediately repeated.

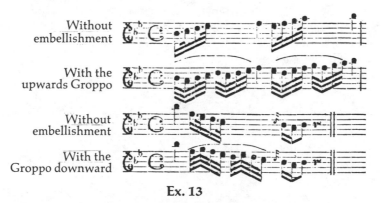

Without embellishment

With the upwards Groppo

Without embellishment

With the Groppo downward

Ex. 13

19. The Circle and Half-circle are little different from the Groppo. If they are of only four notes, they are called Half-circle; if there are eight notes, it is a full circle. These figures are customarily so-called because the notes have the appearance of a circle.

Without embellishment

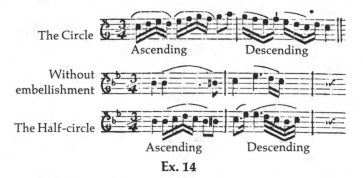

The Circle   Ascending   Descending

Without embellishment

The Half-circle   Ascending   Descending

Ex. 14

20. Those who are much interested in etymology have also a desirable counter-term in the word *Tirata,* which some determine to be from *tirare,* which means to pull, and use it in making many different sayings; others take it from *tirata,* a shot, *tirare,* to shoot, which is taken in a figurative sense and is indeed a foreign expression. Both are right.

And since the *Tirata* is nothing other than a row of stepwise notes, either ascending or descending, which are arbitrarily between two notes that are some distance apart, there can be fast or slow *Tirate,* depending on whether the tempo is fast or slow, and on how far apart the [end] notes are from each other.

If the *Tirata* is slow, it is called a *Zug,* and comes from *tirare, ziehen;* for one pulls the melody through a number of tones one note after another and links the two extreme notes through the intervals lying between. If the *Tirata* is fast, however, the connection is the same; only it happens so quickly that one can liken it to the shooting of an arrow or shot.* Here are examples.

Without ornament

With a slow descending Tirata   Adagio.

Without ornaments

With a slow descending Tirata   Adagio.

* What? Banish the Shot from the realm of music? I would not attempt it; for it has penetrated not only the *beaux arts* but all places. Yes, where one does not want it, there it reeks strongly of powder. *Quis suos patimur Manes.*—Virgil

Ex. 15

21. One can however apply the *Tirata* in many other ways. I will give one or two of these here.

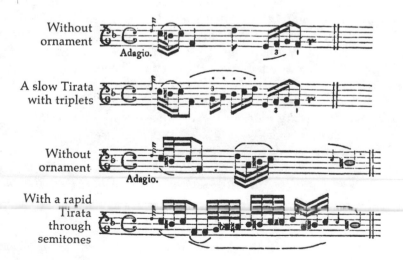

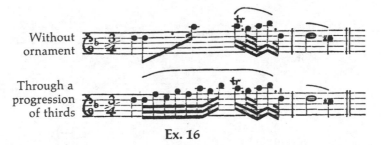

Ex. 16

22. All these ornaments are used only if one is playing a solo, and then very moderately, at the proper time, and only in order to vary several passages that are often repeated. Let one look well at the composer's instruction, for in the application of such embellishments one betrays his ignorance. Principally, let one guard against all optional ornaments when several persons are playing from one part. What confusion would arise if each one were to befrill the notes according to his taste? And finally, one would no longer understand the melody because of the clumsy "beauties" mixed in! I know how frightened one becomes when one hears the most singable piece maimed so pitifully by such unnecessary decoration.

Daniel Gottlob Türk (1756–1813), the German theorist and composer, contributed a number of works on theory and performance that became widely known in his time and for some years thereafter, being used as manuals of instruction. One such was his Clavierschule *of 1789, which became a standard work that went through a number of editions. It is a comprehensive work, combining technical instruction for playing the clavier with general music instruction. His book is based on C. P. E. Bach's famous* Versuch über die wahre Art das Clavier zu spielen *(1753, 1762) and on the instructions of F. W. Marpurg as set forth in his* Anleitung zum Clavierspielen *of 1765; but Türk includes in it his own observations, especially those conveying the necessity for sensitive performance, above all in the "characters" of music. In this respect he still holds to the earlier* Affektenlehre *to some degree.*

By "clavier" Türk meant primarily the clavichord, his preferred instrument, and his ideas of expression were often based on the capabilities and possibilities of that instrument; nevertheless his instructions and remarks are applicable to the fortepiano, by 1789 the more generally used instrument.

The extract given here shows how important the expression of emo-

tions and feelings was in Türk's time and gives some of the measures prescribed to achieve expressive performance.

SOURCE: *Daniel Gottlob Türk,* Clavierschule *(Leipzig u. Halle, 1789),* Ch. VI, sec. 5.

DANIEL GOTTLOB TÜRK
from *Clavierschule*

On the Proper, Correct Feelings for All Expressive Emotions and Passions in Music

60. The final and indispensable requirement for a good performance is without doubt a proper and correct feeling for all expressive passions and emotions. If one does not have this feeling, or possesses it only in small degree, the given sign will be for him useless for the most part. A spoken direction would be somewhat more effective for such a person than the best written instruction, although even the most assiduous and knowledgeable teacher would find it difficult to obtain a good rendition from the student who has no feelings for Nature.

61. There are persons who have such dull feelings that even the most moving piece of music makes little or no impression on them. These can never achieve a good performance in accordance with the usual movements of Nature. Particular pieces that the teacher has played many times for him, he can perhaps learn in some degree tolerably well, even very well, and present the appearance of expression. But this is not his own, only a borrowed feeling, a kind of mechanical imitation, like a little piece a trained bird whistles for better or worse, according as it has heard its master play it. Without new instructions such a trained musician would play a new piece of the same character, still unknown to him, without expression.

62. Others have only feeling for certain emotions. They will be moved to happiness, for example, by a piece of jolly character, whereas an *Adagio mesto* has no effect on them. Then there are others, one of whom will play only an *Allegro* well, another only an *Adagio*. Although this one-sided feeling is better than none, it remains nevertheless incomplete. For the true professional musican must be able to project himself into every mood, or have a sense for all expressive passions and

emotions in music, because he not only must express gay or happy emotions, but often in the same piece quite opposite ones. However, no one can be induced to play well at all times and under all conditions, since the mood of the mind has a very perceptible influence on performance.

63. If the composer of the required expression conveys it as well as possible throughout the work and in specific places, and the player has suitably employed all the aforementioned means given in the previous sections, there still remain particular cases in which the expression can be heightened by exceptional means. I count it here as preferable (1) playing without strict measure, (2) hurrying and drawing back, (3) the so-called *Tempo rubato*—three methods, which can be employed with great effect only rarely and in the right place.

64. Apart from the free fantasy, cadenzas, fermatas, etc., also the recitative with text, certain passages should be played more according to feeling than to strict time. One finds here and there in sonatas, concertos, and the like, certain pieces of this kind; for example, in the *Andante* of the first Sonata by C. P. E. Bach, dedicated to the King of Prussia. Such passages would give a bad effect if one played them according to the actual note values. The important notes must be slower and stronger, but the less important ones must be played lighter and faster, approximately as a sensitive singer would sing them or a good orator would declaim them.

65. The places where hastening or holding back may occur are difficult to describe; however I will at least attempt to make some of them discernible. I presume, however, that one will avail himself of the aforementioned means only if he plays alone or with very observant companions.

66. In music whose character is impetuosity, anger, scorn, rage, frenzy, and the like, one can perform the most forceful passages somewhat *accelerando*. Also, some ideas which are to be intensified when repeated require that one take into consideration to some extent the velocity. If occasionally gentle emotions are interrupted by a lively passage, one may play the passage somewhat hurriedly. Also in the case of an idea that causes an unexpected passionate emotion, hastening is permitted.

67. In exceptionally tender, languishing, melancholy places, where the emotion is brought to a point, so to speak, the effect may be unusually strengthened by an increasing *ritardando*. Also, in the expression before certain fermatas, one takes the movement a bit slower, little by little, just as if its strength were exhausted by degrees. Places toward the end of a piece (or a section), which are marked *diminuendo, diluendo, smorzando*, and the like, can also be played somewhat *ritardando*.

68. A tender, moving passage between two lively, fiery ideas (as in

the first part of my easy Clavier Sonata pp. 10, 11, 25ff.) can be played somewhat lingeringly; only in this case one does not slow the movement little by little, but at once takes it a little slower (but only a *little*). An especially nice occasion for lingering arises in compositions in which two characters of opposing kinds are represented. [C. P. E.] Bach has written a splendid sonata "which seems to contain a conversation between a Melancholicus and a Sanguineus." In a similar way E. B. Wolf depicts the country bride separated from her bridegroom in the six little Sonatas of 1779. Above all, lingering or delaying can occur intentionally in passages in slow movements .

71. If the composer of a piece does not want the entire piece to be played in strict time, he indicates that by means of the words *con discrezione*. In this case it is left to the feeling of the player whether to hold back somewhat in certain places, or to hasten in others. Here one must apply what I have said in previous paragraphs.

In addition, the expression "play with discretion" appears in many other meanings. Very often it is understood to mean a good performance or refined taste. If, for example, the performer plays with proper insight, refinement, and judgment as to the composer's ideas, one says: he plays with discretion. "To play with discretion" also often means much the same as yielding, or conforming to others. Thus one who is playing with a poor performer hurries from courtesy and continues, omitting several measures from necessity, and puts matters right, etc., is said to play (or accompany) "with discretion." And unfortunately one must be thus discreet all too often.

72. The so-called *Tempo rubato* or *robato* (properly stolen time) was mentioned in para. 63 as the last resource to be applied in the feeling and judgment of the player. This expression appears in more than one meaning. Generally it is understood to be a kind of shortening and lengthening of the notes, or a displacement of them. It is a kind of stealing time from one note and adding it to another, as in the following example [Ex. 1]. The simple notes are in (a); in (b) *Tempo rubato* is achieved by anticipation; and in (c) through retardation. One sees here that by this kind of execution the overall rhythm is not displaced. Accordingly, the usual, but ambiguous German expression *Verrücktes Zeitmass* is not applicable, for the lowest voice goes its way in measured

Ex. 1

rhythm; only the notes of the melody are shifted from their normal position. More correct would be the expression: "displacement of the notes or parts of the measure." Further, if in the melody several notes are displaced, as in examples (e) and (f) [Ex. 2], both parts must come together correctly at the beginning of the measure. Therefore in this case also there is no real displacement of the measure.

This distortion of notes, as it is otherwise called, must be used with care, for small errors in the harmony can arise from it. The anticipation in example (f) would be possible only in rather slow movement.

Ex. 2

In addition to the indicated meaning of *Tempo rubato*, the expression sometimes means a particular kind of performance, when the accent is shifted from strong notes to weak notes, or in other words: when one plays the note on the weak beat more strongly than those notes that normally fall on the strong beat of the measure, as in this example.

Ex. 3

Still another kind of *Tempo rubato* may be written by the composer himself, as for example in Pergolesi's *Stabat Mater* [Ex. 4] or in the following way [Ex. 5].

Ex. 4

Ex. 5

Liberties, or many distortions, cannot be permitted without the express direction of the composer.

18. The Dance

Jean-Georges Noverre (1727–1810), of Swiss ancestry, passed his whole life mainly in Paris, studying dancing with the ballet master of the Paris Opéra Ballet, and then as a member of the corps de ballet. Noverre made a successful debut at a popular Parisian theater, but soon opened at the Opéra Comique in a ballet that he wrote and choreographed. He made numerous appearances in other European capitals, among them London, Vienna, and Stuttgart, where for some time he was maître de ballet to the Duke of Württemberg. In 1776 he returned to the Paris Opéra as ballet master.

His work is of fundamental importance in the history of ballet, especially his Lettres sur la danse et sur les ballets (1760). Noverre decried purely technical dancing in favor of more expressive kinds and deprecated the purely virtuoso techniques for the same reason. His ideas on dance costume were equally revolutionary. In a time when the dancers' dress was too often heavy, cumbersome, and purely decorative, he wanted to substitute for them light costumes that would give the dancer freedom of movement. His new ideas influenced European theatrical dancing for many generations.

Noverre created and performed many ballets during his career at the Opéra. Unfortunately none have survived, and we have only a record of them.

SOURCE: Jean-Georges Noverre, Lettres sur la danse et sur les ballets (Lyon: Delaroche, 1760), Letter I; extracts from Letters II, VI, VIII.

JEAN-GEORGES NOVERRE
from *Letters on the Dance*

Letter I

Poetry, painting, and the dance, Sir, are only, or should be only a faithful copy of beautiful Nature; it is by the truth of this imitation

344

that the works of the Racines, the Raphaels, have come down to posterity, after having obtained (which is still rarer) the approval of their own times. Would that we could join to the names of these great men those of the Masters of Ballet who were the most celebrated of their time! But they are scarcely known. Nevertheless it is not the fault of the Art. A ballet is a picture; the stage is a canvas; the gestures of the participants are the colors; their faces, if I dare express myself in this manner, are the brush; the ensemble and the vivacity of the scenes, the choice of the decor and the costumes are its pigments; and finally the Director is the painter. If Nature has given him the fire and the enthusiasm, which are the very soul of painting and poetry, his immortality is also assured. The artist has here, if I dare say so, more obstacles to surmount than in the other arts; the paintbrush and colors are not in his hands; the tableaux must be varied and endure only an instant. In a word, he must revive the art of gesture and pantomime, so well known in the century of Augustus. All of these difficulties have no doubt frightened my predecessors. Bolder than they, perhaps with less talent, I have dared embark upon new roads; the indulgence of the public has encouraged me; it has sustained me in crises capable of destroying my trust in myself; and my success seems to authorize me to satisfy your curiosity about an art which you cherish and to which I consecrate every moment of my time.

The ballets have been up till now only feeble sketches of what they can be one day. This art, entirely controlled by taste and genius, can be embellished and varied *ad infinitum*. History, legend, poetry, painting all extend their arms to draw it from that obscurity where it has been buried, and one is rightly astonished that the *régisseurs* have disdained such precious help.

The programs of the ballets which have been presented during the last hundred years or thereabouts, in the different courts of Europe, would make one believe that this art, far from making progress, has lost a great deal; these kinds of tradition, it is true, are always suspect. There are different ballets as there are different fêtes in general; nothing so beautiful and elegant on paper, nothing so tedious and so badly conceived very often in performance.

I think, Sir, that this art has remained in infancy because its effects have been limited to those of fireworks, designed only to amuse the eyes. Though it shares with the best dramas the advantage of interesting, moving, and captivating the spectator with the charm of the most perfect illusion, it has not been suspected of speaking also to the soul.

If the ballets in general are feeble, monotonous, and spiritless, if they are devoid of that kind of expression which is its very soul, it is less the fault of the art itself than of the artist: should he ignore that the dance is an art of imitation? I would be tempted to believe it, since great numbers of the composers sacrifice the beauties of the dance in order to copy servilely a certain number of dance figures that the public has found to be stale for a century past, so that a ballet about Phaeton, or any other ancient opera revived by a modern composer, differs so little from those that had been created when the opera was a novelty, that one would imagine they were all the same.

Indeed, it is rare, not to say impossible, to find any genius in the ballets, any elegance in the form, any lightness in the grouping and precision, any cleanness in the ways which lead to the different figures; they scarcely are aware of the ancient art of disguising old things and giving them an air of novelty.

The ballet masters should consult the pictures of the great painters. This examination would doubtless bring them nearer to Nature; they could avoid then, as much as would be possible for them, the symmetry of the figures which, by repeating the same thing, gives the same canvas two exactly similar pictures.

To say that I condemn in general all similar figures, to think that I have the pretention of abolishing their use totally, is to make me look like a strange person and a reformer, a role I wish to avoid.

The abuse of the best things is always harmful; I disapprove only of the too-frequent and too-often-repeated use of this kind of figure, a use of which my confrères will feel the viciousness when they devote themselves to copying Nature faithfully and in painting on the stage the different passions with the nuances and the coloration that each particular one demands.

These symmetrical figures from right to left are supportable only in the entrances, which have no expressive character and are made only to give time to the premier dancers to catch their breath. They can take place in a general ballet which terminates a festival; they can also pass in the *pas d'exécution* of four, six, etc., although in my opinion it is ridiculous to sacrifice, in this kind of passage, expression and feeling in the adroitness of the body and the agility of the legs. But symmetry should make place for nature in action scenes. One example, weak as it is, will make me more intelligible and will suffice to support my feeling.

A troupe of nymphs, at the unexpected sight of a troupe of young fauns, takes flight rapidly and fearfully; the fauns on the contrary pursue the nymphs with that eagerness that ordinarily gives the impression of pleasure; soon they stop to examine the impression they are making on the nymphs; they in turn stop their flight; they consider the fauns fearfully, they try to make out their intentions, and to assure themselves that by running away they will find some shelter which will protect them from the danger they fear; the two troupes join, the nymphs resist, defend themselves, and escape with a skill that is equal to their quickness, etc.

That is what I call an action scene, where the dance must speak with fire, with energy, where the symmetrical and formal figures cannot be used without changing the truth, without injuring verisimilitude, without weakening the action and cooling off the interest. That is, I say, a scene where the art of the choreographer should not be evident except to embellish Nature.

A ballet master without intelligence and taste will treat this piece of the dance mechanically and will deprive it of its effectiveness because he will not understand its spirit. He will place the nymphs and fauns in several parallel lines; he will demand scrupulously that all the nymphs are posed in uniform attitudes; and that the fauns should raise their arms to the same height; he will see to it that in this distribution he will not put five nymphs at the right and seven nymphs at the left; this would be a sin against all the old rules of the Opera. And he will make a cold and rigid exercise of an action scene which should be full of fire.

Ill-humored critics who do not know enough about the art to judge its different effects will say that the scene should offer only two tableaux; that the dances of the fauns should trace one and the fear of the nymphs should paint the other. But how many different nuances there are to show in this fear and this desire! How many varied brush strokes! How many contrasts! How many gradations and shadings to be observed, for a multiplicity of tableaux to be derived from these emotions, each more animated than the others.

Since the passions are the same among all men they differ only in proportion to their sensations; they are imprinted and act upon some with more or less force than upon others, and manifest themselves outwardly with more or less vehemence and impetuosity. This principle once granted, and Nature demonstrates it every day, it would be nearer the truth to diversify attitudes and give shadings to the expressions, and immediately the pantomime gestures of each personage would cease to be monotonous. It would be just as faithful an imitator as an excellent painter to show the variety of expression in the faces, to give some of the fauns a ferocious expression, to some of them less eagerness, to others a more tender air, to others a voluptuous character, which would allay or share the fear of the nymphs; the sketch of one tableau determines naturally the composition of the other; I see the nymphs then hesitating between pleasure and fear, I see others who show me by their attitudes the different movements by which their souls are agitated; some are more proud than their companions; some nymphs mix curiosity with their fright, which makes the tableau more piquant; this diversity is the more seductive as it is the very image of Nature. Agree with me, Sir, that symmetry, daughter of Art, will ever be banished from the active dance.

I will ask everyone who retains the prejudices of habit if they would find symmetry in the actions of a flock of sheep trying to escape the murderous teeth of a wolf, or in peasants abandoning their fields and their huts to evade the furor of a pursuing enemy. *No,* doubtless! But art is able to disguise Art. I do not preach disorder and confusion, on the contrary I want regularity to be found in irregularity itself; I am asking for ingenious groups, for strong situations, but always natural, a manner of composing that hides the work of the choreographer. As for the figures of the dance, they are capable of pleasing only when they are presented rapidly and designed with as much taste as elegance.

From Letter II

The well-composed ballet is a living picture of the feelings, the manners, the usages, the ceremonies, and the costumes of all the peoples of the earth; in consequence it must be pantomime of every kind and speak to the soul through the eyes. If it is devoid of expression, of striking tableaux, of powerful situations, it offers then only a cold and monotonous spectacle. This sort of performance cannot endure mediocrity; like painting it demands a perfection the more difficult to attain since it is subordinate to the faithful imitation of Nature, and as it is hard, not to say impossible, to seize this sort of seductive truth, which gives an illusion to the spectator, which transports him in an instant to the spot where the scene must have occurred, which places his soul in the same situation where it would be if he were looking at the action, of which Art presents only the imitation. What precision you must have, not to place yourself either above or below the object you wish to imitate? It is as dangerous to embellish your model as to make it ugly; these two faults are equally in opposition to resemblance; one makes Nature simper, the other degrades it.

Since ballets are performances they should contain the parts of drama. The plots that are performed in dancing are for the most part empty of sense and offer only a confused mass of scenes, as badly knit together as they are disagreeably acted; however it is in general indispensable to submit to certain rules. Every ballet plot should have its exposition, its central idea, and its denouement. The success of this kind of spectacle depends in part on a good choice of subject and its arrangement.

From Letter VI

The gradation of colors and heights is unknown in the theater; it is not the only part that is neglected, but this negligence appears inexcusable to me in certain circumstances, above all in the opera, theater of fiction; theater which, often denuded of strong action and deprived of interest, should be rich in tableaux of all genres, or at least ought to be.

A scene of whatever kind is a large picture prepared to receive some figures. The actors and actresses, the dancers, are the personages who must ornament and embellish it; but in order that this picture should please and not shock the sight, it requires just proportions, equally brilliant in the different parts of which it is composed.

If, in a scene representing a temple and a palace of gold and blue, the dresses of the actors are blue and gold, they destroy the effect of the décor, and in its turn the décor deprives the costumes of the effect they would have had against a more tranquil background. Such a distribution of colors will eclipse the tableau, the whole will only form a monotone painting, a cold and monotonous genre that men of taste will always regard as an illegitimate child of Painting.

The color of the drapery and clothing ought to stand out against the scenery; I compare it to a beautiful background; if it is not tranquil it is not harmonious; if the colors are too bright and lively it will destroy the charm of the picture. It will deprive the forms of the relief they should have; nothing will detach itself because nothing will be done artistically, for nothing will have been treated with Art, and the garishness which will result from a poor understanding of colors, will present only a panel of cutouts, illumined without taste and intelligence.

In scenes of beautiful simplicity and with little variation of colors, rich and striking costumes can be admitted, as well as those that are varied by bright and solid colors.

In tasteful and well-imagined scenes, like Chinese palaces, or the public square of Constantinople decorated for a fête, a genre of composition which does not submit to any severe rules, leaves the field free for genius, whose merit grows in proportion to the singularity the poet gives it. In these kinds of scenes—gleaming with colors, loaded with fabrics, enhanced with gold and silver—the clothing must be draped suitably, but it must be simple and in shades entirely opposed to those that most stand out in the décor. If this rule is not carefully observed all will be destroyed because of shadows or oppositions; everything should agree, should be harmonious in the theater; when the scenery is made for the costumes, the costumes for the scenery, the charm of the representation will be complete.

Gradation of sizes should be observed not less scrupulously in the moments where the dance becomes part of the scene. Olympus or Parnassus are among such pieces, where the ballet forms and composes three-fourths of the tableau, pieces which cannot please if the painter and the ballet master are not in agreement on the proportions, the distribution, and attitudes of the personages.

In a spectacle as rich in resources as that of our Opera, is it not shocking and ridiculous to find no gradation in the heights [of figures], when one pays attention to and is concerned with it in the parts of the painting which are accessories to the picture. Jupiter, for example, or Apollo at the summit of Parnassus, should they not appear smaller because of the distance, for the muses and the divinities who are below them are closer to the spectators? If the painter, to make the illusion, submits to the rules of perspective, how does it happen that the ballet master, who is a painter himself, throws off the yoke? How can the tableaux be pleasing if they are not realistic, if they are without proportion, and if they sin against the rules that Art has drawn from Nature by the comparison of objects? It is in the fixed, tranquil tableaux of the dance that gradation ought to be used. It is less important in those that vary and are formed in dancing. I mean by a *fixed tableau* all that makes a group in the distance; all that is dependent on the scenery, and accords with it, forms a large machine to be true.

But how, you will say to me, to observe this gradation? If it is a Vestris who dances Apollo, must the ballet be deprived of this resource and sacrifice all the charm it will lavish to the charm of a single moment? No, Sir, but one will take for the quiet tableau an Apollo proportionate to the different parts of the machine, a young man of fifteen who will be dressed in the same way as the true Apollo; he will descend from Parnassus and by means of the wings he will be made to disappear, so to speak, in substituting in his place the good form and superior talent.

It is by reiterated trials that I am convinced of the admirable effects of gradation.

From Letter VIII

Let us speak of costume. Variety and truth in costume are as rare as in music, in the ballets, and in the simple dance. Stubbornness is present in all parts of the opera: it presides as sovereign to the spectacle: Greek, Roman, shepherd, chauffeur, warrior, faun, sylvan, games, pleasures, smiles, tritons, winds, fires, dreams, grand priest, and sacrificers—the costumes of all these personages are cut on the same pattern and differ only in the color and the embellishments that lavishness rather than taste adds by chance. Tinsel gleams everywhere: the peasant, the fisherman, and the hero are equally laden with it; the more a costume is garnished with gewgaws, sequins, gauze, and net, the more it gives merit in the eyes of the actor and the spectator without taste. Nothing is so singular as to see at the Opera a troupe of warriors who have just fought, disputed, and carried off the victory. Do their faces and glances appear still terrible? Is their hair disarranged? No, Sir, nothing of the kind. They are groomed most scrupulously and they resemble effeminate men coming from the hands of the bath-man rather than warriors escaped from the fray.

What becomes of truth? Where is credibility? From what is illusion born? And how not to be shocked by an action so badly done? Decorum in the theater is necessary, I agree, but there must also be some truth and naturalness in the action, some tension and vigor in the tableaux, and certainly some disorder in whatever demands it. I would like no more of those [stiff skirts] like little kegs, which in certain positions of the dance place the hip at the shoulder, so to speak, and which hide all contours.

I would banish all symmetrical arrangements in the costumes, a dull arrangement which shows Art without taste and which has no grace. I would prefer draperies that are simple and light, contrasting in colors, and distributed in such a way as to allow me to see the form of the dancer. I would like them to be light, without the material being skimpy, with pretty folds, lovely masses, that is what I ask, with the ends of these draperies turning and taking new forms as the action becomes more lively and accentuated; all should have a light aspect. A leap, a quick step, a flight would agitate the drapery in different ways; that is what would approach painting, and consequently Nature: that is what would lend attractiveness to the attitudes and elegance to the positions. Finally, it would give the dancer the lithe air that is not possible under the Gothic trappings of the Opera.

I would reduce by three-fourths the ridiculous hoopskirts of the female dancers: they oppose equally the liberty, swiftness, and prompt action of the dance. They also deprive the form of its elegance and of the just proportions it should have; they diminish the attractiveness of the arms, they *bury*, so to say, the graces, they constrain and hinder the dancer to such a point that the motion of her hoop affects and occupies her more seriously than the movement of her arms and legs. Every actor in the theater should be free. . . .

19. On Vocal Music

Observations on the Florid Song; or, Sentiments on the Ancient and Modern singers (1742) is J. E. Galliard's translation of Pier. Francesco Tosi's Opinioni dei cantori antichi e moderni, o sieno Osservazioni sopra il Canto figurato, written in 1723. Tosi (1654–1732) was a soprano singer who was, in Galliard's words, "a Singer of great Esteem and Reputation. He spent the most of his Life travelling and by that means heard the most eminent Singers in Europe, from whence, by the Help of his nice Taste, he made the following Observations. Among his many Excursions, his curiosity was raised to visit England, where he resided for some time in the Reign of King James the Second, King William, King George the First, and the beginning of his present Majesty's: He dy'd soon after, having lived to above Fourscore. He had a great deal of Wit and Vivacity, which he retained to his latter Days. His manner of singing was full of Expression and Passion; chiefly in the Stile of Chamber-Musick. The best performers in his Time thought themselves happy when they could have an Opportunity to hear him. After he had lost his voice, he applyed himself more particularly to Composition; of which he has given Proof in his Cantatas, which are of an exquisite Taste, especially in the Recitatives, where he excels in the Pathetick and Expressive beyond any other. He was a zealous Well-wisher to all who distinguished themselves in Musick; but rigorous to those who abused and degraded the Profession. . . ."

Tosi's little treatise, one of the earliest to deal exclusively with the art of singing, remains today a precious witness to the ideals of taste and style in the late Baroque. In its ten chapters Tosi presents the esthetic approach of his generation and remarks on the general method of teaching, placement of the voice, ornaments of all kinds, recitative, and arias. He also condemns the "modern style" ca.1710–20. He describes the "perfect virtuoso," who is well grounded in musical composition and literature, who is able to sing in all three styles—church, theater, and chamber—and who always comports himself with a dignity suitable to his position. Tosi's little volume appears to have had wide circulation and considerable influence, for besides Galliard's translation, as late as 1757 Johann Friedrich Agricola translated the work into German as Anleitung zur Singkunst.

SOURCE: Observations on the Florid Song; or, Sentiments on the Ancient and Modern singers, . . . by Pier. Francesco Tosi . . . Translated into English by Mr. Galliard . . . (London, 1743), Ch. IX, Ch. X.

PIER. FRANCESCO TOSI

from *Observations on the Florid Song*

Observations for a Singer

38. The most admired Graces of a Professor ought only to be imitated, and not copied; on condition also, that it does not bear even so much as a shadow of resemblance of the original; otherwise, instead of a beautiful imitation, it will become a despicable copy. . . .

41. Whoever does not know how to steal the time in singing, knows not how to compose, nor to accompany himself, and is destitute of the best taste and greatest knowledge.

42. The stealing of time, in the *Pathetick,* is an honourable theft in one that sings better than others, provided he makes a restitution with ingenuity.

43. An exercise, no less necessary than this, is that of agreeably *putting forth* the voice, without which all application is vain. Whosoever pretends to obtain it, must hearken more to the dictates of the heart, than to those of art.

44. Oh! how great a master is the Heart! Confess it, my beloved Singers, and gratefully own, that you would not have arrived at the highest rank of the profession if you had not been its scholars; own, that in a few lessons from it, you learned the most beautiful expressions, the most refin'd taste, the most noble action, and the most exquisite Graces; own, (though it be hardly credible) that the Heart corrects the defects of nature, since it softens a voice that's harsh, betters an indifferent one, and perfects a good one; own, when the Heart sings you cannot dissemble, nor has Truth a great power of persuading; and lastly, do you convince the world, (what is not in my power to do) that from the Heart alone you have learned that *Je ne sais quoi,* that pleasing charm, that so subtly passes from vein to vein, and makes its way to the very soul. . . .

50. It may seem to many, that every perfect singer must be a perfect instructor, but it is not so; for his qualifications (though ever so great) are insufficient, if he cannot communicate his sentiments with

ease, and in a method adapted to the ability of the scholar; if he has not some notion of composition, and a manner of instructing, which may seem rather an entertainment than a lesson; with the happy talent to shew the ability of the singer to advantage, and conceal his imperfections; which are the principal and most necessary instructions. . . .

52. [A Master] knows, that a deficiency of ornaments displeases as much as the too great abundance of them; that a singer makes one languid and dull with too little, and cloys one with too much; but of the two, he will dislike the former most, though it gives less offence, the latter being easier to be amended.

53. He will have no manner of esteem for those who have no other graces than gradual *Divisions*; and will tell you, embellishments of this sort are only fit for beginners.

54. He will have as little esteem for those who think to make their auditors faint away, with their transition from the sharp third to the flat.

55. He'll tell you, that a singer is lazy, who on the stage, from night to night, teaches the audience all his songs; who, by hearing them always without the least variation, have no difficulty to learn them by heart. . . .

63. He will marvel at that singer, who, having a good knowledge of time, yet does not make use of it, for want of having apply'd himself to the study of composition, or to accompany himself. His mistake makes him think that, to be eminent, it suffices to sing at sight; and does not perceive that the greatest difficulty, and the whole beauty of the profession consists in what he is ignorant of; he wants that Art which teaches to anticipate the time, knowing where to lose it again; and, which is still more charming, to know how to lose it, in order to recover it again; which are the advantages of such as understand composition, and have the best taste. . . .

65. What will he not say of him who has found out the prodigious art of singing like a *Cricket*? Who could have ever imagin'd, before the introduction of the *Mode*, that ten or a dozen quavers in a row could be trundled along one after the other, with a sort of *tremor* of the voice, which for some time past has gone under the name of *Mordente Fresco*?

66. He will have a still greater detestation for the invention of laughing in singing, or that screaming like a Hen when she is laying her egg. Will there not be some other little animal worth their imitation, in order to make the profession more and more ridiculous? . . .

71. He will have no great opinion of one, who is not satisfied with his part, and never learns it; of one, who never sings in an Opera without thrusting in one *Air* which he always carries in his pocket; of one, who bribes the Composer to give him an Air that was intended for an-

other; of one, who takes pains about trifles, and neglects things of importance; of one, who, by procuring undeserved recommendations, makes himself and his patron ridiculous; of one, who does not sustain his Voice, out of aversion to the *pathetick*; of one who gallops to follow the *Mode*; and of all the bad singers who, not knowing what's good, court the *Mode* to learn all its defects.

72. To sum up all, he will call none a Singer of Merit, but him who is correct; and who executes with a variety of graces of his own, which his skill inspires him with unpremeditately; knowing that a Professor of eminence cannot, if he would, continually repeat an Air with the self-same Passages and Graces. He who sings premeditately, shews he has learned his lesson at home.

Of Passages or Graces

1. Passages or Graces being the principal ornaments in singing, and the most favourite delight of the judicious, it is proper that the singer be very attentive to learn this art.

2. Therefore, let him know, that there are five principal qualifications, which being united, will bring him to admirable perfection, *viz.* Judgment, Invention, Time, Art, and Taste.

3. There are likewise five subaltern Embellishments, *viz.* the Appoggiatura, the Shake, the putting forth of the Voice, the Gliding, and Dragging.

The principal Qualifications teach:

4. That the Passages and Graces cannot be form'd but from a profound Judgment.

5. That they are produced by a singular and beautiful *Invention*, remote from all that is vulgar and common.

6. That, being govern'd by the rigorous, but necessary, precepts of *Time*, they never transgress its regulated measure, without losing their own merit.

7. That, being guided by the most refined Art on the Bass, they may there (and no where else) find their center; there to sport with delight and unexpectedly to charm.

8. That, it is owing to an exquisite *taste*, that they are executed with that sweet *putting forth* of the Voice, which is so enchanting.

From the accessory Qualities is learn'd:

9. That the Graces or Passages be easy in appearance, thereby to give universal delight.

10. That in effect they be difficult that thereby the art of the inventor be the more admired.

11. That they be performed with an equal regard to the expression of the words, and the beauty of the art.

12. That they be *gliding* or *dragging* in the *Pathetick*, for they have a better effect than those that are mark'd.

13. That they do not appear studied, in order to be the more regarded.

14. That they be softened with the *Piano* in the *Pathetick*, which will make them more affecting.

15. That in the *Allegro* they be sometimes accompanied with the *Forte* and *Piano*, so as to make a sort of *Chiaro Scuro*.

16. That they be confin'd to a group of a few notes, which are more pleasing than those which are too numerous.

17. That in a slow *Time*, where may be a greater number of them (if the Bass allows it) with an obligation upon the singer to keep to the point propos'd, that his capacity be made more conspicuous.

18. That they be properly introduc'd, for in a wrong place they disgust. . . .

23. That they be stol'n on the *Time*, to captivate the soul.

24. That they never be repeated in the same place, particularly in *Pathetick Airs*, for there they are most taken notice of by the judicious. . . .

27. But it is now time that we speak of the *Dragging*, that, if the *Pathetick* should once again return into the world, a singer might be able to understand it. The explanation would be easier understood by notes of music than by words, if the printer was not under great difficulty to print a few notes; notwithstanding which, I'll endeavour the best I can, to make myself understood.

28. When on an even and regular movement of a Bass, which proceeds slowly, a singer begins with a high note, dragging it gently down to a low one, with the *Forte* and *Piano*, almost gradually, with inequality of motion, that is to say, stopping a little more on some notes in the middle, than on those that begin or end the *Strascino* or *Dragg*. Every good musician takes it for granted that in the Art of Singing there is no invention superior, or execution more apt to touch the heart than this, provided however it be done with judgment, and with putting forth of the voice in a just *Time* on the Bass. Whosoever has most notes at command, has the greater advantage; because this pleasing ornament is so much the more to be admired, by how much greater the fall is. Perform'd by an excellent Soprano, that makes use of it but seldom, it becomes a prodigy; but as much as it pleases descending, no less would it displease ascending. . . .

33. Finally, O ye young singers, hearken to me for your profit and advantage. . . . He that studies, let him imitate the ingenious Bee, that

sucks its Honey from the most grateful flowers. From those called Ancients, and those supposed Moderns, (as I have said) much may be learn'd; it is enough to find out the flower, and know how to distill, and draw the Essence from it.

For biographical information see selections by Quantz in Chapter 17.

SOURCE: *Johann Joachim Quantz*, Versuch einer Anweisung die Flöte traversière zu spielen *(Berlin, 1752), Ch. XVIII, secs. 11, 12.*

JOHANN JOACHIM QUANTZ
from *Versuch einer Anweisung die Flöte...*

Requirements of a Good Singer

11. The requirements of a good singer are: that he first of all have a good, clear, pure tone and an equal scale from bottom to top, which, without those defects that originate in the nose and throat, should be neither hoarse nor hollow. The voice and the use of words are the only things that enable a singer to take precedence over instrumentalists. Further, a singer should know how to join the falsetto to the chest voice in such a way that one cannot observe where the latter ends and the former begins. He should have a good ear and pure intonation so that he can produce all the notes in their proper relationships. He must know how to draw out the voice (*il portamento di voce*) and to sustain long notes (*messa di voce*) in an agreeable way; he must therefore possess a firmness and security of voice and not, in a moderately prolonged note, either begin to tremble or, when he wishes to strengthen the tone, change the pleasant sound of the human voice into a disagreeable screech of a reed pipe, as frequently occurs among singers who are inclined to haste. The good singer further will have a good trill that is not a bleat and that is neither too fast nor too slow; and he must be careful to observe a suitable breadth of trill and distinguish whether it should be of whole- or half-steps.

The good singer must also have good enunciation. He must present the words clearly, and not pronounce the vowels *a, e,* and *o* all the same way in passagework so that the words become unintelligible. When he makes an ornament on a vowel, he must continue it to the end and not mix another vowel with it. Also in producing the words he must take care not to change one vowel into another, such as to transform *e* into *a* and *o* into *u*; for example, in Italian pronouncing *genitura* instead of *genitore*, causing laughter among those who understand the language. On *i* and *u* the voice should not weaken; no lengthy passages should be made in the low register on these two vowels, and almost no graces in the upper register.

A good singer must have dexterity in reading and sounding the notes, and he must know the rules of generalbass. He must not emit the high tones either by a hard attack or by a forcible breath of air from the chest; even less should he howl them out, for this changes the sweetness into brutality. Where the words demand certain emotions to be expressed, he must know how to raise and moderate his voice at the right time and without affectation. In a sad piece he should not introduce as many trills and rapid ornaments as in a cantabile or jolly one, for very often by this means the beauty of the melody is obscured and destroyed.

He should sing the Adagio in a moving, expressive, caressing, grace-ful, cohesive, sustained manner, with lights and shadows, both in the *piano* and *forte* as well as in the addition or ornamentation, in con-formity with the words and melody. He must perform the Allegro in a lively, brilliant manner and with lightness. He must make the passage-work clearly, neither pushing it too hard nor dragging it in a lame and lazy manner. He must be able to moderate his voice from bottom to top, and thereby be able to make a difference between theater and chamber styles, and between strong and weak accompaniment, so that his singing in the higher register does not change into a bawling. He must be very sure of his tempos, and not sometimes hurry and sometimes, particularly in the passages, drag. He must take breaths at the proper times, and quickly. Should this become rather difficult to do, he must nevertheless seek to hide it as much as possible; above all he should never allow himself to be thrown off the beat.

Finally, he must seek to learn that whatever he adds as embellish-ments must be his own, and not be, as are most, like a parrot who listens to others. A soprano and a tenor may permit themselves more embellish-ments than an alto and a bass. To the two latter belong a noble sim-plicity; the portamento of the voice and use of the chest voice are more suitable than the use of the very high register and superfluity of ornaments. True singers have respected and practiced these precepts at all times.

12. If all these possible good qualities are found together in one singer, one can confidently say that he not only is a good singer and justly de-serves the title of virtuoso but also is one of Nature's wonders. Anyone

who wishes to gain the name of a singer of excellence can and should provide himself with the aforementioned qualities; however, a man with all the virtues is as rare as a singer with all these shining merits. For this reason one cannot judge the singer as strictly as the instrumentalist; rather one must be content if one finds only some of the good qualities enumerated above, along with various deficiencies, and not deny him the usual title of virtuoso.

20. Travelers' Reports

For biographical information on Charles de Brosses see his letter quoted in Chapter 15.

Source: *Charles de Brosses,* Lettres familières écrites en Italie en 1739 et 1740, *ed. Romain Colomb (Paris, 1835; 4th ed., 1885).*

CHARLES DE BROSSES
from *Lettres familières*

Letter from Venice

29 August, 1739

The carnival begins after the 5th of October, and there is another short one of two weeks at Ascension; one can therefore count on about six months when everyone goes about masked, priests as well as others, even the Nuncio and the Superior of the Capucines. Do not think that I am joking, it is the prescribed attire; and it is said the parish priests would not be recognized by their parishioners, the archbishop by his clergy, if they did not have a mask in their hand or on their nose. I regret this singularity, and even more the operas and spectacles of the time. It is not that I am wanting for music; there is almost no evening when there is not an Academy somewhere; the people go on the Canal to hear it with as much enthusiasm as if it were for the first time. The rage of the country for this art is inconceivable. Vivaldi has become one of my intimate friends in order to sell me his concertos at a good price. He has partly succeeded, and I, as I desired, was able to hear him and often to have excellent musical entertainments. He is an old man, who has a prodigious fury for composition. I heard him undertake to compose a concerto, with all the parts, with greater dispatch than a copyist can copy it. I found, to my great astonishment, that he is not as much esteemed as he should be in this country, where everything is in fashion, where his works have been heard for a very long time, where last year's music no longer attracts.

The famous Saxon [Hasse] is today the man who is fêted. I heard him at his residence, as well as the celebrated Faustina Bordoni, his wife, who sings with great taste and charming agility; but hers is no longer a fresh voice. She is without doubt the most agreeable woman in the world, but she is not the best singer.

The transcendent music here is that of the hospitals. There are four, composed of orphan or illegitimate girls and those whose parents cannot afford to educate. They are educated at the expense of the State, and they are trained only to excel in music. So they sing like angels, and play the violin, flute, organ, oboe, violoncello, bassoon, in brief, there is no instrument so large as to frighten them. They are cloistered in the manner of religious. They alone perform, and each concert is composed of about forty girls. I assure you there is nothing so agreeable as to see a young and pretty nun, in a white habit, with a bouquet of flowers over her ear, conduct the orchestra and beat the measure with all the grace and precision imaginable. Their voices are adorable both for their quality and agility; but here one does not know about the roundness and spun-out tones *à la française*. La Zabaletta of the Incurabili is astonishing above all for the range of her voice and the *coups d'archet* [bow strokes] she has in her throat. For my part, I have no doubt that she has swallowed Somis's violin.[1] She is the one who receives all the applause, and anyone who calls another equal to her would be attacked by the public. But hear, my friends (I believe no one is listening) and I will whisper in your ear that the Margarita of the Mendicanti is just as good as she is, and pleases me more.

The hospital where I go most often and amuse myself the most, is the Pietà; it is also the first for the perfection of symphonies. What precision of execution! There only one hears that *premier coup d'archet*, so falsely vaunted at the Opera in Paris. La Chiaretta would surely be the leading violin of Italy, if Anna-Maria of the Ospedaletti did not surpass her. I was very fortunate to hear this last, who is so fantastic that she scarcely plays once a year. They have here a kind of music that we do not know at all in France. . . . These are the large concertos where there is no *violino principale*. . . .

---

1. Giovanni Battista Somis, brilliant Italian violinist at Turin.

Sojourn at Naples

24 November, 1739

. . . That evening there occurred the grand opening of the large theater of the palace with the first performance of the opera *Parthenope* by Domenico Sarri. The King attended; he talked during half of the opera, and slept during the other half.

"This man certainly does not love music" [Molière].

He has his loge on the second balcony, opposite the actors: it is much too far, in view of the immense size of the hall, in one part of which one can barely see, and in another one cannot hear at all. The Aliberti and Argentina theaters in Rome are much smaller, more commodious, and better arranged. In truth, we should be ashamed of not having in all of France a hall for performances, unless it is that of the Tuileries, which is not very comfortable and which is almost never used. The Opera hall, which is good for a private person who had it built in his own house to play his tragedy *Mirame*, is ridiculous for a city and a people like those of Paris. Be assured that the theater proper in Naples is longer than the whole Opera of Paris and wide in proportion, and that is what is needed to set up the decorations; though I have been told that the rear of the stage was closed only by a simple partition, which opens on the gardens of the palace; and in case they want to present performances with large scenery, this partition is removed and the decoration is lengthened the whole length of the garden. Judge of the effect of perspective that must create; it is in this respect that Italian painters excel today, as they always have. . . .

This was the first grand opera that we had seen. The work by Sarri, a clever musician, but dry and sad, was not very good, but as a reward, was very well played. The famous Senesino played the main role; I was enchanted with the tastefulness of his singing and his bearing on the stage. But I felt with astonishment that the natives were not at all satisfied. They complained that he sang in a *stile antico*. I must tell you that musical taste changes here at least every ten years; all the applause was reserved for the Baratti woman, a new actress, pretty and easygoing, who was playing a man's part, a touching circumstance which perhaps contributed not a little to her getting such support. In truth, she deserved it, even as a girl; but the liveliness with which she was applauded has raised her stock so high that when I left she was worth 180 sequins a role.

The construction of the poem in Italian operas is somewhat different from ours. One of these days I will treat of that subject as a professional with Quintin, who in his last letter asked me several questions about performances. They play up to the taste of the common people. An opera would not please at all if there were not, among other things, a pretended battle; one hundred rascals on both sides perform it, but they are careful to put in the first rows a certain number of swashbucklers who know how to handle weapons. This is always amusing, at least it is not as ridiculous as our combatants in *Cadmus and Theseus*, who kill each other in a dance. In this opera, *Parthenope*, there was an effective cavalry skirmish, which I liked very much. The two captains, before starting to fight, sang on horseback a duet, a kind of debate, chromatically perfect, and quite capable of rivaling the long harangues of the *Iliad*. We had four operas at the same time in four different theaters. After having tried them all successively, I left three of them one after the other, so as not to miss a single performance of *La Frascatana*, a dialect comedy by Leo.

What invention! What harmony! what excellent musical jesting! I shall bring this opera to France, and I want Malateste to send me news of it. But will he be able to understand it? Naples is the capital of the musical world; there are numerous schools where the young people are educated in this art and from them most of the famous composers have come: Scarlatti, Leo, Vinci, the true god of music; the Zinaldo, Latilla, and my charming Pergolesi. All of these have concerned themselves only with vocal music, instrumental music reigns in Lombardy. . . .

Dr. Charles Burney (1726–1814), English organist, composer, and music historian, was also an amateur astronomer, connoisseur of painting, and something of a poet. He is best known for his History of Music *(1776), but his* Musical tours in Europe *constitute the most informative—and delightful—reading imaginable. The indefatigable Dr. Burney, having decided to write a history of music, found that in order to obtain the necessary information, he would have to travel widely. Accordingly, he started his first tour in 1770, visiting France and Italy. He heard music wherever he went; he visited prominent musicians and scholars, libraries, churches, museums, and art galleries as well, and made the acquaintance not only of all the important musicians in those countries but also the outstanding literary men, artists, and scientists. In 1772 he undertook another such tour, this time through the Low Countries, Germany, and Austria, and again he was welcomed wherever he went and saw and heard everything of interest.*

Unlike his History, *in which a more scholarly and impersonal tone is* preserved, the accounts of his tours are lively, the tone almost conversational, and the range of his observations incredibly wide.

Fortunately for us today, Dr. Burney included many details, many small descriptions and bits of information that bring his narrative to life. He provides the reader with many insights and almost the sense of being there himself. His comments, too, are very pertinent, contributing much to our knowledge of attitudes and opinions of the day, as well as details of performance, kinds of music played and sung, and the like.

The four extracts included here are only a very small sampling of what Dr. Burney saw, heard, and noted down. They present four different kinds of musical events or concerts, little vignettes that show some of the musical life of the eighteenth century.

SOURCES: The Present State of Music in France and Italy, *by Charles Burney, Mus. D. The second edition, corrected (London: T. Becket & Co., 1773). The Present State of Music in Germany, the Netherlands and the United Provinces . . . by Charles Burney, Mus. D., F.R.S. The second edition, corrected (London: T. Becket & Co., 1775).*

CHARLES BURNEY

from *The Present State of Music in France and Italy*

A French Organ Performance

June 18, 1770

This evening I went to St. Gervais, to hear M. Couperin,[1] nephew to the famous Couperin, organist to Louis XIV, and to the regent Duke of Orleans; it being the vigil of the Feast of the Dedication, there was a full congregation. I met M. Balbastre and his family there; and I find that this annual festival is the time for organists to display their talents. M. Couperin accompanied the *Te Deum*, which was only chanted, with great abilities. The interludes between each verse were admirable. Great variety of stops and style, with much learning and knowledge of the instrument, were shewn, and a finger equal in strength and rapidity to every difficulty. Many things of effect were produced by the two hands, up in the treble, while the base was played on the pedals.

1. Armand Louis Couperin (1725–89).

M. Balbastre introduced me to M. Couperin, after the service was over, and I was glad to see two eminent men of the same profession, so candid and friendly together. M. Couperin seems to be between forty and fifty; and his taste is not quite so modern, perhaps, as it might be; but allowance made for his time of life, for the taste of his nation, and for the changes music has undergone elsewhere, since his youth, he is an excellent organist; brilliant in execution, varied in his melodies, and masterly in his modulation.

It is much to be wished that some opportunity, like this annual meeting, were given in England to our organists, who have talents, and good instruments to display. It would awaken emulation, and be a stimulus to genius; the performer would be sure of being well heard, and the congregation well entertained.

The organ of St. Gervais, which seems to be a very good one, is almost new; it was made by the same builder, M. Cliquard,[2] as that of St. Roque. The pedals have three octaves in compass; the tone of the loud organ is rich, full and pleasing, when the movement is slow; but in quick passages, such is the reverberation in these large buildings, every thing is indistinct and confused. Great latitude is allowed to the performer in these interludes; nothing is too light or too grave, all styles are admitted; and though M. Couperin has the true organ touch, smooth and connected; yet he often tried, and not unsuccessfully, mere harpsichord passages, smartly articulated, and the notes detached and separated.

A Milanese Accademia: Padua

July 30, 1770

A private concert in Italy is called an *accademia*; the first I went to was composed entirely of *dilettanti*; *il padrone*, or the master of the house, played the first violin, and had a very powerful hand; there were twelve or fourteen performers, among whom were several good violins; there were likewise two German flutes, a violoncello, and small double bass; they executed, reasonably well, several of our Bach's[3] symphonies, different from those printed in England; all the music here is in MS. But what I liked most was the vocal part by *la padrona della casa*, or lady of the house; she had an agreeable well-toned voice, a good shake, the right sort of taste and expression, and sung sitting down, with the

2. François Henri Cliquot (1728–90), one of a famous French family of organ builders.

3. Johann Christian Bach.

paper on the common instrumental desk, wholly without affectation, several pretty airs of Traetta.

Upon the whole, this concert was much upon a level with our own private concerts among gentlemen in England, the performers were sometimes in and sometimes out; in general, however, the music was rather better chosen, the execution more brilliant and full of fire, and the singing much nearer perfection than we can often boast on such occasions; not, indeed, in point of voice or execution, for in respect to these our females are, at least, equal to our neighbours, but in the *portamento* or direction of the voice, in expression and in discretion.*

On my arrival at Padua I was extremely desirous of seeing the famous church of Saint Antonio, as well as of hearing the service performed in it; and, supposing my Reader to be possessed of a small portion of my impatience, I shall hasten to give him a short description of this fabrick, and an account of its musical establishments.

It is a large old Gothic building, and is called here by way of excellence, *il Santo*, the Saint. It has six domes or cupolas, of which the two largest compose the nave; but though it is only the second church in rank, it is the first in fame and veneration at Padua. It is extremely rich, and so much ornamented, as to appear crowded with paintings and sculpture. At the entrance into the choir the majestic appearance of four immense organs is very striking, of which the front pipes are so highly polished as to have the appearance of burnished silver; the frames too are richly carved and gilt. These four organs are all alike; there are no pannels to the frames, but the pipes are seen on three sides of a square.

There are on common days forty performers employed in the service of this church: eight violins, four violetti or tenors, four violoncellos, four double basses, and four wind instruments, with sixteen voices. There are eight *castrati* in salary, among whom is Signor Gaetano Guadagni, who, for taste, expression, figure, and action is at the head of his profession. His appointment is four hundred ducats a year, for which he is required to attend only at the four principal festivals. The first violin has the same salary. The second *soprano*, Signor Casati, has a feeble voice, but is reckoned to sing with infinite taste and expression. The famous Antonio Vandini is the principal violoncello, and Matteo Bissioli Bresciano the first hautbois in this select band.

---

* It is humbly hoped that my fair countrywomen will not take offence at the use of the word *discretion*, as its acceptance here is wholly confined to music, in which the love for what is commonly called *gracing* is carried to such a pitch of *indiscretion*, as frequently to change passages from good to bad, and from bad to worse. A *little* paint may embellish an ordinary face, though a great deal would render it hideous; but true beauty is surely best in its natural state.

August 2, 1770

This morning ... I went to St. Anthony's church, where, it being the *Day of Pardon*, there was a mass, with solo verses of Padre Vallotti's composition, who was there to beat the time; but the two principal singers, Signor Guadagni, and Signor Casati, being absent, little remains to be said of the execution of this music, as far as the vocal was concerned; the writing, however, was good, the harmony pure, the modulation masterly, and the stile grave and suitable to church. But I found that two of the four organs were more than sufficient to overpower the voices; and Padre Vallotti told me that the noise used to be still more intolerable, but that he had reduced, by one at a time, the four organs, which were formerly played all at once, to two; the whole four never play now but for the common service, when there are no other performers than the priests. ...

Though it was not a great festival, yet the band was more numerous than ordinary. I wanted much to hear the celebrated hautbois Matteo Bissioli, and the famous old Antonio Vandini, on the violoncello, who, the Italians say, plays and expresses *a parlare*, that is, in such a manner as to make his instrument *speak*; but neither of these performers had solo parts. However, I give them credit for great abilities, as they are highly extolled by their countrymen, who must, by the frequent hearing of excellent performers of all kinds, insensibly become good judges of musical merit. People accustomed to bad music, may be pleased with it; but those, on the contrary, who have been long used to good music, and performers, *cannot*. It is remarkable that Antonio, and all the other violoncello players here, hold the bow in the old-fashioned way, with the hand under it.

The choir of this church is immense; the basses are all placed on one side, the violins, hautbois, french-horns, and tenors on the other, and the voices half in one organ-loft and half in another; but, on account of their distance from each other, the performers were not always exact in keeping time. ...

The day before my departure from Padua, I visited Signor Tromba, Tartini's scholar and successor. He was so obliging as to play several of his master's solos, particularly two which he had made just before his death, of which I begged a copy, regarding these last drops of his pen as sacred relics of so great and original a genius.

from *The Present State of Music in Germany, the Netherlands and the United Provinces*

A Concert in Munich

August 22, 1772

After [a visit to the Elector of Bavaria] M. de Visme was so kind as to carry me back to Munich as fast as possible, in order to attend a concert, which Signora Mingotti obligingly made for me, of the best musicians which she could get together upon short notice, whom I had not heard before. M. Kröner, whose performance I had only heard at Nymphenburg in full pieces, was first violin. There was M. Sechi, a very good hautboy, who, if I had not lately heard Fischer, would have charmed me: M. Rheiner, the bassoon, who, when in England was so ill that he was unable to play more than once in public, and whom I had not yet heard, was here tonight, and had quite recovered his health. His tone is sweet, and execution neat, and he must be allowed by every competent and impartial judge, to be a very able and pleasing performer.

Madame la Presidente, a lady of fashion, a friend and neighbor of Signora Mingotti, opened the concert by a lesson on the harpsichord, which she executed with uncommon rapidity and precision. A *quintette* was played next, that was composed by M. Michel, a young man that had been brought up at the Jesuits music school. He has a genius that wants only the pruning knife of time and experience to lop off luxuriance; every performer in this piece had an opportunity of shewing the genius of his instrument, and his own powers of execution. There was, in the solo parts, the brilliant, pathetic, and graceful, by turns; and the *tutti* parts had no other imperfection than being too learned, and *recherchées* in modulation. I hardly ever heard a composition, that discovered more genius and invention, one that required more abilities in the execution, or that was better performed; it was made for a violin, a hautboy, tenor, bassoon, and violoncello.

Signor Guadagni and Signor Rauzzini were both at this concert, and the latter, whom I had only heard in one song, with full accompaniments, was so obliging as to sing a very pretty air of his own composition, and another admirable one, by Signor Sacchini, in the *Eroe Cinese*. In the execution of these airs, he manifested great and captivating powers: a sweet and extensive voice, a rapid brilliancy of execution, great expression, and an exquisite and judicious taste. I was today even surprised by the strength of his voice, which had before appeared rather too feeble for a great theatre; but it was want of exertion, for now it made its way through all the instruments, when playing *fortissimo*.

A duet by Sechi and Rheiner, which finished the concert, put me in mind of the two Bezzozzis, at Turin; as their instruments, so their genius and abilities seem made for each other, there being a like correspondence in both.

After these charming performances were over, I hastened to the comic opera, at which were the Elector, and all the electoral family. Count Seeau, intendant of the Elector's music, had most obligingly changed the opera, in order to afford me an opportunity of hearing Signora Lodi in her best character. The burletta of tonight was the *Moglie fedele*, composed by Signor Guglielmi; her voice is brilliant, and style of singing charming; but as I had, in London, seen Signora Guadagni in the same character, her acting did not strike me so much as it would otherwise have done. After the opera, there was a long dance, which was an ingenious and entertaining pantomime, and of which, the scenes and decorations were well-contrived, and splendid.

The next day, which was that of my departure from Munich, at nine o'clock in the morning, Signora Mingotti, who was indefatigable in rendering me every service in her power, had prepared another small but select band, for me at her house, in order to afford me an opportunity of hearing two scholars of Tartini on the violin; M. Holtzbogn, and Lobst, which political reasons had prevented her from inviting the day before. They are both good performers; had been in the service of the late Duke of Bavaria, and have still a pension, though but few opportunities of being heard.

Holtzbogn has a great hand, a clear tone, and more fire than is usual, in one of the Tartini school, which is rather remarkable for delicacy, expression, and high finishing, than for spirit and variety. This performer writes well for his instrument, and played a very masterly concerto of his own composition. Lobst played a concerto of Tartini with great delicacy; he is naturally timid, and want of practice added nothing to his courage; however, through these disadvantages, he discovered himself to be a worthy disciple of the great Tartini.

After these pieces Signora Rosa Capranica, in the service of this court, and scholar of Signora Mingotti, brought hither from Rome by the Electress Dowager of Saxony, sung a very difficult song by Traetta, with great neatness, and in a pleasing and agreeable manner. This performer is young, and has natural powers capable of great things, at which if she does not arrive under such a mistress as Signora Mingotti, it must be totally attributed to want of diligence.

At the Court of Frederick the Great

September 29, 1772

This morning Mr. Nicolai did me the favour of introducing me to M. Joseph Benda, brother of the celebrated violin player of that name, who is master of his Prussian majesty's band. This able musician was so obliging as to play to me a very pleasing solo, composed by his brother, which he executed with great neatness and delicacy. He was accompanied by his son, under whose direction there is an *Academia* of *Dilettanti*, every Friday night, to which I had the honour of an invitation.

Upon quitting M. Benda, we called on M. Lindner, an eminent performer on the German flute, and scholar of M. Quantz. His Prussian majesty's attachment to this instrument has rendered the practice of it very general at Berlin. . . .

After this I made a second visit to M. Agricola,[1] accompanied still by my obliging friend M. Nicolai, who dedicated this whole day to my service. I was now presented to Signora Agricola, whose name before marriage, was Benedetta Emilia Molteni; she is now near fifty years of age, and yet sings songs of *bravura*, with amazing rapidity. The thinness of some parts of her voice discovers the loss of youth, but yet she has fine remains of a great singer; her compass extends from A in the bass, to D in *alt*; and she has a most perfect shake and intonation; she was born at Modena, and had instructions from all the great masters of her time, among whom she numbers Porpora, Hasse, and Salimbeni. She has been upwards of thirty years settled at Berlin, and in the service of the court. She now performs the second woman's part in his Prussian majesty's serious opera. During this visit she was so obliging as to favour me with three airs in different styles, a *Grazioso*, an *Allegro*, and an *Adagio*, all composed by M. Agricola.

From hence we went to the great opera-house; this theatre is insulated in a large square, in which there are more magnificent buildings than ever I saw, at one glance, in any city in Europe. . . .

1. John Frederic Agricola, composer of serious opera to Frederick the Great.

A considerable part of this edifice forms a hall, in which the court has a repast on *ridotta* days; the rest is for the theatre, which, besides a vast pit, has four rows of boxes, thirteen in each, and these severall contain thirty persons. It is one of the widest theatres I ever saw, though it seems rather short in proportion.

The orchestra is very large, and arranged after that at Dresden. The band consists of about 50 performers, among whom are:

Two composers	One harp
The concert-master	Four tenors
Eleven violins	Four flutes
Five violoncellos	Four hautboys
Two double basses	Four bassoons, and
Two harpsichord players	Two french horns.

The most eminent professors in his majesty's service are:

M. John Joachim Quantz, composer and chamber-musician in ordinary to the king; no less celebrated for his performance and compositions, than for having had the honor of instructing his Prussian majesty on the German flute. But few of his *Concertos* for that instrument are published; however, he has composed more than three hundred for the use of his royal scholar.

M. Joh. Frederic Agricola, composer and director of the opera, mentioned above; his name is well known in Germany by his writings on the subject of music, as by his compositions.

M. Franci Benda, musician in ordinary to his majesty, and master of his concert, has acquired a great reputation in his profession, not only by his expressive manner of playing the violin, but by his graceful and affecting compositions for that instrument.

His Prussian majesty's favorite operas are those of his late *maestro di capella*, Charles Henry Graun, to which he is so much attached, as to hear, unwillingly, those of any other master; and the overtures and concertos of his brother, the concert master, M. Joh. Gottlieb Graun, but lately deceased, are still in high reputation at Berlin, though not of the first class for taste or invention.

The chief singers of this serious opera, in the female parts, are Mademoiselle Schmeling, Signora Agricola, and Signora Gasparini, seventy-two years of age; a time of life, when nature seldom allows us any other voice than that of complaint, or second childhood.

The principal male parts are performed by Signor Ant. Uberti Porporino, whose voice is a *Contralto;* he has been more than twenty years in the service of his Prussian majesty, and is extremely admired for his taste and expression, particularly in singing *adagios*. And Signor Carlo

Concialini, a *soprano;* his voice is feeble, but extremely sweet, and his manner of singing slow movements is delicate and touching.

Besides the composers and performers just mentioned, the theatre royal employs twenty-four chorus singers, a ballet master, a great number of dancers of both sexes, and the Abate Landi, as poet.

The King being at the whole expence of this opera, the entrance is *gratis,* so that anyone, who is decently dressed, may have admission into the pit. The first row of boxes is set apart for the royal family and nobility; the boxes that are even with the pit, and those of the second and third row, are appropriated to the use of the ministers of state, foreign ministers, and persons of rank, who have offices about the court; and a stranger of distinction, by application to the baron Pölnitz, chamberlain and director of public spectacles, is sure of being accommodated with a place in the theatre, according to his rank.

The performance of the opera begins at six o'clock; the king, with the princes, and his attendants, are placed in the pit, close to the orchestra; the queen, the princesses, and other ladies of distinction, sit in the front boxes; her majesty is saluted at her entrance by two bands of trumpets and kettle drums, placed one each side the house, in the upper row of boxes.*

The king always stands behind the *maestro di capella,* in sight of the score, which he frequently looks at, and indeed performs the part of *director-general* here, as much as of *generalissimo* in the field.

Such is the present state of the opera at Berlin. . . .

---

* This species of music, as it is the most ancient, so it seems to be that for which the northern inhabitants of Europe have, in spite of new fashions and refinements in music, the greatest passion. There is scarce a sovereign prince in Germany, who thinks he can dine comfortably, or with proper dignity, without a flourish of drums and trumpets; and this love of noise, perhaps first introduced music at our city entertainments, at my lord mayor's feast, and at the feast of every mayor in the kingdom.

21. On the Performance of Famous Men

Rarely do performers speak of their manner of playing, and very few accounts by eyewitnesses exist that provide any real information. In the following extracts, however, considerable information is given; from them one may gain some insight into the manner of playing or style of each composer.

Johann Nikolaus Forkel's description of "Bach the Clavier Player," from his work on Bach's life and music, may be considered reliable, for he gathered a great deal of information from Bach's sons, Emanuel and Wilhelm Friedemann Bach, that could not have been found elsewhere.

SOURCE: *Johann Nikolaus Forkel, On Johann Sebastian Bach's Life, Genius and Works, 1802; trans. A. C. F. Kollman (?) 1820, Ch. III.*

JOHANN NIKOLAUS FORKEL
from *On Johann Sebastian Bach's Life*

Bach the Clavier Player

John Sebastian Bach's manner of managing the clavier was admired by all those who had the good fortune to hear him, and envied by all those who might themselves claim to be considered as good performers. That this mode of playing on the clavier, so generally admired and envied, must have been very different from that in use among Bach's predecessors and contemporaries may easily be imagined; but hitherto nobody has explained in what this difference properly consisted. . . .

According to Sebastian Bach's manner of placing the hand on the keys, the five fingers are bent so that their points come into a straight line, and so fit the keys, which lie in a plane surface under them, that

373

no single finger has to be drawn nearer when it is wanted, but every one is ready over the key which it may have to press down. What follows from this manner of holding the hand is:

1. That no finger must fall upon its key, or (as also often happens) be thrown on it, but only need to be *placed* upon it with a certain consciousness of the internal power and command over the motion.

2. The impulse thus given to the keys, or the quantity of pressure, must be maintained in equal strength, and that in such a manner that the finger be not raised perpendicularly from the key, but that it glide off the forepart of the key, by gradually drawing back the tip of the finger towards the palm of the hand.

3. In the transition from one key to another, this gliding off causes the quantity of force or pressure with which the first tone has been kept up to be transferred with the greatest rapidity to the next finger, so that the two tones are neither disjoined from each other nor blended together.

The touch is, therefore, as C. Ph. Emanuel Bach says, neither too long nor too short, but just what it ought to be.

The advantages of such a position of the hand and of such a touch are very various, not only on the clavichord, but also on the pianoforte and the organ. I will here mention only the most important.

1. The holding of the fingers bent renders all their motions easy. There can therefore be none of the scrambling, thumping, and stumbling which is so common in persons who play with their fingers stretched out, or not sufficiently bent.

2. The drawing back of the tips of the fingers and the rapid communication, thereby effected, of the force of one finger to that following it produces the highest degree of clearness in the expression of the single tones, so that every passage performed in this manner sounds brilliant, rolling, and round, as if each tone were a pearl. It does not cost the hearer the least exertion of attention to understand a passage so performed.

3. By the gliding of the tip of the finger upon the keys with an equable pressure, sufficient time is given to the string to vibrate; the tone, therefore, is not only improved, but also prolonged, and we are thus enabled to play in a singing style and with proper connection, even on an instrument so poor in tone as the clavichord is.

All this together has, besides, the very great advantage that we avoid all waste of strength by useless exertion and by constraint in the motions. In fact, Seb. Bach is said to have played with so easy and small a motion of the fingers that it was hardly perceptible. Only the first joints of the fingers were in motion; the hand retained even in the most difficult passages its rounded form; the fingers rose very little from the keys, hardly more than in a shake, and when one was employed, the other remained quietly in its position. Still less did the other parts of his body take any share in his play, as happens with many whose hand is not light enough. . . .

The natural difference between the fingers in size as well as strength frequently seduces performers, wherever it can be done, to use only the stronger fingers and neglect the weaker ones. Hence arises not only an inequality in the expression of several successive tones, but even the impossibility of executing certain passages where no choice of fingers can be made. John Sebastian Bach was soon sensible of this; and, to obviate so great a defect, wrote for himself particular pieces, in which all the fingers of both hands must necessarily be employed in the most various positions in order to perform them properly and distinctly. By this exercise he rendered all his fingers, of both hands, equally strong and serviceable, so that he was able to execute not only chords and all running passages, but also single and double shakes with equal ease and delicacy. He was perfectly master even of those passages in which, while some fingers perform a shake, the others, on the same hand, have to continue the melody.

To all this was added the new mode of fingering which he had contrived. Before his time and in his younger years, it was usual to play rather harmony than melody, and not in all the 24 major and minor keys. As the clavichord was still *gebunden*, which means that several keys struck a single string, it could not be perfectly tuned; people played therefore only in those keys which could be tuned with the most purity. Through these circumstances it happened that even the greatest performers of that time did not use the thumb until it was absolutely necessary in stretches. Now when Bach began to unite melody and harmony so that even his middle parts did not merely accompany, but had a melody of their own, when he extended the use of the keys, partly by deviating from the ancient modes of church music, which were then very common even in secular music, partly by mixing the diatonic and chromatic scales, and learned to tune his instrument so that it could be played upon in all the 24 keys, he was at the same time obliged to contrive another mode of fingering, better adapted to his new methods, and particularly to use the thumb in a manner different from that hitherto employed. Some persons have pretended that Couperin taught this mode of fingering before him, in his work published in 1716 under the title of *L'Art de toucher le Clavecin*. But, in the first place, Bach was at that time above 30 years old and had long made use of his manner of fingering; and, secondly, Couperin's fingering is still very different from that of Bach, though it has in common with it the more frequent use of the thumb. I say only "the more frequent," for in Bach's method the thumb was made a principal finger, because it is absolutely impossible to do without it in what are called the difficult keys; this, however, is not the case with Couperin, because he neither had such a variety of passages, nor composed and played in such difficult keys as Bach, and consequently had not such urgent occasion for it. We need only compare Bach's fingering, as C. Ph. Emanuel has explained it, with Couperin's directions, and we shall soon find that, with the one, all passages, even the most difficult and the fullest, may be played distinctly and easily, while with the other we can, at the most, get through Couperin's own compositions, and even then with difficulty. Bach was, however, acquainted with Couperin's works for the harpsichord of that period, because a pretty and elegant mode of playing may be learned from them. But on the other hand he considered them as too affected in their frequent use of graces, which goes so far that scarcely a note is free from embellishment. . . .

From the easy, unconstrained motion of the fingers, from the beautiful touch, from the clearness and precision in connecting the successive tones, from the advantages of the new mode of fingering, from the equal development and practice of all the fingers of both hands, and, lastly, from the great variety of his figures of melody, which were employed in every piece in a new and uncommon manner, Sebastian Bach at length acquired such a high degree of facility and, we may almost say, unlimited power over his instrument in all the keys that difficulties almost ceased to exist for him. As well in his unpremeditated fantasies as in executing his compositions (in which it is well known that all the fingers of both hands are constantly employed, and have to make motions which are as strange and uncommon as the melodies themselves), he is said to have possessed such certainty that he never missed a note. He had, besides, such an admirable facility in reading and executing the compositions of others (which, indeed, were all easier than his own) that he once said to an acquaintance while he lived at Weimar, that he really believed he could play everything, without hesitating, at the first sight. . . .

He had an equal facility in looking over scores and executing the substance of them at first sight at the keyboard. He even saw so easily through parts laid side by side that he could immediately play them. This he often did when a friend had received a new trio or quartet for stringed instruments and wished to hear how it sounded. He was also able, if a single bass part was laid before him (and often it was a poorly figured one), immediately to play from it a trio or quartet; nay, he even went so far, when he was in a cheerful humor and in the full consciousness of his powers, as to add extempore to three single parts a fourth part, and thus to make a quartet of a trio. For these purposes he used two clavichords and the pedal, or a harpsichord with two sets of keys, provided with a pedal.

He liked best to play upon the clavichord; the harpsichord, though certainly susceptible of a very great variety of expression, had not soul enough for him; and the piano was in his lifetime too much in its infancy and still much too coarse to satisfy him. He therefore considered the clavichord as the best instrument for study, and, in general, for private musical entertainment. He found it the most convenient for the expression of his most refined thoughts, and did not believe it possible to produce from any harpsichord or pianoforte such a variety in the gradations of tone as on this instrument, which is, indeed, poor in tone, but on a small scale extremely flexible.

Nobody could install the quill-plectrums of his harpsichord to his satisfaction; he always did it himself. He also tuned both his harpsichord and his clavichord himself, and was so practiced in the operation that it never cost him above a quarter of an hour. But then, when he played from his fancy, all the 24 keys were in his power; he did with them what he pleased. He connected the most remote as easily and as naturally together as the nearest; the hearer believed he had only modulated within the compass of a single key. He knew nothing of harshness in modulation; even his transitions in the chromatic style were as soft and flowing as if he had wholly confined himself to the diatonic scale. His *Chromatic Fantasy*, which is now published, may prove what I here state. All his extempore fantasies are said to have been of a similar description, but frequently even much more free, brilliant and expressive.

In the execution of his own pieces he generally took the time very brisk, but contrived, besides this briskness, to introduce so much variety in his performance that under his hand every piece was, as it were, like a discourse. When he wished to express strong emotions, he did not do it, as many do, by striking the keys with great force, but by melodical and harmonical figures, that is, by the internal resources of the art. In this he certainly felt very justly. How can it be the expression of violent passion when a person so beats on his instrument that, with all the hammering and rattling, you cannot hear any note distinctly, much less distinguish one from another?

Sir John Hawkins's description of Handel's playing is less detailed than Forkel's account of Bach's, but it does convey a good impression of his organ playing (which agrees generally with all other accounts on his performances). It also shows Handel's musical abilities in another light.

SOURCE: *Sir John Hawkins*, A General History of the Science and Practice of Music *(London, 1776), vol. II, Book XX, Ch. CXCVII, pp.912–13.*

SIR JOHN HAWKINS

from *A General History of the Science and Practice of Music*

On Handel's Playing

As to [Handel's] performance on the organ, the powers of speech are so limited, that it is almost a vain attempt to describe it otherwise than by its effects. A fine and delicate touch, a volant finger, and a ready delivery of passages the most difficult, are the praise of inferior artists; they were not noticed in Handel, whose excellencies were of a far superior kind; and his amazing command of the instrument, the fullness of his harmony, the grandeur and dignity of his style, the copiousness of his imagination, and the fertility of his invention were qualities that absorbed every inferior attainment. When he gave a concerto, his method in general was to introduce it with a voluntary movement on the diapasons, which stole on the ear in a slow and solemn progression; the harmony close wrought, and as full as could possibly be expressed; the passages concatenated with stupendous art; the whole at the same time being perfectly intelligible, and carrying the appearance of great simplicity. This kind of prelude was succeeded by the concerto itself, which he executed with a degree of spirit and firmness that no one ever pretended to equal.

Such in general was the manner of his performance; but who shall describe its effects on his enraptured auditory? Silence, the truest applause, succeeded the instant that he addressed himself to the instrument, and that so profound that it checked respiration, and seemed to control the functions of nature, while the magic of his touch kept the attention of his hearers awake only to those enchanting sounds to which it gave utterance.

Wonderful as it may seem, this command over the human passions is the known attribute of music. . . .

There seems to be no necessary connection between those faculties that constitute a composer of music, and the powers of instrumental performance; on the contrary, the union of them in the same person, seems as extraordinary as if the poet should be able to write a fine hand; nevertheless in the person of Handel all the perfections of the musical art seemed to center. He had never been a master of the violin, and had discontinued the practice of it from the time he took to the harpsichord at Hamburg; yet, whenever he had a mind to try the effect of any of his compositions for that instrument, his manner of touching it was such as the ablest masters would have been glad to imitate. But what is more extraordinary, without a voice he was an excellent singer of such music as required more of the pathos of melody than a quick and voluble expression. In a conversation with the author of this work, he once gave a proof that a fine voice is not the principal requisite in vocal performance; the discourse was upon Psalmody, when Mr. Handel asserted that some of the finest melodies used in the German churches were composed by Luther, particularly that which in England is sung to the hundredth psalm, and another, which himself sang at the time and thereby gave occasion to this remark. At a concert at the house of Lady Rich he was prevailed on to sing a slow song, which he did in such a manner, that Farinelli, who was present, could hardly be persuaded to sing after him.

Mozart left no "method" of playing the clavier, nor any instructions for keyboard players. However one can glean from certain passages in his letters much about Mozart's concept of what a good pianoforte should be, his own playing, and his standards of good and bad playing. Mozart is not charitable, and often cruel in his remarks, but by observing his criticisms it is easy to see what he himself would have done. His own technique was flawless, so he scorned a poor or faulty technique; he was able to maintain a steady tempo and played with utmost precision, so he ridiculed those who were less accomplished; and so it went. His comments reveal, however, what he would expect of a good performer.

Sources: Mozart's Letters, trans. and ed. E. Anderson (London: Macmillan, 1966), Letters of Oct. 17–18, 1777; Oct. 23, 1977. Letters of Wolfgang Amadeus Mozart, selected and edited by Hans Mersmann, trans. M. M. Bozman (London: J. M. Dent, 1928), Letters of Nov. 14–16, 1777; Jan. 17, 1778.

WOLFGANG AMADEUS MOZART
Four Letters

MOZART TO HIS FATHER, OCT. 17–18, 1777

This time I shall begin at once with Stein's pianofortes. Before I had seen any of his make, Späth's claviers had always been my favorites. But now I prefer Stein's, for they damp ever so much better than the Regensberg instruments. When I strike hard, I can keep my finger on the note or raise it, but the sound ceases the moment I have produced it. In whatever way I touch the keys, the tone is always even. It never jars, it is never stronger or weaker or entirely absent; in a word, it is always even. . . . His instruments have this special advantage over the others that they are made with escape action. Only one maker in a hundred bothers about this. But without an escapement it is impossible to avoid jangling and vibration after the note is struck. When you touch the keys, the hammers fall back again the moment after they have struck the strings, whether you hold down the keys or release them. [Stein] told me that when he has finished making one of these claviers, he sits down to it and tries all kinds of passages, runs and jumps, and he polishes and works away until it can do anything. For he labors only in the interest of music and not for his own profit; otherwise he would be finished almost immediately. He often says: "If I myself were not such a passionate lover of music and had not myself some slight skill on the clavier, I should long ago have lost patience with my work, but I do like an instrument that never lets the player down and which is durable." And his claviers really do last. He guarantees that the sounding board will neither break nor split. When he has finished making one for a clavier, he places it in the open air, exposing it to rain, snow, the heat of the sun and all hell, in order that it may crack. Then he inserts wedges and glues them in to make the instrument very strong and firm. He is delighted when it cracks, for he can then be sure that nothing more can happen to it. Indeed, he often cuts into it himself and then glues it together and strengthens it in this way. He has finished making three pianofortes of this kind. . . . Here and at Munich I have played all my six sonatas by heart several times. . . . The last one, in D, sounds exquisite on Stein's pianoforte. The device, too, which you work with your knee is better on his than on other instruments. I have only to touch it and it works; and when you shift your knee the slightest bit, you do not feel the least reverberation.

FROM AUGSBURG, OCT. 23, 1777
. . . When I was at Stein's house the other day he put before me a sonata by Beecke—I think I have told you that already. That reminds me, now, for his little daughter. Anyone who sees and hears her play and can keep from laughing, must, like her father, be made of stone. For instead of sitting in the middle of the clavier, she sits right up opposite the treble, as it gives her more chance of flopping about and making grimaces. She rolls her eyes and smirks. When a passage is repeated, she plays it more slowly the second time. If it has to be played a third time, then she plays it even more slowly. When a passage is being played, the arm must be raised as high as possible, and according as the notes in the passage are stressed, the arm, not the fingers must do this, and that too with great emphasis in a heavy and clumsy manner. But the best joke of all is that when she comes to a passage which ought to flow like oil and which necesitates a change of finger, she does not bother her head about it, but when the moment arrives, she just leaves out the note, raises her hand and starts off again quite comfortably—a method by which she is much more likely to strike a wrong note, which often produces a curious effect. I am simply writing this to give Papa some idea of clavier-playing and clavier teaching, so that he may derive profit from it later on. Herr Stein is quite crazy about his daughter, who is eight and a half and who now learns everything by heart. She may succeed, for she has great talent for music. But she will not make progress by this method—for she will never acquire great rapidity, since she definitely does all she can do to make her hands heavy. Further, she will never acquire the most essential, the most difficult and the chief requisite in music, which is, time, because from her earliest years she has done her utmost not to play in time. Herr Stein and I discussed this point for two hours at least and I have almost converted him, for now he asks my advice on everything. He used to be quite crazy about Beecke; but now he sees and hears that I am the better player, that I do not make grimaces, and yet play with such expression that, as he himself confesses, no one up to the present has been able to get such good results out of his pianofortes. Everyone is amazed that I can always keep strict time. What these people cannot grasp is that in *tempo rubato* in an Adagio, the left hand should go on playing in strict time. With them the left hand always follows suit. . . .

MOZART TO HIS FATHER, NOV. 14–16, 1777

. . . Three days ago I began to teach Mlle. Rose [Cannabich] the sonatas. We finished the first allegro today. We shall have most trouble with the andante, for it is full of expression and must be played accurately with *gusto, forte* and *piano* just as it is written. But she is very apt and learns very easily. The right hand is excellent, the left unfortunately has been quite spoiled. I can tell you that I often feel very sorry for her when I see her make so great an effort that she is quite out of breath, and that not from stupidity but because long habit, her whole previous training, has made it impossible for her. I have told both her mother and herself that were I formally her music-master I would lock up all her music, cover the clavier with a handkerchief and make her play, at first quite slowly, nothing but passages, shakes, *mordanten extra* exercises with the right and left hands till the hand was fully trained. After that I trust I could make a real pianist of her. For it is a pity. She has so much talent, reads quite passably, has much natural facility and much feeling. They both agreed with me. . . .

MOZART TO HIS FATHER, JAN. 17, 1778

. . . About eleven in the morning the Herr Councillor came to see me bringing Herr Vogler. The latter desired *absolument* to make my better acquaintance—he had plagued me so often already to come to him, and had finally conquered his pride so far as to make me the first visit. . . . Accordingly I went upstairs with him at once; the other guests began to arrive and we did nothing but chatter. After dinner, however, he sent to his house for two claviers, tuned to one another, and also for his tedious published sonatas. I was forced to play them and he accompanied me on the other clavier. At his urgent request I was then obliged to send for my own sonatas. N. B. before dinner he bungled through my concerto (the one which the daughter of the house plays— Mme. Litzau's) *prima vista*. The first movement went *prestissimo*, the andante *allegro* and the rondo still more *prestissimo*. He played the bars for the most part not as it is written and from time to time entirely changed both harmony and melody. At that pace nothing else is possible; the eyes cannot see the music nor the hands perform it. But what kind of sight-playing is that?—Useless. The listeners (I mean those of them who are worthy to be so named) can only claim to have *seen* music and clavier playing. They hear, think and *feel* as little during the performance as the player himself. You may easily conceive how insupportable it was, for I could not well say to him "Much too fast!" Moreover, it is much easier to play a thing quickly than to play it slowly. In the former case certain notes can be dropped out of the runs without being missed; but is that desirable? In rapid playing the right and left hands can be changed without anyone seeing or hearing it; but is *that* desirable? And in what does the art of *prima vista* playing consist? In this—in playing the piece in correct time, as it should go, with appropriate expression and taste in every note, phrase, etc., so that one would suppose the performer had composed it himself. His fingering, moreover, is wretched. His left thumb is like that of the late Adlgasser, and he executes all descending runs in the right hand with the first finger and thumb.

Like Mozart, Beethoven left no method of instruction, and what is known of his teaching and playing stems from his contemporaries, students, and friends.

From Carl Czerny's Autobiography comes his recollections of his earliest encounter with Beethoven and the master's comments and procedure in teaching the talented ten-year-old boy.

SOURCE: *Carl Czerny, "Recollections from my life,"* Neue Beethoven Jahrbuch, *vol. 9, 1939.*

CARL CZERNY

from "Recollections from My Life"

I was about ten years of age when Krumpholz took me to meet Beethoven. . . . It was on a wintry day that my father, Krumpholz, and I journeyed from Leopoldstadt (where we were then living) to Vienna, to a street called *der tiefe Graben,* where we mounted endless steps to the fifth and sixth floors, where an ill-kempt servant announced us to Beethoven. . . .

At that time . . . he did not give the slightest sign of deafness. I was told to play something at once, and as I was timid about beginning with one of his own compositions, I played Mozart's great C major Concerto, which begins with a number of chords. Beethoven very soon turned his attention to me, drew closer to my chair and, in those passages where I played only an accompaniment, played the orchestral melody with me, using his left hand. His hands were thickly covered with hair, and his fingers, particularly at the ends, were very broad. When he expressed satisfaction, I was encouraged to play his *Sonata pathétique,* which had just been published, and at the last, his *Adelaide,* which my father sang in his quite good tenor. When I had finished, Beethoven turned to my father and said, "The boy has talent; I will teach him myself and accept him as my pupil. Send him to me once a week. But first of all, get him Emanuel Bach's book on *The True Art of Playing the Pianoforte,* which he must bring with him next time."

All those who were present then congratulated my father on this favorable decision, Krumpholz especially, who was delighted, and my father immediately hastened away to obtain Bach's book.

During the first lessons Beethoven kept me exclusively on scales in all the keys, and showed me the only correct position of the hands, something still unknown to most players at that time, and the position of the fingers and especially how to use the thumb; useful rules which I did not fully appreciate until a much later time. He then had me play through the studies given in the manual and pointed out especially the *legato,* which he himself had mastered to such an incomparable degree, and which all other pianists of that time considered to be impossible to execute on the fortepiano, as it was still the fashion (as in Mozart's time) to play in a detached, abrupt manner. Beethoven himself told me in later years that he had heard Mozart play on several occasions, and that Mozart had developed a mode of playing on the claviers of that time that was not at all suitable to the fortepiano. Some years later I also made the acquaintance of several persons who had studied under Mozart, and found Beethoven's remark borne out by their playing. . . .

Anton Schindler's discussion of Beethoven's Op. 14 piano sonatas is both interesting and instructive. His descriptions of Beethoven's playing are of great interest, as are his reminiscences and remarks on Op. 7 and Op. 10.

Sources: *Anton Schindler,* The Life of Beethoven, including the biography by Schindler, Beethoven's correspondence with his friends . . . *ed. Ignace Moscheles (London, 1841; Boston: O. Ditson, 1841), pp. 153–62;* Biographie von Ludwig van Beethoven, *4th ed. (Münster, 1871), Musicalischer Teil, pp. 232, 234, 236–40; Suppl. M, pp. 358–62.*

ANTON SCHINDLER

from *The Life of Beethoven*

Now, with regard to the sonatas, I have further to observe that the hints which I received from Beethoven on the subject of their composition, and the proper style of their performance, had direct reference to only a few of those compositions. Still, no doubt, many persons will be gratified by what I have to communicate. To the intelligent lover of music, these hints will afford matter for reflection, whereby he may not only more thoroughly comprehend the works in question, but also, by the help of the key thus obtained, open for himself a path to the knowledge of other compositions of the like kind, imbued with the like soul and spirit.

Among the most rich in materials, and unfortunately, among the least known, are the two sonatas comprised in Op. 14. The first is in E major, and the second in G major. Both these sonatas have for their subject a dialogue between a husband and wife, or a lover and his mistress. In the second sonata [Op. 14, No. 2], this dialogue, with its signification, is very forcibly expressed; the opposition of the two principal parts being more sensibly marked than in the first sonata. By these two parts, Beethoven intended to represent two *principles,* which he designated the *entreating* and the *resisting*. Even in the first bars [Ex. 1] the contrary motion marks the opposition of these principles.

Ex. 1

By a softly gliding transition from earnest gravity to tenderness and feeling, the eighth bar introduces the entreating principle alone [Ex. 2].

Ex. 2

This suing and flattering strain continues until the middle part is taken up in D major, when both principles are again brought into conflict, but not with the same degree of earnestness as at the commencement. The resisting principle is now relaxing, and allows the other to finish without interruption the phrase that has been begun.

In the following phrase [Ex. 3], both approximate, and the mutual understanding is rendered distinctly perceptible by the succeeding cadence on the dominant.

Ex. 3

In the second section of the same movement, the opposition is again resumed in the minor of the tonic, and the resisting principle is energetically expressed in the phrase in A flat major. To this succeeds a pause

Ex. 4

on the chord of the dominant, and then in E flat the conflict is again resumed till the tranquil phrase [in Ex. 4] comes in as it were like a preparation for mutual concord, for both repeat several times the same idea, resembling an interrogation, beginning slowly, and with lingering pauses, then over and over again in rapid succession. The introduction in the tonic of the principal motive renews the conflict, and the feelings alternate as in the first part; but, at the conclusion of the movement, the expected conciliation is still *in suspenso*. It is not completely brought about until the end of the sonata, when it is clearly indicated, and as it were expressed, on the final close of the piece, by a distinctly articulated "Yes!" from the resisting principle.

Ex. 5

Then was not Beethoven justified in saying, that the poetic idea which had stimulated his imagination in the composition of this work was quite obvious? In fact, is not the explanation of every individual phrase perfectly natural? Of this let any one convince himself, by comparing the above indication of the design with the sonata itself.

But the reality and certainty of the composer's intention is fully obtained only on the performance of the piece, the difficulty of which, be it observed, is much greater than it is generally believed to be. For example, words directing the quickening or retarding of the time, such as *accelerando, ritardando,* etc. do not, in their ordinary acceptation, convey an adequate idea of the wonderfully delicate shading which characterized Beethoven's performance. . . .

M. Ries, alluding to the "Sonata Pathétique," p. 106 of his "Notizen," makes the following remarks on the performance of Beethoven: "In general, he played his own compositions in a very capricious manner; he nevertheless kept strictly accurate the time, occasionally, but very seldom, accelerating the *tempi.* On the other hand, in the performance of a *crescendo* passage, he would make the time *ritardando,* which produced a beautiful and highly striking effect. Sometimes in the performance of particular passages, whether with the right hand or the left, he would infuse into them an exquisite, but altogether inimitable expression. He seldom introduced notes or ornaments not set down in the composition." Yes, it may be truly said that the expression was inimitable! What the "Sonata Pathétique" became under the hands of Beethoven—though he left much to be desired on the score of pure execution—can only be conceived by those who have had the good fortune to hear it played by him. . . . In short, all music performed by his hands appeared to undergo a new creation. These wonderful effects were in a great degree produced by his uniform *legato* style, which was one of the most remarkable peculiarities of his playing.

All the pieces which I have heard Beethoven himself play were, with few exceptions, given without any constraint as to the rate of the time. He adopted a *tempo-rubato* in the proper sense of the term, according as subject and situation might demand, without the slightest approach to caricature. Beethoven's playing was the most distinct and intelligible declamation, such, perhaps, as in the same high degree can only be studied in his works. . . .

I will now, as far as verbal description may permit, endeavor to convey an idea of the manner in which Beethoven himself used to play the two sonatas contained in Op. 14. His wonderful performance of these compositions was a sort of musical declamation, in which the two principles were as distinctly separated as the two parts of a dialogue when recited by the flexible voice of a good speaker.

He commenced the opening allegro [of Op. 14, No. 2] with vigor and spirit, relaxing these qualities at the sixth bar, and in the following passage [Ex. 6]. Here a slight *ritardando* made preparation for gently intro-

Ex. 6

Ex. 7

ducing the entreating principle. The performance of the phrase [in Ex. 7] was exquisitely shaded; and to the following bars [Ex. 8], Beethoven's

Ex. 8

manner of holding down particular notes, combined with a kind of soft, gliding touch, imparted such a vivid coloring, that the hearer could fancy he actually beheld the lover in his living form, and heard him apostrophizing his obdurate mistress. In the following groups of semi-quavers [Ex. 9] he strongly accented the fourth note of each group, and gave a

Ex. 9

joyous expression to the whole passage; and, at the succeeding chromatic run, he resumed the original time, and continued it till he arrived at this phrase [Ex. 10], which he gave in *tempo andantino*, beautifully accenting

Ex. 10

the bass, and the third notes of the upper part of the harmony, as I have marked them in the last two bars of the subjoined example, thereby rendering distinct to the ear the separation of the two principles. On arriving at the ninth bar [Ex. 11], he made the bass stand out prom-

Ex. 11

inently, and closed the succeeding cadence on the dominant in the original time, which he maintained without deviation to the end of the first part.

In the second part, Beethoven introduced the phrase in A flat major, by a *ritardando* of the two preceding bars. He attacked this phrase vigorously, thus diffusing a glow of color over the picture. He gave a charming expression to the following phrase in the treble by strongly accenting and holding down longer than the prescribed time the first note in each bar [see Ex. 12], whilst the bass was played with gradually increasing softness, and with a sort of creeping motion of the hand.

Ex. 12

The passage next in succession was touched off brilliantly; and, in its closing bars, the *decrescendo* was accompanied by a *ritardando*. The following phrase [Ex. 13] was begun in *tempo andante*.

Ex. 13

At the fifth bar, there was a slight *accelerando*, and an increase of tone. At the sixth bar, the original time was resumed. Throughout the remainder of the first movement, Beethoven observed the same time as that which he had taken in the opening bars.

Various as were the *tempi* which Beethoven introduced in this movement, yet they were all beautifully prepared, and, if I may so express myself, the colors were delicately blended one with another. There were none of those abrupt changes which the composer frequently admitted in some of his other works, with the view of giving a loftier flight to the declamation. . . .

With regard to the second Sonata in E major [Op. 14, No. 1] the subject of which is similar to that of the first, I shall confine myself to the
description of Beethoven's manner of performing a very few passages.
In the seventh bar of the first *allegro* movement as well as in the eighth
bar, he retarded the time, touching the keys more *forte*, and holding
down the fifth note, as marked [in Ex. 14]. By these means he imparted
to the passage an indescribable earnestness and dignity of character.

Ex. 14

In the ninth bar [Ex. 15], the original time was resumed, the powerful
expression still being maintained. The tenth bar was *diminuendo* and
somewhat lingering. The eleventh and twelfth bars were played in the
same manner as the two foregoing.[1]

Ex. 15

On the introduction of the middle movement [i.e., mm 22ff.; Ex. 16],

Ex. 16

the dialogue became sentimental. The prevailing time was *andante*, but
not regularly maintained; for, every time that either principle was introduced, a little pause was made on the first note, thus [Ex. 17]

---

1. Schindler's numbering from the seventh through the twelfth bars is incorrect
and has been corrected.

Ex. 17

At the following phrase [mm 39ff.; Ex. 18], a joyous character was expressed. The original *tempo* was taken, and not again changed till the close of the first part.

Ex. 18

The second part, from this passage [mm. 65ff.; Ex. 19] forward, was characterized by an increased breadth of rhythm, and augmented power of tone, which, however, was further on shaded into an exquisitely delicate *pianissimo*; so that the apparent meaning of the dialogue became more perceptible without any overstrained effort of imagination.

Ex. 19

The second movement *allegretto* was, as performed by Beethoven, more like an *allegro furioso*; and until he arrived at the single chord [m 43; Ex. 20], on which he made a very long pause, he kept up the same *tempo*.

Ex. 20

In the *maggiore*, the *tempo* was taken more moderately and played by Beethoven in a beautifully expressive style. He added not a single note;

but he gave to many an accentuation which would not have suggested itself to any other player. On the subject of accentuation, I may state, as a general remark, that Beethoven gave prominent force to all appoggiaturas, particularly the minor second, even in running passages; and, in slow movements, his transition to the principal note was as delicately managed as it could have been by the voice of a singer.

In the rondo of the sonata to which I am here referring, Beethoven maintained the time as marked until he arrived at the bars introducing the first and third pauses. These bars he made *ritardando*.

from *Biographie von Ludwig van Beethoven*

On the occasion of Cherubini's and Cramer's communications about Beethoven in the second period, we promised to set forth later the opinions these two authorities held of the master's piano playing; these now follow. The bluff Cherubini characterized it with one word: rough. The gentleman, Cramer, however, was less offended by the rough playing than by the unreliable readings of one and the same composition; one day he would play it with great spirit and characteristic expression, the next day whimsically, and often confused to the point of unclarity. For this reason, several friends had expressed the desire that Cramer be permitted to perform in public several works, some of them still unpublished—which touched Beethoven's very sensitive side. His jealousy was aroused and, according to Cramer, a certain mutual tension resulted.

It appears to me that Cherubini, already crowned with fame in Europe and ten years older than Beethoven, must have had a strong influence on our Beethoven, and many things bear me out. When we met, Cherubini used to say that he could not forbear to draw Beethoven's attention to the Clementi "School," i.e., to Clementi's style of piano playing, and that Beethoven had always thanked him for these suggestions, with the promise that the next time he played he hoped Cherubini would be pleased. Clementi's judgment of Beethoven's piano playing, which he communicated to this author in Baden in 1827, was confined to a few words. He said, "His playing was only somewhat polished, and not a little impetuous, like himself, yet always full of spirit." It was in 1807 that Clementi had heard Beethoven play various works in Vienna. . . .

There are still a few outstanding traits of our master's playing, which are supported by accounts of Cramer and Clementi, to call to notice. These were: his hands held quietly, as was the upper portion of his body; a sustained style; and his exceedingly remarkable accentuation. In regard to his sustained style, in which we can recognize the former organist, the master distinguished himself, and was said in earlier times to have surpassed Hummel, who was, like John Field, a model for this style. . . .

As for Beethoven's individual style of accentuation, the author can speak partly from Beethoven's critical remarks on Czerny's playing, partly from the piano instruction Beethoven gave to him directly. Above all it was the rhythmic accent that he most strongly called to attention and that he wanted others to stress. On the other hand, he treated the melodic (grammatic, as usually called) accent mostly according to circumstances. He ordinarily emphasized all retardations, especially that of the diminished second in *cantabile* sections, more than others. Therefore his playing acquired a significantly personal character, far from the shallow blandness that never reaches tonal eloquence. In *cantilenas* he turned to the methods of cultivated singers, who do neither too much nor too little; further, he recommended that appropriate words be put to a debatable passage and then sing it, or listen to a good violinist or wind player play it. He held to be important the manner of striking the keys, and its significance: the physical or material and the psychological, to which Clementi had directed his attention. By this last, Clementi meant the sensation of calculated fullness of tone, before the fingers even strike the keys. Whoever is a stranger to this sense will never play an Adagio with feeling. Above all, our master was a declared opponent of miniature painting in all musical performance, and accordingly demanded strength of expression throughout. Even the performances of the Schuppanzigh Quartet bore witness to this. In a *forte* the four men gave the impression of a small orchestra, in complete contrast to the lifeless, mannered tones of the celebrated quartets of our day.

An even more important aspect of Beethoven's piano language was the rhetorical pause and the caesura, both received from Clementi. In order not to misunderstand this aspect, we must call to mind what Beethoven taught with respect to the art of declamation. The caesura, a sudden break in the flow of speech, is in music more related to the concept of rhetorical pause than in poetry, where it must appear in a specific foot of the line; for example, in a pentameter distich it always falls on the third foot. The idea of the rhetorical pause, according to Beethoven, had only the characteristic of lengthening a written note without an expressly designated pause. Both these technical devices are not greatly different, and both have the aim of heightening the effect of what follows. To be sure, this is to be used only in suitable phrases, and therefore will be of more or less significance to the discourse. Examples will be given.

All the idioms of Beethoven's rhetoric can be found in detail in his first sonatas; for example, in the first movement of the first sonata in F minor; in all four movements of the one in E flat, Op. 7; in all three movements of the one in C minor, Op. 10; in all four movements of the D major of the same opus; in the *Pathétique*; and in the sonatas of Op. 14. All the characteristic gradations from naïve, sentimental, serious, and gay to passionate are to be expressed in these sonatas. A few glimpses into the first movement of the C minor sonata [Op. 10, No. 1] and the first of the *Pathétique* will convey the concept of the rhetorical pause and the caesura. The passages in the latter sonata are given in the Supplement.

The contrast between vigor and gentleness that appears at the very beginning of the C minor sonata, or, more expressively, between passion and tenderness, are the expressive principles that appear in the first and third movements, which move together with suitable variations in tempo. It is one of the most hazardous contests between emotion and intellect, which, if it succeeds, is of indescribable aesthetic and deeply moving effect.

From the thirteenth to the twenty-first measures we find the rhetorical pause. This is the passage [Ex. 1]. The written quarter rests in the upper voice are all to be increased to about twice their length, and the abrupt phrases thrown out impetuously. Increased tension is the objective. With the twenty-second measure, the continuation of the passionate discourse

Ex. 1

is resumed in a regular rhythm until the general pause in measure thirty. How what follows from there until the *Cantilena* in E flat major (second subject) is to be performed must be passed over, "because it is not easy to express it in words," as Czerny says. But one should refer to Ph. E. Bach's precepts.

The cadence before the coda of the first part of this movement, together with the beginning of the coda itself, shows the application of Beethoven's precepts, namely rests, where the composer has not expressly marked them. These rests also have the purpose of setting off the coda more sharply. The passage referred to is this [Ex. 2]. The passage moves downward impetuously and stops abruptly on B flat. The coda calms down, and continues deliberately in keeping with the Allegro. At the beginning of the *Cantabile* in F minor, with the thirteenth measure of the second part, the quarter rest in the twelfth measure is to be lengthened. The caesura is clear in this measure. The gentleness of it requires a very marked separation from the passionate movement.

Ex. 2

Sonate Pathétique

In the first, second, and third measures [of Ex. 3], after the opening chords have been struck firmly, they should then die away almost completely. The continuation in long and short notes is to be done with a light touch and in a free rhythm; the dotted sixteenth-note rest in the bass in each of these three measures should be lengthened somewhat. The last three chords of the third measure are to be played in a measured tempo, likewise those in the fourth measure, up to the *fermata*. They are to be performed very freely in the final group, in the same way the Italian

Ex. 3

singer treats each *fermata*. The composer's directions merely indicate a certain measure length, without wishing to impose on the performer the duration of the notes any more than the poet will set the syllable meter for the orator. Both must be determined only by the cultivated taste of the singer, musician, or orator.

Beginning in the fifth measure, the tender *cantilena* with its abruptly contrasting *fortissimo* moves steadily through four measures in strict rhythm. The [high] octave F in the ninth and the [high] C in the tenth measure are held somewhat longer, and the following groups of notes are to be breathed out with tenderness, a beautiful rounding out, as it were. Special attention must be given to the short notes in this *Cantilena*, so that their character will not be lost. Therefore they must be played softly and almost broadly. That this hint does not apply to the contrasting passages is obvious.

Numerous experiences have taught me that it is difficult, even for well-trained musicians, not to play any piece of music like clockwork, however deeply the composer felt it and however obvious the indications given for a correct understanding of it; the 4/4 time signature has therefore misled musicians in the unconstrained expression of their feelings. But the change of time signature in this introduction to 2/4 has sometimes had desirable results, for the thirty-second notes are removed from the conditioned eye. . . .

Secondary Theme of the First Movement Allegro

Although the two principles (or opposites) were only hinted at in the introduction, they appear in this secondary theme in a crowded form,

Ex. 4

uttered in close succession. Even the most dried-up piano teacher would not hesitate to recognize a particular significance in this theme, if he had heard it in a thoroughly thought-out artistic performance. The necessary nuances as marked opposite [Ex. 4] are clear as day. The frequently repeated sign V indicates not merely a stronger accent but also a short pause on the note so marked, but a pause not to be observed by the accompanying voice, which moves in strict rhythm to the last measure of the period. (See the conclusion of C. P. E. Bach's thesis, II, 227.)

In the second movement of the *Pathétique* (the Adagio), many dynamic markings are lacking in all editions. In the principal theme, the expression rises from *piano* to a *mezzo forte* in the sixth measure, and falls back with a *diminuendo* to *piano* in the eighth measure. The warm emotion of the performer will enable him to restore the missing markings to their correct place without difficulty. Holding back the tempo, for instance, in the songlike section in F minor from the 17th to the 23rd measure, and advancing the tempo, from the 37th measure until the return of the principal theme in A flat major, are proper in this case, as in every other Adagio, to the essential requirements of the performance in the spirit of the composition. Only cultivated artistic taste will choose the correct measure of holding back and of forward movement, frequently only after several trials. Emotion alone is not to be trusted. Further, in this Adagio he employs many examples of both the rhetorical pause and the caesura. Such a pause is essential before the beginning of the *Cantilena* in F minor, and a caesura should come before the A flat minor section in measure 37.

In the third movement, "Rondo," none of the necessary performance markings are missing, if one considers only the usual signs. But the thoughtful performer will soon find additional places where he has applied other means to enhance the musical oration. To make the humorous character of the main motive evident in this movement, as Beethoven himself performed it, resists every effort with words and signs.

Let the gentlemen "clavier-masters" continue to count this and all the sonatas of the first period and most of the second, simply because they contain no finger-breaking passages, as "minor" sonatas; and for this reason alone they will continue to give them to their pupils, talented or not, to play badly. After all I have said, it is not my belief that they will want to be undeceived. For if they do not want to be advised, or do not possess the capacity for mending their ways, they are beyond the help of positive proof. . . .

22. Opinion and Criticism

Charles Avison (1709–1770) was an English organist and writer on musical subjects. The son of musical parents, he was trained in his native Newcastle-on-Tyne, and perhaps, though this is problematical, in Italy. He occupied various church positions in his native city, and introduced subscription concerts into Newcastle, to his own great profit.

His best-known work, An Essay on Musical Expression *(1752), caused some controversy, for it was the first English work on musical criticism and contained views often quite different from those generally accepted at the time. His rather outspoken critical remarks and his blunt objections to many common practices did nothing to endear him to his readers; on the other hand, it must be said that many of his comments are perfectly valid. In his second edition of 1753 he softened a good many of them.*

These brief selections from his book will show that his views were possibly not as outrageous as his readers thought them.

SOURCE: *Charles Avison,* An Essay on Musical Expression, *2d ed. (London, 1753), pp. 81, 88, 92, 121, 128, 131, 132.*

CHARLES AVISON

from *An Essay on Musical Expression*

. . . The energy and grace of Musical Expression is of too delicate a Nature to be fixed by words; it is a matter of taste, rather than of reasoning, and is, therefore, much better understood by example than by precept. It is in the works of the great masters, that we must look for the rules and full union of *Air, Harmony, & Expression.*

. . . Our Church music is equally capable of improvements from the same sources of taste and knowledge. We seem, at present, almost to have forgot, that devotion is the original and proper end of it. Hence that ill-timed levity of Air, in our modern anthems, that foolish pride of execution in our voluntaries, which disgusts every rational hearer, and dissipates, instead of heightening true devotion.

If our Organist is a lover of poetry, without which, we may dispute his love for music; or indeed, if he has any well-directed passions at all, he cannot but feel some elevation of mind, when he hears the Psalm preceding his Voluntary, pronounced in an aweful and pathetic strain. It is then he must join *his* part, and with some solemn Air, relieve, with religious chearfulness, the calm and well-disposed heart. Yet, if he feels not this divine energy in his own breast, it will prove but a fruitless attempt to raise it in that of others: nor can he hope to throw out those happy instantaneous thoughts, which sometimes far exceed the best concerted compositions, and which, the enraptured performer would often gladly secure to his future use and pleasure, did they not as fleetly escape as they arise. He should also be extremely cautious of imitating common songs or airs, in the subjects of this latter kind of performance; otherwise he will but too much expose religion to contempt and ridicule.

It may not derogate from our subject of Church-Music, just to mention the present method of singing the common Psalm tunes in the parochial service, which are every where sung without the least regard to *Time* or *Measure*, by drawling out every note to an unlimited length. It is evident that both the *Common* and *Proper* Tunes were originally intended to be sung in the Alla-Breve time, or the regular pointing of two, three, four Minims in a bar:—a kind of movement which every ear, with the least practice, may easily attain: nor when they are sung in parts, should there be any more than three, i.e. one Treble, Tenor, and Bass; as too complete an harmony would destroy their natural *Air*.[1] And, in this style, our Psalm tunes are capable of all the solemnity that can be required from such plain and unadorned Harmony.

However trifling it may appear to consider this species of music, I cannot but own, that I have been uncommonly affected with hearing some thousands of voices hymning the Deity in a style of harmony adapted to that aweful occasion. But sorry I am to observe, that the chief performer in this kind of noble Chorus [i.e., organist] is too often so fond of his own conceits; that with his absurd graces, and tedious and ill-connected interludes, he misleads or confounds his congregation, in stead of being the rational guide and director of the whole.

1. By *Air* Avison sometimes means subject (as in fugue or theme) and sometimes the handling of the thematic material.

It may be thought, perhaps, by thus depriving our Organist of this public opportunity of shewing his dexterity, both in his voluntary and Psalm tune, that all performers indiscriminately, might be capable of doing the Duty here required; but it will be found no such easy matter to strike out the true sublimity of style, which is proper to be heard, when the mind is in a devout state; or, when we would be greatly solemn, to avoid the heavy and spiritless manner, which, instead of calmly relieving and lifting up the heart, rather sinks it into a state of deprivation.

We might soon arrive at a very different style and manner, as well in our compositions as performance, did we but study the works of the best Chapel-Masters abroad, as Caldara, Lotti, Gasparini, and many others, whose excellent compositions ought surely to be better known. . . .

On Expression and Indications for It

The different species of music for the Church, the Theatre, or the Chamber, are, or should be, distinguished by their peculiar Expression. It may easily be perceived, that it is not the Time or Measure, so much as Manner and Expression, which stamps the real character of the piece. A well-wrought Allegro, or any other quick movement for the Church, cannot, with propriety, be adapted to theatrical purposes; nor can the Adagio of this latter kind, strictly speaking, be introduced into the former: I have known several experiments of this nature attempted, but never with success. For, the same pieces which may justly enough be thought very solemn in the Theatre, to an experienced Ear will be found too light and trivial, when they are performed in the Church. And this, I may venture to assert, would be the case, though we had never heard them but in some Anthem, or other divine performance: and were, therefore, not subject to the prejudice, which their being heard in an opera might occasion.

It is also by this efficiency of musical expression, that a good ear doth ascertain the various terms which are generally made use of to direct the performer. For instance, the words Andante, Presto, Allegro, &c are differently apply'd in the different kinds of music above-mentioned. For the same terms which denote Lively and Gay, in the Opera, or Concert Style, may be understood in the practice of Church-Music, as Chearful and Serene, or if the reader pleases, less lively and gay; wherefore the Allegro &c in this kind of compositions, should always be performed somewhat slower than is usual in Concertos or Operas.

On the Expressive Performance of Music in Parts

Having said so much with regard to the expressive performance of music in general, I shall now conclude with a few hints which may be of service in the performance of full music: especially of such concertos as have pretty near an equal share of Air and Expression in all their parts.

The first material circumstance which ought to be considered in the performance of this kind of composition, is, the number and quality of those instruments that may produce the best effect.

And, first, I would propose, exclusive of the four principal parts which must be always complete, that the chorus of other instruments should not exceed the number following, viz., six *Primo*, and four *secondo Repienos*; four *Repieno Basses*, and two *Double Basses*, and a *Harpsichord*. A lesser number of instruments, near the same proportion, will also have a proper effect, and may answer the composer's intention, but more would probably destroy the just contrast, which should always be kept up between the Chorus and Solo: for in this case the effect of two or three single instruments would be lost and overpowered by the succession of too grand a Chorus; and to double the *Primo*, and *secondo Concertino*, or Violoncello in the Solo, would be an impropriety in the conduct of our musical economy, too obvious to require anything to be said on that head. It may be objected, perhaps, that the number of basses, in the above calculation, would be found too powerful for the Violins: but as the latter instruments are in their tone so clear, sprightly, and piercing, and as they rather gain more force by this addition, they will always be heard: however if it were possible, there should never be wanting a Double Bass; especially in a performance of full concertos, as they cannot be heard to any advantage without that NOBLE FOUNDATION of their harmony.

As to Wind-Instruments, these are all so different in their Tone, and in their progressions through the various keys, from those of the stringed kind, besides the irremediable disagreement of their rising in their pitch, while the others are probably falling, that they should neither be continued too long in use, nor employed but in such pieces as are expressly adapted to them, so that in the general work of concertos, for Violins &c. they are almost always improper; unless we admit of the Bassoon, which, if performed by an expert Hand, in a soft and ready tone, and only in those passages that are natural to it, may then be of singular use, and add fullness to the harmony. . . .

Secondly, in the four principal parts there ought to be four performers of almost equal mastery; as well in regard to time as execution; for however easy it may seem to acquire the former, yet nothing more shews a master than a steady performance throughout the whole movement, and therefore chiefly necessary in the leading parts. . . .

Thirdly, the same rule will serve for all the other instruments except the Harpsichord; and as this is only to be used in the Chorus, the Performer will have little else to regard but the striking the just chords, keeping the time, and being careful that no jangling sound or scattering of the notes be continued after the pause or cadence. During this interval of rest, he should also attend with the utmost exactness the leading off again [of] the remaining part of the movement, that when all the parts are thus instantly struck, his own may be found to pervade and fill the whole: and if there are any rests succeeding the pause, his attention to the leading instrument will direct him when these are to commence. The same care is necessary at the return of each double strain, when there are no intermediate notes to introduce the repeat. In fine, a profound silence must be always observed wherever the composer has intended a general respite, or pause in his work. I am the more particular in giving this caution to performers on the harpsichord, as they are the most liable to transgress in this way; because their instrument, lying so commodious to their fingers, is ever tempting them to run like wildfire over the keys and perpetually interrupt the performance. As compositions of this nature are not calculated for the sake of any one instrument, but to give a grand effect by uniting many, each performer ought therefore to consider his particular province, and so far only to exert himself as may be consistent with the harmony and expression in his part. . . .

The use of the *Acciaccatura,* or sweeping of the chords, and the dropping or sprinkling notes, are indeed some of the peculiar beauties of this instrument. But these graceful touches are only reserved for a masterly application in the accompaniment of a fine voice, or single instrument; and therefore, besides the difficulty of acquiring a competent skill in them, they are not required in the performance of full music.

William Jackson (b. 1730) was an English organist and prolific composer as well. His songs, melodious and refined, were popular in his time, and his many cantatas, hymns, and organ works were widely used. Every English church organist, no matter how small his choir, was familiar with Jackson's Te Deum, *known to the profession as "Jackson in F." In 1777 he was appointed Master of the Music at Exeter Cathedral, where he remained throughout his life.*

Jackson was also a critic and historian. His Thirty Letters on Various Subjects *(1782) was favorably received and went through three editions. In 1791 his* Observations on the Present State of Music, in London *appeared. This small work of thirty-five pages shows Jackson to have been extremely conservative and to have found it difficult to accept the newer musical styles of the end of the century. He complains that modern music has no "air," laments the good old days, censures composers then writing (Haydn, Vanhall, Mozart, Pleyel—whom he never mentions by name), and criticizes music of all genres. Dr. Burney wrote a devastating review of this book in the* Monthly Review *(October 1791) in which he criticizes Jackson's statements and principles severely; he does, however, give Jackson credit where credit is due, namely in his observations on the abuse of embellishments in solo songs and in his remarks on trios and quartets.*

The following extracts reflect attitudes of a large portion of musicians from the provinces in contrast to the more enlightened taste of the London musical public.

SOURCE: *William Jackson,* Observations on the Present State of Music, in London *(London, 1791), pp. 10, 15, 20, 22, 24–25.*

WILLIAM JACKSON

from *Observations on the Present State of Music, in London*

Vocal music had once nothing but Harmony to subsist on; by degrees, melody was added; and now it is very near to being lost again.

In the Grand Opera, songs may be considered as *pathetic, bravura,* something between the two which has no name, and airs called *Cavatina.* Generally the last have most melody, and the first sort have least; but it is scarce worth while to ascertain which has most, where all are defective. If it were not for some passages that have been worn to rags, how few of these songs possess the least trace of real Melody! This must remain an assertion without proof unless I can define melody, which I really cannot, as to be intelligible to those who have no ear; and, to those who have, a definition would be needless. But let me observe, where *sounds* follow each other in that arrangement we call Tune, besides immediate pleasure, there is always joined with it an *Impression*, which enables us to remember passages, and sometimes an entire Air. But this is never the case in a fortuitous or unmeaning succession of sounds. Let the Music of the present day be "weighed in the balance," and the greater part will be found "wanting."

These observations will do for the Opera Buffa, omitting the term *pathetic* and substituting *comic* in its room. But it is using Thalia very ill to call the nonsensical folly of this drama *comic*.

In the English Opera the composers very wisely adapt some of the songs to tunes which were composed when melody really existed: and it is curious to observe how glad the Audience are to find a little that is congenial to their feelings, after they have been gaping to take in some meaning from the wretched imitations of Italian bravura and pathetic song; which, alas! are but "the Shadows of a Shade."

If our Vocal Music has dismissed Melody as unnecessary, our Instrumental Music has closely followed the bad example.

The old Concerto is now lost, and modern Full-pieces are either in the form of Overtures or Symphonies. The Overture of the Italian Opera never pretends to much; that of the English Opera always endeavors to have an Air somewhere, and the endeavor alone makes it acceptable. As the first movement of the overture is most commonly like that of a Symphony, what I have said of the latter will do for both.

When Richter introduced among us this style of music, it was justly admired, being the first instance of attention to the different character of instruments: a nicety unknown to Handel or to any of his predecessors. Richter was very successfully followed by Abel, and by many others. But later composers, to be grand and original, have poured in such floods of nonsense, under the sublime idea of *being inspired*, that the present Symphony bears the same relation to good music as the ravings of a Bedlamite do to sober sense. Sometimes the Key is perfectly lost by wandering so far from it that there is no road to return—but extremes meet at last of themselves. The measure is so perplexed by arbitrary divisions of notes, that it seems as if the composer intended to exhibit a table of twos, threes, and fours. And, when discords get so entangled that it is past the art of men to untie the knot, something in the place of Alexander's sword does the business at once. All these paltry shifts to conceal the want of Air, can never be admitted to supply its place.

Where there is *really* Air it will exist under all disadvantages of performance. But, what would become of our sublimities, if it were not for the short cut of a *Pianissimo* so delicate as almost to escape the ear, and then a sudden change into all the *Fortissimo* that Fiddling, Fluting, Trumpeting, and Drumming can bestow. . . .

The Quartet and Trio are in a much more respectable style: as are Concertos for *particular instruments,* those for the Piano to be excepted; which, of late, seem to have abandoned that style of melody so peculiarly the property of the instrument, and exchanged the easy flow of execution, which it has cost so many years to establish, for staggering Octaves. The Cadences are invariably the same, and the worst that could be invented by an imagination perverted in the extreme. The Performer, no doubt, ought to be able to run from the bottom to the top of the keys, in semitones, but let him be satisfied with having the power without exerting it, for the effect of the passage is to the last degree detestable.

The most pleasing of all instrumental compositions is the Concertante, for three, four, or five principal performers supported by the Ripieno. Whether the contrast of the different instruments becomes a sort of substitute for melody, and is received as such, or whether we are more interested because of the excellence of the Performer, I know not; but it seems as if an Air subsisted more in this than in any other species of instrumental music. . . .

The Performance of single songs was perhaps never more removed from Truth than at present. If there were a possibility of writing down the sounds which issue from the mouth of the singer, my remarks would be fully justified—but, unfortunately, lines and spaces will only express musical intervals. Words seem as little suited to the purpose, for how can one describe the encompassing a note with frippery flourishes that prevent the real sound from meeting the ear, until the time in which it should be heard, is past? How can one express the filling up of an interval with something composed of a slide and a shout, but which means there is no interval at all?

There are some things, however, which *may* be described; such as forcing the voice in the upper part, where it ought ever to be soft; and singing the lower tones faint, which should always be full. Cadences with, for ever, a concluding shake—though sometimes it seems as if it would *never* conclude—and every shake with exactly the same turn after it. . . .

Whatever objections may be made to the composition of Symphonies, the performers of them are entitled to the highest praise. The performer plays just what he sees, and nothing else, as is generally the case with most instrumental music, which is incomparably more pure in its execution, at present, than Vocal. Is it not rather uncommon, that two branches from the same stock should be so different?

The notes of a song are broken into so many parts that they actually lose their existence: on the contrary, the performance of a Symphony etc. is pure and simple. In the one everything is cut up; in the other—to borrow a phrase from painting—the parts are kept broad: and breadth of effect is as necessary in music as in painting.

Instrumental music has been of late carried to so great perfection in London, by the consummate skill of the performers, that any attempt to beat the time would be justly considered as entirely needless. I am sorry to remark that the attention of the Audience at one concert, has been interrupted by the vulgarity of this exploded practice, which is unworthy of the supreme excellence of the Band, and highly disgusting to the company.

Johann Friedrich Reichardt (1752–1814) was the son of a Königsberg musician and trained as a musician. At the University of Königsberg he continued his study of violin, piano, and composition as well as philosophy and literature. Before settling in a position, he spent the years 1771–74 traveling, visiting the great centers of music in Germany and Austria. The result of this tour was a book, Vertraute Briefe eines aufmerksamen Reisenden *(1774 and 1776), in which he showed his talents as a musical critic and writer. In 1775 he became* Kapellmeister *and court composer at the court of Frederick the Great, where he remained until 1785. During his tenure there he established a* Concert spirituel *modeled on the more famous Parisian group. He returned to Berlin after Frederick's death in 1786, but his sympathies with the French Revolution made enemies for him at court; also his many absences and journeys were not looked on favorably. He was dismissed in 1794.*

Reichardt was something of a composer, producing Singspiele *and operas that were very well received. He was also a* littérateur *and man of the world, a keen observer and a very good critic. He wrote two other important works of reportage and criticism:* Vertraute Briefe aus Paris . . . , *1804, and* Vertraute Briefe aus einer Reise nach Wien . . . , *1810. His books are interesting, not only for his accounts of music but also for the wealth of information he gives on society, politics, literature, the theater, and personalities in the cities he visited.*

Source: *Johann Friedrich Reichardt,* Vertraute Briefe aus Paris geschrieben in der Jahr 1802 und 1803 *(Hamburg, 1804), Fourth Letter, pp. 94–99, 109–16.*

JOHANN FRIEDRICH REICHARDT
from *Vertraute Briefe aus Paris*

PARIS, NOVEMBER 15, 1802

[Reichardt has mentioned that he has made calls on several people, dined with others, and begun to participate in musical life.]

Among the early return visits I have received, I am happy to mention Paisiello, Gossec, Cherubini, Lalande, and Caillard. Paisiello, whom I last saw twelve years ago, has certainly not aged; he still has a stately, manly appearance. His large figure has acquired a colossal air because of a very considerable *embonpoint,* so that with his fiery, black eyes and thick black hair, it suggests that the pleasant, charming, gracious composer is in excellent condition. About a year ago the first Consul sent to Naples for him in order that he might compose a great French opera here in Paris. The affair did not appear very attractive to Paisiello; however, more acceptable were the conditions under which he is here. He receives three thousand *livres* monthly (about eight hundred *Thaler*), free residence, servants, and carriage. For this he composes and conducts the Consul's private Mass. Meanwhile he calls himself *M. da capella* of the King of Naples, and is only here by the King's permission.

He was given at first a poem by Lemercier to compose, but Paisiello declined it because he did not believe that a Spirit, who played the most important role in it, could sing interestingly throughout the whole opera. Now he has been given an old poem by Quinault, *Proserpine,* prepared after Marmontel, and he is now working on the second act. The opera will be given right after New Years.

You will still remember the old, small, round, blond, friendly Gossec, who within and without is so completely the opposite of Paisiello. He is still the cordial, sympathetic person and doesn't look his seventy-one years. He is one of the most efficacious Inspectors of the Conservatoire de Musique and promises me many good things from it; he also thinks that several young talents that the Conservatoire has recently supplied to the Opera will enable me sufficiently to make peace with the singing of the Opera. Paisiello likewise has stipulated that of the older singers he will use only Lais in his *Proserpine;* all the other roles will be taken by those younger singers.

You will remember well how, seventeen years ago, the amiable Cherubini came to Paris as a fine young man with Babini, and there in the *Concert spirituel* and the splendid *Concert d'amateurs à la Loge*

Olympique he heard Haydn's symphonies for the first time; how astonished and enchanted he was, and finally stood there pale and almost petrified. That beautiful moment certainly was decisive in his later taste and artistic style. And although he was the leading Italian vocal composer, who often sacrificed the vocal parts to the instrumental accompaniment, he is still the first and only one of his countrymen who was in a position to produce such orchestral effects and to create such an individual and artistic genre. But what exertion it has cost him to go against his natural agreeable talent for pleasing song, and to hold to a different path and keep pace with Haydn, can be seen unfortunately and only too well in his appearance. In his face and bearing there is no longer the happy youthful exuberance which then impressed us; he appears weak, sickly, and melancholy. But that does not disfigure him at all; it makes him much more interesting. He told me that he has completely withdrawn from society; he lives at home with a lovely wife and two dear children. Here [in Paris] injustice and ungratefulness have their part in the way this rare artist is treated. Throughout his entire ten-year stay in Paris he still has not been able to have an opera performed in the great Opera theater. Several years ago he had composed a small opera for it, but it has always been put aside for other operas by the most favored composers, as now happens with Paisiello's *Proserpine*. All his beautiful works, which we admire so much in Germany, were composed for the little Théâtre Feydeau. It is the same with Méhul, who, like Cherubini, is Inspector and teacher at the Conservatoire de Musique, which began to furnish better voices at the Opera. If the prize of a great opera, that would be approved, were not so important, then I would be surprised that such men could even conceive of wanting to compose for any bawler; for the primary roles are not made for old singers except when forced by an authoritative decree, as the report was in the case of Paisiello. However, no more for now about these *parties honteuses* that otherwise administer the Parisian theater world.

Men of taste and experience who find occasion in their travels to get to know the better vocal music, or who clearly favor the attractive Italian song, take almost no notice of the present grand Opera. This is, for example, the case with Caillard, who is himself musical, and Lalande. He dismisses with French vehemence and one-sidedness the entire so-called French or declamatory genre. On that score he is even a declared antagonist of Gluck, and allows only Piccini and Sacchini to be of worth. Also he detests the unmusical texts of French opera, and the entire lyric poetry of the French, which certainly is not intended for the song forms of the newer Italian music. But I will allow myself to return to the Opera later, about which I cannot yet speak in detail. . . .

In the last several days I have seen at the Opera *Les Prétendus* by Le Moine and *Le Jugement de Paris,* one of the great pantomimic ballets by Gardel. The first one, that only through recitative was powerful enough to obtrude on this large theater, is a very pleasing, attractive piece that could provide opportunity for a bright and delightful score.

The music of Le Moine, who has been at the theater since 1789, does not fill the expectations that the reading of the work suggests. It is an awkward imitation of the usual Italian comic music, and just as colorless and monotonous as the music of the little Italian comedians always is.

In the magnificent ballet I saw and felt more than ever that among all the riches of individual artists, the large pantomimic ballet has lost much. The former noble grace is no longer there, the dignity and perfection of the ensemble is lacking. Vestris, and all those with him, leap and stretch and extend themselves on all sides; but that does no good. The Paris ballet is no longer the single great inexpressible artistic performance, about which no one could ever give anyone else an idea in words. It is the same as that one sees in the great theaters in other capital cities, only better, richer, larger; it is a merry, dancing world, in which everything is calculated in terms of single, pleasing, attractive, voluptuous tableaux. Among Gardel's new compositions this is also the single thing that has worth; in this he has succeeded: the grouping and arrangement of the whole stage, the opulence and charm in single scenes, and the finely combined movement of everything to make the most delightful effect for the eye, is unsurpassed. But the whole composition, as great ballet and particularly this ballet, is small, often quite childish.

Also, I am no longer pleased as formerly with the stage decor. They have set up splendid gardens and effective backgrounds, but the front and middle ground are used merely for tricks, leaps, and the endless running and chasing of the dancers, against all true and large theater effects. No! No! One recognizes the great uneducated public, for whose approval the artist now has to strive, not only by untimely applause and senseless raving and uproar but also one recognizes it by the entire artistic production itself.

What would our respectable [German] theater managers, who often find the apparel of our actresses and dancers indecent, say if they saw the costumes in the ballets today! The beautifully formed dancers appear almost naked. The thin, fine veils of their costumes cover barely a fourth of their lovely bodies; they are completely transparent in the bright lighting, and, through the violent movement and countless turns, like a top, twenty, thirty times one after another, even in the noblest character parts, often blow completely away from their bodies. In elegance and splendor, where it is suitable, the ballet costumes are incomparable.

The lighting also is most beautiful, which, as an article of *virtù* according to the rules of optics and artistic lighting, is treated with great art and attention. In "fire scenes" especially one sees inconceivable effects.

What spoils my enjoyment of these ballets the most is the rhapsodic, often senselessly put-together music, which the ballet master himself has patched up from single movements of quartets, symphonies, sonatas, or opera arias. After the most beautiful pieces by Haydn—which are rarely played in their proper intrinsic movement but, according to the whim of the dancer, considerably faster—one hears frequently the dullest, most commonplace things, without any harmonic or rhythmic order. Also, the good things are often performed completely unsuitably. So, in the ballet of *Le Jugement de Paris*, at Jupiter's decree *Ein männchen und ein Weibchen* from Mozart's *Zauberflöte* was played! Another time, I have forgotten exactly where, but on a serious occasion, *Als auf meiner Bleiche*, by our Hiller. And that in Paris, where ballet music under Rameau has reached such a high degree of artistic perfection!

I have seen in the Theatre Feydeau four pieces in two evenings; two of them interested me extraordinarily and in very different ways. Both were by Méhul. The one, *L'Ariodan*, a big serious work that in itself as a poem is not interesting, and in the actual performance turned out to be insignificant. But Méhul's music has great, splendid things in it, particularly a duet between two lovers, which in fervor, warmth, and voluptuous beauty of expression surpasses almost everything of its kind. Overall one hears great intentions, often very happily executed; but often, unfortunately, through excess and through the unfortunate striving to be harmonious and to please still more, it becomes distorted and fails. Thus there ran throughout the Overture an ingenious treatment of a bass theme, at first presented simply, then led back and forth in many ways to boredom; and the same kind of thing often spoiled the most attractive songs. Because of the songs I became acquainted again with two fine and interesting singers, Mme Scio Messié, a real singer with a beautiful, expressive voice, especially in the low and middle notes. From her I heard for the first time here in Paris some real singing; she is also a good actress for tragic opera roles. Besides her, Mlle Pingenet the elder sang, who had a pleasing, or rather, a somewhat stronger voice with good range; and also, not least, she even undertakes *bravura* only occasionally rather than too often. She is also very pretty and not a bad actress.

Also I have come to know another very pleasant tenor and good actor in Gavaudan and an excellent bass and actor in Solié. What a wealth of talent there is in an opera theater! And there is also a crowd of good supporting actors behind them.

In a small, pretty, unimportant piece with dull music by Devienne, *Le valet de deux maîtres*, the same evening, a couple of outstanding comic talents appeared—Dozainville and Batiste—whom I am eager to see in important roles.

The second work by Méhul, which in its way pleased me almost as much as *Ariodan*, was *Une Folie*, a very entertaining, amusing work of intrigue with a completely charming and florid score, particularly in the part of the lively orchestra accompaniments. It was also admirably played by Ellevion, Martin, Solié, Dozainville, and the elder Mlle Pingenet. But everyone around me said that the piece had lost much by the departure of Mlle Phillis, who went to Petersburg a short time ago. She must have been completely captivating and peerless in naïve, lively roles and in interesting musical delivery.

Ellevion is one of the handsomest and most attractive men in figure, face, and bearing that I have ever seen; to me he is the most perfect portrayer of a lover to appear anywhere, even in the French theater. Along with that he has a very pleasing, true, although not strong, tenor voice and a brilliant exuberant delivery. In this, however, he is surpassed by Martin, who is also a good comedian. His voice is more of a baritone (high bass) than tenor; in his performance one recognizes a good musician, which he really must be. One can say that he, and perhaps Ellevion, overdo the wealth of colorful ornamentation; others also say this. In this little jolly genre, where the audience enjoys first-rate entertainment of the most agreeable kind, the change and variety in performances is also a great merit. So it is that a piece that pleases at the beginning is given almost daily for several weeks, and subsists on it afterwards for ten or twelve years in such a way that it appears at least once a month. The first loges are subscribed mostly for an entire year, and often limited to those persons only who have paid the subscription; so there are always the same persons in them. For others, who pay for their seats each time, it is now fashionable to attend frequently a piece that is very pleasing. This is very agreeable, for it enables one to hear the new embellishments of the singers.

Hector Berlioz (1803–1867) told the story of his own life in his immense autobiography, which was published in two substantial tomes two years after his death. He seems to have been one of those Protean figures such as the Romantic movement often produced. He was a copious composer of music, and a theorist, who in his Traité d'instrumentation et d'orchestration modernes *was extremely influential during the nineteenth century. This work is important even today and still in use. In addition to his orchestral music, Berlioz wrote operas, cantatas and religious choral compositions of great power, and many beautiful songs.*

Besides his musical activity, Berlioz was also a critic, very prolific and extremely well informed. He claims to have become a critic because of poverty and to have written only to keep the wolf from his door. If one chooses to believe him, his critical writings are of no importance; but he underrates his work. He wrote on the subjects he knew best, on music and musical performance, and his essays are unbiased, intelligent, and interesting. His feelings for Romanticism and the Romantic composers are under control so as not to be obtrusive.

For nearly fifty years, spurred on by personal need, Berlioz wrote for several Paris newspapers, his chief outlet being the prestigious Journal des Débats, *under the editorship of Louis Bertin, who was able to tame the wild man and help him to produce masterly writings. These productions consisted of chats, reviews, letters from the editor, learned articles, anecdotes—a massive production of more than 650 items. Many of these were later collected in four volumes—*Les soirées de l'orchestre *(1832),* Voyage musical *(1844),* Les grotesques de la musique *(1859), and* À travers chants *(1862, with its curious punning title). Much of Berlioz's journalistic criticism remains to be salvaged. While he continually laments the time wasted on literary production, his output was prodigious and of high quality.*

In the articles we have chosen to reprint the critical sense of the musician and performer overshadows that of the journalist to a large extent.

SOURCES: Hector Berlioz, "On Gluck's System of Dramatic Music," in Voyage musical (Paris, 1844); "On the Present State of Singing in the Lyric Theaters of France and Italy . . ." and "Bad Singers, Good Singers, the Public, the Claque," in À travers chants (Paris, 1862).

HECTOR BERLIOZ

from *Voyage musical*

On Gluck's System of Dramatic Music

Here are the terms in which Gluck himself explains his system of dramatic music, in a preface to the Italian edition of *Alceste* now become very rare. He published it first in Vienna in 1749.

"When I undertook to set the opera *Alceste* to music, I tried to avoid the abuses which the mistaken vanity of the singers and the excessive compliance of the composers had introduced into the Italian opera and which, out of the most stately and the most beautiful of all spectacles, had made the most boring and the most ridiculous; I tried to bring music back to its true function, that of assisting the poetry, to strengthen the expression of the feelings and the interest of the situations without interrupting the action and cooling it with superfluous ornamentation. I thought that the music should add to the poetry what is added to a correct and well-composed drawing by the liveliness of colors and the happy agreement of the light and shade, which serve to animate the figures without altering their contours.

"So I took good care not to interrupt an actor in the heat of dialogue, to make him wait for the end of a *ritornello*, or to stop him in the middle of a discourse on a favorable vowel, either to show in a long passage the agility of his beautiful voice or to wait for the orchestra to give him time to catch his breath to make an organ point.

"I imagined that the overture should warn the spectators of the character of the action that was to be presented before their eyes and indicate its subject, that the instruments should be brought into action only in proportion to the degree of interest and passions, and that, above all, in the dialogue one must avoid leaving too great a disparity between the air and the recitative so as not to cut off the sentences, and not to interrupt *mal à propos* the movement and the heat of the scene. I thought also that the best part of my work should be to seek a fine simplicity, and I avoided exhibiting a series of difficulties at the expense of clarity. I gave no worth to the discovery of novelty, unless it came up naturally as a consequence of the situation, and was attached to its expression; there is not a single rule that I thought might not be sacrificed willingly to effectiveness."

This profession of faith seems to us admirable for its frankness and common sense. The points of doctrine which form its foundation are based on the strictest reasoning, and on a deep sense of real dramatic music. Aside from a few exaggerated conclusions, which we will point out presently, these principles are so excellent that they have been adopted by most of the great composers of all nations. Piccini himself, whom people for a long time opposed to Gluck, was entirely in the system of Gluck. His *Iphigenia in Tauris* and his *Dido* prove it; the case was the same with Sacchini, Salieri, Cherubini, among the Italians; Méhul, Berton, Kreutzer, among the French. (I will not cite M. Lesueur; he has followed a route parallel to that of the illustrious author of *Alceste* but which differs from it enough so it cannot be mistaken for it.) Among the Germans I know of no dramatic composer who has departed in any perceptible way from Gluck's doctrine. Among those who have adopted and developed it, one must cite Mozart, who, in *Don Giovanni*, the *Marriage of Figaro*, *The Magic Flute*, and the *Abduction from the Seraglio*, has written only a few songs in bad taste and false expression when he was forced against his will by the sometimes irresistible caprice of his singers. It has been said that Mozart borrowed much from the old Italian school; the fact may be true for the pattern of some of his airs, as well as the Raphaël-like beauty of his melodic design, the variety of his harmony and his instrumentation so rich and expert, scarcely allow one to perceive those so-called borrowings; but as to the general plan of the musical drama, the profundity of the expression with which every character is traced and sustained, one is forced to recognize that he has followed and accelerated the movement given to the art, in this direction, by the power of Gluck's genius.

The same thing is true of Beethoven and of Weber. Both have applied themselves equally to the development of the faculties which Nature has granted them, the simple and luminous code of that Aeschylus of music. At present Gluck, in promulgating these laws whose correctness is demonstrated by the smallest feeling for it, or even by simple common sense, hasn't he exaggerated their application somewhat? This is impossible to mistake after an impartial examination. So, when he says that the music of a lyric drama has no other function but to add to the poetry what color adds to drawing, I think that he deceives himself. The task of the composer in an opera, it seems to me, is important in quite another way. His work contains both drawing and color, and, to continue the comparison of Gluck, the words are the subject of the picture, scarcely anything more. It is very important to hear them, or at least to know them, for the same reason that one should have present in his mind the historical event depicted on the canvas by the painter, to be able to judge the merit of the truth and the expression with which the painter has brought the characters to life. But Gluck, by placing the design in the words and only the coloration in the music, places very high the authors of the libretti; he must have consented to seeing his equal in Le Bailli du Roullet. Certainly one cannot carry modesty further, and I very much doubt that he would have been contented in such company. Besides, expression is not the sole aim of dramatic music; it would be just as pedantic as clumsy to scorn the purely sensual pleasure we find in certain effects of melody, harmony, rhythm, or instrumentation, quite independent of all kinship with the depiction of feelings or the passions of the drama. In addition, if one wished to deprive the hearer of this source of enjoyment and not allow him to stimulate his attention by turning it away for a moment from the main subject, one could still cite numerous cases where the composer is called upon to bear, he alone, the weight of the interest of the scene. In the character dances, for example, in the pantomimes, in marches, finally in all the bits of music where instrumental music bears the burden alone and which, as a result, have no words, what then becomes of the importance of the poet? The music must contain both the design and the coloring. No, one cannot fail to see Gluck's error on this point, an error that one has difficulty in understanding, unless one knew that at the time when he wrote, many people still, as in the time of Louis XIV, "went to see the opera only for the verse."

This opinion could not fail to exercise a destructive influence on this genius, who adopted it without calculating the consequences. It conceals a dangerous trap, one from which he could not always protect himself. No musician more than he has been endowed with a penetrating charm, with a noble and graceful simplicity in his melody; no one has surpassed the elegance of some of his songs, the freshness of his choruses, and the charming *desinvoltura* of his dances; so it would be tedious to prove it by quotations. The joy of his women has a ravishing modesty about it, and their sorrow, even in its most violent paroxysms, still retains the beauty of the ancient forms. No matter what has been said about it by the Marquis de Caracioli, that evil inventor of "bons mots," that powdered dilettante of the last century, who judged music absolutely as do today the perfumed adorers of the divas *à la mode*—*Alceste* and the two *Iphigenias* are still, even in tears, as beautiful as Niobe.

Well! it has frequently happened to Gluck to allow himself to be so occupied with seeking expressiveness that he has forgotten the melody. In some of his airs, after the exposition of the theme, the song turns into measured recitative; it is a fine recitative, I am far from denying it, but finally, because of the very slight interest of the vocal part, it seems that the tune has been interrupted until the reentrance of the main motif. Gluck probably did not see any error in this. On the contrary, he declares formally, in the preface that we are commenting on, that he has tried to avoid too great a disparity between the recitative and the airs. None of his disciples, Salieri excepted, has thought that he must adopt this rule. It is certain that its application has spread widely over many parts of the works of the great tragic writer a uniform and monotone tint which fatigues the attention of the most robust spectator; fatigues uselessly the nervous system of the listener, at length irritates his sensibility, and has done more damage to Gluck than the barbs and the pamphlets of people like Caracioli, Marmontel, and the other clowns. Music lives by contrasts, nothing is clearer; all the efforts of modern art tend to produce more modern art; not that I propose as models certain orchestral effects from a celebrated school whose sudden violence surprises the listener, almost like a sudden pistol shot near his ear. Such contrasts, which cause cries of fright by nervous people, might be regarded as schoolboy farces if they were not really acts of absurd brutality. But it is clearly recognized today that well-organized variety is the very soul of music. It is done to give to the composers every means in obtaining this precious variety, which is the principal talent of the clever writers of libretti. They take care not to place two bits of the same character next to each other; they avoid as much as possible having one air succeed another air, one duo next to another duo, one chorus next to another chorus. So in the old symphonic style an allegro moderato was followed by an andante in two-four or six-eight; the andante was followed by the minuet, allegretto in three-four time; this was followed by the finale in two-four, very animated; and this was highly regarded.

To try to erase the difference which, in an opera, separates the recitative from the singing, is to try, in spite of reason and common sense, to deprive one's self, with no compensation, of a source of variety which stems from the very nature of this sort of composition. Mozart was so far from sharing Gluck's opinion on this point that, to draw the line of demarcation more clearly, he insisted that the recitative in *Don Giovanni* be accompanied on the piano, accepting at the same time, the necessary recitative, in which the situations make the presence of the orchestra obligatory. In a vast hall like that of the great opera house in Paris, the effect of the piano is so feeble and so thin that this kind of accompaniment has been completely abandoned. It may seem preferable, however, to the one that Gluck uses constantly in the same cases, and which consists of four-note chords, sustained without interruption by the whole string section the length of the entire musical dialogue. This stagnant harmony produces for the ear an effect of torpor and irresistible boredom, and ends by plunging the listener into a heavy somnolence that makes him indifferent to the rarest attempts of the composer to move him emotionally. It was truly impossible to find anything more antipathetic to the French than this long and obstinate buzzing; one should not be astonished that the greatest number of them felt at the performances of Gluck as much boredom as admiration. What should be surprising is, that this genius should make such a mistake about the accessories, to such an extent as to employ ways that an instant of reflection would make him reject as insufficient or dangerous, and in which resides the obscure cause of the cruel miscalculations that his most magnificent productions make him too often undergo.

If one makes exception of some of the brilliant sonatas by the orchestra where the genius of Rossini shows itself so gracefully, it is certain that most of these instrumental compilations, honored by the

Italians with the name of "overture," are grotesquely nonsensical. But how much more pleasant it must have been, sixty years ago, when Gluck himself, encouraged by example, was not afraid to let fall from his pen that incredible asininity, the *overture* to *Orpheus*. It was only after much reflection and many talks with his poet, Calzabigi, the gentleman best fitted to understand him, that he finally acknowledged that the overture should be an important part of an opera, should be a part of the action and clarify its character. Hence the radical changes noted in his manner, dating from the overture to *Alceste*; hence the fine instrumental compositions that he wrote to precede his two *Iphigenias*; from this came the impulse which later produced the symphonic masterpieces, which, in spite of the failure or the deep forgetfulness of the operas for which they were written, have remained standing, superb peristyles of ruined temples. But here again, by exaggerating a good idea, Gluck parted from reality; not this time by restraining the power of music, but by attributing to it, on the contrary, one that it never possessed: it is when he says that the overture should show the subject of the piece. Musical expression would never be able to go that far; it can reproduce joy, sorrow, seriousness, playfulness, and even the delicate nuances of each of the numerous characters that constitute its rich domain; it will establish a striking difference between the joy of a pastoral people and that of a warlike one, between the sorrow of a queen and the chagrin of a simple village dweller; between the serious and calm meditation and the ardent dreaming that precedes an outburst of passion. Taking from different peoples and even from individuals the musical style proper to them, whatever certain critics say whose merit I recognize, it can distinguish the song of a mountaineer from that of a dweller on the plains, the serenade of a brigand from the Abbruzzi from that of a Scotch hunter or a Tyrolian, the nocturnal march of pilgrims with mystical habits from that of a band of cattle merchants coming home from the fair; it might even go so far as to represent extreme brutality, triviality, the grotesque, by opposition to angelic purity, nobility, and candor. But if it desires to leave this immense circle, music should of necessity have recourse to the word, sung, recited, or read, to fill the gaps it leaves in a work whose plan addresses itself at the same time to the mind and to the imagination. Thus the overture to *Alceste* will announce scenes of desolation and of tenderness, but it cannot tell either the object of this tenderness nor the causes of this desolation. It will never tell the spectators that Alceste's husband is a king of Thessaly condemned by the gods to lose his life if some other guilty person does not sacrifice himself; however, *that is the subject of the play*. Perhaps people will be surprised to find that the author of this piece of writing imbued with certain principles, thanks to certain persons who have pretended to believe it, in their opinions about the expressive power of music, are as far away from the truth as they are in another direction; they have, consequently, generously given to him their share of ridicule. Let this be said, without malice, in passing.

The third proposition that I have allowed myself to underline in Gluck's preface, in which he declares that he attaches no value to the discovery of a novelty, seems to me also equally difficult to justify. Already in 1749 lots of lined paper had been scribbled on, and any musical discovery whatsoever, even if it was only indirectly connected with scenic expression, did not seem so bad as to be scorned.

For all the others I do not think that they can be combatted with any chance of success, even the latest one, which announces an indifference for the rules, and which many professors would find blasphemous and impious. Luckily these gentlemen have never read the preface to *Alceste;* perhaps they do not even know that it exists; without their ignorance the glory of Gluck would be in terrible danger.

from *À travers chants*

On the Present State of the Art of Singing in the Lyric Theaters of France and Italy and on the Causes Which Have Brought It About

It seems to ordinary common sense that one should, in the so-called lyrical establishments, have singers for the operas; but it is just the opposite that occurs: one has opera for the singers. One must always adjust, re-cut, patch up, piece out, lengthen, shorten a score to put it in a state (and what a state!) to be performed by the artists to whom it has been given. One finds his part too high; another finds his too low; another has too many pieces; still another has not enough; the tenor wants "i"s at the end of each song; the baritone wants "a"s; another finds an accompaniment that is awkward for him; elsewhere his competitor complains about a chord that provokes him; this part is too slow for the prima donna; this other is too fast for the tenor. In the end an unfortunate composer who took it into his head to write a C scale in a middle range in a slow movement, without accompaniment, cannot be certain to find singers to sing it without *changes;* most of them would claim that the scale *did not lie in their voices* because it had not been written *for them.*

At the present time in Europe with the fashionable system of singing (it must be said), out of ten persons who call themselves singer, it might be possible to find at most two or three capable of singing well—really well, correctly, exactly, expressively, with good style and a pure and sympathetic voice, a simple romance. Suppose one were to take one of these people at random and say to him: "Here is an old air, very simple, very touching, whose sweet melody does not modulate and remains in the modest range of one octave; sing it for us"—it is quite possible that your singer, who might be illustrious, will wipe out the poor musical flower, and in listening to him you would regret some fine village girl you have heard humming the old tune.

No musical thought, no melodic form, no expressive accent can withstand the frightful kind of interpretation that is becoming more and more extensive today. Even if that were the only thing!—but we have several varieties of anti-melodic songs today. First there is the *innocently stupid,* the insipid song; then the intentionally stupid, the song ornamented with all the stupidities that the singer takes into his head to make; this person is already most blameworthy. Next comes the vicious singing, which corrupts the public and lures it into bad musical paths by the attraction of certain capricious methods of performance, brilliant but with false expression, which is revolting to both good sense and good taste. Finally we have the criminal song, the wicked song that unites with its wickedness a bottomless pit of stupidity, which proceeds only by great howls and enjoys adding noisy *mêlées* to the long drum rolls, to the somber dramas, to the murders, poisonings, curses, anathemas, to all the dramatic horrors that provide the occasion to show off the voice. It is this last which, I am told, reigns supreme in Italy. But the cause, what is the cause? one will say. The cause, or the causes, I will answer, are easy to find; it is the remedy that we know less about, or to speak freely, it is the remedy that will never be applied, even if it were known and its efficacy were clearly demonstrated. The causes are both moral and physical, all of them dependent upon each other; and if the theatrical enterprises had not, from the beginning and almost everywhere, been in the hands of people greedy for money and ignorant of the necessities of art, these causes would not exist.

These are: the excessive size of most of the lyric theaters;

The system of applause, paid or not;

The preponderance, which has been allowed to grow, of performance over composition, of the larynx over the brain, of matter over mind, and finally the all too often cowardly submission of genius to stupidity.

The lyric theaters are too large. It is proved, it is certain that sound, in order to act musically on the human organism, should not be made at too great a distance from the hearer. One is always ready to answer when anyone talks about the sonority of an opera house or a concert hall: "You can hear everything very well."

But I also can hear very well from my study the cannon fired on the esplanade of the Invalides; nevertheless this noise, which is really outside of musical conditions, does not strike me, does not move me, does not disturb my nervous system in any way. Well then! it is this blow, this emotion, this disturbance, this shock which sound must absolutely give to the hearing organism in order to move it musically, which one does not receive from groups of voices or instruments, even the most powerful, when one listens at too great a distance. Some savants think the electrical fluid is powerless to cross a space bigger than a certain number of thousands of leagues; I do not know if this is the case, but I am sure that the musical fluid (I ask permission to designate thus the unknown power of musical emotion) is without power, without warmth, without life at a certain distance from its point of departure. One *hears*, one does not *vibrate*. Well! one must *vibrate* with the instruments and the voices, and because of them, in order to perceive true musical sensations. Nothing is easier to demonstrate. Place a small number of persons, well organized and with some knowledge of music, in a medium-sized room, not too well furnished or carpeted; play seriously for them some real masterpiece, by a real composer, truly inspired, a work really free from the insupportable conventional beauties that the pedagogues and the prejudiced enthusiasts extol; play for them a simple trio for piano, violin, and bass, the trio in B-flat by Beethoven, for example; what is going to happen? The listeners are going to feel that little by little they are filled with an unaccustomed emotion, they will feel a pleasure, intense and deep, which at one moment will agitate them deeply, soon will plunge them into a delicious calm, in a true ecstasy. In the middle of the andante, at the third or fourth return of that sublime theme, so passionately religious, one of them may not be able to control his tears, and if he lets them flow for a moment, he will end (I have seen this phenomenon occur) by weeping violently, furiously, explosively. This is a real musical effect! Here is a hearer intoxicated by the art of sound, a hearer borne to immense heights above the ordinary regions of his life. He adores music, this one; he does not know how to express what he feels; his admiration is ineffable and his gratitude to the great poet-composer who has just delighted him matches his admiration.

Now, suppose that in the middle of this same piece, played by these same virtuosi, the room in which they are playing could gradually enlarge, and then as a result of the enlargement of the room, the audience were little by little to become farther and farther away from the players. Well, now your salon is big as a theater; our hearer who a moment earlier felt emotion overcome him, begins to regain his poise; he still *hears* but he *vibrates* almost not at all; he admires the work, but with his reasoning powers alone, no longer with sentiment nor as the result of being carried away irresistibly. The salon grows bigger, the hearer is farther and farther from the source of the music. He is now as far away as he would be if the three players were grouped together on the stage of the opera and he were seated in the balcony among the first *loges de face*. He still *hears*, not a sound escapes him; but he is no longer moved by the *musical fluid*, which no longer reaches him; his emotion is dissipated; he becomes cool again; he even feels a sort of disagreeable anxiety, the more painful as he makes more efforts to pay attention so as not to lose the thread of the musical discourse. But his efforts are in vain, insensitivity paralyzes him, ennui overcomes him, the great master, fatigue, obsesses him, the masterpiece is to him now no more than a ridiculous noise, from the giant there rises a dwarf, art is a deception; he grows impatient and listens no longer. Here is another experiment.

Follow a military band playing a brilliant march down the Rue Royale perhaps: you hear it with pleasure, you march gaily following it, its rhythm carries you along, its warlike fanfares animate you, and you already dream of glory and battles. The military band enters the Place de la Concorde, you can still hear it, the reflectors of sound are no longer there, its prestige is dissipated, you no longer vibrate and you let it go its way, and you no longer care about it any more than a clown band.

Now, to return to the core of our subject; how many times has it happened to me, during the time when they still had the goodness to produce, and not badly, the works of Gluck at the Opera, to remain cold, but irritated with my coldness, when I heard the first act of *Orpheus*? I knew, I was sure, however, that it is a marvel of expression, of poetic melody; the performance lacked none of the essential qualities. But the scenery representing a *sacred grove* was open on every side; the sound was lost in the rear, at the right, at the left of the stage; there were no reflectors and therefore no effect; Orpheus seemed actually to be singing in a plain of Thrace; Gluck was wrong. This same role of Orpheus sung by A. Nourrit, these same choruses sung by the same choristers, the same pantomime music played by the same orchestra, but in a hall at the Conservatoire, regained their magic; people were in ecstasy, breathing in the poetry of antiquity; Gluck was right.

The symphonies of Beethoven, which overwhelm everyone in the hall of the Conservatoire, have been played several times in the Opera; there they produced no effect; Beethoven was wrong. *Don Juan* of Mozart, so ardent, so passionate, and so impassioned at the Théâtre Italien when the performance is good, is glacial at the Opera, everybody agrees. The *Marriage of Figaro* would be even colder there. So Mozart is wrong at the Opera!

The masterpieces of Rossini's first manner, the *Barber, Cenerentola,* and so many others, lose their piquant physiognomy and their wit at the Opera. You still enjoy them, but coldly, from a distance, like a garden that you look at through a telescope. Is Rossini wrong?

And *Freischütz,* look how it drags at the Opera, this lively musical drama with such savage energy. So Weber is wrong!

I could easily multiply instances. What is a theater in which Gluck, Mozart, Weber, Beethoven, and Rossini are wrong if not a theater built with bad conditions for music? Sonority is not lacking however. No! but like all the other theaters with the same dimensions, the Opera is too large. The *sound* fills it easily, but not the *musical fluid* that the ordinary means of performance emit. Someone will doubtless object that many fine works produce a fine effect, that a clever singer, when he has the talent of concentrating the attention of the audience upon himself, can successfully attempt the *chant doux.* But I will answer that this precious singer would impress his public much more in a hall less vast, and that it would be the same with these fine works, written especially for the Opera theater; further, that out of twenty fine ideas contained in the exceptional scores (scores written even today for the Opera) scarcely four or five survive, all the rest are lost. Even these beauties appear only veiled and belittled by distance and never in all their aspects, never in all their liveliness, never in all their *éclat.*

Hence the necessity, so much sneered at, but nonetheless there, to hear a fine opera many times to savor it and discover its merit. At its first performance everything seems confused, vague, colorless, formless, without nerves; it is only a picture half effaced, and one must follow its design line by line. Listen to the judgment of the foyer between the acts at the first performance; the new work, according to the critics, is invariably boresome or detestable. I have been listening to them for twenty-five years without having heard a more favorable judgment. It is much worse at the dress rehearsal, when the hall is half empty; then nothing survives, everything disappears; no graceful melody, no harmonic science, no colorful instrumentation, no love, no anger does anything; it is a vague noise, more or less tiresome, which irritates or bores you and you leave the hall cursing the work and the author.

I shall never forget the dress rehearsal of *Les Huguenots,* when I met M. Meyerbeer on the stage after the fourth act. I could say only this to him: "There is a chorus in the next to the last scene which, it seems to me, should have an effect." I wanted to speak of the chorus of monks, of the scene of the benediction of the daggers, one of the most striking inspirations of all time. It *seemed to me* that it should make a sensation. I was never so much struck by anything. . . .

Musical dramatic composition is a double art; it results from the association, the intimate union of poetry and music. The melodic accents can doubtless have a special interest, a charm that is all their own resulting from the music alone; but their power is doubled if they are seen to be contributing to the expression of a fine passion or a lovely sentiment indicated by a poem worthy of the name; the two arts united help each other. Now this union is destroyed mostly in rooms which are too vast, where the hearer, in spite of his attention, can hardly understand one line out of twenty, where he can scarcely make out the faces of the actors, where, as a consequence, it is impossible to understand the delicate nuances of the melody, the harmony, the instrumentation, and the motifs of these shadings, and their connection with the dramatic element determined by the words, since he cannot hear these words.

The music, I repeat, must be heard nearby; at a distance its principal charm disappears; it is at best strangely *modified* and weakened. Would anyone take pleasure in the conversation of the wittiest people in the world if one were obliged to sustain it at a distance of thirty paces? The sound, beyond a certain distance, though one can hear it, is like a flame that one can see but whose heat one cannot feel.

This advantage of small halls over large ones is evident, and it is because he had noticed it that a director of the Opera said with pleasing naïveté and a little pique: "Oh, in your hall at the Conservatoire everything has a good effect." Yes? Well, just try to get people to understand dirty words, brutal platitudes, nonsense, misconceptions, discordances, cacophony, which one hears *tant bien que mal* in your hall at the Opera, and you will see the kind of effect they produce.

Now let us examine another side of the question, the one that is concerned with the art of singing and with the art of the composer; we shall quickly find proof of what I said in the beginning; that is, if the art of singing has become what it is today, the art of yelling, the too-large dimension of the theaters is its cause; you will also find that from this one excess many others have come that dishonor modern music.

The theater La Scala, at Milan, is immense, that of the Cannobianna is very vast also, the theater of St. Charles at Naples, and many others which I could cite, also have enormous dimensions. Well! whence came that school of singing that is blamed so openly and so correctly today?— from the great musical centers in Italy. The Italian public being also in the habit of talking during the performances as loudly as we talk at the Bourse, the singers have gradually been brought to the point, as are the composers, of seeking any means of concentrating on themselves the attention of the public who pretend to like *its* music. Since that time sonority has been the aim; to attain it the use of nuances has been suppressed, the mixed voice, the head voice, and the lower notes of the scale in each voice as well; for the tenors the only notes admitted are the high ones called "de poitrine"; the basses, singing only in the high notes of their range, have been transformed into baritones; the men's voices, not really gaining at the top what they lose in the lower part, have deprived themselves of a third of their range; the composers, when writing for the singers, have had to limit themselves to one octave, and, being restricted to the use of eight notes at most, produce only melodies of a monotonous and discouraging vulgarity; the highest women's voices, the most piercing, have been preferred above all the others. These tenors, these baritones, these sopranos going at full speed, alone have been applauded; the composers have helped them as much as possible by writing in the direction of their stentorian pretensions. Duets in unison, trios, quartets, choruses in unison have been produced; this manner of composing, since it was easier and faster for the *maestri* and comfortable for the singers, has prevailed; and, helped by the bass drum, we have seen the system of dramatic music that we enjoy establish itself in a large part of Europe.

I have made this limitation because it does not really exist in Germany. There are no cavernous halls there. That of the Grand Opera at Berlin has no disproportionate dimensions. The Germans sing badly, they say, and it might be true in general. I don't want to bring up the question of whether their language is the cause, and if Madame Sontag, or Pischek, or Titchachek, or Mademoiselle Lind, almost a German, and many others, do not constitute magnificent exceptions; but as a whole, the immense majority of German singers sing and do not howl, the school of the yell is not theirs; they make music. How does this happen? Because doubtless they have a finer feeling for music than do many of their emulators in other nations, but also because their lyric theaters, being all of small dimensions, the *musical fluid* reaches everywhere in them; because the public shows itself always silent and attentive, the shameful efforts of the voices and instruments become here of no use and appear even more odious than with us.

There, you will say, is the indictment of the large theaters; one can no longer get 10,000 francs income, nor have 1800 people at the Opera in Paris, at Covent Garden in London, at La Scala, at San Carlo, nor anywhere else without running the risk of criticism from the musicians.

We do not hesitate to answer in the affirmative. You have uttered the big word: *The receipts!* You are speculators, we are artists, and we are not talking of the art of coining money, which is the very art that interests you.

True art has its conditions of power and beauty; speculation, which I shall take good care not to confuse with industry, has its own success more or less moral, and in the last analysis, art and speculation execrate each other mutually. Their antagonism is everywhere, at all times, it will be eternal; it lies at the very heart of the questions. Speak to the director of a spectacle, ask him what is the best hall for opera; he will answer, or at least he will think if he does not dare say it, that it is the hall from which you get the *most income*. Talk to a musician, or to a knowledgeable architect, a friend of music, they will tell you this: "A hall for opera, if one wants the essential qualities of the art of sound to be appreciable; should be a *musical instrument*; well, it is not, if its builders have not in its construction taken into consideration certain laws of physics, whose nature is well known. All other considerations are not applicable and have no authority. Stretch metal wires across a packing case, fit a keyboard to it—you will not have a piano that way. Stretch gut strings or silk strings on a wooden sabot, you will not get a violin that way. The skill of the pianists or the violinists will be incapable to change these ridiculous contrivances into real musical instruments, even if the body were of rosewood, or the shoe of sandalwood. It would be quite in vain for you to blow up a tempest in a stovepipe; the sound may be very energetic but it will not be an organ pipe, nor a trombone, nor a tuba, nor a hunting horn. All the imaginable reasons, reasons of perspective, reasons of splendor, reasons of money when it is a question of constructing an opera house, all give way to the laws of acoustics and those of the transmission of the *musical fluid,* for these laws do exist. It is a fact, and the stubbornness of a fact is proverbial." That is what they will say, these . . . artists. But they want to make music and you want to make money.

As for the effect of the orchestra in these halls which are too large, it is defective, incomplete, and false in the sense that it is different from what the composer imagined when he wrote his score, even if the score was written expressly for the large hall where it is heard.

Since the range of the *musical fluid* of the different projectors of sound is unequal, it follows necessarily that the instruments that can be heard at a great distance will on many occasions have a power too great for the importance the composer has assigned to them, whereas those with little power will disappear or will be inadequate for the use which was assigned to them in order to reach the aim of the composition. For in order for the *musical action* of the voices and the instruments to be complete, all the sounds should reach the hearer simultaneously and with the same vitality of vibration. In a word, the sounds written in the score (musicians will understand me) should reach the ear *en partition*.

Another consequence of the extreme size of the hall in the lyric theaters, a consequence of which I gave a glimpse a moment ago when I reminded the reader of the use of the bass drum, has been the introduction of all the auxiliary instruments of the ordinary orchestra. And this abuse carried now to its utmost limits, while it ruins the power of the orchestra itself, has contributed not a little to introducing the deplorable system of singing by exciting these singers to fight violently with the orchestra in the production of sounds.

Here is how the reign of the percussion instruments has come about.

My readers who are friends of music will please pardon me for going into such long explanations, I hope! As for other people, I do not fear to bore them; they will never read me.

It was, or I am greatly mistaken, in Gluck's *Iphigenia in Aulis* that the bass drum was heard for the first time at the Paris Opera, but alone, without cymbals nor any other percussion instrument. It appears in the last chorus of Greeks (a chorus in unison, let us note in passing), of which the first words are "Let us go, let us fly to victory!" This chorus is in marching movement with repeats. It was used for the passage of the Thessalian army. The bass drum beats the strong beat of each measure, as in ordinary marches. This chorus having disappeared when the denouement of the opera was changed, the bass drum was no longer heard until the beginning of the following century.

Gluck also introduced the cymbals (and we know to what admirable effect) in the chorus of the Scythians in *Iphigenia in Tauris*—the *cymbals alone*, without the bass drum, which the routine musicians of all countries think are inseparable. In a ballet of the same opera he uses the triangle alone with the happiest effect. And that was all.

In 1808, Spontini admitted the bass drum and the cymbals into the gladiator's dance in *La Vestale*. Later he used it again in the march of the cortège of Telasco in *Fernando Cortez*. Up until that time the use of this instrument, if not ingenious, had been at least suitable and very rare. But Rossini came to present at the Opera *The Siege of Corinth*. He had noticed, not without some chagrin, the sleepiness of the public in our great theater during the performance of the most beautiful works, sleepiness brought about more by physical causes contrary to the musical effect, which I have just pointed out, than by the style of the fine works of the period; and Rossini swore not to endure this insult. "I will prevent you from sleeping," he said. And he put bass drums everywhere, and cymbals, and the triangle, and trombones and ophicleids in groups of chords, and striking with might and main he caused such lightning bolts of sonority, if not harmony, such thunderclaps to burst forth from the orchestra that the public, rubbing its eyes, liked this new kind of emotion, more lively if not more musical than those it had felt before. Encouraged by success, he pushed this abuse still further by writing *Moses*, where, in the famous finale of the third act, the bass drum, the cymbals, and the triangle strike in the *fortes* the four beats of the measure and consequently play *as many notes as voices*, which fit together as one can imagine in such an accompaniment. Nevertheless the orchestra and the chorus are constructed in such a way that the sonority of the voices and instruments arranged in this way is so overwhelming that the *music* survives in the middle of the racket, and that the *musical fluid* projected in waves to all parts of the room, in spite of its vast dimensions, takes hold of the audience, shakes them, makes them vibrate; and one of the greatest effects ever to be pointed out in the hall of the Opera since it came into existence, is produced. But do the percussion instruments contribute to this? Yes! if you consider them as exciting the other instruments and the voices furiously; no! if you consider only the part they play in the musical action, for they overwhelm the orchestra and the voices and substitute a noise violent enough to drive you crazy for a fine energetic sonority.

However that may be, dating from Rossini's arrival at the opera, the instrumental revolution of the theater orchestras was accomplished. The great noises were used on any occasion and in all the musical works, whatever was the style demanded by the subject. Soon the kettledrums, the bass drums, the cymbals, and the triangle were no longer sufficient, and to them were added another drum, then two cornets came to the aid of the trumpets, the trombones, and the ophicleid; the organ was installed in the wings beside the bells, and soon military bands came on the stage, and finally those great instruments of Sax, which are to the other voices of the orchestra what a cannon shot is to a rifle shot. Finally, Halévy in his *Magicienne* added to all the violent instruments, the tam-tam. The new composers, irritated by the obstacle that the immensity of the hall imposed on them, thought that on pain of death for their works, they must make a change. Now have we in general remained in dignified and worthy artistic conditions, by using extreme means to avoid the obstacle, thinking we are destroying it? No, certainly exceptions are rare.

The judicious use of the most common instruments, even the clumsiest, may be admitted by art, may really serve to increase its richness and power. Nothing is to be scorned in the instruments we have gained today, but the instrumental horrors we have witnessed become all the more odious, and I think I have demonstrated that they have greatly contributed to bringing about the vocal excesses that have motivated these too long and, I fear, useless reflections.

Add that these same excesses, introduced gradually in the Opéra Comique, and those with regard to the special conditions of the theater, of its orchestra, of its singers, of the general tone of its repertory, are incomparably more revolting.

I thought that I should meet this question face to face, for the first time, this question on which the life of theatrical music evidently depends; these truths might displease the great artists, the excellent and powerful minds; but I think that in their own minds they will recognize that these are truths.

I have pointed out, at the beginning, the moral causes of the immense disorder, the physical causes of which I have just studied. The influence of applause and of what the dramatic artists above all still have the astonishing naïveté to call *success* should take first place in this study. The ridiculous importance accorded to performers who are or who one believes to be indispensable, the authority that they have usurped, should not be forgotten either. But this is not the place to indulge ourselves in examining these questions; there is a book to be written about it.

Bad Singers, Good Singers, the Public, the Claque

I have already said, a man or woman capable of singing only sixteen measures of good music in a natural voice, well placed, pleasing, and singing them effortlesly without distorting the phrasing, without over-stressing the accents, without platitudes, without primness, without mistakes in the French, without dangerous slurs, without omissions, without insolent changes in the text, without transposition, without howling, without bleating, without false intonation, without maiming the rhythm, without ridiculous ornaments, without nauseating appoggiaturas—to sum up, in such a way that the phrasing written by the composer becomes comprehensible and remains quite simply *what he has written*, this singer is a *oiseau rare*, very rare, extremely rare.

His rarity will become still greater if the aberrations in the public's taste continue to become clear, as they do now, strikingly, passionately, with hatred for common sense.

If a man has a big voice without knowing in the least how to use it, without having the most elementary ideas of the art of singing; if he produces a sound violently he is applauded violently for the *sonority* of this note.

If a woman possesses only an exceptional vocal range, when she produces, *à propos* or not, a *sol* or a lower *fa* more like the dying moan of a sick person than a musical sound, or a high *fa* as agreeable as the yelp of a little dog when you step on his paw, that is enough for the whole hall to resound with acclamations.

The woman who could not produce the smallest simple tune without giving you the fidgets, whose warmth of spirit is equal to a block of Canadian ice—if she has the gift of instrumental agility, as soon as she sends off her fireworks, with sixteen sixteenths to the measure, when she pierces your ear drum with her infernal trill with ferocious insistence for a whole minute without catching a breath, you are certain to see the monstrous claque sitting in the parterre jump up and howl with pleasure.

If a ranting actor has taken it into his head that the accentuation—whether true or false, but exaggerated—is everything in dramatic music, that it may take the place of sonority, of measure, of rhythm; that it suffices to replace singing, form, melody, movement, tonality; that, to fulfill the needs of such an inflated, bombastic, turgid style with exaggerated emphases, one has the right to take strange liberties with the most admirable productions—when this system is put into practice before a certain kind of audience, the greatest and the most sincere enthusiasm rewards him for having disemboweled a great master, ruined a masterpiece, torn to shreds a beautiful melody, destroyed utterly a sublime passion.

Those people have one quality which in any case would not be enough to make singers out of them, but which they have transformed into a fault, a repulsive vice, by exaggerating it. It is no longer a beauty spot; it is a wart, a polyp, a tumor that spreads over a perfectly insignificant face—if it is not absolutely ugly. People who do this are the bane of music; they demoralize the public, and it is an evil action to encourage them.

As to the singers who have a voice, a human voice, who really sing, who know how to vocalize and who sing, who know the music and who sing, who know French and who sing, who are able to accentuate properly and who sing, and who—as they sing—respect the work and the author, whose attentive, faithful, and intelligent interpreters they are—the public, all too often, has only proud disdain for them or lukewarm encouragement. Their regular faces have no beauty spots, no warts, no defects. They do not show off. They do not dance on a phrase. These are nonetheless the true singers, useful and charming, who, staying within the limits of their art, deserve the support of men of taste in general and the gratitude of composers in particular. It is through them that the art exists; for the others it dies. But, you will say, will anyone dare to be bold enough to say that the public does not applaud, and very warmly, the great artists, masters of every resource of dramatic song, endowed with sensitivity, intelligence, virtuosity, and that rare faculty called inspiration? No; doubtless the public applauds *them* also. The public at that time resembles those sharks that follow a ship and which men fish for; it swallows everything—the piece of fat and the harpoon.